RECEIVED

APR 26 2014

BROADVIEW LIBRARY

D0090547

NO LONGER PROPERTY OF
SEATTLE PUBLIC LIBRARY

Supreme Commander

ALSO BY SEYMOUR MORRIS JR.

American History Revised

SUPREME COMMANDER

MacArthur's Triumph in Japan

SEYMOUR MORRIS JR.

HARPER

www.harpercollins.com

SUPREME COMMANDER. Copyright © 2014 by Seymour Morris Jr. All rights reserved. Printed in the United States of America. No part of this book may be used or reproduced in any manner whatsoever without written permission except in the case of brief quotations embodied in critical articles and reviews. For information, address HarperCollins Publishers, 10 East 53rd Street, New York, NY 10022.

HarperCollins books may be purchased for educational, business, or sales promotional use. For information, please e-mail the Special Markets Department at SPsales@harpercollins.com.

"Assistant Cooks" cartoon: Fred O. Siebel cartoon is reproduced with permission of the *Richmond Times-Dispatch*. Further reproduction prohibited without permission.

"Japanese thinking" illustration: from Courtney Whitney, *MacArthur: His Rendezvous with History*, page 252.

MacArthur/Marshall cartoon: 1951 Herblock Cartoon, © The Herb Block foundation.

FIRST EDITION

Library of Congress Cataloging-in-Publication Data has been applied for.

ISBN: 978-0-06-228793-9

14 15 16 17 18   OV/RRD   10 9 8 7 6 5 4 3 2 1

To Alexander C. Hoyt

Acknowledgments

THE FIRST QUESTIONS people often ask when they meet an author are: How did you choose to write this book? How long did it take you to write it?

First things first. When I applied to Harvard Business School many years ago, there was an interesting essay question on the application: If you had not chosen a career in business, which career would you choose? To which I answered, "Write American history" (my major in college). So, after thirty years in business and deciding I wanted to do something new and different with my life, I plunged in and became an author. And, lo and behold, I got my first book published by a major publisher. I was on my way. . . . In late 2012, I was talking with my literary agent about what to do next. There is so much fascinating history out there that often the hardest task for a historian is to try to narrow down all the options and choose a particular subject/theme to focus on. I had a particular topic I had spent several months developing and was passionate about. When I presented it to Alex Hoyt, he cast me a skeptical eye and shot his bullet: "No, no, there's no market." (You're a businessman, remember? You may have a brilliant idea, but if there's no market . . .) "So what do you suggest?" I asked.

"In your business career you've always dealt with CEOs and government leaders," he said. "So why don't you write about one of the greatest feats of American leadership: Douglas MacArthur in Japan?" If only he knew: Just the week before I had resolved to clean up my library of unread books groaning on the bookshelves, and I had donated to a charity William Manchester's *American Caesar*, figuring I'd never get around to reading it.

Properly humbled, off I went to the Argosy Bookstore in New York City, a treasure trove of secondhand books, to buy another copy. When Alex introduced me to Adam Bellow of HarperCollins, I made a two-minute pitch, and he said, "I like it!" and invited me to submit the obligatory forty-page proposal to secure a commitment. In so doing, I realized I had a particular advantage few authors have that can be all-important: an open mind. I was not in love with my subject, I was just intrigued with it. I was able to approach it with a tabula rasa.

It was an unusual proposal that I submitted. I explained that although many books had been written about MacArthur, and many books about the occupation, no book had been written analyzing why it had been so successful—a sharp contrast to our hard-fought, frustrating effort in Iraq and Afghanistan.

As a management consultant who had spent many years working with large organizations and subsequently as an entrepreneur running my own international business, might there be lessons here worth noting? Unlike academics, I must also bring to the task the hands-on lessons I had learned (and not learned) over many years about what it takes to run an organization in which you are on the firing line and responsible for delivering results. I must put myself, as much as possible, in MacArthur's shoes. What's your policy? What's your strategy? How much time do you have? Do you take on two or three objectives, or do you take on ten? What kind of people do you hire? How quickly do you get rid of people who don't deliver even though they have powerful allies who could stir up trouble?

What do you tell your investors/bosses (in MacArthur's case, the president and the Joint Chiefs) when you fundamentally disagree with their priorities? Do you voice your concerns, or do you keep them secret and go ahead and do what you want to do anyway (like MacArthur did in imposing a new Japanese constitution)? How do you handle malcontent employees? Try an extreme example: How do you handle dissidents—like MacArthur did—who actually try to kill you? (Hint: MacArthur invited him for a cup of tea and let him go free.)

Most difficult of all, how do you handle a host country president or prime minister who doesn't cooperate as you would want him to? No matter how much you want to pack up and go home, you have to hang in there and keep negotiating.

The problems of running an organization—especially a military occupation where nobody wants you around—go on and on, they never stop. The pressure is incessant and unrelenting What most impressed me about Douglas MacArthur is that he remained above the fray and always maintained control. He eventually got dismissed, but the fact remains that he had performed his job so well, he might as well leave, there was nothing more for him to do. He had outlived his usefulness.

And left behind a treasure of achievement worth exploring.

Second question: "How long did it take you to write it?" It took me exactly one year, only because I had set a deadline for myself: one year, and no more. (Time is money, remember.) In one year I read some 250 books and countless articles, pored through several archives, interviewed several people still alive, and cranked out four hundred pages. I worked day and night. There is a saying in business: "If you want something done, give it to your busiest man." I was now that busiest man. You'd be amazed how efficient you suddenly become.

I met my deadline, my book is great (so I thought), nothing more needed to be done. Really? HarperCollins associate editor Eric Meyers and copy editor Susan Llewellyn got their hands on my document and put it through the wringer; it was agonizing, it was awful, there was blood on the floor. After two more months, when all was said and done, they destroyed 10 percent of my book—and made it 30 percent better. Never underestimate what a top book publisher can do for you. (Amazon: Please take note. Those of you thinking of self-publishing, take double note.)

I had the benefit of superb research facilities provided by the New York Public Library—my office (especially the Milstein Room)—and the Japan Society of New York Library and the MacArthur Archives in Norfolk, Virginia. As I undertook this writing effort, a number of close friends provided unswerving personal support: Arthur, Bob, Bruce, Buz, Copey, Craig, my wife, Gabriela, JC, John, Larry, Lindsay, Nina,

Peter, Sandra, and Tony. And of course, Alex Hoyt, a man who does what few literary agents do: he specializes. He knows more history than I will ever know.

Left out, only because I don't know who you are, is you, the reader. Author acknowledgments—so far as I can tell—never acknowledge this. Yet praise (and helpful criticism) is the highest honor an author can receive. I only hope you enjoy reading this book as much as I did writing it.

Douglas MacArthur was a man of major personal flaws and gigantic achievements. When he returned home in 1951, he was the biggest celebrity in America, the man who had saved Japan. Actually, he did more: quite possibly, he saved all of Southeast Asia. Today, because of his failure in Korea, he is largely forgotten (including by me, who had tossed out the Manchester biography of him). How wrong I was! Only by writing this book did I realize what he had accomplished in Japan was what I now conclude was "the greatest achievement by America's greatest general." To be sure, not everyone agrees that he was our greatest general, but certainly he was our most decorated—by a huge margin.*

That we don't have men like him today in times of critical need is our nation's loss. How wonderful it might have been to be able to sit down and talk with him. . . .

Permit me to close with a real-life coincidence. In the course of my research, I stumbled on a 1947 *Fortune* article with a photo of Col. William T. Ryder. I was blown away: I knew William Ryder well. He was a founder of the American paratroopers, I had stayed at his home many times. He was the father of one of my closest prep school friends at St. George's School, who turned out to be MacArthur's godson! (I never knew this, and the Ryders never name-dropped this fact.) When I tracked down my long-lost classmate and asked him about his godfather, he regretted he had never inquired deeply.

So I say to you: Whenever you meet a great man, do not—do not—let the moment slip by. History missed is history forgotten.

—Seymour Morris Jr.

---

* For his honors and medals, see page 54. For a critical view of MacArthur as a general, see books by Eric Larrabee (1987) and Thomas Ricks (2012).

Contents

Preface

IN LATE 1943 Winston Churchill received a confidential memo from a British officer serving as UK liaison to Gen. Douglas MacArthur. Churchill wanted to know what kind of man this was who was commanding the American campaign in the South Pacific.

"He is shrewd, selfish, proud, remote, high-strung and vastly vain. He has imagination, self-confidence, physical courage and charm, but no humor about himself, no regard for truth, and is unaware of these defects. He mistakes his emotions and ambitions for principles. With moral depth he would be a great man: as it is he is a near-miss, which may be worse than a mile . . . his main ambition would be to end the war as a pan-American hero in the form of generalissimo of all Pacific theatres."

Less than two years later this man did become the generalissimo of all Pacific theaters, responsible for leading Japan away from militarism and feudalism and toward democracy.

The American occupation of Japan was without question the most successful—and possibly the only—successful occupation of a defeated nation ever attempted. The fact that after it was over and the defeated country eventually went on to become a world power in its own right tends to color our view of history. We think of Japan's path to democracy and economic prosperity as obvious, something to be expected of such a hardworking and diligent people.

It was not. When the war ended no one knew what path Japan would take. It was a country living on the edge. Totally destroyed and humiliated, with hardly a friend in the world after all the brutality it had inflicted on its neighbors in Southeast Asia and the Southern Pacific, its prospects were bleak. Its most likely future appeared to be either a return to fascist repression, or a Communist revolution.

Into this huge void fraught with danger, the United States sent Gen. Douglas MacArthur, the most decorated military general of World War I and World War II. Knowing the magnitude—not to mention the difficulty—of this mission, President Truman gave him a majestic title never given any American before or since: Supreme Commander for the Allied Powers. Victorious in battle, he must strive to be victorious in peace.

Never before in the history of the United States "had such enormous and absolute power been placed in the hands of a single individual." Certainly no general faced a more awesome task, one that generals normally are not prepared for.

His five-year rule of Japan before the Korean War ranks as one of America's greatest feats of leadership, a guide to how to occupy another country that our military failed to employ in later occupations such as Iraq. He achieved his occupation of a bellicose country notorious for assassinations and kamikaze warriors with only a relative handful of troops and masterful use of leadership and psychology. "The greatest gamble in history," he said. It was more than that, it was a first: the only occupation, said the prime minister of the defeated country, "without a single shot being fired."

Many people believed that a twenty- or fifty-year occupation would be needed to reform Japan; instead MacArthur did it in five—just as he had predicted. The Americans expected treachery and resistance; the Japanese, for their part, expected rapine and pillage. What emerged was a happy surprise for both the conqueror and the conquered. Almost everything MacArthur set out to do, he achieved. He demonstrated that Rudyard Kipling was wrong about occupier country and subject country: The twain *did* meet. No man rose higher, stirring people with his powerful oratory, than MacArthur. Yet, coming at a time when most of the world's attention was focused on Europe, what he accomplished ended up being "one of the worst-reported stories in history," observed renowned journalist John Gunther. Today MacArthur is largely forgotten, just as he predicted: old soldiers fade away. His accomplishment, which stands at the pinnacle of military occupations, is a remarkable story where America performed well.

AS GEN. DOUGLAS MACARTHUR surveyed the devastation and poverty of broken-down Japan, he may have reflected—as he frequently did—on how he was almost always right. At the beginning of the year, in January 1945, he had sent President Roosevelt a forty-page memorandum containing five top-secret Japanese peace overtures, two obtained through American channels and three through the British, all contingent on the United States guaranteeing to preserve the emperor. And what had he gotten in return? A backhanded slap from FDR: "MacArthur is our greatest general and our poorest politician."

Do presidents have better judgment than generals? Unlike the president, as Japan's plight worsened in the waning days of World War II, MacArthur had come to view the atom bomb as unnecessary. When the new president, Harry Truman, consulted his advisors about the military need to use the atom bomb or not, he never consulted the man who knew the Japanese situation better than anybody, Douglas MacArthur. To complete the conquest of Japan, the president and the army chief of staff, George C. Marshall, planned for the one-million-man Operation Downfall, an invasion of Japan to be led by MacArthur. Once again MacArthur disagreed.

He thought Japan was on its knees because of the Jimmy Doolittle raids and the naval blockade engineered by Admiral Nimitz. Japan's surrender was just a matter of time as the U.S. Navy continued to sink Japanese ships and cut off imports of food and essential supplies. No bomb or invasion was necessary; just keep hammering away and wait it out. In this bold view MacArthur was not alone. Joining him were no less than the five-star admirals Chester Nimitz, William Leahy, and Ernest King, the five-star air force general Henry "Hap" Arnold, and the former ambassador to Japan for ten years, Joseph Grew. A greater lineup of expertise could hardly be assembled.

Their strategy for ending the war: a siege. It lacks the drama of a battlefield victory or a city blown to smithereens by a bomb, but it works. It is the professional soldier's weapon of choice. It saves lives, both for the attacker as well as the defender.

In Washington, President Franklin Roosevelt—like Secretary of War Henry Stimson, Secretary of State James Byrnes, Assistant Secretary of State Dean Acheson, and Army Chief of Staff Marshall—thought differently. And so President Truman would claim he had acted on the urgent advice of his military advisors. Not true. He relied on Marshall and the civilian advisors.

WHEN MACARTHUR AND the admirals arrived in Japan for the surrender, they would find the Japanese people suffering from massive hunger and disease even worse than they—or anybody in Washington—ever imagined. They were stunned to learn that had there been no atom bomb and no invasion, just a blockade, within two months ten million Japanese might have starved to death. So said the Japanese minister of finance to the United Press. Even if the minister was wrong by a month or two, still, ten million of the enemy killed with no American casualties might have been a better way to bring the war to an end.

No point making an issue about it. The American generals and admirals would be quiet, and the American public would never know. Let the public be told, as President Truman said, that the bomb had been dropped to save American lives. The public would not be told that the bomb had saved a lot more Japanese lives than otherwise. And that maybe it hadn't been necessary in the first place (other than serve as a warning that such a weapon never be used by anybody ever again).

Every great enterprise begins with a philosophy, a mission statement. Now entering Japan to occupy and rule the country was the larger-than-life "I shall return!" general the Japanese feared the most. Yet he would not be the man they expected: a man on a white horse. To the contrary, he—who knew Japanese brutality firsthand—would bear no ill will. By his generosity to a vanquished militaristic nation and the ideals he espoused through his magnificent oratory, he would demonstrate the better angels of human nature and push for the Japanese abolition of war, though he was no pacifist.

Yet when he died in 1964, he would not be remembered for these deeds. Newspaper and magazine articles would extol his military exploits, with nary a word said about his greatest achievement, for which he had hoped to be remembered.

PART ONE

TAKING CONTROL

1

A President Rolls the Dice

H E HAD NEVER met the man. Never even talked to him . . . not once.

   In 1945, on August 12, the president of the United States was about to make a decision. A decision based on incomplete information, yet one that had to be made one way or another whether he liked it or not. To procrastinate would only be another form of decision. Japan was now defeated: the Tokyo air raids, the two atom bombs, and the naval blockade had assured closure. Peace negotiations were well under way; any moment an agreement would be reached. There was one stumbling block: the Japanese demand that there be no occupation of their country, which of course was totally unacceptable to the United States. There would be an occupation, and to make sure the Japanese got the message, Truman would appoint as head of it America's most successful general, the man the Japanese feared most: Gen. Douglas MacArthur, the man who had conquered the Philippines and electrified the nation—and terrified the Japanese—with his poignant slogan, "I shall return!"

   There was a small problem: not only had the president not met him, he didn't like him.

   Essentially a president makes two kinds of decisions. Easy decisions where he knows exactly what he wants to do and he is convinced he is right, and hard decisions where he has little information to go on or where the alternatives are unpalatable and he's basically groping in the dark. He will never admit this, of course; he will put on a show that he knows what he's doing, showing the world how decisive—and what a good actor—he is. Truth be told, at times he is really rolling the dice.

The personnel file on MacArthur contained many papers, including a curriculum vitae used for press releases.

1880 Born January 26, son of a general, grandson of a U.S. Supreme Court justice

1897 Class valedictorian, West Texas Military Academy

1903 Graduated first in class from West Point, with a 98.14 average—one of the three highest grades ever recorded in the history of the academy (one of the two other high achievers being Robert E. Lee)

1904–13 Posted to the Philippine Islands, the Panama Canal Zone, and the United States as engineering officer; promoted to first lieutenant, 1904; as aide-de-camp to his father, Gen. Arthur MacArthur, inspected Japanese military bases, 1905, and toured China, Siam, Java, the Malay States, Burma, India, and Ceylon in 1906; spent year as White House military aide to President Theodore Roosevelt; promoted to captain

1914 Conducted hazardous reconnaissance mission during U.S. occupation of Veracruz, Mexico; recommended for the Medal of Honor (did not receive it)

1914–19 Served on the general staff of the War Department; head of the Bureau of Information conducting press relations for the secretary of war; promoted to major, 1915; initiated and implemented plan to form a twenty-thousand-man National Guard division comprising units from several states, known as the Forty-Second Infantry, or "Rainbow" Division, American Expeditionary Force; chief of staff of the Rainbow Division, with the rank of colonel; served in France, 1918: led the Rainbow Division into battle, promoted to brigadier general; awarded two Distinguished Service Crosses, seven Silver Stars, and two Purple Hearts; awarded by France two Croix de Guerre and made a Commandeur of the Légion d'Honneur; recommended for the Medal of Honor (again passed over); participated in the occupation of the Rhineland in Germany

1919–22 Superintendent of the U.S. Military Academy (West Point): modernized curriculum, replaced summer camp (mostly a social activity) with basic infantry training; curbed practice of excessive hazing; formulated the honor code to be administered by the cadets; promoted intercollegiate athletics and initiated a new program of intramural sports; maintained four-year program despite cost pressures to reduce it to three

1922　Commander of the Military District of Manila, Philippine Islands

1923　Commander of a brigade in the Philippine Division

1925　Awarded second star, promoted to major general

1925–28 Served in various U.S. postings; served as one of the judges of the court-martial that tried Brig. Gen. Billy Mitchell; president of the American Olympic Committee during the 1928 Summer Olympics in Amsterdam

1928–30 Commander of the Philippine Department, Manila; developed plans for a large Filipino self-defense force

1930–35 Chief of staff, U.S. Army: led resistance to budget cutbacks during a time of widespread pacifism; on the instructions of President Herbert Hoover, led forcible expulsion of the so-called Bonus Army protesters from Washington, D.C., 1932; appointed by President Roosevelt to head the Civilian Conservation Corps; in 1933, appointed chief of staff; term extended one year (first time this was ever done); awarded citation (Bronze Oak Leaf Cluster) for distinguished service, 1935

1935–41 Returned to the Philippines at the request of Manuel Quezon, first president of the new Commonwealth of the Philippines, as military advisor and field marshal to create a strong Filipino army; retired from the U.S. Army, 1937

1941　Recalled by President Roosevelt to active duty as major general and commander of U.S. Army Forces Far East, responsible for managing U.S. troops and a fleet of B-17 bombers, and training ten new Filipino divisions; promoted to lieutenant general, subsequently promoted to general

1942　After three months of leading fierce ground resistance to superior Japanese forces, ordered by President Roosevelt to escape to Australia to plan counterattack; received the Medal of Honor; appointed Commander of Allied Forces, Southwest Pacific (troops mostly Australian)

1944 Appointed Commander of American Southwest Pacific Area by President Roosevelt; led the assault on Japanese territories in the Pacific; conducted victorious New Guinea campaign: upon reaching the Philippines, waded ashore at Leyte on October 20 and fulfilled promise, "I shall return!" Awarded third Distinguished Service medal; appointed by the Australian government an honorary Knight Grand Cross of the Order of the Bath; promoted to new five-star rank of General of the Army (along with George Marshall and Dwight Eisenhower).

No question, this man was in illustrious company, not only with Marshall and Eisenhower but also with other five-stars like General Arnold and Admirals Halsey, Leahy, King, and Nimitz. Plus this man had been the army chief of staff and superintendent of West Point—to which President Truman had once sought admission and been rejected. Most impressive of all, this man was a recipient of the vaunted Medal of Honor (and had been recommended for it three times, not just once—that, too, must set a record).

The Medal of Honor. How proud the president would have been in his place! A World War I veteran himself, an avid reader of military history and admirer of great generals, Harry S Truman often thought he would rather be a Medal of Honor recipient than be a president of the United States.

The position was a political and administrative one: commander of the Allied Powers occupying Japan. Though it reported to the president and the army chief of staff, its powers were far greater than those granted to the president under the Constitution. Its occupant would have total and complete dictatorial control over a nation of nearly eighty million people who had knifed America in the back at Pearl Harbor and waged a bitter war—replete with atrocities—for four and a half years. It would not be an easy assignment, and called for a man of extraordinary leadership skills to bring peace and democracy to a sullen, devastated nation.

Was MacArthur the right man? Brilliant though he had been on the battlefield, he was known as one who marched to the beat of his own drum, hard to control, full of himself. Harry Truman was a person with no pretensions, just a lot of good common sense and a politician's knack for reading people. His own military service in France, seeing the stupidity of generals and the senseless slaughter of grunts like himself, had sharpened his smoldering resentment of pompous generals and the military caste system, a feeling he put to good use as a senator when he headed the Senate Special Committee to Investigate the National Defense Program, went after all the wasteful military spending, and saved the United States a staggering three billion dollars. He had made such a good name for himself and the so-called Truman Committee that FDR chose him to be his running mate.

Enough scuttlebutt had filtered up to the White House to make the president leery about this man. In his personal diary of June 17, he had written: "discussed . . . Supreme Commander and what to do with Mr. Prima Donna, Brass Hat, Five Star MacArthur. He's worse than the Cabots and the Lodges—they at least talked with one another before they told God what to do. Mac tells God right off."

That wasn't all. The president also went on to call him "a play actor and a bunco man" and wonder "how a country can produce such men as Robert E. Lee, John J. Pershing, and Eisenhower & Bradley and at the same time produce Custers, Pattons, and MacArthurs."

The problem with MacArthur was that he had a majestically high opinion of himself, almost to the point of having a Mount Rushmore complex. Over the past fifteen years he had referred to himself not in the first person but in the third as if he were an institution: "MacArthur says" . . . "MacArthur requests" . . . "MacArthur thinks."

Was he too smart for his own good? Too independent? In the 1925 trial of Gen. Billy Mitchell, MacArthur had been the sole judge to vote for acquittal, saying that "a senior officer should not be silenced for being at variance with his superiors in rank and with accepted doctrine." Fair enough, but on two occasions MacArthur had demonstrated a tendency to let his independence veer into insubordination. The first was the 1932 attack on the Bonus Army marchers in Washington: when ordered by Secretary of War Patrick Hurley to clear out the area in a controlled manner, MacArthur had used excessive force that resulted in national headlines and a public relations disaster for President Hoover. A second dereliction was even more serious. Within hours of the Pearl Harbor attack he had been ordered to execute the emergency war plan, Rainbow Five. What a debacle that was! MacArthur, confident that the Japanese wouldn't dare attack, had done nothing. He was wrong: Seven hours later the Japanese launched a surprise raid on the Philippines, and MacArthur lost almost half his air force—ninety-six planes, mostly sitting on the ground.

Douglas MacArthur hadn't been in the United States since 1937. Had he "gone native"? Truman had no idea. What a strange situation this was! A president of the United States is supposed to meet and personally sign off on every cabinet officer and senior advisor in his administration, and here was Harry Truman, a man who prided himself on his people skills and gut instincts, appointing a stranger to one of the most powerful positions in his administration. Unfortunately there was no time to order MacArthur to Washington for a face-to-face meeting.

Two days earlier the president had received a call from Senator Tom Connally telling him he was "making a mistake in appointing Dugout Doug as Allied Commander in Chief to accept the Jap surrender." The senator warned him that MacArthur would run against him for president in 1948 if he built him up. The president told the senator that whatever MacArthur might or might not do didn't bother him in the least because he didn't want to run in 1948 anyway.

The president knew Admiral Nimitz wanted this post, Supreme Commander for the Allied Powers (SCAP). Truman liked and admired Nimitz, fleet commander of the U.S. Navy in the Pacific. But Truman had been president for only a short time—exactly four months now—and was highly reluctant to appear to countermand President Roosevelt's 1944 selection of MacArthur over Nimitz as the lead strategist for the Pacific theater. In his capacity as Commander for the American Southwest Pacific Area, MacArthur had delivered on his promise. For the general who had done the most to bring Japan to its knees, the SCAP position would be a logical reward.

The president knew he really had no choice. "The buck stops here," famously proclaimed a sign on his desk. He must make a decision. After his secretary came back with the necessary papers, he reached for his pen and signed his name, authorizing the appointment. He was not thrilled: MacArthur was a wild card, a "bunco man." The president would have to watch him carefully and make sure he didn't cause any trouble.

U.S. presidents make decisions all the time, some they are comfortable with, some they are most definitely not. Truman always said he slept peacefully on the night he made the decision to drop the atom bomb. History does not tell us how he slept on the night he made the decision to appoint MacArthur, but this we do know: It was a superb decision, perhaps the best he ever made.

Even though, in the end, he would have to fire him.

2

Flying Nine Hundred Miles
from Okinawa to Atsugi

CHIEF OF STAFF: *My God, General, the emperor is worshipped as a real god, yet they tried to assassinate him. What kind of a target will that make you?*
MACARTHUR: *I'm going.*

THE MAN ON the plane held the most powerful military position ever created: SCAP, or Supreme Commander for the Allied Powers that had won World War II and now controlled practically the entire globe. His directive from President Truman had been short and sweet: "You will exercise your authority as you deem proper to carry out your mission."

Oh, how MacArthur loved those words! "As you deem proper." This would be his show, a job he always wanted. Back in February when he was concluding his victorious swath through the Philippines, he had announced: "Manila is ours . . . on to Tokyo." It was well understood that when the Americans undertook Operation Downfall, their massive million-man invasion of Japan, he would be the lead general in charge of what was expected to be a ruthless, kamikaze-filled campaign lasting weeks and months down to the last man, even woman. (Reports from his G-12 spy apparatus warned about housewives armed with gasoline-filled bottles and knife-sharpened broomsticks made into bayonets. In such a case the fight for Japan could end up in hand-to-hand combat in the kitchens.)

Fortunately the devastation of Hiroshima and Nagasaki had stunned the Japanese, enabling the emperor to overrule the militarists and announce Japan's compliance with the nonnegotiable surrender terms.

Instead of fighting his way into Japan with a massive horde of men that would have made D-Day look like a skirmish, MacArthur was about to arrive as a victor in peace. Or so he hoped. As he looked around his new personal plane, a C-54 marked *Bataan* on the outside to honor the prisoners of war in the Philippines who endured the notorious death march, he noted that his officers and troops were all heavily armed.

A flash of inspiration went through his head: How about—? The more he thought about it, he more he liked the idea. But knowing how his men would react, he kept his mouth shut. He saw his closest advisor three rows away, Maj. Gen. Courtney Whitney. How about bouncing the idea off him? No, not a good move. How about Maj. Gen. Charles Willoughby, his lovable, crazy "Baron von Willoughby"? Again, probably best not. Leadership is a lonely position: just when you most need reassurance, you must not seek it lest you reveal your fears and destroy the delicate equilibrium that keeps a leader above his followers.

His idea, sure to shock everyone, must remain in his fertile brain, a brain he regarded as second to none and capable of great bursts of creativity like this particular inspiration. Or like the time in Manila when all the telephone lines in Japan were down after the Nagasaki bombing and he single-handedly devised a way to communicate with the Japanese government by using a secret code on the one channel still functioning, the weather channel. No one else in the entire U.S. military had come up with this clever solution.

He won a prize in 1904 from the War Examining Board for his creativity. The written test: suppose he were on an island with a small force of men, and the enemy was about to invade the harbor with a large group of ships, portending certain death. What to do? Other students were stumped. Not MacArthur. His solution? He would paint lots of damaged signs reading "Harbor mined" and throw them into the ocean in front of the harbor. The enemy would stay away, afraid to attack.

On the other hand, too much creativity resulted in crackpot ideas. The military was always coming up with schemes he had to stomp on and make sure never saw the light of day. Like the phosphorescent foxes. That brainchild came from William "Wild Bill" Donovan's OSS, picking up on the Japanese superstition that "a ghostly fox seen at night carries an evil spirit." The OSS plan went as follows: to make the Japanese think that the gods were about to smite them, the Americans would paint a skulk of foxes with bright phosphorescent paint, toss the animals overboard, and watch them swim to shore and cause panic and fear among the Japanese. MacArthur told the OSS guys the idea was nuts, and told them why. So they made a bet, and a huge shipment of foxes was delivered to Chesapeake Bay for a trial run. The OSS men slapped paint on the squealing animals, then dumped them into the water. Sure enough, MacArthur was right: by the time the foxes reached shore most of the paint had washed off in the salt water. Once on the beach, instead of running into the enemy formations and causing havoc, the foxes lay down on the sand and licked off the remaining paint. MacArthur had a good laugh over that one.

As he looked around the plane, he spotted his aide with the marvelous name of Bonner Fellers, his chief of psychological operations. Fellers had been magnificent: when the OSS had told him about the crackpot phosphorescent fox scheme and rambled on about how their experts understood the Japanese peasant psychology, Fellers had put them in their place so ruthlessly they never uttered a peep again. "Our experts," Fellers had informed them, "state that your experts are obviously superficial observers."

His latest idea, thought MacArthur, was no phosphorescent fox. It had merit. But he would keep it close to his vest. He would wait until the last minute before making his announcement, when it would be too late for anyone to object. In the meantime he relished his lunch, munching on an American creation he was unlikely to enjoy again for a long time: a grilled ham-and-cheese sandwich.

THIS TRIUMPHANT, LONG-AWAITED plane ride to Japan reminded him how quickly he had risen from the ashes. When he had arrived in Australia in 1942, he was one of the most thoroughly defeated generals in history, his reputation in tatters, his nickname "Dugout Doug" for leaving behind a starving army of some 78,000 men on Bataan and Corregidor (albeit on President Roosevelt's orders). In a conference with FDR and Admiral Nimitz in July 1944, the odds were against him.

The favored strategy was the navy's plan to bypass the Philippines and approach Japan directly across the Pacific. The man making the final decision was the president, a navy man. MacArthur was to be retired gracefully, at sixty-four. Instead, in a brilliant two-hour presentation with no notes whatsoever, MacArthur had dazzled the president and Nimitz with a plan so persuasive that he beat out Nimitz and talked himself back into the war. As the new commander, in eight months he won the land, air, and sea battle for Leyte, then Luzon and Manila, becoming the conqueror of more territory than any general since Darius I in 540 B.C. Oh, how he loved history!

Yet how much war had now changed! Had he not told George Kenney, his commander of the Far East Air Forces: "The winner of the next war is going to be some 2nd lieutenant who pulls the string on the A-bomb"? If technology was this powerful, what did the world need generals for? Were not men like him an endangered species, potential dinosaurs?

On his silver C-54, an hour had gone by. MacArthur got up and paced the aisle, due to land in two hours at Japan's Atsugi airfield, the training base for kamikaze pilots. He was confident there would be no trouble, because the emperor had so decreed. He also had confidence in his head general now on the ground making sure everything was okay: Robert Eichelberger, the man to whom he had entrusted the most important part of his Philippine campaign; "Take Buna, or not come back alive."

Bob Eichelberger had come back alive, mission accomplished. He was MacArthur's kind of general, a man who went up to the front and personally inspected the situation instead of relying on subordinates and written reports. When promoted to brigadier general on the same day as his West Point classmate George Patton, Eichelberger received a wire from Patton saying they were "the two best damn officers in the U.S. Army"—an assessment with which MacArthur wholly agreed.

MacArthur and Eichelberger had something specific in common: Both had held the rarefied position of superintendent of West Point— one of the three positions in the army FDR stipulated that only he could fill (the other two being chief of staff and chief of engineers). Like MacArthur, Eichelberger had instituted major reforms to modernize the academy and toughen the training. Gone were the polite newspaper photographs of cadets jumping horses over hurdles or smiling at pretty girls at a dance—instead, there were "pictures of cadets making river crossings under smoke barrages." Perhaps most important of all, the two men were passionate football fans and believed the sport to be an essential part of the West Point experience. For MacArthur, who never made the varsity team and had to settle for the position of manager, the highlight of the year was the Army-Navy game, when he would put on headphones, listen to the broadcast over long-range radio, and yell, "Go, Army, go!" So passionate was MacArthur that he had cabled the coach after Army won the 1944 game 24–7: "We have stopped the war to celebrate your magnificent success." The reason Army was now a football powerhouse was Eichelberger, who—after two disastrous seasons and a 48–0 drubbing in one game—decreed that the Army cadets "deserved a team that would teach them to be good warriors." Eichelberger recruited the legendary Earl "Red" Blaik, a West Point graduate then coaching at Dartmouth. More important, he single-handedly eliminated the rule stating no cadet could weigh more than 175 pounds. The regulation had been instituted by the U.S. surgeon general on the theory that life expectancy is greater for a slender man. While this may have been true from an actuarial viewpoint, it was one hell of a way to run a football team. Eichelberger won the argument by going down to Washington and pointing out that life expectancy in battle is just about the same for big or little men.

MacArthur hated bureaucratic thinking. Rules had their place, but adding more and more rules for the sake of convenience was a cowardly and lazy way to run an organization. His experience had taught him several precepts:

1. There is no substitute for adequate preparation. "Had there been a trained and well equipped army of some 20,000 men at Bull Run, the Civil War never would have been fought," he had told a 1933 congressional committee. A keen student of history, he was absolutely right: Had the Union won its first major battle, the Civil War would have been over in a day. "To build an army to be defeated by some other

fellow's army is my idea of wasting a great deal of money," he had told the committee, "and if you are defeated you will pay a billion dollars for every million you save in inadequate preparation." MacArthur had won the post of Supreme Commander of the Pacific over Admiral Nimitz because he had been better prepared and made a better presentation to President Roosevelt, and he had won his campaign by studying every map thoroughly and figuring out how to surprise the enemy.

2. In battle the greatest enemy is personal fear, those awful moments when stomach butterflies nervously flap their wings. The most important job of a leader in life-and-death situations is to communicate with his men and provide reassurance. In civilian jobs, obviously, such reassurance is not so germane, but in Japan, amid some seventy-eight million hostile people, it would be essential. He must use all means available to communicate, pronounce, and strengthen his command. He would do this by conducting his office in a forceful manner and using his powerful mastery of rhetoric.

3. Speed and decisiveness are more important than mass. MacArthur's stunning conquest of the Philippines was due primarily to his speed and use of highly mobile forces to proceed from one island to the next. MacArthur always had to keep moving forward before bad weather set in or the enemy counterattacked with reinforcements. In civilian contexts the need for such urgency is rare, and managers generally value prudence over recklessness. In Japan he would be in a race against time before the inevitable resentment against military occupation set in. He would have only two years at best. His organization, a peacetime one, would have to run at a wartime pace.

4. Put as little as possible in writing, especially rules and regulations. In war, for reasons of security, where possible he always issued his directives in person. The same for peacetime: He would eschew bureaucracy and especially its love of cover-your-butt written reports. One of his dicta as superintendent of West Point had read: "To take up a painful matter by letter or other written communication is not only the rankest cowardice but the ruination of morale." The organization he would create would be a lean one managed by decision makers all

the way down the line. In his view, "Too many executives indolently dispense with a problem by sending out a form letter or looking up a precedent in a book, an action any child could do." His organization, SCAP, would be entirely different. It would be big, of course, but it would act like a lean one: He would make all the key decisions.

5. Military occupations never last long because nobody likes living under another country's thumb. For the occupation of Japan to work, extraordinary efforts must be made to understand Japanese psychology and work with it to mutual advantage.

MacArthur was extremely proud of the job his cadre of officers was doing. Just ten days earlier they caught a horrendous mistake by Washington that could have upset the entire surrender and enabled the Japanese in several years to renounce it as improper and invalid. All because the provincial bureaucrats in Washington didn't know what everyone who knows a bit of French knows, the difference between *vous* and *tu*. One is a formal, impersonal form of "you," the other is a more personal, intimate one. Many languages make this distinction, which English does not. In Japanese the distinction is as wide as a chasm.

The surrender documents prepared by Washington had used the wrong pronoun, *watakushi*, meaning "I"—a word never used by someone so important and dignified as the emperor. The proper word is *chin*, which translates, for lack of a better term, into "we." Using the wrong word was more than just incorrect, more than just degrading and humiliating to the emperor: It was a mistake with profound legal implications.

Fortunately the head of the four-thousand-man Allied Translator and Interpreter Section, Col. Sidney Mashbir, had caught it and gone to his boss, General Willoughby. Willoughby, German-born and a master of several languages, immediately set up a meeting for Mashbir to see MacArthur. They spent an hour together, discussing the distinctions between "temporal power" and "spiritual power" and how the emperor fitted in. At the end of the meeting MacArthur had given Mashbir complete authority to rewrite the surrender document to conform to Japanese usage, and closed the meeting with the words: "If at any time you feel that there is anything I should know, I want you to come straight to me with it. Don't hesitate." That's how MacArthur ran his organization: If someone had a serious problem, come straight to him.

MacArthur was no lawyer, but he had the brains of a good one. In fact, if he hadn't admired his father enough to follow in his footsteps and become a general, his choice of career would have been law. The legal implications of this translation error may have escaped the non-lawyer or the incompetent one, but they didn't escape MacArthur. Someone in Washington had screwed up, big-time. Had the surrender documents contained language improperly prepared under Japanese law, then at any time in the future the Japanese government could have said the surrender was invalid. . . .

It was all a page out of Santayana, about people not remembering the past being condemned to repeat it. Wasn't this exactly how the Nazis had justified themselves: by repudiating the legality of the Treaty of Versailles? Their argument, which had merit, was that Germany—technically speaking—had never surrendered, which in turn meant that the reparations demands had no legal standing and therefore were improper.

Looking out the window and far off into the distance, where Japan must be, he had his fingers crossed, hoping that the Eighth Army under General Eichelberger had everything under control. How ironic that his top general in Japan was the holder of two medals from the Japanese government: the Imperial Order of Meiji, aka the Order of the Rising Sun, and the Order of the Sacred Treasure. As a member of the American Expeditionary Force in Siberia in 1919–20, Eichelberger had been awarded these medals for helping the Japanese fight the Bolsheviks. Imagine what the Japanese would think if he were to wear these medals on his army uniform now!

MacArthur knew the Japanese were playing possum. They had been ordered to lay down their arms, and every report from his commanders on the ground had confirmed this. Even Eichelberger said so. But he knew Eichelberger well enough to know that Eichelberger slept with one eye open. Especially when it came to the Japanese. Eichelberger understood the Japanese militarists better than anyone in America: He had served with them for two and a half years in Siberia and had not come home brimming with affection. Quite the contrary; after watching the

Japanese surprise everyone by bringing in 125,000 men instead of 12,000, Eichelberger had warned his superiors in Washington, his two Japanese medals notwithstanding: "The Japanese High Command . . . managed to achieve for itself a record of complete perfidy, of the blackest and most heinous double-dealing."

Can't get more blunt than that.

MacArthur reflected on the report he had received from Col. Charles Tench, his aide who had led the fleet of planes that landed on August 26 to prepare the Atsugi airstrip for MacArthur's arrival on August 30. One of the people greeting Tench was a Russian: "I am Commander Anatoliy Rodionov, Naval Attaché of the Soviet Union in Japan. Welcome." What the heck were the Russians doing here? Outrageous, these Russians, having declared war only one day after the bombing of Nagasaki, already trying to grab a piece of the victor's spoils. MacArthur never liked them anyway. Now he loathed them. Then to top it all off, they had handed Tench a letter from Jacob Malik, Russian ambassador to Japan, to be delivered to MacArthur, asking for passes to the surrender ceremonies. What nerve!

MacArthur had tossed the letter aside. Many people back in Washington may have been pleased that the Russians were joining the war against Japan; MacArthur was not one of them. The Russians weren't needed, they were just crashing the victory party.

MacArthur had good reason to abhor the Russians. Ostensible allies in the war against Germany, they had almost cost MacArthur his life. In October 1944, a senior official in the Russian Foreign Ministry had tipped off the Japanese ambassador in Moscow that the American forces were getting ready to attack in the Philippines. Four days later a top Japanese general and the country's legendary hero, Gen. Tomoyuki Yamashita, arrived in Manila. Every bit as arrogant and self-confident as MacArthur, Yamashita electrified everyone by declaring that he was going to teach MacArthur a lesson and dictate surrender terms in the Philippines.

In due course MacArthur would have the immense pleasure of dealing with the butcher Yamashita, but he would never forgive the Russians for having put this general against him, thus causing many needless American deaths.

MacArthur was not a man who, once he made a decision or developed a plan, was racked with self-doubts or what-ifs. He had to be pleased with himself that day, having just received a cable from Secretary of War Stimson calling him the "principal architect" of the Pacific victory and citing him for "brilliant planning" and an "enterprise [that] has grown in scope and boldness." *Boldness*, he liked that word. His plan to land in Japan and take it over was a daring one: to hit his first area of occupation with sizable forces and pour men in rapidly behind the first troops. The Japanese would have no room for surprise maneuvers. In keeping with his tactics of what the *New York Times* would soon tout as his "fool-proof"occupation, he would establish a beachhead and seal off Tokyo and annex the great port of Yokohama, without actually taking over Tokyo. This had now been done. Next, he would extend his lines to take in Tokyo and adjacent areas. Then, and only then, would he gradually fan out, as more divisions came ashore to take over all of Honshu Island.

War Department officials had warned him to be completely on guard against Japanese treachery. Yes, that was a serious possibility, but MacArthur was betting on another trick up his sleeve, a psychological one. The Japanese had yet to receive the full details of American surrender terms. Everything was very much up in the air, meaning there was nothing specific for Japanese militarists to focus their rancor on. Everyone in Japan was waiting to see what MacArthur would do. He had, if you could call it that, a grace period. By the time it expired, MacArthur would have so many troops in Japan that the Japanese would realize the futility of last-ditch resistance.

But for this plan to work it was essential that this landing at Atsugi go off perfectly.

Corncob pipe in hand, he spent forty minutes of the three-hour flight walking up and down the aisle, deep in thought. Speaking out to his fellow generals, he astonished them by giving a lecture and announcing his major priorities for the occupation—as if he had no concern about kamikazes and assassins waiting for them in Japan:

First destroy the military power ...
Then build the structure of representative government ...

Enfranchise the women . . .
Free the political prisoners . . .
Liberate the farmers . . .
Establish a free labor movement . . .
Encourage a free economy . . .
Abolish police oppression . . .
Develop a free and responsible press . . .
Liberalize education . . .
Decentralize the political power.

That was it: eleven priorities. Eleven major tasks to accomplish, with the entire world watching. From the tone of his voice, everyone on the plane knew he was not shooting the breeze or thumping his chest, he was dead serious. He had a plan. He was thoroughly prepared.

They were impressed—as MacArthur wanted them to be. In his *Reminiscences* he wrote: "From the moment of my appointment as supreme commander, I had formulated the policies I intended to follow, implementing them through the Emperor and the machinery of the imperial government."

Had he really? As was often the case with MacArthur, he was guilty of exaggeration. The day before, he had received via military radio from Washington the fifth draft of *Initial Post-Surrender Policy for Japan*, a policy document under development for more than a year. What MacArthur had actually done was take a poorly written document and translate its key points into language everyone could understand.

Helping people better understand Washington government memorandums is all well and good, but as a general on a dangerous mission, MacArthur's major objective was to ensure the safety of his people and himself. He couldn't admit it, but he had good reason to be as terrified as his men about the security at Atsugi. Had the Japanese, as ordered, subdued the thousands of kamikaze pilots and removed the propellers from all the airplanes? He knew the country they were flying into was heavily armed, with 2.2 million soldiers at beck and call. More specifically he was flying directly into the dragon's mouth, the headquarters of the so-called Divine Wind Squadrons. He had only 4,000 American troops in the immediate area of Atsugi; the Japanese had more than 300,000. Up until two days before, diehard Japanese pilots had been dropping leaflets over the cities and countryside, urging the people to carry on the fight. "Resist with tooth and nail!" . . . "Destroy MacArthur's plane!" . . . "The American army devils are coming!" . . . "Send the women and children to the mountains!" The country was swarming with disgruntled militarists and terrorists for whom killing was an act of honor. He, Douglas MacArthur, was the "Most Wanted Man" in this nation; it would take only a single bullet. And he was not the only one. Already, on August 15, there had been an attack by thirty-two young Japanese officers on the emperor's palace after the emperor had made his concession statement. They claimed he was not the real Hirohito and that his radio announcement was a fake masterminded by the Americans.* They killed the commanding general of the Imperial Guard Division, and set fire to and machine-gunned the home of the prime minister, Kantaro Suzuki. By the time the bloodbath was over, all thirty-two rebels and six guards were dead. American troops were now in Atsugi and Yokohama, but not yet in Tokyo; they had been warned by the Japanese army that it needed a few more days to clean up the city and ensure there were no renegades running around. In the meantime another group of ultra-nationalists, belonging to the Black Dragon Society, had made two attempts to assassinate the prime minister. When those failed, they tried to kill the head of the Privy Council (an advisory board to the emperor). When would this all end? The only comfort for MacArthur was that the U.S. Navy under Admiral Halsey had an armada offshore consisting of twelve American battleships, two British battleships, and seventeen aircraft carriers with a hundred-plus planes to darken the sky—enough firepower to decimate the Japanese into oblivion should they try any funny business at Atsugi.

Still, all it takes to start complete mayhem—and a full-scale invasion—is one lunatic with a gun or a grenade. It was a chance he

---

*This claim was not as preposterous as it seems. The Japanese people had never before heard the emperor's voice on the radio. (For most of the American military, used to American radio and FDR's "fireside chats," this came as a shock.)

would have to take. All his life he had taken risks on the battlefield and never gotten hit. Worry would do him no good, he must get ready for the big moment, so he finally took a nap. He was the only one. None of the other generals and officers on the plane dared think of sleep, they were so uptight and racked with tension and fear.

Down on land the Japanese were just as nervous as the men in the plane. Never in twelve hundred years had Japan been invaded. Who knew what these Americans would do? In Gifu City, the mayor ordered all girls aged fifteen to twenty-five to flee into the mountains to avoid American soldiers. At several Japanese companies such as Kanto Kyogo and Nakajimo Aircraft, cyanide capsules were being handed out to female workers should American soldiers try to rape them.

Only an incurable romantic would do what MacArthur was doing, descending unarmed onto a kamikaze airfield like a swashbuckling Errol Flynn. Reckless and foolhardy? At the age of twenty-five, MacArthur had visited Japan as aide to his father, a prominent general and Medal of Honor recipient (like his son was to become).* At the 1905 Battle of Mukden, where 140,000 men were killed in the biggest land battle of the Russo-Japanese War, MacArthur had watched a Japanese battalion trying five times to take a Russian position. Like an artist impelled to seize the brush of a fumbling student, MacArthur couldn't bear watching it anymore: He took command of the (undoubtedly startled) Japanese battalion and led it by a new route to capture the Russian battery on top of the hill. Had he been Japanese, he would have gotten a medal.

Now he was being equally reckless, perhaps? He did not think so, based on his reading of the emperor's hold over the Japanese people. MacArthur had met the emperor at the time, Hirohito's grandfather Mutsuhito, and written: "I met all the great Japanese commanders: Oyama, Kuroki, Nogi, and the brilliant Admiral Heihachiro Togo— those grim, taciturn, aloof men of iron character and unshakeable

---

*The only other father-son besides Arthur MacArthur and Douglas MacArthur who have received the Medal of Honor are the son Theodore Roosevelt Jr. and then his father (posthumously).

purpose. It was here that I first encountered the boldness and courage of the Nipponese soldier. His almost fanatical belief in and reverence for his Emperor impressed me indelibly."

What most impressed MacArthur was a particular small incident. A Japanese general was ordering his soldiers to take pills every four hours to fight a battlefield sickness. MacArthur teased the general, saying that his Japanese soldiers wouldn't take the pills any more than American GIs would, they'd throw the capsules into the first ditch. The Japanese general was offended: "My soldiers will never do that. You wait and see. Orders will be carried out."

They weren't. The Japanese soldiers threw away the pills, happy to be alive. Frustrated, the Japanese general issued a new order: "The Emperor requests that each soldier take one capsule every four hours."

This time the soldiers obeyed.

MacArthur knew that when the emperor issued a pronouncement, it was called the Voice of the Crane (an imperial command that, like a crane's call, could still be heard in the sky after the bird had passed). In the 1945 Japanese deliberations about how to respond to the Potsdam Declaration, setting forth the terms of the Japanese surrender, the vote in the Supreme War Council had been 3–3, until the emperor cast the deciding vote in favor of surrender, 4–3 (in effect, 7–0). Hirohito recited his surrender announcement twice, each one a separate recording for the sake of security. It was the first time the emperor had ever spoken directly to the people. The emperor's statement was a masterpiece of pettifoggery:

We declared war on America and Britain out of our sincere desire to ensure Japan's self-preservation and the stabilization of East Asia, it being far from our thoughts either to infringe upon the sovereignty of other nations or to embark on territorial aggrandizement. But now the war has lasted for nearly four years. Despite the best that has been done by everyone, the war situation has developed not necessarily to Japan's advantage, while the general trends of the world have all turned against her interest.

Moreover, the enemy has begun to deploy a new and most cruel bomb. . . .

Such being the case, how are we to save the millions of our subjects, or to atone ourselves before the hallowed spirits of our imperial ancestors? This is the reason why we have ordered the acceptance of the provisions of the Powers of the joint declaration.

We cannot but express the deepest regret to our allied nations of East Asia, who have consistently cooperated with the Empire towards the emancipation of East Asia. . . .

Full of half-truths and equivocations, the document contains not a word about "defeat," "surrender," or "capitulation." The emperor says Japan was taking the initiative "in effecting a settlement of the present situation by resorting to an extraordinary measure" (that is, agreeing to surrender). His comment on the bomb is equally self-serving: "The enemy has begun to employ a new and most cruel bomb, the power of which to do damage is indeed incalculable, taking the toll of so many innocent lives. Should we continue to fight, it would not only result in an ultimate collapse and obliteration of the Japanese nation, but it would lead to the total extinction of human civilization." In other words, Japan—the most militarist nation on earth, a nation that had killed seventeen million people, most of them innocent civilians—was saving the rest of the world. And to say Japan couldn't "continue to fight" because of the bomb was totally incorrect from a military point of view. Japan was getting clobbered in the last few months of the war: Everyone in the government knew it. All the bomb did was bring the war to a sharp conclusion.

Clearly SCAP had a job to do: Educate the Japanese people about the real facts.

As the plane neared Mount Fuji, MacArthur was awakened to admire the beautiful view. It was spectacular, but where was the snow? The snow-capped peak of Fujiyama, so familiar to everyone from photographs, postcards, and paintings, was bare. One of the generals grumbled that he was willing to bet the Japanese had melted the snow off on purpose.

After passing Mount Fuji the *Bataan* dipped down over Kamakura, the home of the great forty-four-foot-high Buddha built in 1352, more than a hundred years before Columbus discovered America. As the plane swung down toward Atsugi, MacArthur's chief aide, Gen. Courtney Whitney, was gripped by fear. "I could see numerous anti-aircraft emplacements. . . . Here was the greatest opportunity for a final and climactic act. The anti-aircraft guns could not possibly miss at this range. Had death, the insatiable monster of the battle, passed MacArthur by on a thousand fields only to murder him at the end?

"I think the whole world was holding its breath. But as usual he had been right," wrote Whitney in his 1956 memoir. "He knew the orient. He knew the basic Japanese character too well to have thus gambled blindly with death." What MacArthur was doing, Whitney knew, was listening to the Voice of the Crane.

The *Bataan* hit the runway. They had reached Atsugi. As the plane slowed to a stop, MacArthur gathered his generals around him and said in a voice loud enough to be heard by everyone on the plane, "Gentlemen, I have an announcement to make."

The men leaned forward, anxious to capture the general's every word. His message was brief: Men, remove your guns.

3

"The Most Courageous Act
of the Entire War"

THE *BATAAN* LANDED by mistake on the wrong end of the runway. Not an auspicious start for this all-important day, the beginning of MacArthur's reign. As a man used to dramatic landings on enemy beaches, he liked everything perfect. At least there was no gunfire—yet.

Gen. Hugh Johnson, the former head of Roosevelt's National Recovery Administration and 1933 *Time* Man of the Year, had once marveled at MacArthur, one of his West Point classmates—a man, he said, "simply born without the emotion of fear."

When Gen. Masahara Homma reported to Tokyo headquarters that with MacArthur in Corregidor he had possession of the bottle and MacArthur trapped inside the bottleneck, MacArthur replied with exuberance, "Homma may have the bottle—but I've got the cork!"

Sure enough, three months later MacArthur escaped Corregidor. When he returned to the Philippines, the Japanese sent to face him their best general, the conqueror of Singapore, General Yamashita. Other American generals might have cringed at the prospect of fighting the Tiger of Malaya, but not MacArthur. He was delighted: "I'm glad to meet the champion." When the fight was over and MacArthur had recaptured Manila, the tiger was on the run. Any moment now he would have to come out of the woods and surrender. How sweet that would be.

Even sweeter was the moment about to begin on August 30. For the past forty-eight hours American troops had worked nonstop with the

Japanese military to secure the Atsugi area. The kamikaze pilots had been rounded up and given their marching orders not to try anything glorious. The war was over: Stay home or you'll be arrested. Their three hundred planes on the airfield had been stripped of their propellers and the gas tanks drained. What a strange sight, all those planes looking naked without propellers, symbolizing Japan's helplessness.

No American claimed to understand Japan better than Joseph Grew, the U.S. ambassador from 1932 to 1941. In a CBS radio address after he returned to the United States, Grew said:

> I have had many friends in Japan, some of whom I admired, respected and loved. They are not the people who brought on this war. As patriots they will fight for their Emperor and their country, to the last ditch if necessary, but they did not want this war and it was not they who began it. . . . But there is another side to the picture, the ugly side of cruelty, brutality, and utter bestiality, the ruthlessness and rapaciousness of the Japanese military machine which brought on this war. That Japanese military machine and military caste and military system must be utterly crushed.

How to explain this dichotomy between the two Japans? It had to do with the old Japanese expression, "When dogs are frightened, they bark, and the more they are frightened, the louder they bark." In his memoirs, published in 1944, Grew wrote:

> The naïveté of the Japanese is really amazing. They love high-sounding formulas and slogans to cover whatever they want and intend to do, with the idea of imparting to their plans the most perfect righteousness, lulling even themselves into the belief that their acts are wholly righteous. . . . A Japanese friend said to me the other day: "The trouble with you Anglo-Saxons is that you regard and deal with the Japanese as grown-up people, whereas the Japanese are but children and should be treated like children. An encouraging word or gesture immediately inspires confidence."

MacArthur was too sophisticated a man to take this literally, but he knew what Grew was referring to. Japan was an underdeveloped, feudal society controlled by a militarist government, like a child raised by a brutal parent. Give people a taste of democracy, give the child room to grow, and you will have the kind of people Grew had come to like and admire. As a general MacArthur knew the value of intelligence: 80 to 90 percent of winning the battle is figuring out what the other side's moves will be. Get into the head of your enemy.

Of course it was easy to lose your temper and blow up when Japanese newspapers like *Nichi Nichi Shimbun* came out with articles charging America with acting "like a prostitute, whispering on dark corners," but what was really going on here? The solution was not to come down hard on frightened people—the atom bombs had been enough—what was needed was a show of empathy to give them self-respect and confidence. He must give the Japanese a sense of security.

What better way than to arrive unarmed?

THE DOOR OF the plane opened, and there stood Douglas MacArthur at his photogenic best, hat at a rakish angle, dark aviator sunglasses, corncob pipe in his mouth, about to descend the stairs and set foot on his realm like a god coming out of the skies. MacArthur, as he always did, had been careful to instruct his ground forces to have photographers ready. A lot of film would be used that day, more than a hundred rolls. A moment in history, to survive, must be photographed vividly.

The heavily armed Japanese soldiers, fingers twitching on the triggers of their rifles at the slightest appearance of trouble from a kamikaze pilot or some angry warrior, were stunned. They were even more amazed as numerous generals poured out of the plane, all smiling as if they were arriving at a college reunion. They were totally unarmed. Winston Churchill, when he heard about it, called it "the most daring and courageous act of the entire war."

Waiting to greet MacArthur was the head of the vaunted Eighth Army, the force now in charge of Japan, Robert Eichelberger, the brilliant general who had won Buna.

MacArthur thrust out his arm and gripped Eichelberger hard: "Bob, this is payoff time."

The cameras clicked away furiously. This was what Buna was for.

Observed the Japanese historian Kazuo Kawai: "It was a masterpiece of psychology, which completely disarmed Japanese apprehensions. From that moment, whatever danger there might have been of a fanatic attack on the Americans vanished in a wave of Japanese admiration and gratitude."

So far, so good.

The party moved forward to where lunch was being served. A young American sergeant reached for his rifle to present arms, the customary salute when a soldier has a weapon. Only problem was, the poor fellow was so nervous and intimidated he picked up the first thing his hand reached for. The supreme commander stopped and stared at the sergeant holding a bamboo stick in his arm, transfixed like a pillar of salt, knowing he had screwed up big-time. MacArthur's stern countenance slowly turned into a smile: "Son, I think you're in the wrong army"— and he gave him a wink.

The head Japanese general had a lot more to be worried about: something goes wrong, the Japanese prime minister had warned him bluntly, you commit suicide. Lt. Gen. Seizo Arisue, director general of Japanese intelligence and chief of what euphemistically might be called "the welcoming committee," nervously motioned the conquerors to the carefully laid-out tables. A scrumptious buffet had been prepared. He hoped the Americans would appreciate the miracles he pulled off, getting his hands on so much food in a destitute country . . . not to mention a quiet airfield, free of gunfire.

Col. Sidney Huff, chief of counterintelligence and the man in charge of security, suddenly stepped forward, panic-stricken. It was fine for MacArthur to pull off this PR stunt arriving unarmed, but what was this orange juice all about? The Japanese waiters were offering trays with glasses of juice. Huff grabbed the first glass before anyone else and quickly gulped it. He put his hand to his heart, then he felt his stomach while everyone watched, some of them starting to laugh—they knew the Japanese wouldn't dare do something so stupid as resort to poison. Lieutenant General Arisue also grabbed a glass and raised it to the Americans, as if making a welcoming toast. The orange juice passed the test, and everyone started drinking.

The buffet, also vigorously tested by Huff's men, was excellent, and the Americans enjoyed themselves thoroughly. After lunch they gathered for a lengthy photo-op. Ever the peacock, MacArthur stayed at the base for an extra half hour, posing for photographers.

It was now time to push on to Yokohama. The Japanese army had assembled a motorcade of fifty dilapidated cars, mostly coal burning—the best they could find, led by an old beat-up red fire engine. For MacArthur the Japanese had come up with a Lincoln. The Americans boarded the cars, and the procession moved forward. Instead of an eighteen-mile trip taking a half hour, this one took an excruciating two hours, interrupted by the fire engine breaking down every ten minutes and starting up again. Once in a while one of the cars sputtered to a halt, a vivid precursor of what happens when a country runs out of oil. A Japanese ran over and dumped some more coal into the engine in the trunk (apparently there was such a severe shortage of petroleum in Japan that the gasoline engines in the front couldn't be used).

For the stunned Americans—who had ever seen a coal-fired car before?—the biggest shock was the lineup of 30,000 Japanese soldiers guarding the road. Armed with bayonets and rifles, they stood with their backs to the motorcade, both for security and to show the same respect to the Americans they habitually showed the emperor.

Just a week earlier, when the emperor had issued his radio announcement that Japan would surrender, a group of Japanese militarists had tried to shoot their way into the palace. Thirty-eight people had been killed. The next day, in a separate incident, ten young men calling themselves the Sonjo Gigun—the Righteous Group for Upholding Imperial Rule and Driving Out Foreigners—had seized a hill within sight of the American Embassy and set off five grenades, killing themselves. Might similar militarists be embedded in the 30,000?

It was like running the gauntlet, said one of the generals: Any one of these guys can turn around and shoot us. Or toss a grenade. MacArthur was firm in his response; there could be no other way: "The gauntlet must be run."

The two-hour journey passed without incident. At the end of the day MacArthur and other senior members of his staff had dinner in a small dining room off the lobby in the New Grand Hotel, 80 percent destroyed in the war. Steak was served. Whitney warned that the steak might be poisoned. MacArthur laughed it off: "No one can live forever." The next course was fish, a most unappetizing-looking concoction, embalmed in a gray sauce. For the next twelve days the hotel would serve the same fish, first with brown sauce, then a yellow sauce, and finally a plain white sauce. It became so depressing that many of the officers looked for any possible excuse to go aboard one of the U.S. Navy ships in the harbor and eat in the mess hall.

That day, in Tokyo, thirty-two members of secret societies committed hara-kiri in public to atone for "their inability to win the war."

The next morning at breakfast MacArthur ordered eggs. It turned out that the hotel kitchen had no eggs. Men of the Eleventh Airborne rushed into the city looking for eggs; after an hour, they returned—with just one egg. MacArthur realized he had a humanitarian crisis on his hands: The Japanese had no food. Making a mental note, he issued his first order of the occupation, the first of the 2,185 orders later called SCAPINS (SCAP instructions): Troops were forbidden to eat local food. They were to eat only what the navy and air force brought in. Local food must be reserved for the locals who desperately needed it.

He had been in Japan only one day, and already the occupation had a huge task on its hands nobody ever thought of: food. He finished eating his fried egg and left to start working on preparations for the big day coming up the day after tomorrow.

4

Sword Sheathed,
but Gleaming in Its Scabbard

The right use of a sword is that it should subdue the barbarians while lying gleaming in its scabbard. If it leaves its sheath it cannot be said to be used rightly. Similarly the right use of military power is that it should conquer the enemy while concealed in the breast.

—IEYASU TOKUGAWA (1543–1616),
the greatest shogun of them all

SEPTEMBER 2, 1945, would be MacArthur's day of glory, the day Japan signed the surrender. Ever since the day after Pearl Harbor, this was the moment he had been waiting for.

Most Americans thought of Pearl Harbor, December 7, as the biggest day of the war. Not MacArthur. He had his own demons to exorcise.

For him it was December 8, when he had failed to follow Gen. George Marshall's warning about a potential attack in the Philippines. On that day—only nine hours after MacArthur had heard about Pearl Harbor and been ordered to go on full alert—the Japanese Air Force had found MacArthur's B-17s lined up on the airfield like sitting ducks and bombed them to bits. Had he not been such a high-ranking general and able to obfuscate the incident with vague and uncorroborated claims about orders passed down the line and mysteriously not obeyed, he might well have been court-martialed for dereliction of duty (like Admiral Kimmel and Admiral Short at Pearl Harbor). It was only because FDR was so desperate for some good news to give the American public that the whole incident had been papered over, no formal investigation undertaken, and MacArthur given the Medal of Honor to make the American public feel proud that America was fighting back. For MacArthur, it had been a close call. He must never underestimate the Japanese again.

But he had. He had encountered Japanese fighting prowess at Corregidor and suffered humiliating defeat, forcing him to flee to Australia. Two years later he had returned, conducting a brilliant campaign covering seven thousand miles and attacks on over forty islands without a single defeat. He was now a hero, acknowledged by Winston Churchill, Franklin Roosevelt, Gen. George Marshall, and Field Marshals Bernard Montgomery and Sir Alan Brooke as the ablest American commander of World War II. Some even called him the greatest American general since Ulysses Grant. And what was MacArthur most proud of? Not that he had captured so much territory and killed so many men, but that he had lost so few of his own. In fact, he had lost fewer men than Eisenhower had in a single battle, the Battle of the Bulge. Great generals are not butchers.*

He was a warrior. There was the famous scene at Leyte where he had stood over a pile of dead Japanese soldiers and exclaimed with glee, "A good Jap is a dead Jap!" He had witnessed the atrocities performed by Japanese soldiers in Manila, raping women, impaling babies on their bayonets, treating prisoners like vermin. He had seen the men he left behind in Bataan, emerging from captivity like walking skeletons—at least those who were still alive. He had every reason to hate the "Japs" for what they had done, but he could not. Warriors have a code of honor. It was now time for peace, and like Tokugawa he would keep his sword sheathed in its scabbard, gleaming and ready to flash at a moment's notice.

*MacArthur was unusually solicitous of the lives of his men. He believed in outsmarting the enemy, not bludgeoning the enemy with superior numbers of manpower at the cost of heavy casualties. In this he was the opposite of Grant, who could lose ten thousand men in a battle and not think twice about it. The first thing most commanders do when they start their day is study the latest battlefield reports and where their troops and the enemy's are configured. Not MacArthur. He would study the latest fatality reports, slowly reading the name of every soldier killed, line by line. It was his way—painful though it might be—of reminding himself of his fundamental responsibility as a general: to protect his men. They all knew this, and respected him for it. To serve under MacArthur was considered a privilege, as good a chance as any they would return home alive.

He had a job to do on this day: to send the Japanese a message. A message so powerful they would never forget it.

MacArthur thought Eisenhower was sometimes a bore: Eisenhower who had been his underling in the Philippines for seven years, Eisenhower who had never fought a battle on the front lines or risked his life as he had, Eisenhower the typical "desk general." At the critical once-in-a-lifetime moment when Germany formally surrendered, Eisenhower had performed the signing in a remote schoolhouse at three in the morning, observed by no one, allowing the defeated Germans to slink away in the dark of night. What a cop-out way to treat an enemy! What a moment of history missed!

What's the point of history if the world can't see it?

He, Douglas MacArthur, would show the world how to conduct a surrender. But he would astonish and impress everyone. Like Grant at Appomattox, he would not humiliate the enemy as everyone expected—he would be respectful, he would uplift them. It would be a huge ceremony, like the coronation of a king, promising better days to come.

Most important of all, he would make absolutely sure they never forgot who won.

In all the armaments of war, nothing is quite so imposing as a battleship, a big, cold, gray battleship with huge guns threatening the skies. For two weeks now, Douglas MacArthur had planned every single last detail of this event. He had to make a lot of people happy, make them think they were vital. To keep the navy happy, he had asked for their best battleship, and President Harry Truman—a lowly captain in World War I—had jumped in and provided the *Missouri*, named after the president's home state and christened by none other than his daughter, Margaret. Again to keep the navy happy, MacArthur had made Bull Halsey the official master of ceremonies, though of course there could be only one lead actor in the play. To remind the Japanese of the brutality they had inflicted in the war, he arranged for two men to be standing on the other side of the desk, facing the Japanese delegation: Jonathan Wainwright, the walking-skeleton general who had endured so much suffering in Bataan, and the equally emaciated Arthur Percival, the British general who had surrendered Singapore.

The Japanese surrender would be signed by two people from Japan, one representing the military, the other representing the government. The surrender document would be brutal and short—just one page long, with a second page for the eleven signatures of the entities participating. To sign for the office of SCAP was MacArthur; to sign for the United States was Admiral Nimitz, the man who had sought the job MacArthur now held. Surrounding the ship would be the greatest naval armada the world had ever seen, with massive cannons ready to unleash their firepower should there be any trouble. Photographers would be present, along with fifteen hundred soldiers and seamen enjoying the fruits of their hard-earned victory, witnessing the spectacle as if in a Roman forum, only there was to be no cheering whatsoever. Everyone invited had been thoroughly instructed to be totally quiet and not say a word, ever. Twenty minutes of dead silence can make twenty minutes seem like a long, long time.

It was now almost nine o'clock in the morning, and everyone was assembled outside. MacArthur was in his cabin, getting his final thoughts together, when there was a gentle knock on the door: "General, we are ready." One moment, said MacArthur, as the messenger turned around and his footsteps retreated into the distance. MacArthur rose from his chair, his hands shaking, walked over to the toilet in the bathroom, leaned down, and threw up.

THE LINEUP OF important American naval officers on board the *Missouri* was notable for the absence of the number-three man, Adm. Raymond Spruance, the winner of the Battle of Midway and soon to be commander of the U.S. Pacific Fleet. Nimitz, fearful that rather than surrender, the Japanese might attack the *Missouri* and kill all the high-ranking Americans aboard, had ordered Spruance to stay in Okinawa and take command of the navy if need be. At the most memorable moment of his career, all Spruance could do was listen to the radio, praying he would never be called.

IT HAD BEEN a wearying morning for Toshikazu Kase. The forty-two-year-old Japanese diplomat, a graduate of Amherst College and a research fellow at Harvard in 1927, had been up since 4:30. Unlike MacArthur, he had no role other than to simply observe. But because of his fluency in English and his trusted role as secretary to the foreign minister, he had been assigned to prepare a report on the day's proceedings to be delivered personally to the emperor.

At 5:00 a.m. four cars joined up to leave Tokyo, a city of desolation. The skyline was gone, reduced to clusters of bomb-ravaged villages. One million of the city's 1,650,000 buildings had been demolished. Debris clogged the streets, and piles of rotting garbage polluted and fouled the air, a dark haze at this early hour. Two-thirds of the 1940 population of nearly seven million were missing, many of them presumably dead. Cats and dogs roamed the streets, looking for food. When daylight rose, children, too, would be scavenging. Half the city's 250 square miles had been wiped out by fire. From the piles of bricks and twisted metal people had assembled thousands of shantytown structures pretending to offer shelter from the rain and cold in a desperate bid for survival—after reading the millions of pamphlets that had rained down on the city blaming their plight on the militarism of people like the men in the four cars.

The cars sped quickly on the war-torn road to Yokohama. Inside were eleven Japanese on their way to the *Missouri* for the signing. They must move quickly, stealthily, in the still-dark light lest assassins were waiting by the roadside to kill them. A defeated nation is an angry land, and millions of people had guns and explosives. "There were few men on the road," observed Kase, "and probably none recognized us." Which was just as well. "Our journey had been kept wholly secret lest extremists attempt to impede us by violence."

Yet most of the road was unpaved, forcing them to slow down to five miles an hour lest one of the cars hit a big pothole in the road and have a flat tire or break its suspension. There was no conversation in any of the cars, just glum silence in the shadow of defeat. "Were we not sorrowing men come to seek a tomb for a fallen empire?" thought Kase. Had not the time come, as the emperor put it, to "bear the unbearable"?

Two men in the small procession of cars were particularly nervous. Their identity deliberately had been kept top secret. Had their identity become widely known as the assigned signers of the surrender document, they could well be waylaid and killed on the spot. All the other men in the cars knew this, fearing, too, for their own lives. So when they finally arrived at 7:00 a.m. in Yokohama and saw the heavily armed soldiers of General Eichelberger's Eighth Army, they were much relieved. They had made it.

After an hour's wait the cars were instructed to follow a jeep and proceed down streets guarded by American sentries, now armed with rifles and bayonets. By now the Japanese officials were extremely nervous. They were not aware that most of the American soldiers bore little vengeance, that only the day before three American infantrymen patrolling the streets had stumbled on a woman knocked down by a streetcar, jumped out of their jeep, rushed to her aid, and taken her to a hospital. Japanese bystanders were amazed. Equally amazed were the Japanese kids whenever the GIs flashed a smile and tossed them pieces of gum and candy. This was not the rapine and pillage they had been told to expect.

At the dockside were four destroyers marked A, B, C, and D. The Japanese flags were removed from the cars, and the military members of the delegation were ordered to leave their samurai swords behind. They boarded destroyer B, the *Lansdowne*, and proceeded fourteen miles out into Tokyo Bay where they met what Kase would describe as "a majestic array" of gray warships, "the mighty pageant of the Allied navies that so lately went forth into battle, now holding back their swift thunder and floating like calm seabirds on the waters." No fewer than 260 ships were in the harbor, almost all American: aircraft carriers, destroyers, battleships, cruisers, and minesweepers.

Equally gray was the sky. It was overcast, the sun nowhere to be seen, but at least it wasn't raining. Protected by the flotilla of many ships, and planes circling overhead, sat the *Missouri*. Destroyer B slowed to a stop so a motor launch could take on the Japanese and deliver them to their assigned places. Coming on board to greet them was Colonel Mashbir, MacArthur's chief translator. The Japanese delegates were very anxious; they had no idea how they should present themselves when they got up to the deck and met their victors. Should they salute, bow, or shake hands? Should they smile? Mashbir said the military members of the group should salute, the others should take off their hats and bow. There was to be no handshaking; this was not a meeting of equals but a formal occasion: "I suggest that all of you wear a *shivan kao* [neutral face]."

There was a problem. The head delegate for the Japanese government, Mamoru Shigemitsu, had a wooden leg, so he could not handle the stairs leading from the ship down to the launch bobbing in the water. The captain of the *Lansdowne* quickly rigged up a bosun's chair to let the man over the side. Foreign Minister Katsuo Okazaki asked Mashbir if he would kindly prevent the photographers from taking pictures of Shigemitsu "in this particularly undignified position." Mashbir turned to the photographers and asked them to put down their cameras, out of respect. They did so.

One of the Japanese delegates, Gen. Yoshijiro Umezu, made a deliberate point of not helping Shigemitsu walk. But an American gunnery officer, Horace Bird—knowing it was not right that the man be unnecessarily humiliated—rushed forward and offered the struggling diplomat his assistance.

Now in the launch, the eleven Japanese—"diplomats without flag and soldiers without sword"—stared in awe at the ship towering twenty stories above them. At the top fluttered the Stars and Stripes, claimed by many to have been the same flag that had flown over the White House the day of Pearl Harbor and been hoisted over Rome in 1943 and Berlin in 1945 (not true, it turned out, but it made a good story).

The guns were awesome. The Japanese men looking up could only feel the horror of war, whose evidence lay strewn throughout Tokyo. They would have been even more depressed if they had spoken to the guards and learned that each of the guns weighed a massive 230,000 pounds, and that despite carrying the weight of nine of these guns, the *Missouri* had engines so powerful it could travel forty miles an hour— and twenty miles an hour backward: In other words this monster could move backward faster than most Japanese ships could move forward.

Even more awesome than this ship were the many hundreds of sailors and soldiers packed on board, pointing and staring down at them as if they were an exotic species from a zoo.

From where they stood the eleven men had an excellent view of the

American battleship *Iowa* and the British battleship *King George V*, each a mere 45,000 tons (like the *Missouri*), poignant reminders of the fate of the even mightier 70,000-ton *Yamato* and its sister ship *Musashi*, both now resting on the bottom of the sea.

As instructed, the Japanese made their way up the gangway and proceeded to their assigned positions on the deck, where they saw mounted on the bulkhead, under glass, the thirty-one-star American flag used by Matthew Perry when he entered Tokyo Bay in 1853. The walk was very slow and difficult for them, led by Foreign Minister Shigemitsu with his prosthetic leg. Some fifteen years earlier his left leg had been blown off in a terrorist attack in Shanghai. Fortunately there happened to be a Canadian doctor available at the time, one whose quick work had saved Shigemitsu's life. The man's name was Moore Cosgrave.

Facing the Japanese delegation were the representatives of nine Allied nations and the Supreme Command. Shigemitsu stared ahead, then saw a man he thought he recognized, smiling at him. Shigemitsu blinked with disbelief. His heart leaped with joy.

It was Moore Cosgrave, now the signatory for Canada.

FOR THE JAPANESE there was nothing to do but stand and wait, as one of them later put it, "like penitent boys awaiting the dreaded schoolmaster . . . subjected to the torture of the pillory. A million eyes seemed to beat on us with the million shafts of a rattling storm of arrows barbed with fire. . . . Never had I realized that staring eyes could hurt so much." Observed one of the American officers on the ship: "The whole scene was as if a huge lion had cornered a tiny, helpless-looking mouse in a cage. If there ever was a scene that brought home to me how sad a defeated nation can be—this scene was it." For Kase, what was to come was as much of a surprise as what had just happened to Shigemitsu. Kase, who had studied for six years in the United States, undoubtedly knew of the Gettysburg Address. Had he been a student of history, he might well have wondered what it must have been like in 1863 to hear Lincoln utter his memorable words.

What he didn't know was that inside the ship was a very serious student of history, Gen. Douglas MacArthur, getting ready to give his speech. As an expert on America, Kase certainly knew who Arthur Vandenberg was: the powerful Michigan senator and member of the Senate Foreign Relations Committee who had urged a conciliatory attitude toward Japan in the late 1930s, only to be rebuffed by President Roosevelt and Secretary of State Cordell Hull.

Vandenberg, after hearing what Kase was now about to hear in person, would call MacArthur's speech the greatest American speech since the Gettysburg Address.

It was now nine o'clock. The door of the bulkhead opened, and out emerged Admiral Halsey, Admiral Nimitz, and General MacArthur. They had rehearsed this event at least a dozen times, scheduling the next twenty minutes with military precision, even to the point of using a stopwatch. Halsey and Nimitz took their assigned places. MacArthur stepped up to the microphone near the table and began to speak.

> We are gathered here, representative of the major warring powers, to conclude a solemn agreement whereby peace may be restored. The issues, involving divergent ideals and ideologies, have been determined on the battlefields of the world and hence are not for discussion or debate. Nor is it for us here to meet, representing as we do a majority of the peoples of the earth, in a spirit of distrust, malice or hatred.
>
> But rather it is for us, both victors and vanquished, to rise to that higher dignity which alone benefits the sacred purposes we are about to serve, committing all our people unreservedly to faithful compliance with the understanding they are here formally to assume.
>
> It is my earnest hope and indeed the hope of all mankind that from this solemn occasion a better world shall emerge out of the blood and carnage of the past—a world founded upon faith and understanding—a world dedicated to the dignity of man and the fulfillment of his most cherished wish—for freedom, tolerance and justice.
>
> The terms and conditions upon which the surrender of the

Japanese Imperial Forces is here to be given and accepted are contained in the instrument of surrender now before you.

As Supreme Commander for the Allied Powers, I announce it my firm purpose, in the tradition of the countries I represent, to proceed in the discharge of my responsibilities with justice and tolerance, while taking all necessary dispositions to insure that the terms of surrender are fully, promptly and faithfully complied with.

What stirring eloquence, what a noble vision! thought Kase, who later wrote in his memoir: "Here is the victor announcing the verdict to the prostrate enemy. He can exact his pound of flesh if he so chooses. He can impose a humiliating penalty if he so desires." Yet he does not. Instead, he pleads for freedom, tolerance, and justice. "For me, who expected the worst humiliation, this was a complete surprise. I was thrilled beyond words, spellbound, thunderstruck." Instead of suffering unbearable embarrassment, Kase found the scene on the quarterdeck of the *Missouri* to have been "an altar of peace" and MacArthur an extraordinary man.

MacArthur continued for a few more minutes, then motioned for the Japanese to come forward to sign the surrender. There were two documents, one for Japan and one for the United States. Foreign Minister Shigemitsu, dressed in London-style top hat, cutaway coat, and striped trousers, hobbled forward, escorted by Kase, holding his left arm for additional support. He took off his silk hat, laid it on the table, took off his white gloves, put his hat back on his head, and finally put both hat and gloves down. He was trembling. He looked at one signature page, then the other, wondering which one—the American or the Japanese—to sign first. The seconds went by, the stopwatch must be ticking.

"Sutherland," MacArthur's voice rang out like a pistol shot, "show him where to sign!" MacArthur's chief of staff stepped forward, showed the poor gentleman where to sign, and Shigemitsu eagerly affixed his signature on behalf of the emperor of Japan and the Japanese government. Next, for the Japanese Imperial General Headquarters, was General Umezu, dressed in the olive garb of a general officer and making it abundantly clear by his unpressed pants and scruffy shoes that for him this was no purgatory. He signed. MacArthur cast him a look of contempt. Little did he know that this was probably the most honorable Japanese general of the entire war, a man who single-handedly had stopped Japan from unleashing on America its biological weapons of mass destruction.

It was now eight minutes past nine, time for MacArthur to sign. He called on Wainwright and Percival—survivors of brutal Japanese captivity—to stand behind him as he sat down and pulled five pens from his shirt pocket. He was to sign in his capacity as Supreme Commander for the Allied Powers. He signed his name using one pen for "Doug" and gave it to Wainwright, another pen for "las" and gave it to Percival. With the third pen he wrote "Mac," this one to be given to West Point. With the fourth he wrote the end part of his last name—"Arthur"—for his aide General Whitney. With the fifth he wrote his full name, this pen for the U.S. government. He was not finished. Reaching into another pocket, he pulled out a sixth pen and signed his full name again, this pen for his wife and son. Even MacArthur, it seemed, wanted a souvenir.

Now the Allied nations signed. Admiral Nimitz signed for the United States. Eight other nations followed: China, the United Kingdom, the USSR, Australia, Canada, France, the Netherlands, and New Zealand. There was an embarrassing moment—causing the proceedings to fall behind schedule specified by the rehearsal stopwatch—where one of the representatives signed on the wrong line. "Fix it!" barked MacArthur, whereupon an American aide rushed up, crossed out the signature, and had the man sign his name again in the proper space. Two of the Japanese delegates managed a smile: Even momentous events like this could have a moment of levity.

When all the representatives finished signing, MacArthur stepped forward and announced: "Let us pray that peace be now restored to the world and that God will preserve it always." He paused for a dramatic moment, then proclaimed: "These proceedings are now closed."

No one said a word. It was a ceremony conducted with extreme dignity, words carefully chosen—no gloating, no military bands, no thumping of drums. As the Japanese turned around and began to file out, MacArthur leaned over and whispered in Admiral Halsey's ear,

"Start 'em up, Bill." Halsey gave the signal. From the east came a tremendous roar: Overhead a massed flight of four hundred silver B-29 Superfortress bombers and fifteen hundred blue navy fighters started to appear, coming closer and closer as everyone looked up at them flying overhead on their way to Tokyo—a loud display of American power to the Japanese nation. The calm, flat ocean reverberated with the sound: The thunder was deafening.

Then the clouds broke suddenly and the sun came out, a perfect symbol to capture the spirit of the day. No doubt, joked an American reporter, MacArthur ordered that one, too. It was like Babe Ruth pointing to the exact spot in right field before hitting a home run, said a Japanese reporter.

As the thunder faded and people returned their gaze to the surrender desk, there was no MacArthur. He had vanished. He was inside the ship, on his way down to the radio room to broadcast the major portion of his speech for the day, this one for the American people. This speech, probably even more than his words before the signing, was his real Gettysburg Address. Speeches in print never have the resonance they do when heard, but here is a speech worth quoting in its entirety. It is one man's attempt to put the surrender event in its full context. Because it was written and delivered by a victorious general enjoying unprecedented authority, it was read and reread countless times by millions of Japanese, looking for hidden meanings portending their future.

> Today the guns are silent. A great tragedy has ended. A great victory has been won. The skies no longer rain death—the seas bear only commerce—men everywhere walk uptight in the sunlight. The entire world lies quietly at peace. The holy mission has been completed and in this reporting to you, the people, I speak for the thousands of silent lips, forever stilled among the jungles and the beaches and in the deep waters of the Pacific which marked the way. I speak for the unnamed brave millions homeward bound to take up the challenge of that future which they did so much to salvage from the brink of disaster.
>
> As I look back on the long, tortuous trail from those grim days

of Bataan and Corregidor, when an entire world lived in fear; when democracy was on the on the defensive everywhere, when modern civilization trembled in the balance, I thank a merciful God that He has given us the faith, the courage and the power with which to mould victory.

We have known the bitterness of defeat and the exultation of triumph, and from both we have learned there can be no turning back. We must go forward to preserve in peace what we won in war.

A new era is upon us. Even the lesson of victory brings with it profound concern, both for our future security and the survival of civilization. The destructiveness of the war potential, through progressive advances in scientific discovery, has in fact now reached a point which revises the traditional concept of war.

Men since the beginning of time have sought peace. Various methods through the ages have attempted to devise an international process to prevent or settle disputes between nations. From the very start workable methods were found in so far as individual citizens were concerned, but the mechanics of an instrumentality of larger international scope have never been successful. Military alliances, balances of power, Leagues of Nations all in turn failed, leaving the only path to be by way of the crucible of war.

The utter destructiveness of war now blots out this alternative. We have had our last chance. If we do not now devise some greater and more equitable system Armageddon will be at our door. The problem basically is theological and involves a spiritual recrudescence and improvement of human character that will synchronize with our almost matchless advance in science, art, literature and all material and cultural developments of the past two thousand years. It must be of the spirit if we are to save the flesh.

We stand in Tokyo today reminiscent of our countryman, Commodore Perry ninety-two years ago. His purpose was to bring to Japan an era of enlightenment and progress by lifting the veil of isolation to the friendship, trade and commerce of the world. But alas the knowledge thereby gained of Western science was forged into an instrument of oppression and human enslavement. Freedom of expression, freedom of action, even freedom of thought were denied through suppression of liberal education, through appeal to superstition and through the application of force.

We are committed by the Potsdam Declaration of principles to see that the Japanese people are liberated from this condition of slavery. It is my purpose to implement this commitment just as rapidly as the armed forces are demobilized and the other essential steps taken to neutralize the war potential. The energy of the Japanese race, if properly directed, will enable expansion vertically rather than horizontally. If the talents of the race are turned into constructive channels, the country can lift itself from its present deplorable state into a position of dignity.

To the Pacific basin has come the vista of a new emancipated world. Today, freedom is on the offensive, democracy is on the march. Today, in Asia as well as in Europe, unshackled peoples are tasting the full sweetness of liberty, the relief from fear.

In the Philippines, America has evolved a modern era for this new free world of Asia. In the Philippines, America has demonstrated that peoples of the East and peoples of the West may walk side by side in mutual respect and with mutual benefit. The history of our sovereignty there has now the full confidence of the East.

And so, my fellow countrymen, today I report to you that your sons and daughters have served you well and faithfully with the calm, deliberate, determined fighting spirit of the American soldier and sailor based upon a tradition of historical trait, as against the fanaticism of an enemy supported only by mythological fiction, their spiritual strength and power has brought us through to victory. They are homeward bound—take care of them.

In this speech MacArthur sent several powerful messages. He recognized that the atom bomb had made the "traditional concept of war" obsolete. He reminded the Japanese that he came only as Matthew Perry had, to open up Japan and help it become a major power. He assured them that their talents, properly utilized, could lead to a new era of "dignity," "liberty," and "relief from fear."

Nobody listened more intently than the eleven Japanese in the radio room of the destroyer taking them back to shore, Toshikazu Kase doing his best to provide a simultaneous translation. "Is it not rare good fortune," asked Kase when the speech was finished, "that a man of such caliber and character should have been designated as the supreme commander who will shape the destiny of Japan?"

In the meantime, crowded into Admiral Halsey's cabin after the speech were all the Allied commanders. They wanted a drink. "If ever a day demanded champagne, this was it, but I could serve them only coffee and doughnuts," recalled Halsey. The *Missouri*, per MacArthur's orders, would be a dry zone.

Upon arriving back in Tokyo, Kase prepared his written report for Shigemitsu to deliver to the emperor. At the end of the report he raised a question: Whether it would have been possible for Japan, had it been the victor, to embrace the vanquished with a similar magnanimity? His answer was no. Returning from his audience with the emperor, Shigemitsu told Kase that Hirohito agreed.

Thinking about what MacArthur had tried to communicate on board the *Missouri*, Kase concluded: "We were not beaten on the battlefields by dint of superior arms. We were defeated by a nobler ideal. The real issue was moral."

5

"Down but Not Out"

*If we allow the pain and humility to breed within us the dark
thoughts of future revenge, our spirit will be warped and perverted
into a morbidly base design. . . . But if we use this pain and humiliation as a spur to self-reflection and reform, and if we make this
self-reflection and reform the motive force for a great constructive
effort, there is nothing to stop us from building, out of the ashes of
our defeat, a magnificent new Japan.*

—*NIPPON TIMES*
(on the surrender ceremony)

FOR YEARS THE Japanese people had been spoon-fed a panoply of
lies breathtaking in audacity. According to the relentless propaganda of the militarists, Japan had conquered the Philippines, the
Netherlands East Indies, New Guinea, Australia, Hawaii, even the West
Coast of the United States.

The specifics would have astounded even those masters of lies, the
Nazis and the Soviets. The Japanese navy was on a roll. Midway was
just a blip on the horizon. As the American navy attempted to cross the
Pacific, the Japanese propaganda drums continued their relentless beat
of fabrications. Believing what they were being told, hundreds of Japanese villages erected *Charen Kensho-tu*—monuments to the victorious
dead—as though Japan's enemies had already surrendered. Little did
they know that most Japanese warships were resting on the bottom of
the deep Pacific. The more specific the claim, the more outrageous the
lie. Okinawa, the government announced, would be the war's *sekigahara*
(decisive battle). (Certainly it had better be, given that Okinawa was
only one day's sail from the southern Japanese islands.)

Lies, once started, inevitably grow into bigger lies—impossible lies.

The Japanese Imperial General Headquarters, after the news of the American invasion of Okinawa, insisted there was nothing to worry about, the 180,000 American soldiers and marines had been allowed to land so Japanese kamikazes could sink their supporting ships and isolate the invaders on the island, where they would be destroyed.

When U.S. broadcasts announced on June 21 that Okinawa had surrendered, people in Japan realized that the war had not been going like they were being told and invasion of the homeland was imminent. For months now, many had suspected as much, beginning with the March 9 raid on Tokyo by Gen. Jimmy Doolittle. It was the greatest single destruction in the history of warfare. Conventional bombs were used. In the ensuing firestorm, in just a few hours 84,000 people burned to death and one million people were left wandering the streets, their homes and apartment buildings reduced to rubble.* Fifteen square miles were totally destroyed.

The knowledge that the homeland was open to attack must have hit Japan like a thunderbolt. Yet Japan did not surrender, even though the imperial headquarters had concluded in mid-1944 that the cause was hopeless. Japan's stubbornness was extraordinary. Five months later, after the Tokyo raids, with the knockout weapon finally perfected and made available, President Truman must have reflected on how the destruction of Tokyo had failed to get the message across. It certainly had not been for want of trying. Before bombing Tokyo the United States had sent planes over the city to drop leaflets warning civilians to evacuate immediately. Titled "Appeal to the People," the leaflet stated: "You are not the enemy of America. Our enemy is the Japanese militarists who dragged you into the war." No response.

After the first atom bomb, the Americans again dropped leaflets, threatening more destruction. Again no response. So Truman went ahead and ordered the second bomb.

The Japanese people, unlike three of the six government ministers who still voted no after the second bomb, were stunned. How could this happen? How could there exist an enemy capable of such devastation?

---

*In Hiroshima and Nagasaki, the death tolls were originally estimated to be 80,000 and 40,000. More recent estimates place the total for the two cities at over 200,000.

When a bomb as powerful as the one at Hiroshima or Nagasaki is dropped on a defenseless city, one would expect an outpouring of national outrage. MacArthur certainly thought so, which is why he had opposed the measure. Only it didn't happen. The national outrage over the atom bomb was directed not at the Americans but at the Japanese militarists who had undertaken such a brutal war and lied to the people.

To salvage their pride in the shame of defeat, the Japanese elevated the Americans: The militarists brought it on us! How could we have possibly beaten a country as strong as America? There would be no hatred for the destruction America had brought about, no hatred of the conqueror. The time had come for Japan to reject the past.

MacArthur would go after the militarists. He would purge them and throw them in jail. He had a secret weapon in mind: women. On the plane ride to Atsugi he had discussed the fate of Japan with General Fellers. "It's very simple," said MacArthur. "We'll use the instrumentality of the Japanese government to implement the Occupation."

Fellers was baffled: What in the world was MacArthur talking about?

"We're going to give Japanese women the vote."

"The Japanese men won't like it," responded Fellers.

"I don't care. I want to destroy the military. Women don't want war." End of discussion.

The militarists, MacArthur knew, were up to no good. In the two weeks of grace between the surrender announcement on August 15 and the August 29 arrival of Col. Charles Tench's C-47s at Atsugi and Admiral Halsey's fleet of 263 vessels in Tokyo Bay, vast stockpiles of food and industrial raw materials had disappeared into black markets and secret warehouses—the work of militarists hoping to win political support by giving away free supplies. Even more outrageous were the actions of the War Ministry, complicit in this subterfuge: It had ordered its officials and field commanders to destroy all records of where these supplies were located. These ministry officials would soon find themselves out of a job and probably arrested and put on trial for war crimes. But in the meantime MacArthur had a crisis on his hands. People in the streets were starving. After his one-egg breakfast on his second day, he had immediately sent a cable to Washington ordering the shipment of 3.5 million tons of food. Getting no quick response, he sent a second message: "Give me bread or give me bullets."

He got the food. Within weeks American planes, followed by ships, arrived with thousands of tons of flour, rolled oats, canned goods, rice, blankets, even medical supplies. Commented Maj. Gen. William Marquat, later the head of SCAP's Economic and Scientific Section: "The Japanese are prisoners of war, and we don't let our prisoners starve, do we?" Nor would the soldiers have to consume precious local food supplies. To ensure that Americans wouldn't have to use the local food markets, the U.S. Army constructed a large hydroponics farm for growing produce.

MacArthur had already had a fight with one of his military officers over food. It started when he heard a complaint from a delegation of Japanese fishermen that they were no longer being allowed to fish. Apparently a SCAP officer had gotten suspicious that the fishermen were planting mines in Tokyo Bay. How paranoid do military people have to get? MacArthur canceled the regulation on the spot. Overnight he became the god of the fishermen, the Poseidon of Japan.

The sight of people scrounging for food was heartrending, a shortage so bad that one woman was seen using a pair of tweezers to pick up seeds spilled on the street. Tokyo's Ueno train station was crawling with orphans collecting cigarette butts to sell. Japan was reduced to an "onionskin economy" in which people peeled off more and more layers of their remaining family belongings and took them out to the countryside to sell to farmers for scraps of food to survive. More than 10 percent of the people in Japan were homeless. Nagasaki lost 74 percent of its buildings; Hiroshima lost 59 percent, Tokyo, 65, Osaka, 57. Observed one journalist: "This city now is a world of scarcity in which every nail, every rag, and even a tangerine peel has a market value. A cupful of rice, three cigarettes, or four matches are all a day's ration. Men pick up every grain of rice out of their tin lunch boxes; there are too few to be wasted. . . . On the Ginza, once the show street of Tokyo . . . hungry kids and young women beg for gum and chocolate and peanuts from soldiers."

But to think of Japan as an utterly beaten nation—an easy conclusion to draw from the pictures of the devastation of its major cities—is an oversimplification. Horrendous damage notwithstanding, Japan was still an industrial power compared with other nations in Asia. Railways were largely intact, the electric power system remained, and hydro-electric plants outside cities were still functioning. Even in Hiroshima, within forty-eight hours of the atomic bomb, trains were running through the city. The government was still in place and operating.

An expression emerged that was to be used frequently during the occupation: "Dempsey damage." It referred to the famous 1926 heavy-weight championship match in which Jack Dempsey knocked down Gene Tunney, yet thanks to "the long count," Tunney was able to get up and go on to win the fight. Tunney later described himself as being "down but not out." So, no matter how devastated Japan looked, the country was not out. Everyone in the major cities was busy cleaning the streets, looking for salvageable items, and rebuilding their burned-down houses.

MacArthur had his game plan in mind. He would assign his men to go after the militarists and make a show of their criminality; he would remain above the fray and address the people of a defeated, bewildered nation sorely in need of hope and idealism. America's mission was not to keep Japan down, but to get it on its feet again.

IT HAD BEEN a long day, this September 2, and MacArthur was beat and emotionally exhausted. He was not about to rest on his laurels, however; he had work to do.

If Mamoru Shigemitsu, who must have had an even more emotion-ally draining day on top of all his physical difficulties, thought he might have a peaceful afternoon, he was sorely mistaken. Late that afternoon, when he might otherwise be having his cup of tea, he was summoned to a meeting at MacArthur's temporary office and informed by one of MacArthur's aides that the general was about to issue three directives, the most important of which was the first, announcing that Japan was now under military government. The directives would go into effect within twenty-four hours.

Shigemitsu was stunned. This was not the deal as he understood it from the Potsdam Declaration, promising a Japan based on the free will of the people. If Japan had surrendered, why did it need a new form of government?

He requested a meeting to discuss the situation before any directives went into effect. To his surprise and relief, he was granted one for 10:30 the next day, and it would be with the supreme commander himself. One imagines Shigemitsu must have had a sleepless night thinking how to present his case. It would be the most important meeting of his entire life. As foreign minister he knew what the United States was doing in Germany under the Morgenthau Plan: Germany was being partitioned and all its heavy industry destroyed. Assuming the powerful U.S. secretary of the treasury had developed a similar plan for Japan, it was only reasonable to assume MacArthur intended to follow it to the fullest. Might he be planning to put Japan back into the Stone Age?

There was no one in the State Department he could talk to. The supreme commander had total and complete power: He was President Truman's sole delegate, a secretary of war and secretary of state rolled into one—with an occupying army at his fingertips. For the past two days American planes had been landing every five minutes, disgorging troops at the rate of 10,000 a day. The total humiliation of Japan, the full invasion, was now a fact.

At 10:30 a very nervous Shigemitsu was ushered into a temporary conference room in the New Grand Hotel in Yokohama. Upon meeting the supreme commander he was "joyfully surprised" by MacArthur's "graciousness." For more than an hour they talked, and it became apparent that their differences were more of perception than of content. Issuing a directive "to the People of Japan," argued Shigemitsu, would undermine people's confidence in the Japanese government and lead to domestic disorder. No one was questioning the ultimate authority of the conquering power, and it was the government's full intention to follow SCAP's wishes, but to do so and be abjectly humiliated was neither reasonable nor acceptable.

Basically what Shigemitsu was pleading for was that the Japanese government be given a chance to prove its worth as an obedient supplicant. "Should the government fail to fulfill its duties, or should the occupation authorities feel the government's policies are unsatisfactory," he promised MacArthur, "then direct orders could be issued by occupation officials." MacArthur responded by assuring the Japanese foreign minister that he had no intention of "destroying the nation or making slaves of the Japanese people." The purpose of the occupation was "to assist Japan in surmounting its difficulties, and if the government showed 'good faith,' problems could be solved easily."

In the room with the two men and an interpreter was MacArthur's chief of staff. MacArthur turned to his aide and ordered the three directives to be scrapped.

UPON ARRIVING AT the American Embassy in Tokyo five days later, MacArthur ordered the American colors to be raised. "General Eichelberger, have our country's flag unfurled, and in Tokyo's sun let it wave in its full glory as a symbol of hope for the oppressed and as a harbinger of victory for the right." Standing rigidly at attention in front of the flagpole were two men. As the flag reached the top, they saluted, tears coming to their eyes, so powerful was the moment.

"Well, Bill . . . ," said MacArthur.

"We really did it," said Admiral Halsey.

Going inside the building for the first time, MacArthur saw a big portrait of George Washington on the wall: "We are home now," he said. Seeing the portrait of the great American general, he reflected later, "moved me more than I can say."

It was now time to let the Japanese—especially the emperor—know he had arrived. He assembled a huge motorcade of trucks and jeeps for the ten-minute drive from the embassy past the Imperial Palace to the Dai Ichi Insurance Building, where he would have his office. Under cover of fighters and bombers he proceeded in a thundering display of strength to his office. Observed one of the American officers: "I'll never forget the experience till the day I die. Even today, it sets the hairs rising on my back thinking about it. You see, there wasn't a single person in the streets to see all this—but we knew they were all watching."

While in Tokyo, Admiral Halsey had a mission to perform. Having heard weeks earlier that the emperor owned a magnificent white horse, Halsey made it known to several reporters that he wanted to borrow it and take it for a ride. One of his aides went to MacArthur and told him Halsey wanted the horse—the emperor's white horse.

"No!" shouted MacArthur. He couldn't believe it. Not even he, the king of vanity, the ultimate narcissist, would dream of asking for such a thing. "Never underestimate a man just because he overestimates himself," *Time* magazine once said of MacArthur. He, Douglas MacArthur, who had won more medals than any other general or admiral,* never wore his medals in public. The only indication when a visitor met him was a small circle of five stars on his shirt collar. Such modesty, he mused with delight, would surely befuddle his enemies (of which he had many).

Halsey's aides came to the rescue. One of the perks of being a fleet admiral is having a lot of aides eager to accommodate the boss' whims. The aides scurried around Tokyo to find a substitute, and got their hands on an old gray mare that had obviously seen better days. They fed the animal a lot of hay and oats, then informed the admiral they had a "white" horse. Fine, said the admiral; he'd take whatever they had. At the appointed hour Halsey came out for a formal inspection of the troops, then eagerly mounted the horse while a bevy of American reporters clicked their cameras. The horse looked very white indeed, a perfect photo-op, white enough to fool some of the reporters. What happened? "Oh," said one of the naval aides, "we washed her up with G.I. soap and water and then covered her with white foot powder from the hospital."

Halsey was a man who liked to have a good time. What greater fun than pretending he was emperor? One night he and his men had a huge celebratory meal at their Tokyo hotel, and when the check came, Halsey signed it, "Hirohito."

MacArthur and Halsey started talking about the Japanese soldiers.

---

*By the time his career was over, five-star general Douglas MacArthur would be the recipient of forty medals and decorations: the Medal of Honor, a Presidential Unit Citation, a UN Service Medal, the Distinguished Service Cross, the Army Distinguished Service Medal, the Navy Distinguished Service Medal, the Air Medal, the Silver Star, the Distinguished Flying Cross, a National Defense Service Medal, the Bronze Star, and a Purple Heart, along with thirty-four orders, decorations, and service medals from foreign countries. The changing nature of warfare today from total to limited wars means that there will never be a general so decorated as MacArthur.

He is not, however, the highest-ranking general. That distinction belongs to George Washington, who was posthumously awarded six stars by Congress in 1976, with the understanding that no general may ever outrank him.

The supreme commander had just issued an order forbidding confiscation of Japanese officers' ceremonial swords. Halsey considered this a mistake. He told MacArthur: Look at Germany, where people proudly kept in their home a bust of some general, with a sword reverently hung above it. Such displays kept the Prussian militarist sprit alive.

"But I was thinking of Appomattox, when Grant allowed Lee's troops to keep their side arms," replied MacArthur.

"Grant was dealing with an honorable foe. We are not."

The supreme commander mulled that one over for a moment, then nodded, told Halsey he was absolutely right, and countermanded the samurai directive. Coming right after his meeting with Shigemitsu, this was the second time in several days he had shown a flexibility unusual for a man widely reputed to be arrogant and cocksure.

The following week, in the private upstairs dining room of the American Embassy, MacArthur had dinner with his two intelligence advisors, General Fellers and Colonel Mashbir. He told them, referring to the former ambassador to Japan: "Grew sat in this identical chair for ten years living in regal splendor. What did he or the whole diplomatic corps do in those ten years to prevent this war?"

And what had Grew done to prevent the use of the atom bomb? Like MacArthur, Grew had felt FDR's "unconditional surrender" to be shortsighted: It stiffened Japanese resolve not to surrender and lengthened the war unnecessarily—requiring the use of the atom bomb. At a meeting of the so-called Committee of Three (Secretary of War Stimson and Secretary of the Navy James Forrestal, and Grew as acting secretary of state), he had suggested that a provision be inserted stating, "We do not exclude a constitutional monarchy under her present dynasty." Doing so, he said, would "substantially add to the chances of acceptance." When President Truman subsequently removed this sentence, the Japanese government had no assurance as to the emperor's fate and dismissed the Potsdam Declaration as just a hollow promise.

The State Department had wanted to bring Grew back to Japan, but he couldn't come back as ambassador because MacArthur as supreme commander already held that rank. Might he come back as an advisor? Grew, who had served for one week as U.S. secretary of state back in June-July and then retired, indignantly refused to consider such a status, and went on to complain that MacArthur "would not want much advice." That's right, thought MacArthur, he most definitely would not. Unlike the diplomats in their fancy striped trousers and cutaways, MacArthur was a general, confident he knew what he was doing and determined to do it, not just talk about it.

The commonly accepted way to run an occupation is to impose a strict regime. MacArthur had other ideas. In March, while in Manila, he had received a visit from the renowned playwright Robert Sherwood, President Roosevelt's emissary, to discuss his ideas for Japan. If the United States treated the Japanese fairly and liberally, and weren't overly restrictive, he told Sherwood, "We shall have the friendship and cooperation of the Asian people far off into the future."

Having Colonel Mashbir at the table made MacArthur grateful to have a loyal subordinate who kept him abreast of enemies in Washington. Back in 1942 after MacArthur had arrived in Australia, Mashbir had informed him about the Baldwin incident. Apparently a U.S. intelligence officer and military attaché in Australia, Col. Karl Baldwin, had received a directive from Washington "to report at once what decorations are being worn by General MacArthur." Baldwin was trapped, because any telegram would have to be sent through General MacArthur's headquarters. Baldwin also knew that people in Washington would be after him if he failed to deliver. Yet MacArthur was his boss. What to do? Looking for a way to protect MacArthur without appearing to do so, Baldwin cabled back: "Those authorized by Army Regulations."

MacArthur must never forget, he had enemies, people watching his every move, ready to pounce at the slightest misstep. To heck with people like Grew who claimed, "The best we can hope for in Japan is the development of a constitutional monarchy, experience having shown that democracy would never work." That was the problem with people who had lots of experience: They could always come up with a dozen reasons why something wouldn't work. Sometimes it takes someone who doesn't know what he doesn't know, to make things happen.

MacArthur hadn't risked his life and fought a war to preserve the old Japan; his job was to change it. He had plans—big plans—full of surprises for the folks back in Washington. They saw the devastation of Japan and the need to play it safe, he saw potential and opportunity. He would seek nothing less than remaking the entire political, social, cultural, and economic fabric of a defeated nation.

At his age, what did he have to lose?

6

Harry Truman Throws a Fit

W AIT A MINUTE, w-a-i-t a minute."
So said President Harry Truman about firing MacArthur
after just three weeks on the job in Japan. Truman, despite
the drama that was to end their relationship five and a half years later,*
was not a man given to impulsively losing his temper or firing people.
In fact, despite his fondness for barroom language, he was actually quite
temperate when he was angry.

So it was on September 18, 1945. He had always imagined he might
have a problem with this bunco man too brilliant for his own good, but
never that it would happen so soon. Eighteen days! That must set some
kind of a record. It really would have been laughable had it not been so
serious. Nonetheless, he could manage. In the meantime Undersecretary
of State Dean Acheson was fuming. The day before, MacArthur—10,000
miles away in Tokyo—had announced that the smooth progress of the
occupation in Japan enabled a drastic cut in the number of troops from
500,000 to 200,000 in six months. For a man on the job for such a short
time to be able to make such a pronouncement was remarkable. Did
he have a crystal ball? More amazing was for a mere general to utter a
statement out of the clear blue that would have major repercussions on
the eight cosigning nations of the *Missouri* surrender pact, let alone the
major signatory, the United States. Already the cable lines were sizzling

---

* MacArthur ruled Japan for slightly less than five years (from August 30, 1945, to June
25, 1950). After the Korean War started, his efforts were devoted almost entirely to the
war, until he was relieved on April 11, 1951.

with urgent messages of consternation from the governments of the United Kingdom and New Zealand seeking clarification. Editorial writers were in a frenzy trying to read the tea leaves of American Far Eastern foreign policy. Some writers went so far as to predict that MacArthur was secretly laying the groundwork for a 1948 presidential run at a time when "bring the boys home" would be a sure vote getter.

Acheson issued a statement—a shot across MacArthur's bow—saying that nobody could foresee the number of troops needed in Japan and that "the occupation forces are the instruments of policy and not the determinants of policy." Such a public rebuke would surely put MacArthur in his place. As for the man whose opinion counted—the president—budget director Harold Smith spoke with Truman and found that he viewed MacArthur's issuance as "a political statement." The White House press secretary reported the president as vowing "to do something about that fellow."

At a press conference on the eighteenth President Truman kept his cool and passed off MacArthur's statement as no big deal. "I'm glad the general won't need as many as he thought. He said first 500,000, later 400,000, and now 200,000. It helps to get as many more men out of the Army as possible." The president was absolutely right: Everyone in America wanted the boys home. The following day Truman announced that more than two million men would be discharged by Christmas, and several days later he released to the press the government's planning document titled *United States Initial Post-Surrender Policy for Japan* (an advance copy of which had been cabled to MacArthur before he arrived at Atsugi).

Originally drafted by the State Department in the spring of 1944 and submitted to the Subcommittee for the Far East (SFE) under the State-War-Navy Coordinating Committee (SWNCC), this document after review by various agencies had gone through seven versions before finally being signed by the president as document SWNCC150/4/A. To be expected of a document emanating from many fathers, it was bureaucratese to the core, so vague and poorly organized as to be virtually useless to the man entrusted with implementing it, Douglas MacArthur. To summarize the document, the objectives of the occupation were to ensure that Japan did not become a menace to the world, and to impose a democratic self-government consistent with the freely imposed will of the people. The occupation would accomplish this by disarming and demilitarizing the country, promoting democratic and representative organizations, and strengthening the economy. Should there be differences among the Allied Powers, "the policies of the United States will govern." The supreme commander (appointed by the United States) would exercise sole executive power, and would work with the existing Japanese government to whatever extent he deemed feasible in reforming its "feudal and authoritarian tendencies." Militarists would be removed from office and war criminals put on trial. War production factories would be dismantled and large economic monopolies broken up. Democratic parties and groups would be encouraged, and citizens' individual rights would be protected.

Thus ended what was essentially a wish list. How it was to be achieved was up to MacArthur. It was his job to clarify the policy, develop the strategy, set priorities and deadlines, and manage the operation. The most important line in the document was the one that defined his role: "The authority of the Emperor and the Japanese Government will be subject to the Supreme Commander, who will possess all powers necessary to effectuate the surrender terms and to carry out the policies established for the conduct of the occupation and the control of Japan."

"All powers necessary. . . . " The next sentence is interesting: It talks about "the desire of the United States to attain its objectives with a minimum commitment of its forces and resources." That is exactly what MacArthur was doing when he talked about how he hoped to reduce American troops from 500,000 to 200,000: He was exercising his powers in trying to fulfill a major "desire of the United States"—demobilization. President Truman may not have been happy about MacArthur stating U.S. policy so forcefully and revealing specific dates and troop numbers, but it was a lot better than if MacArthur had said he needed a million men.

To use examples from the Civil War, generals can be divided into those like the infamous George McClellan, who need twice as many men as the enemy before they dare attack, and others like Grant, who don't complain and make do with whatever they've got. MacArthur was the latter. At a time when Americans were weary of war, and mothers, wives, and girlfriends wanted their boys back home, the size of forces available for MacArthur would have to be lean. One month later, in October, the issue of how many troops MacArthur needed came up again. He received a wire from the army chief of staff, General Marshall, saying Truman wanted to know whether MacArthur could *reduce* the minimum of 200,000 which he had contemplated. MacArthur chuckled over that one. In a conversation with General Eichelberger he said: "It seems funny that they should now be asking me to reduce below 200,000 when you think of all the fuss they made when I advanced the idea that 200,000 would be enough."

But MacArthur still wasn't out of the doghouse with the president. He had been invited by Truman to make a trip back to the United States for a meeting and "to receive the plaudits of a grateful nation." To Truman's surprise, MacArthur passed, claiming it would be "unwise" to leave Japan because of "the delicate and difficult situation which prevails here." In October, Truman issued a second invitation for MacArthur "to make a trip home at such time [as] you feel you can safely leave your duties." The president even offered an enticement: Would the general like to address a joint session of Congress? Again MacArthur passed, citing "the extraordinarily dangerous and inherently inflammable situation which exists here."

From the president's point of view, only a man of MacArthur's oversize ego could dare such effrontery—a slight the president would not forget. Truman could only wonder how MacArthur would have reacted if one of his subordinates had said he was too busy to see him.

Except that Truman totally missed the point. Japan was conquered, but was it really? MacArthur was the commander of a hostile nation known for kamikazes. At any moment a bomb could go off or someone prominent be assassinated, and the war on Japan would resume in a second. Guerrilla bands of terrorists could strike anytime. To suggest ("order") your general in Japan to come home for a week of celebration was pipe-dreaming, in MacArthur's view. He had no choice: He must stay on duty. He had a job to do, and he could not afford to leave, much though he might have relished returning home to a hero's welcome. In

Japan, MacArthur was beginning the role of a lifetime, an opportunity few people ever get, one that must be seized and savored in its fleeting fullest. For Douglas MacArthur, the key operating words out of the numerous instructions he got from Washington came from the president himself: "Your authority is supreme."

Supreme.

Now, when a word like that is attached to a man, especially a general, it can quickly go to his head (one thinks of Mussolini in this regard). For someone who had spent his entire life cloistered in the bowels of the military, his every expense and personal whim paid for by the government, MacArthur—most curiously—had a fervently negative view of socialism and big government. Consider an argument he once had in the Philippines with his chief of staff, Lt. Col. Richard Sutherland. They were at a dinner party, and Sutherland was espousing strong views about the advantages a dictatorship had in waging war. According to one of the other officers present:

> General MacArthur told Sutherland he was wrong; that democracy works and will always work, because the people are allowed to think, to talk, and to keep their minds free, open, and supple. He said that while the dictator state may plan a war, get everything worked out down to the last detail, launch the attack, and do pretty well at the beginning, eventually something goes wrong with the plan. Something interrupts the schedule. Now, the regimented minds of the dictator command are not flexible enough to handle quickly the changed situation. They have tried to make war a science when it is actually an art.

In a democracy, MacArthur was saying, there will be hundreds of free-thinking people to spot a dictator's errors and devise better methods. A democracy may be at a disadvantage at first when war comes, but eventually it will win. It may be inefficient and wasteful, but in the end it always will perform best.

By "democracy" he did not mean a chorus of voices having equal weight regardless of their merits. Leadership in a democracy meant being first among equals, and if he didn't consider the people he had to deal with to be equals, he could be ruthless in cutting them off. To appease the feelings of other nations, and fearful of what it regarded as MacArthur's dangerous appetite for power, the State Department had created two advisory organizations. However, if President Truman thought these organizations would rein in MacArthur, he was mistaken.

The first was the Far Eastern Commission (FEC), consisting of the United States and the eight other signatories to the surrender document, plus China and the Philippines (with Burma and Pakistan added later, in 1948). Formed in the gallant spirit of the United Nations, its purpose was to give those countries that had suffered from Japan's aggression a chance to influence the rehabilitation of their former enemy. In late November 1945 MacArthur invited the commission to visit Japan to see actual conditions firsthand and to provide him the "greatest possible aid." The delegates arrived the day after Christmas and got treated to a tour of eight Japanese cities in addition to extensive briefings by SCAP officials, plus extensive time with the supreme commander himself. His charm could be overwhelming. Back in Washington, the commission chairman wrote a letter to Secretary of State James Byrnes that sounded as if it could have been written by MacArthur himself:

> The most satisfactory result of the Commission's visit, from the point of view of the United States, was the feeling of confidence in the Supreme Commander engendered in the minds of the foreign representatives. Regardless of their views concerning the policies established by the United States for the control of Japan, all delegates are convinced that these policies are being carried out effectively and with the utmost wisdom by the Supreme Commander and his staff. They were all impressed by General MacArthur's grasp of the problems which face him and by the statesmanship he has shown in performing his difficult task.

Because it was based in Washington the commission could really do nothing but send memos, which more often than not were read quickly

and promptly filed away in some basement storage room. When significant issues came up MacArthur could be fearless in using his power. He
got into a major row with Australia and China when he allowed Japan to
conduct deep-sea whaling off the coasts of China and the Philippines;
even the British got aroused when he permitted Japanese whalers to
go as far south as the Antarctic. The protesting nations lodged formal
complaints with the State Department, only to be told nothing could be
done to counteract whatever MacArthur decreed, his authority being
inherent in his position as supreme commander.

The other advisory organization was the Allied Council for Japan
(ACJ), based in Tokyo and consisting of the United States, the USSR,
China, and the United Kingdom (representing itself, Australia, New
Zealand, and India). Whereas the FEC was to set the general policy
of the occupation, the ACJ was to advise on its execution. The council
would meet once a week to "consult and advise" MacArthur. The idea
was that if any members had disagreements of a fundamental nature
with the supreme commander, he would seek their agreement before
issuing his orders. Here MacArthur proved himself to be a master of
the hidden dagger. In his April 5, 1946, address to the ACJ, he put the
members—especially the Soviets—in their place:

I welcome you with utmost cordiality in the earnest anticipation
that . . . your deliberations throughout shall be governed by goodwill, mutual understanding and broad tolerance. As the functions
of the Council will be advisory and consultative, it will not divide
the heavy administrative responsibility of the Supreme Commander as the sole executive authority for the Allied Powers in
Japan, but it will make available to him the several viewpoints of
its members on questions of policy and action. I hope it will prove
to be a valuable factor in the future solution of many problems.

In other words, take it or leave it. The delegates nodded in agreement
that their views would be consulted, but the Russians knew toughness
when they saw it. Their response was one of grudging admiration: "Now
there's a man!" The council met for more than 160 sessions; MacArthur

never attended any of them, leaving the United States to be represented by one of his officials. With the State Department he was more blunt: He told the department he would do things his way, otherwise he might as well "quit and go home."

Even Japan felt the ax of his decisiveness. As supreme commander he exercised his full power to withhold his support of the Japanese government when he felt it appropriate, like the time he told the Japanese foreign minister: "Baron Shidehara may thereafter be acceptable to the Emperor as the next Prime Minister, but he will not be acceptable to me."

Asked if he understood what MacArthur meant, the minister replied: "Too clear!"

MacArthur would be a strongman, but he would not be a dictator seeking to stay in power forever. He had too great an appreciation of history not to recognize that military occupations are never popular and never last long. Bismarck had once said, "Fools say they learn by experience. I prefer to learn by other people's experience." MacArthur preferred the ultimate source of Bismarck's quote, the saying by the ancient Greek historian Polybius (200–118 B.C.): "There are two roads—one through the misfortune of their own, the other through those of others; the former is the most unmistakable, the latter the less painful."

He knew Japan was a country like Germany in World War I, a country that had never been defeated on its own soil. He was ruling a nation in a state of shock that would soon wear off. Japan had no choice but to accept whatever reforms he imposed, no matter how drastic they might seem. It was a great experiment he was undertaking, he wrote, "the world's greatest laboratory for an experiment in the liberation of a people from totalitarian military rule and for the liberation of government from within. . . . Yet history clearly showed that no modern military occupation of a conquered nation had been a success."

"Military occupation was not new to me," he continued:

I had garrisoned the West Bank of the Rhine as commander of the Rainbow Division at the end of World War One. At first hand I had seen what I thought were basic and fundamental weaknesses in prior forms of military occupations: the substitution of civil by military authority; the loss of self-respect and self-confidence by the people; the constantly growing ascendancy of central-ized dictatorial power instead of a localized and representative system; the lowering of spiritual and moral tone of a population controlled by foreign bayonets; the inevitable deterioration of the occupying forces themselves as the disease of power infiltrated their ranks and bred a sort of race superiority.

If any occupation lasts too long, or is not carefully watched from the start, one party becomes slaves and the other masters. History teaches, too, that almost every military occupation breeds new wars of the future. I had studied the lives of Alexander and Caesar and Napoleon, and great as these captains were, all had suffered when they became the leaders of the occupation forces. I tried to remember the lessons my own father had taught me, lessons learned out of his experience as military governor of the Philippines, but I was assailed by the greatest misgivings. With such hazards as I anticipated, could I succeed? My doubts were to be my best safeguard, my fears my greatest strength.

7

The Photograph That Saved
a Thousand Ships

O N SEPTEMBER 27, a meeting took place that would shape the destiny of both victor and vanquished. Unlike the public glare of the deck of the *Missouri*, this meeting was held inside an embassy. Unlike the treaty signing, known well in advance, nobody in the outside world knew this meeting had taken place until it was over. No transcript was ever made. There were no witnesses, just a single Japanese translator who kept his mouth shut and wrote no memoir. Unheard of for such a pivotal meeting, there was no specific agenda or clear concept of goals and objectives. It was more a touchy-feely exercise of two men groping in the dark, checking each other out. The real communication lay not in what one man said, but in how the other man responded.

The two men, of course, were the supreme commander and the emperor.

At the meeting a photograph was taken. It caused a sensation, for never before had the Son of Heaven permitted himself to be photographed with a mere commoner, much less with an enemy. Like Helen of Troy, "the face that launched a thousand ships," this photograph—more than anything else—kept the peace and saved the United States from having to launch a massive invasion to keep Japan subdued.

Coming so soon after his Atsugi landing and the Missouri surrender ceremony, it demonstrated MacArthur at his best in terms of his flair for the dramatic.

"Welcome, Sir." The emperor, dumbfounded, a man not used to shaking hands, stepped out of his limousine and found himself greeted by General Bonner Fellers, MacArthur's chief of counterintelligence. Little did he know what this man had written about him: "As Emperor and acknowledged head of the State, Hirohito cannot sidestep war guilt. He is part of and must be considered an instigator of the Pacific war . . . whether or not Pearl Harbor was against the Emperor's will is of little consequence . . . inescapably he is responsible." In other words, Hirohito might as well get ready for the hangman's noose.

Fortunately for the emperor, this man so anxious to meet him in person and look into his eyes was also the one who, more than any other American advisor to MacArthur, would save his life. For it was this general with the unusual name who had been advocating from day one, both in Washington when he worked for the Office of Strategic Services (OSS, now the CIA) and when he served as chief of psychological warfare in the Pacific before joining MacArthur in the Philippines, that the emperor should not be hanged as a war criminal. To the Japanese, said Fellers, hanging the emperor "would be comparable to the crucifixion of Christ to us. All would fight to die like ants."

If the emperor didn't know how precariously his life hung in the balance, he certainly had been reminded of it ten minutes earlier, when his car stopped at a traffic light. A traffic light! Emperors' cars do not stop at traffic lights; traffic lights stop for them. Not this time. The American GI acting as traffic cop—security was especially tight that morning— flashed a smile at the waiting imperial Daimler while making sure the next street was clear before waving the three cars on. Understandably the emperor's stomach was churning at this brazen demonstration of his smallness. He had no idea what to expect other than that when he arrived at the American Embassy he would be greeted, as befitted an emperor, by General MacArthur himself.

But MacArthur was not there.

"I am honored to meet you," said Fellers. The two men shook hands.*

Fellers ushered the emperor and his entourage into the building,

*Upon returning to his palace, the emperor asked who that friendly man was who had put out his hand to greet him when he got out of his limousine. He reciprocated by sending Fellers a signed photograph of himself.

where Maj. Faubion Bowers, fluent in Japanese, shocked the group by instructing the entourage of Japanese officials to wait downstairs while he escorted Hirohito and his personal interpreter upstairs to meet MacArthur alone. The emperor, observed Bowers, looked "frightened to death. As I took his top hat, I noticed his hands were trembling. On meeting MacArthur on the threshold, he bowed low, very low, a servant's bow."

In fact he bowed so low that the startled supreme commander found himself holding the emperor's hand over Hirohito's head. MacArthur escorted the emperor into the drawing room, where a photographer snapped three pictures one after the other, and quickly departed. The only other person in the room was Hirohito's translator. As at Atsugi, MacArthur put all his trust in the Japanese: He had no translator of his own to ensure his words weren't being misstated. To make his guest feel at ease, MacArthur began by relating how he had at one time been received by the emperor's father at the end of the Russo-Japanese War. The emperor, hands still trembling, declined to touch his cup of coffee lest he spill it. MacArthur, seeing his distress, pulled out his gold cigarette case and offered an American cigarette; Hirohito, no regular smoker, eagerly accepted, and MacArthur leaned forward and flicked his cigarette lighter.

The two men were not entirely strangers; under less traumatic circumstances there were a number of things they could have talked about. They had met once before, back in 1937 when Manuel Quezon of the Philippines met with the emperor and MacArthur sat next to Quezon as his military advisor. Had either Hirohito or MacArthur been invited into the other's private office, he might have been thrilled to discover a mutual idol, Abraham Lincoln: MacArthur had pictures of Lincoln and Washington on the wall; Hirohito had busts of Lincoln, Napoleon, and Darwin. Both men had exalted military titles, MacArthur as Commander of the American Army of the Southwest Pacific and now Supreme Commander for the Allied Powers, Hirohito as emperor and commander of the Japanese armed forces. Both men were well traveled: The general had visited Japan and the Far East in 1905–6 and lived in Asia since 1937; in 1921 the emperor had taken a six-month royal tour of

Hong Kong, Singapore, Egypt, Malta, England, France, Belgium, Holland, and Italy. Finally, and not least, each man was absolutely convinced that he alone was a man of destiny and represented God's favored race.

Normally in a meeting of the conqueror and the vanquished, the vanquished must be the more nervous: Is he going to have his head cut off? Thrown into a dungeon for the rest of his life?

Actually, in this case it was MacArthur who was the more tense. Japan was prostrate, what more could the emperor lose? But for MacArthur, having won a war, he could easily lose the peace—a grim prospect after such a hard-fought war. He had to tread carefully, for he had politicians and generals back in Washington snapping at his heels. A lot of people back home wanted vengeance. He had to be careful. While he enjoyed unprecedented power as a supreme commander, he knew his standing with President Truman and Army Chief George Marshall was hardly rock solid and could be taken away at a moment's notice.*

Ever since the surrender on the *Missouri* he had known he would have to move with utmost delicacy. His first test would be what he was going to do with the emperor.

MacArthur also knew that he was in a fairly weak position, like any head of a military occupation. Without the emperor's support, he would need a million soldiers to maintain order. He did not have a million soldiers, at the moment he had barely five hundred thousand—and almost all of them were clamoring to go back home.

MacArthur was a general: The same style of thinking he had used in war he would use in this new form of war called peace: "To avoid the frontal attack with its terrible loss of life; to bypass Japanese strong points and neutralize them by cutting their lines of supply; to thus isolate their armies and starve them in the battlefield; to, as baseball player Willie Keeler used to say: 'hit 'em where they ain't.'" In other words, be clever and outfox them. Be patient. Don't rush into battle, sit back and wait and take advantage of the other side's impatience.

*Which is exactly what happened in America's next major military occupation. In 2003 in Iraq, President Bush abruptly fired Gen. Jay Garner after three weeks and installed the inexperienced, politically connected Paul Bremer as head of the Coalition Provisional Authority.

Urged by his staff weeks earlier to summon the emperor to his head-quarters, MacArthur had refused: "To do so would be to outrage the feelings of the Japanese people and make a martyr of the Emperor in their eyes. No, I shall wait and in time the Emperor will voluntarily come to see me." MacArthur explained: "In this case the patience of the East rather than the haste of the West will best serve our purpose." Asked if the emperor initiated a visit, would he return it, MacArthur again said no: "I shall never call upon the Emperor until a treaty of peace is signed and the occupation comes to a close. To do otherwise would be universally construed as an acknowledgement of the equality between his position and that which I occupy in representation of the Allied Powers—an equality which does not exist."

His position was clear: The emperor must make the first move. The days went by, he waited. He was in no hurry, time was on his side, he had plenty of other things to do. He did, however, make quiet over-tures through two Japanese Quaker friends of Bonner Fellers who were anxious to prove that the emperor was "a lover of peace." Sure enough, after two weeks an inquiry was received by the American Embassy and the highly anticipated meeting quickly arranged. The Japanese were given no clue what to expect other than that the meeting would take place at the American Embassy—not at MacArthur's official office in the Dai Ichi Building. The emperor's visit was to be a courtesy call, nothing more.

Now sitting in the reception hall of the American Embassy, smoking his cigarette and looking at the man across from him, the emperor was dumbfounded at the supreme commander's attire. Here he was, the Son of Heaven, dressed in the full diplomatic outfit of cutaway jacket and striped trousers, calling on a man wearing military khaki trousers and shirt, no jacket or tie. The American's only mark of military power was a small circle of five stars on his right collar. Yet he was the most powerful general in the world.

The emperor had no idea how much MacArthur knew of his involve-ment in the war, how much he had rewarded his military command-ers after the bloody conquest of China, how he had known of the plan to bomb Pearl Harbor and done nothing to stop it, how he could have prevented the beheading of captured American pilots. The emperor knew the Americans were seething with anger over the surprise attack on Pearl Harbor, plus the Japanese atrocities of war. He also knew that his former prime minister, Hideki Tojo, had been arrested two days ago and was now cooling his heels in Sugamo Prison, possibly to be executed any moment. Was that the fate awaiting him?

He had a vague hope that he would be allowed to stay on as emperor, for the Potsdam Declaration had specified that the occupation would be conducted according to the "freely expressed will of the Japanese people." Was not the emperor beloved by his people? Was he not the expression of their will?

He knew that the Hague Convention of 1928 precluded tampering with the political machinery of an occupied country, and that there was also the Atlantic Charter of 1941, which proclaimed America's commitment to the right of all peoples to determine their own form of government. But he also knew that Japan had submitted to unconditional surrender, meaning the victors could do whatever they chose, and that his own army chief of staff had told him unconditional surrender meant the end of the imperial system. He knew further, totally apart from what the Americans' disposition might be, that the Australians, the British, the Chinese, and especially the Russians were out to get his scalp.

MacArthur, for his part, planned to be quiet and hear what the emperor had to say. As Theodore Roosevelt had once said to him when MacArthur was serving as the president's personal military aide in 1903: "You must listen to the grass grow."

What MacArthur didn't want to hear was a plea for mercy. He had already made up his mind to follow the Potsdam Declaration—how could he not?—but he had no intention of revealing his hand. Military men have a code of honor. To forgive someone you must first of all respect him. If the emperor was to be let off the hook, he must earn his way.

The meeting began. "I come to you, General MacArthur, to offer myself to the judgment of the powers you represent . . . as the one to bear sole responsibility for every political and military decision made and action taken by my people in the conduct of war." The key operative word in this sentence was "every." There was no equivocating here, no mea culpa, no skirting the edges about Pearl Harbor, or the Rape of Nanking, or the atrocities of the Bataan March. Everything was on the table.

MacArthur, knowing how deep and dreadful the emperor's humiliation must be, was stunned. "A tremendous impression swept me," he wrote later. "This courageous assumption of a responsibility implicit with death, a responsibility clearly belied by facts of which I was fully aware, moved me to the very marrow of my bones. He was an emperor by inherent birth, but in that instant, I knew I faced the First Gentleman of Japan in his own right." After the meeting he told Faubion Bowers: "To see someone who is so high, reduced to such a position of humility is very painful."

Of course the emperor's admission also suggested he might be talking in riddles to absolve all the generals who engaged in atrocities, but that was a question for another day when SCAP conducted a war crimes trial. For MacArthur what was important now was that the emperor had not begged for mercy or put him on the spot. The emperor—like MacArthur—was a man of honor.

The two men engaged in casual conversation. There was no discussion of politics or war crimes—that was taboo. MacArthur, though he had no idea how true it was, made a specific point of praising Hirohito for his role in ending the war. Then Hirohito dropped a surprise. He told MacArthur that the bombing of Hiroshima was what had impelled Japan to finally surrender: "The peace party did not prevail until the bombing of Hiroshima created a situation which could be dramatized." If MacArthur, who had gone on record opposing the bomb, was amazed by this revelation, he did not admit it, nor did he necessarily believe it. By blaming everything on the bomb, the emperor was protecting himself and the Japanese people. MacArthur would play along. He was there, after all, not as an investigator to unravel deep truths but rather to search common ground on which to base future cooperation and harmony.

The emperor thanked MacArthur for the Americans' occupying Japan so peaceably; MacArthur responded that this was wholly due to Hirohito's cooperation. Hirohito suggested it would be interesting to know what future historians would say about responsibility for the war;

no reply from MacArthur. Hirohito sounded him out on abdication; again no response. The general was being very cagey. In thirty-eight minutes Hirohito had learned nothing about what would come next or what his fate would be.

The meeting was over, and MacArthur escorted the emperor down to his car, then abruptly turned around without shaking hands and walked back into the embassy. The next day the photograph was developed and released. The Japanese government was appalled and banned this picture as insulting to the emperor; MacArthur rejected the ban and ordered the picture to be published in all the newspapers, pronto. It appeared the following day, September 29, and generated a firestorm of controversy: It was "Mahomet going to the mountain." For the first time in his life the emperor was photographed with no advisor present. MacArthur was big, confident, and dead serious, almost grim; the emperor was small and subservient, a man snapping to attention like a waiter. Such was the fate of an emperor "without peer on the land, the sea, and in the air, the direct descendant of the Sun Goddess Amaterasu."

Considered by many to be the most influential single political photograph of the twentieth century, this picture became key in persuading the Japanese not to rise up against their powerful occupier, a man who looked more like an emperor than even Hirohito himself.

Douglas MacArthur was off to a good start.

8

What to Do with the Emperor and the Militarists?

ITH HIS THREE bold moves—the Atsugi landing, the surrender ceremony, and the meeting with the emperor—MacArthur had surprised and impressed the enemy. The emperor and the militarists had good reason to be nervous: They knew full well there was tremendous pressure in the United States to try them as war criminals. Even before he arrived as supreme commander, MacArthur was the most feared of all Americans because of what he had done in the war. Leaving Bataan, he had promised he would return. The local people in the Philippines took his words to heart. On folders, blotters, match covers, leaflets, and cards, the magic words "I shall return" appeared. Japanese officials and soldiers found the words scrawled on signs, windows, and buses. Observed one journalist: The Japanese "erased the words, burned them, stomped them into the ground, but they would not be destroyed. It was a psychological weapon MacArthur had forged in the fight and it worked. *I shall return* was an invisible weapon poised at the heart and brains of the Japanese soldier. It frightened him, worried him, tore down his morale."

So when the man who uttered those powerful words ended up ruling Japan, he possessed the aura Machiavelli said every prince must have: He was feared.

MacArthur was especially pleased by his meeting with the emperor. He had promised nothing, and he had gleaned useful information confirming he was on the right path. A lot of work and thought had gone into this meeting, a lot more than what most people assumed for such a short encounter. Well before the surrender, he had assigned General Fellers to evaluate the situation concerning the emperor. The report he received included the following:

> There must be no weakness in the peace terms. However, to dethrone, or hang, the emperor would cause a tremendous and violent reaction from all Japanese. Hanging of the emperor to them would be comparable to the crucifixion of Christ to us. All would fight to die like ants. The position of the gangster militarists would be strengthened immeasurably. The war would be unduly prolonged. . . . An independent Japanese army responsible only to the emperor is a permanent menace to peace. But the mystic hold the emperor has on his people and the spiritual strength of the Shinto faith properly directed need not be dangerous. The emperor can be made a force for good and peace provided Japan is totally defeated and the military clique destroyed. . . . The Government must have a system of checks and balances. The emperor must be surrounded by liberal civilian leaders. The military must be limited to an internal police force, responsible to the civil authority.

The Potsdam Declaration had implied, but not stated, that the emperor would be spared. In its directive to MacArthur appointing him Supreme Commander for the Allied Powers, the Truman administration had made it clear that the final decision would be his.

Should the emperor be allowed to stay or not? It was the question on everyone's mind—and it was one that must not linger. Immediately after the surrender MacArthur had assigned to his latest chief of counterintelligence, Brig. Gen. Elliott Thorpe, the task of confirming that the emperor's support among the Japanese people was as widespread as MacArthur assumed it was. Would the exemplary behavior of the Japanese at Atsugi be likely to continue? When Thorpe responded affirmatively, MacArthur moved to put some pressure on the emperor for a meeting. He did so by having Thorpe arrest and lock up Marquis

Koichi Kido, the Lord Keeper of the Privy Seal and personal advisor to the emperor, on charges of war crimes. Naturally this set the alarm bells ringing in the royal household.

Thorpe got a visit from Toshikazu Kase, the bilingual delegate at the *Missouri* surrender signing, offering an invitation for Thorpe to have a geisha dinner with Kido's replacement, Marquis Yasumasa Matsudaira. Thorpe agreed to what he knew would be a session of having his tongue pulled for clues and hints. After a lengthy and lavish dinner enjoyed by all, Thorpe related what had happened: "Did I think General MacArthur would grab the Emperor? The Emperor was worried." Thorpe responded vaguely, so as to make the emperor's advisors "sweat a bit." He recalled:

> I told Matsudaira straight out that nothing could save the imperial institution if Japan was to be run on the same old lines. I suggested the Emperor and his government get busy and do something about the plight of the people and not sit there bewailing the firmness of General MacArthur's directives. I reminded the group that there had been monarchies in France and elsewhere that had been swept away on the tide of revolution simply because of such oppressive conditions and do-nothingism as existed in Japan. If such a revolution came in Japan, I warned, no one could stop it, not even the occupation forces. Moreover, we would not try to stop it unless it imperiled our own safety. . . . If you love your Emperor so much why don't you get to work and make him a genuine, worthwhile being?

Matsudaira replied: "How could that be done?"

Thorpe told Matsudaira the emperor was being too aloof—he needed to get out and mix more in public, to exercise some American-style public relations.

This was strong advice to give about a man who had never before ventured out in public except in his military uniform and riding his big white horse, but MacArthur was betting on a trait he had noticed about the Japanese that separated them from all the other countries in Asia:

their tremendous curiosity about the best way to do things. For decades Japan had sent missions to the West to study the building of railroads, ships, dams, and factories. MacArthur was sure the emperor shared this same desire for improvement. Whatever he suggested in the way of subtle hints, Hirohito would do out of respect for him as a conqueror.

As Thorpe himself admitted, "Otherwise we would have had nothing but chaos. The religion was gone, the government was gone, and he was the only symbol of control. Now, I know he had his hand in the cookie jar, and he wasn't any innocent little child. But he was of great use to us." By now MacArthur's decision was clear: The emperor would be allowed to stay so long as he provided a symbol of continuity. MacArthur would separate Hirohito from the militarists, retain him as a constitutional monarch (but only as a figurehead), and use him to bring about a spiritual transformation of the Japanese people. MacArthur made his decision official by notifying Gen. Dwight Eisenhower, the recently appointed army chief of staff, that the emperor was not responsible for the war.

Just as the militarists had used the emperor as their tool, so would MacArthur. "I could have humiliated him, publicly exposed him, but what for?" he told Faubion Bowers. "I fought the war, he ended it. He deserves respect, the magnanimous gesture a noble defeated enemy deserves. Besides, with him as figurehead, our job is so much more easy." Several days earlier he had said: "I was born a democrat; I was reared as a liberal. But I tell you I find it painful to see a man once so high and mighty brought down so low." Of course, not many Americans would have called the Japanese "a noble . . . enemy" or found bringing down the emperor "painful." "I don't trust the vermin," said Admiral Halsey of the emperor. MacArthur was willing to do so: It was part of his strategic game plan to overlook inconvenient truths in pursuit of long-term goals. If he was to lead a successful and peaceful occupation, he would need the emperor just as much as the emperor needed him. Looking back many years later, MacArthur wrote in his memoirs: "The Emperor called on me often after that, our conversation ranging over most of the problems of the world. I always explained carefully the underlying reasons for the occupation policy, and I found he had a more thorough grasp of the democratic concept than almost any Japanese with whom I talked. He played a major role in the spiritual regeneration of Japan, and his loyal co-operation and influence had much to do with the success of the occupation."

However, the emperor still needed to become more assertive and independent. "Hirohito was so controlled by the militarists that he nearly had to get permission to go to the bathroom," MacArthur observed. Those days were over. MacArthur would put the militarists out of business in due course; right now he needed to give the emperor a gentle nudge. No fool, Hirohito caught on quickly. In a subsequent meeting with the supreme commander he asked permission to leave his 240-acre estate and travel around the country and offer blessings and support for his people. MacArthur nodded and suggested, in the same vein, that it might be a good idea for Crown Prince Akihito, who was twelve, to have an American tutor to educate him in American democratic ways. The emperor concurred, and requested that the tutor be an "American woman of cultural background and maturity." MacArthur liked this idea, for much the same reason that he would become such a forceful proponent of women's rights: Many Japanese men were militarists; Japanese women were not. Better the boy have a woman tutor than a man. In 1946 a U.S. educational commission came to Japan to upgrade Japan's school system. MacArthur asked the chairman, George D. Stoddard, to recruit a tutor for the crown prince. Stoddard chose Elizabeth Gray Vining, a Quaker teacher and author of several children's books, who immediately came to Japan and ended up staying for four years.

The emperor, following Thorpe's advice, would undergo a major transformation in his role and public image. In just three months, on January 1, 1946, the emperor would announce to the Japanese people that he was not divine (causing a Texas congressman to remark that "the real reason the Emperor came out and said he wasn't God was because he found that MacArthur was"). To humanize Hirohito, SCAP had him go on extensive inspection tours throughout the country and attend concerts, art exhibits, sports events, and other public gatherings. Gone were the uniform and military medals, leaving a man dressed in a business suit like a civilian. The Japanese were shocked to learn that the emperor owned lots of Western suits, military uniforms, and pairs of shoes, and not one Japanese kimono or a pair of clog shoes. Instead of Japanese miso broth and fish for breakfast, he ate bacon, eggs, and toast. Such revelations did nothing to diminish his stature; instead they only endeared him more to the public. Even the news about the American tutor for the crown prince enhanced the emperor's reputation.

Anybody who thought the emperor was getting off easily, however, was mistaken. MacArthur, after his meeting with Hirohito, assigned Elliott Thorpe to be the official custodian of the emperor and his household, meaning that any foreigner who wanted to meet with the emperor had to go through Thorpe. That was for starters. Next, the supreme commander demanded a complete list of all holdings at home and abroad by the Japanese government and its war allies, plus all Allied properties seized during the war. The list had to include the personal holdings of Emperor Hirohito. Whatever alarm bells had rung in the Imperial Palace when MacArthur arrested Kido now turned into shock waves. The days of Hirohito's vast land holdings were numbered. Gone were the days when he had three thousand servants at his beck and call. A new era of democracy and austerity had arrived, and within months most of the servants were let go.

If the emperor and his translator had been less preoccupied when they came to meet the supreme commander for the first time on September 27, they might have noticed lying on the coffee table a copy of the September 17 issue of *Time* magazine. History does not tell us whether the emperor read a translation of this issue, but for sure someone high up in the Japanese government did, and picked up this story about the U.S. State Department's report on Japanese atrocities:

> The State Department report was a compilation of some 240 separate protests made to the enemy while the war raged. Behind the stiff, formal language was apparent the rage which must have gripped [State] Secretaries Hull and Stettinius every time a new atrocity account came in. The Department had refrained from public outburst as long as the war was on. But now some of the tale could be told.

It covered the familiar stories of lack of hospitals, lack of food and clothing, vermin-infested camp, corporal punishment of prisoners, death by decapitation of a U.S. airman in New Guinea, name not disclosed. (From Korea came a story of U.S. prisoners on Jap ships, crazed with thirst, biting their arms and drinking their own blood, perishing when the ships were bombed by U.S. planes.)

But among all the cases cited in the long and sickening report, one stood out in its barbaric horror.

The date was Dec. 14, 1944. The place was Puerto Princesa in the Philippines. On that date in that place Jap guards drove 150 U.S. prisoners into air-raid tunnels, emptied gasoline into the tunnel openings and set them afire. The victims, enveloped in flames and screaming in agony, swarmed from the shelters. As they did, they were bayoneted or machine-gunned. About 40 who threw themselves over a 50-ft. cliff onto a beach were attacked by sentries on the shore. Many, moaning in agony, were buried alive.

One who swam into the sea was recaptured. A Jap soldier poured gasoline on his foot and set it afire, finally set fire to his other foot and to both his hands. In the end the Japs bayoneted their victim, poured gasoline over him and watched the flames until his body was consumed.

Last week the pestilential camps of the Japanese Empire continued to disgorge their victims (2,900 from Niigata, 3,495 from Nagoya, 1,100 from Tientsin). The record of horror grew.

The number of Americans killed by the Japanese in World War II was 100,997. Among other nations the toll was far greater. From 1931 to 1945 the Japanese Empire had killed 17.2 million people in fourteen countries, ranging from 10 million in China, 3 million in the Netherlands East Indies, 1.5 million in Bengal . . . down to 10,000 in New Zealand. Even worse than the number of deaths was the brutality of many of these deaths and deliberate attacks on innocents. Among the favorite targets of Japanese warplanes, for instance, were field hospitals, plainly marked with the Red Cross sign.

Back in America there was little love lost by the American public for "the Japs." Americans were outraged by the infamous Pearl Harbor attack and the harsh treatment of American war prisoners. A November 1944 Gallup poll showed 13 percent of Americans favored killing *all* the people in Japan after war ended. Even the *New York Times* ran articles on the feasibility of eliminating the Japanese race. Another survey three months before the surrender showed that some 33 percent of Americans were in favor of executing the emperor with no trial, while a majority favored convicting him as a war criminal. In Washington, Representative John Rankin spoke of the Japanese as "savage apes," and Georgia's distinguished senator Richard B. Russell Jr. called them "bestial."

Early in the occupation the Japanese premier, Prince Naruhiko Higashikuni, had caused an uproar in SCAP when he said: "If you in the United States will forget Pearl Harbor, we will forget Hiroshima." The Japanese were astonished at the anger this remark stirred in the Americans: Japan had always started hostilities by surprise attack. To people with a militarist mind-set, Pearl Harbor was normal. What was on trial, in the Japanese view, was not responsibility but defeat. MacArthur's job would be to change this amoral thinking.

Under MacArthur, Hirohito would be spared, but not the militarists. "The surrender terms are not soft, and they won't be applied in kid-glove fashion," MacArthur announced. "The overall objectives for Japan have been clearly outlined in the surrender terms and will be accomplished in an orderly, concise, and comprehensive way."

Immediately after the *Missouri* signing, MacArthur issued an order for the arrest of forty top generals, the most prominent of whom was Hideki Tojo, prime minister from 1941 to 1944. On September 8, the day MacArthur arrived in Tokyo, Tojo was arrested. To beat the rap, he shot himself in the chest but missed his heart. After a life-saving operation by American surgeons, Tojo was in the hospital recovering. Among his other medical needs was a custom-fitted set of dentures—a present from the United States government. Two American military dentists undertook the task, secretly etching on the patient's teeth three words in Morse code: "Remember Pearl Harbor."

PART TWO

VIGOROUS EXECUTION

9

Organizing for Success

I N THE SPRING of 1945, students at a special Civil Affairs Training School at Harvard University played policy games by composing handbooks for a hypothetical military government under "General MacNimitz"—a compound of the two leading contenders for the job after the successful invasion of Japan. Nimitz or MacArthur would suspend the operations of the national government and replace its top-level officers with Americans. Members of the imperial household, including the emperor, would be taken into custody.

Just because MacArthur had had a good meeting with the emperor didn't mean he had solved the emperor problem. The Joint Chiefs asked MacArthur if it was possible to combine the imperial institution with democratic government. He responded that it was possible, so long as great care was taken. Putting the emperor on trial, satisfying though it might be for most people in America, would doom the occupation's prospects. "Underground chaos and guerilla warfare in mountainous and outlying regions would result," and would require a million troops to maintain order.

That kind of number quickly ended the discussion. It was to be the best-kept secret of the entire six and a half years that America ruled Japan: its vulnerability. Military occupations are extremely labor-intensive. One can never have enough troops, meaning that much of an occupation's success depends on political relations with the subject population. This was particularly true in the case of Japan. After a huge world war the U.S. Army was under relentless pressure to release troops from duty. The number of troops available to MacArthur would decrease over time—just when most military occupations would need more troops, not less. Given the winding down of the number of American troops and the first priority being Europe, few troops would be available for a surge should he need it.

How long would the occupation have to last? Some members of Congress said possibly as long as twenty years. MacArthur was more specific. According to his preliminary plan for occupying Japan, known as Operation Blacklist, the military occupation would be for five years and consist of three phases: one year for post-surrender consolidation, three years for demilitarization/disarmament, and one year for peace treaty and withdrawal of military forces from Japan. This proved to be a realistic prediction. By 1950 the United States was ready to end the occupation; the only reason it stayed until early 1952 was international tensions and the 1950 outbreak of war in Korea.

Generals often do their most significant work before the major fighting begins. When it does start, they must have a sixth sense—the mysterious ability to sense battlefield developments. Both traits would serve MacArthur well in his peacetime role as supreme commander. He had strong views about what needed to be done concerning the emperor, political reform, the Japanese constitution, Japanese militarism, and humanitarian aid. He would keep the Japanese government in place and have SCAP function in a supervisory role rather than implement the orders itself. SCAP was to be an advisory organization rather than an executive one (akin to a staff as opposed to a line function). Demobilization, construction, transport, education, health care, banking, and other basic functions—to the fullest extent possible—would be carried out by the Japanese themselves. Speed was of the essence. The faster the Americans got out of Japan, the better. Once Japan fulfilled the requirements of the Potsdam Declaration, there would be little left for a military force to do. Prolonging the occupation would only give rise to a "colonial" psychology and stir local resentment.

Make no mistake about it, thought MacArthur, the occupation must be comprehensive. The British begged to differ. When shown an early draft of U.S. policy, they argued that all the Allies had to do was occupy major military points and put on occasional demonstrations of military power. Sir George Sansom, a leading authority on Japanese history, claimed that sweeping reforms were not needed to convert Japan into an acceptably democratic state. MacArthur, who fancied himself a man with a keen understanding of the Oriental mind, disagreed totally.

Unlike Eisenhower in Germany, MacArthur encouraged his soldiers to mingle and fraternize with the occupied population, and to give out chocolates to children. The Japanese people, surprised by such openness and friendliness, called them "the happy soldiers." "Wherever Americans went," observed Elizabeth Vining, the American writer hired by the emperor to tutor the crown prince, "the children crowded about, shy, curious, friendly, smiling. Children reflect what they hear at home. If there was hatred and bitterness and talk of revenge in the family circle, the children would not swarm with obvious delight about the foreigner."

They were our best ambassadors, MacArthur said of his 500,000 soldiers (eventually reduced to 118,000 in 1948, and 75,000 in 1951). The supreme commander and his officials ran a tight ship, brooking no abuse or offense to Japanese dignity. Knowing how short of food most Japanese people were, the supreme commander forbade soldiers to accept invitations to eat in Japanese homes. Japanese food was reserved for the Japanese. If an American soldier was invited to a Japanese home for dinner, he must bring his own food and he must be back by eleven o'clock. The only cultural items allowed to be purchased by American servicemen were discarded samurai swords; everything else must remain in Japan; there was to be no plundering whatsoever of the country's artistic heritage. When a soldier broke into a Japanese teahouse, MacArthur had him sentenced to ten years' hard labor. Any American caught slapping a Japanese citizen automatically got a five-year jail sentence. When the newspapers publicized this draconian ruling, the Japanese were stunned that a conqueror could be so tough on itself. "That," marveled one Japanese man to an American journalist, "was when we knew we had lost the war."

Equally correct behavior was expected of the Japanese, and Americans let them know it. When the emperor tried to curry favor with an important official from Washington by giving him a solid gold cigarette case with an inscription, the official returned it immediately. When a Japanese government minister visiting Japanese being held in prison by SCAP stated, "I wish to lodge a formal complaint—there is no heat whatsoever in this prison," General Eichelberger responded: "I fully agree, it is a disgraceful state of affairs. You fellows should have had heating installed when our boys were prisoners here."

As in any occupation there were the inevitable incidents of rowdy behavior and a few cases of rape or theft by American soldiers, but by and large the impression they made was very favorable. Likewise, the cooperation and hospitality displayed by the subject Japanese tended to be exemplary.

By treating the Japanese with magnanimity, MacArthur sought to persuade them of the error of their ways in accepting feudalism and militarism. Observed Masuo Kato, one of the two Japanese reporters at the surrender ceremony on the *Missouri*:

> We Japanese were poorly led, but we cannot ascribe our misguidance to the militarists and statesmen alone. We were lacking in a fundamental quality as a people, the understanding of the importance of individual liberty and the will to protect it. In its place was only a feudalistic submission to power, and in that respect the whole nation must accept responsibility for the war.

Added the Japanese historian Toshio Nishi: "The Japanese, accepting defeat, assumed the conqueror must have won because of superior values and institutions."

Every organization begins with a mission statement. MacArthur never put it in writing, but the closest he came to expressing one was when he met with an American visitor shortly after arriving in Japan: "We are trying to sow an idea—the idea of freedom, the freedom that roots in religion. If you sow an idea, an army can't stop it. Secret societies can't stop it. What we want to do is to release into the life of these millions of people the idea of freedom and democracy."

"FROM THE MOMENT of my appointment, I had formulated the policies I intended to follow, implementing them through the Emperor and the machinery of the imperial government," MacArthur wrote in his memoir.

This is only somewhat true. He did develop the specific actions, rules, and regulations. But he already had the Potsdam Declaration of July 26 and a September 6 policy statement known as United States Initial Post-Surrender Policy for Japan (SWNCC 150/4). The main operating document was a November 3 memorandum from the Joint Chiefs known as JCS 1380/15, acknowledged by MacArthur as "one of the great state papers of modern history." Written by Gen. John Hilldring, an aide to Army Chief of Staff George Marshall who later became assistant secretary of state, JCS 1380/15 is organized into two sections, "General and Political," and "Economic, Civilian Supply and Relief, Financial." This 7,500-word document contains fifty specific directives relating to myriad items like dissolution of paramilitary organizations, emphasis on local government, closure of military research laboratories, authorization of banknotes and legal tender, censorship, protection of cultural and religious objects, repatriation of Korean citizens, and foreign exchange controls.

It takes nothing away from MacArthur to give Washington full credit for the planning it did. In accepting these policies (which he agreed with), MacArthur became responsible for putting them into action—and modifying them where necessary.

Several items relating to overall policy are worth noting:

> #2: . . . Unless you deem it necessary, or are instructed to the contrary, you will not establish direct military government, but will exercise your powers so far as compatible with the accomplishment of your mission through the Emperor of Japan or through the Japanese Government.

#3a: . . . The United States desires that the Japanese Government conform as closely as may be to principles of democratic self-government, but it is not the responsibility of the occupation forces to impose on Japan any form of government not supported by the freely expressed will of the people.

#4c: . . . The policy is to use the existing form of government, not to support it. Changes in the direction of modifying the feudal and authoritarian tendencies of the government are to be permitted and favored.

#4e: . . . You will make it clear that military occupation of Japan is effected in the interests of the United Nations and is necessary for the destruction of Japan's power of aggression and her war potential and for the elimination of militarism and militaristic institutions which have brought disaster on the Japanese.

Other paragraphs dealt with MacArthur's power:

#4h: Representatives of civilian agencies of the United States Government or of other United Nations governments shall not participate in the occupation or function independently within Japan except upon your approval and subject as to purpose, time and extent, to decisions communicated to you by the Joint Chiefs of Staff.

#13a: You will not assume any responsibility for the economic rehabilitation of Japan or the strengthening of the Japanese economy. You will make it clear to the Japanese people that: a) You assume no obligations to maintain, or have maintained, any particular standard of living in Japan, and b) That the standard of living will depend upon the thoroughness with which Japan rids itself of all militaristic ambitions . . . and cooperates with the occupying forces and the governments they represent.

#29a: You will assure that all practicable economic and police measures are taken to achieve the maximum utilization of essential Japanese resources in order that imports into Japan may be strictly limited. Such measures will include production and price controls, rationing, control of black markets, fiscal and financial controls and other measures directed toward full employment of resources, facilities and means available in Japan.

Finally, other paragraphs laid out specific policy directives. Paragraph #25 opened the door for land reform, the formation of labor unions, and the breakup of economic monopolies: "It is the intent of the United States Government to encourage and show favor to a) Policies which permit a wide distribution of income and ownership of the means of production and trade, and b) The development of organizations in labor, industry, and agriculture on an economic basis."

JCS 1380/15 was almost like a business plan. It became the bible of the occupation. MacArthur chopped up its 179 paragraphs into fragments and assigned them to his fifteen staff sections for implementation. If it provided a ready checklist, it proved even more valuable in reminding SCAP's senior officers of their purpose for being in Japan: to liberate.

With the occupation's mission and objectives now in place, MacArthur's next task was organization and staffing. But first he had to deal with reporting relationships. In an effort to appease its allies, Washington had established a rather confusing organizational structure:

CHAIN OF COMMAND, SCAP

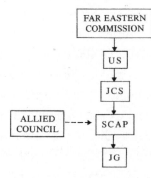

The entity in charge of ruling the Japanese government (JG) was the Supreme Commander for the Allied Powers (the organization, not the man, though the name was used interchangeably for one or the other—in itself an indication of MacArthur's extraordinary power).

Above MacArthur was the U.S. government bureaucracy. The supreme commander reported first to the secretary of the army, then to the secretary of war, then to the army chief of staff, then to the chairman of the Joint Chiefs of Staff, and finally to the commander in chief of the U.S. armed forces, President Truman. Frequently MacArthur as a five-star general would find himself reporting to lower-ranking generals occupying the positions of secretary of the army, army chief of staff, and chairman of the Joint Chiefs, making for an awkward situation. The best way for them to handle this was to let MacArthur do pretty much whatever he wanted.

The occupation of Japan, in duration and in the number of Americans involved, would be the largest foreign policy operation ever undertaken by the United States. The entity running it would be the War Department, not the State Department. To ensure its control and to minimize the role of the State Department, the War Department required all orders to SCAP to go through the Joint Chiefs of Staff (JCS). In a perfect example of how bureaucracies protect their turf, this requirement meant that if the State Department wanted to send a directive and the Joint Chiefs didn't like it, it was never sent.

To get around this JCS filter and give the State Department a vehicle for exercising influence, Secretary of State Byrnes set up the FEC. The State Department maintained that there could be no lasting peace without the consent of all major powers in the Far East. The War Department and MacArthur thought differently: Had not America been the dominant power winning the war in the Pacific? To the victor belong the spoils, and this victor had a major concern: the USSR, which had already shown its true colors by jumping into the war so quickly and taking over Manchuria. The Pentagon arranged for a critical sentence to be inserted in Washington's September 6, 1945, directive to SCAP: "Although every effort will be made . . . to establish policies for the conduct of the occupation . . . which will satisfy the principal Allied powers, in the event of any differences of opinion among them, the policies of the United States will govern."

Protected from above by the Joint Chiefs, and being the only person in the occupation with executive authority, MacArthur was free to do as he wished. When he had to participate in meetings or do things he didn't want to do, he simply ignore them. When accused of friction with the ACJ or FEC, he would issue a soothing denial: "It is difficult to visualize any serious disagreement."

Gnashing their teeth with infuriation, the committee members could do little; MacArthur kept them on the sidelines by using smooth talk and evasion. He attended the first meeting of the Allied Council, told the members he welcomed their input, and left the meeting, never to be seen again. Without MacArthur's personal participation, the council accomplished little.

The Far Eastern Commission was a more serious threat. Three of the members—the USSR, China, and Great Britain—along with the United States, held veto power over SCAP policies. MacArthur saw this as a direct maneuver on their part to get their hands on Japan. He wanted none of it, especially when they attacked his urgent requests to Washington for emergency food shipments for the Japanese. Their argument? That the Japanese should not be permitted a higher standard of living than that of the Chinese or Soviet allies. Imagine!

When Secretary of State Byrnes said control of Japan should be an

Don't need your help, thank you.

Allied responsibility, MacArthur took great exception and claimed that such responsibility belonged exclusively to him. The FEC was nothing more than "a debating society," he said, "a policy-making body with no executive powers, functions or responsibilities." He took care of this nuisance by issuing orders and directives on his own, leaving the FEC to figure out what to do with his fait accompli.

By effectively muzzling these two organizations and keeping Russia's influence to a minimum, MacArthur ensured that SCAP's rule was more about liberation than about punishment. America would run the show. "We do not come in the spirit of conquerors," he said. This attitude was less a statement of personal generosity than an assessment of the Japanese people. A few weeks before the Japanese surrender, Secretary of War Henry Stimson had informed President Truman that the Japanese were an "extremely intelligent people" and their nation building during the eighty years from the late 1850s to the late 1930s had been "one of the most astounding feats of national progress in history." Something, obviously, had gone terribly wrong. America's job was to fix it.

Where to begin? How do you free an entire nation from its militaristic past and do it a way that is acceptable and not overbearing for a people dazed by the ignominy of total defeat? How do you instill in them an appreciation of individual liberty? MacArthur knew how he wanted to do it: by being magnanimous. But lofty principles of liberalism still need vigorous executive action to be translated into effective deeds. This called for a man renowned for his administrative skills.

Organization charts rarely appear in history books, but in management consulting studies they play a prominent role. This would be a substantial operation, eventually growing to 2,800 people in 1949, of which nearly 2,450 were civilians.

There is a reason why this chart is so complicated: It depicts a shadow government. Unlike in Germany, the occupation operated as a supervisory superstructure over an existing country and therefore had to monitor all the activities of the Japanese ministries. SCAP was divided into fifteen staff sections. For each of the forty-six prefectures of Japan, General Headquarters (GHQ) provided a team of seven officers, seven civilians, twenty enlisted

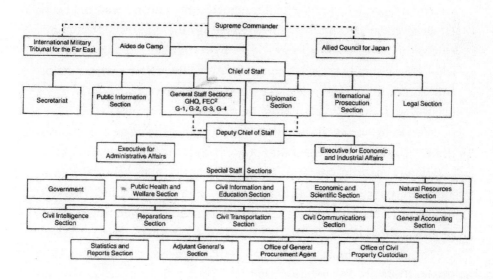

men, and fifty Japanese. These teams, first called "military government teams," were soon called "civil affairs teams." They did no governing per se; rather, they inspected and monitored the subdivisions of the Japanese government to ensure SCAP directives were being properly carried out. These teams helped transmit as much power as possible to the Japanese, giving advice—not orders. To speed up the administration and instill a spirit of camaraderie and partnership, as well as initiative, these suggestions were made in person or by telephone; hardly anything was put in writing. There was to be no paper trail of disagreements or suggestions not followed that might embarrass the Japanese.

The most powerful sections, all headed by members of "the Bataan gang" of generals who had served with MacArthur in the Philippines, were Government, Economic and Scientific, Intelligence, Civil Information and Education, and Public Health and Welfare. Almost all the staffers were provided by Washington. MacArthur loved to complain that Washington had sent him "a boatload of New Dealers," but he was really speaking in jest. He had nothing but the highest regard for the work done by Charles Kades and Alfred Hussey in constitutional reform, Thomas Bisson in politics, and Theodore Cohen in labor unions. MacArthur, who was held in great esteem by conservatives and right-wingers in America for his fervent anti-Communism, was actually quite liberal in his political reform in Japan. He was essentially a nineteenth-century classical liberal: He believed in free markets, in breaking up the entrenched economic trusts (the *zaibatsu*), and in providing more equitable opportunities for laborers and small farmers. Though he was a total dictator whose whims and utterances carried more force than the law, he was opposed to abso-lute rule and wanted to give the country back to the Japanese as quickly as possible. In this regard he was like his idol George Washington: a powerful general who could be trusted with power because he would not abuse it.

He preached the limits of occupation: "After about the third year, any military occupation begins to collapse of its own weight." This fact, drawn from his vast reading of history, dictated his operating philoso-phy: "We won't do for them what they can do for themselves."

The country was a shambles and people were literally starving. How to structure an organization that was comprehensive yet quick and responsive? MacArthur's military experience came in handy. In war, where a campaign is organized by territory and communications with headquarters is often impossible, commanders are responsible for their area in battle. In peacetime this structure requires middlemen to pro-vide coordination. To cut out the middlemen and eliminate the bottle-necks, it is necessary to organize by function. This would be done here.

MacArthur would make all the major decisions. These directives—called SCAPINS—went out under his name and signature. The of-ficial language of the occupation was English. All new Japanese laws and regulations had to be translated and given to SCAP for approval. The amount of paperwork to be translated was massive. Just in the first full month, September 1945, the number of pages to be translated was 278,594—almost 10,000 a day.

The supreme commander moved quickly. He had to—before armed guerrilla bands started operating in the mountains. He gave himself thirty days to get his organization in place and establish firm control over the country. He did it by extending the art of delegation to an extreme form. He was available only to senior members of his staff; the junior members worked through his chief of staff. Observed his air chief, Gen. George Kenney: "It is by avoiding too much that General MacArthur gets so much done." One day the phone rang in the office of Ken Dyke, an air force officer in Yokohama. It was a man he had never met on the other end. "I've been looking over your record," said MacArthur, "and I'm putting you in charge of all public information media and the re-education of the Japanese people. Get copies of the material I have received from the Joint Chiefs of Staff and write your own general orders." Click, end of call. Go write your own job description, and get cracking.

Most of the people MacArthur hired came from the military. When positions became available for which there was no one appropriate in Japan, MacArthur notified Washington. People hired in the United States got a letter from the War Department saying General MacArthur had expressed an urgent need for their services and would they be interested? Overnight these people became celebrities in their hometowns as "advisors of General MacArthur." Observed one senior SCAP official: "With rare exceptions the closest they ever were to him was when they stood in the crowds that daily watched the General arrive and leave the General Headquarters Building in Tokyo."

Unfriendly newspaper correspondents accused MacArthur of surrounding himself with sycophants and mediocrities. "Such sophistry has no place in any serious discussion of MacArthur," wrote Justin Williams, one of SCAP's top lawyers. Certainly if there were a lot of mediocrities, then a man whose occupation administration accomplished so much would have to be an absolute genius. A more modest appraisal of MacArthur would have to dispute this notion and give significant credit to men like Whitney and Kades in government, Marquat in industry, and William Sebald and George Atcheson in foreign affairs. MacArthur commanded great loyalty from his military men who had served with him in the Philippines. Together they had overcome incredible odds. Experiences like that make for strong bonds. They shared a deep distrust of Washington, especially of George Marshall, who had given priority to the European front and failed to deliver the promised troops and ships needed to defend the Philippines. MacArthur's General Headquarters (GHQ) thus had a substantial "us vs. them" siege mentality. Men in this mind-set will develop an extreme need for control and view outsiders with suspicion, which many freshly arrived newspapermen could not understand or relate to. They reserved their particular animus for MacArthur's number two—hatchet man, chief administrator, and public relations man all rolled into one.

He was Maj. Gen. Courtney Whitney, head of the Government Section (GS). An American lawyer and investor who made a fortune in the Philippines in the 1930s, Whitney joined the army in 1940 and became close to MacArthur. Physically he was not an impressive man: Five foot four, puffy-faced and overweight, he looked like "a sharp businessman who had become president of his local Kiwanis Club." "A stuffed pig with a moustache," another detractor called him.

His staff begged to differ. He told them his door was always open:

I want your reaction to every directive to the Japanese government prepared in this section. The junior officers are as well, if not better, qualified to pass judgment on our moves as the higher-ranking ones, including myself. I mean exactly as I say. And I look forward to the time when a lieutenant will barge into my office, bang on my desk and say, "Goddamit, general, such-and-such a proposal directive is preposterous, and you'd be out of your mind to ask General MacArthur to approve it."

More important, noted Kades, a liberal lawyer from Washington: "Everyone felt, at least after General Whitney took over, that we were in a way carrying [on] a crusade." To indicate his stature in the organization, Whitney's office was next to the supreme commander's, and connected by a private door. Whitney saw MacArthur for sometimes as much as three hours a day. He was as smart as MacArthur, a superb administrator of the SCAP organization, and he shared MacArthur's political views. He opposed Japanese conservatives and was a strong advocate of demilitarization, the purge of business leaders, and decentralization of the police.

MacArthur had enormous regard for him. When MacArthur's chief of staff sent a memo announcing that all appointments with the supreme commander would go through him, Whitney went to MacArthur and threatened to quit. MacArthur flashed a big grin, took the aide's memo, struck a match and set the memo on fire, and dropped it in the wastebasket.

MacArthur deliberately avoided making friends with his staff, believing it would affect his professionalism. Whitney was the opposite. When the staff worked overtime and couldn't get to the dining room before it closed at 8:00 p.m., Whitney treated them to the swank Imperial Hotel dining room, where the kitchen always had food available for generals. When one of his officers married another GS staffer in 1946, Whitney demonstrated his joie de vivre by drinking champagne from the bride's slipper.

The most powerful man after Whitney was Maj. Gen. Charles Willoughby, in charge of intelligence, surveillance, and suppression of subversive activities. He was MacArthur's "lovable fascist," otherwise known as "Baron von Willoughby." He was not a baron, but he was pretty close to it, a modern-day version of Baron von Steuben (George Washington's Prussian military advisor). He had been born in Germany as Adolf Karl von Tscheppe-Weidenbach, and allegedly attended the University of Heidelberg and the Sorbonne before immigrating to the United States at age eighteen. Adopting his American mother's maiden name, he graduated from the University of Kansas, then enlisted in the U.S. Army. The author of a 1939 book, *Maneuver in War*, a magisterial four-hundred-page study of 140 battles, he was the occupation's resident intellectual, a man as well-read as MacArthur. At a time when most Americans thought of Stalin as "Uncle Joe" and the USSR as an ally, he stood out for his strong concerns about Communism. His intelligence operation would have its hands full. Its major areas of interest were military weapons, the imperial household, POWs and escapees, chemical and biological warfare, labor organizations, Communist groups and, of course, Soviet spies. He also managed to bring a degree of risqué to the SCAP organization. A bachelor, he was was strikingly good-looking and a magnet for the ladies (though he managed to keep himself out of trouble). Clare Boothe Luce, wife of Henry Luce, the head of Time-Life, worked as a roving journalist and visited the Philippines on two occasions and was immediately smitten with Willoughby. No shrinking violet herself, she found Willoughby to be the sexiest man she ever met, a man who, she said, "made her weak at the knees."

An equally interesting character was the number-four man, Brig. Gen. William Marquat. A professional boxer and newspaper reporter, he had volunteered for the army in World War I and risen through the ranks as an antiaircraft artillery officer. When a business executive slotted for the position of economics chief got blackballed by Washington, MacArthur jumped to fill the position quickly and appointed his friend Marquat, though he had no industry or banking background. It was an enormous job, responsible for supervising industry, banks, and labor—three different ministries of the government. What was expected to be a temporary assignment turned out to be a lot more: a permanent one, as Marquat, an energetic worker and a quick study, proved more than capable of handling the job. He also made himself Japan's baseball commissioner—the game was his true passion. Whenever he could get out of a SCAP meeting, he would head out to the ballpark.

Responsible for military security was Lt. Gen. Robert Eichelberger, whose position does not appear on the organization chart because he was head of the Eighth Army, an organization outside SCAP that also reported to the supreme commander.* He was beloved by everyone, a big teddy bear, genial, honest, uncomplicated, approachable, "as easy, as they say admiringly in the South, as an old shoe." Like MacArthur, he was a former superintendent of West Point and a war hero, having won the pivotal Battle of Buna in the Philippines. Hard-nosed and direct like many generals, he described the Japanese delegation that came to Manila to discuss surrender as a bunch of "goggle-eyed little black-toothed birds." Having served in Siberia in 1918–20 and worked with the Japanese militarists, he had acquired an appreciation of Japanese history. Remembering the surprise attack on Port Arthur in the Russo-Japanese War, the Mukden and Peking incidents, and the treacherous attack on Vladivostok, which he had personally witnessed in 1920, he was leery of the Japanese and didn't trust them one bit. At a banquet in New York three days before Pearl Harbor, he had given a speech predicting that Japan would attack the United States "within a

---

*MacArthur had four titles: SCAP, CINCUNC (Commander in Chief, United Nations Command), CINCFE (Commander in Chief, Far East), and CGFEC (Commanding General, Far East Command). He was running the occupation of Japan, the deployment of U.S. troops in Okinawa and Taiwan, the use of Allied troops in Japan and Korea, and the naval and air forces stationed in the Far East.

few days." He was the only man in America to make this prediction.

He was to appear on the cover of *Time* magazine and be courted by Eisenhower to be his deputy in Washington—not a good way to stay in MacArthur's favor. Though he turned down the offer at MacArthur's insistence (thus blowing an excellent chance to become Eisenhower's successor as army chief of staff), he and MacArthur never had the close relationship they had before.

Not all MacArthur's key men were members of the Bataan gang. One surprising addition was a China expert from the State Department, George Atcheson, chosen by Undersecretary of State Dean Acheson because he was unfamiliar with Japan and would bring a fresh perspective. MacArthur was wary of State Department people because many of them favored the Communists in China. Upon meeting Atcheson, he showed him a letter alleging that Atcheson was "a pink." "I just wanted you to see this so we can start off on a fair and square basis," he told Atcheson. "The cards are now face up on the table." He assured Atcheson that he would hold nothing against him, he would make up his own mind, and everything depended on his job performance.

Atcheson went on to become one of MacArthur's most trusted advisors, including serving as MacArthur's surrogate at ACJ meetings. Unfortunately Atcheson was killed in a 1947 plane crash in the Pacific, when the plane—in a tragedy reminiscent of Amelia Earhart's—missed its assigned refueling island (a tiny dot in the ocean) and ran out of fuel just short of Hawaii.

Another recruit who turned out to be a positive surprise was Maj. Gen. Ned Almond, director of personnel, sent to Japan from Europe. A protégé of George Marshall, after several months he came to admire MacArthur even more than Marshall and was eventually promoted to be MacArthur's chief of staff and one of his two top generals in the Korean War.

His team in place and the organizational structure defined, the supreme commander swung into action.

10

Occupier as Humanitarian

I N T H E S P I R I T of FDR's famous "Hundred Days," MacArthur launched an avalanche of initiatives and activities that left the Japanese astounded; they had never seen a man move so fast (a trait their generals in the South Pacific knew only too well). The supreme commander later called it his Two Hundred Days, not because he wanted to make a grandiose statement—though that was never far from his mind—but because by the time six months had passed, so much had been accomplished. Of the five years (1945–50) he devoted himself fulltime to Japan, the first two hundred days were the most important.

FDR, a liberal Democrat, had viewed MacArthur as a conservative Republican, "one of the two most dangerous men in America" (even though, after saying it in 1932, he kept MacArthur on board and even promoted him). Yet what MacArthur did in Japan was almost like following a script written by the late president: Take over a dazed nation and overwhelm the opposition with countless directives and regulations in pursuit of progressive change. He would be an activist leader, going far beyond the normal parameters of his job. He would be a successful Herbert Hoover. Like Hoover, he would bring to the job an incredible résumé as a skilled administrator; unlike Hoover, however, he would be flexible and willing to try new measures when current efforts were not working or conditions changed. "Above all," FDR had famously said, "do something." Eventually something would work. The supreme commander followed that precept.

Though the U.S. Army had plenty of experience managing occupations, most of it was useless. The standard military government manuals, observed one officer, essentially said, "Bury the dead horses. Appoint somebody as police chief and somebody as mayor, and try to get a good health officer, then you're on your own!" The occupation of Japan had a lot more work to do than just bury dead horses. So much needed to be done right away: Free the American prisoners, demilitarize the country, and bring in food and medical supplies. "Political parties, elections, democracy, the Emperor: all are of academic importance when the rice bowl is empty," said State Department adviser John Emmerson to Secretary of State Byrnes. People in the cities of Japan were starving, living on just 800 calories a day—less than half the normal amount required to be healthy. They were desperate. Impromptu mobs formed on the street. The occupation had to act quickly.

The occupation also had to contend with moving a staggering number of people. It had to bring back from overseas 2.5 million Japanese troops and 2 million Japanese civilians. In the opposite direction it had to return 1.6 million people to Korea and Formosa, most of whom had been forcibly brought to Japan as slave labor to work in the coal mines and steel factories. The war was over; everyone wanted to get home. These people were spread out all over the map, some as far as five thousand miles away. They had to be tracked down, properly identified and processed, and put on ships for the correct destinations. There were not enough ships. By confiscating Japanese warships and merchant ships, and using spare parts and scrap iron from beached and sunken Japanese ships, the occupation was able to repair and put into commission an impromptu fleet of 167 ships capable of carrying 87,600 people—50 percent of the time. Run the numbers: If we assume a fleet of two hundred ships, five hundred people per shipload, and twenty days to load/transport/unload (including 50 percent downtime), such a fleet can move five thousand people a day—or 5.5 million in three years (assuming everyone has been rounded up and cleared for departure when the ship is ready). By adding whatever additional ships it could get from the merchant marine, plus a fleet of a hundred Liberty ships from the United States, SCAP accomplished 90 percent of this transport in one year—without a single ship lost. The boasted logistics of D-Day were child's play compared with this. Eisenhower had to transport 73,000 American troops across the English Channel; in Japan, MacArthur had to transport almost fifty times as many people—and over much greater distances. Plus almost none of these people spoke any English, thereby creating numerous delays and complications.

There was another very urgent problem: disease control. There is no faster way to spread a disease and start a contagion than put people into the confines of a ship. By the time the boat lands, everyone is ill, many dead. In processing people for transport, occupation health officials first had to screen and inoculate passengers for a host of deadly diseases, and where necessary, put sick people into special medical facilities arranged on the spur of the moment.

In managing this postwar chaos, the American occupation team was well prepared: It had a mission, a plan, an organization, and a strong leader. It also had an advantage very unusual for a country in the throes of a total war defeat: a fully functioning local government. The atom bombs had hit so abruptly that the government had no time to fall apart . . . the best way to help it get back on its feet would be to give it something productive to do. MacArthur delegated to the Japanese government the responsibility for the management of these 6.1 million repatriates coming and going. At major ports, under the direction of SCAP, the Japanese government set up repatriation centers to meet exacting security and health standards. Each person was subject to physical examinations, inoculations and vaccinations, screening of baggage for smuggled goods and precious metals, and identification to ensure he or she was not a war criminal.

MacArthur also delegated to the Japanese government the most sensitive assignment of all: disarming the country's 2.2 million troops at home, all trained, armed, and dangerous. Whereas the New York Times back home ran headlines screaming about how "Japan's Fanatics Are MacArthur's Number One Problem," the supreme commander preferred a more measured approach. His gesture permitting self-disarmament astonished and gratified the Japanese military leaders. Expecting humiliation, they got none. They ended up doing their job so well that by mid-October, in less than two months, MacArthur could announce that they had abolished the armed forces and several million men had surrendered their arms. In addition, over the next six months, the

Japanese and Americans working together located and destroyed 10,000 airplanes, 3,000 tanks, 90,000 fieldpieces, three million small arms, and one million tons of explosives; plus all the "eggs" in the harbors (mines laid by American B-29s as part of the economic blockade). That wasn't all. In a country armed to the teeth in preparation for invasion, millions of weapons had been stashed away in remote, hard-to-find places. Tracking down and cleaning up the arsenals, ammunition dumps, and ordnance depots, joint inspection teams stumbled on 100,000 tons of highly sophisticated chemical warfare supplies (a precursor to today's "weapons of mass destruction"). From civilians they confiscated 120,000 bayonets, 81,000 rifles and carbines, 2,240 automatic weapons, and hundreds of tons of makeshift weapons such as crossbows, body armor, plumbing-pipe guns, bamboo bazookas, explosive arrows, even baseball bats. The baseball bats were returned. MacArthur, a left fielder on West Point's varsity baseball team, seized this rare opportunity to promote a common love of both countries. Baseball, introduced to Japan by an American schoolteacher in 1872, had become Japan's national pastime. The supreme commander ordered the resumption of professional baseball games. On a more basic level, General Marquat placed an order with an undoubtedly puzzled War Department in Washington for thousands of baseballs and baseball mitts for Japanese kids playing "stickball." American GIs, usually acting on their own, undertook to teach young boys the finer points of the game.

Airport runways, where feasible, were torn up and turned into fields for growing food. Anything relating to aviation was forbidden. In their zeal to eliminate any kind of military weapon, SCAP personnel drafted rules that were often excessively vague and broad in scope. The Japanese were not allowed to own aeronautical equipment of any kind; even the millions of toy airplanes enjoyed by children were forbidden. MacArthur eliminated this silly rule. Because he had to approve all important decisions, much of his time was spent resolving bureaucratic snafus. Like the one about corn bread. A group of home-economics experts had arrived from the United States to advise the Japanese on how to make corn bread with eggs, milk, and butter. The only problem was there were no eggs, milk, or butter in postwar

Japan. MacArthur sent the consultants home, thank you very much.

MacArthur didn't need teachers, he needed food. The situation grew more and more critical by the day: "You cannot teach democracy to a hungry people," he scowled. There was no threat of revolution—the Japanese were too war weary for that, plus revolutions don't take place when things are at their worst, as MacArthur knew from reading about the American, French, and Russian revolutions; they occur when circumstances are getting better and there is a formation of a middle class. This was not happening in Japan. Still there was danger: people in the cities were starving. Every day saw trains packed with people carrying family heirlooms out to the countryside to barter for food from the farmers.

As bad luck would have it, 1945 was a year of worldwide food shortages. Washington's first priority was delivering food to Germany. MacArthur sent urgent cables: "Thirty million people are threatened by starvation. Disease and unrest will endanger the work of the Occupation." For him the issue was one of fundamental ethics: At a time when the Americans were arresting and planning to execute Japanese generals for their brutality to American prisoners in the infamous Bataan March in the Philippines, namely "ill-treatment including starvation," here the situation was reversed. Every day people were dropping dead in the street. He must act: Not under his watch should a single person die by starvation if it could possibly be helped. His cables to Washington went unanswered, but after several weeks of being badgered, Washington finally got around to sending an International Investigation Commission to Japan to study the problem. MacArthur went into an apoplectic rage: He didn't need a study team, he needed food! Fortunately former president Herbert Hoover—who probably knew more about famines than anyone else in America, from his post–World War I relief work in Europe—was in the Far East in his capacity as chairman of the American Famine Emergency Committee. MacArthur got him to come to Japan and quickly survey the situation. Hoover concluded that if Japan didn't get food imports right away, it would fall down to subsistence level "comparable to a Buchenwald concentration camp." By mid-1946 the grain ships started arriving, delivering $100 million a year of food supplies. It would take another two years for the situation to get back to normal, where people's daily intake was enough to live on, albeit only barely. The amount of grain delivered by the United States was 3.5 million tons, which at eighty million people works out to be almost ninety pounds per person.

Thousands were also dying every day from disease. Under the vigorous leadership of Gen. Crawford Sams, SCAP's Public Health and Welfare Section carried out widespread inoculation programs to stop the spread of diphtheria, smallpox, typhus, typhoid, meningitis, scarlet fever, dysentery, and cholera. The entire Japanese population participated. The results were instantaneous and dramatic. No relief effort anywhere in the world has matched this achievement:

LIFE EXPECTANCY UNDER THE OCCUPATION
(NUMBER OF YEARS, EXCLUDING WAR DEATHS)

	1947	1952	% Increase
MEN:	50.1	59.6	19%
WOMEN:	54.0	63.0	17%

The number one killer in Japan was tuberculosis: In 1945 it killed a greater number of people than all those who died from the bombing, the fire raids, and the two atom bombs put together. Thanks to Sams' doctors and imports of sophisticated American vaccines, by 1950 the number of tuberculosis fatalities was down to 146 deaths per 100,000 population. During 1946–48, dysentery was reduced by 87 percent, typhus by 86 percent, and diphtheria by 85 percent. The most astounding success was with smallpox. After the appearance of 17,800 cases in 1946, the entire population of 80 million was vaccinated. In 1948 only 29 cases of smallpox appeared.

Most histories of the occupation focus on the political aspects of MacArthur's reign, ignoring the humanitarian one. Yet it was there that MacArthur made his greatest impact. According to the historian Eiji Takemae, Crawford Sams' ambitious health-care assistance may have saved as many as three million lives. As for MacArthur's emergency food program, SCAP estimated that the amount of grain and canned goods imported from the United States was enough to save eleven million people. Any way you figure the total—eight, ten, fourteen million—it is a huge number. In addition, SCAP engaged in preventive health care by providing two hot meals a week to 3.2 million schoolchildren to ensure they had a proper diet.

If not the historians, certainly the people remembered, and their hearts and minds followed. MacArthur became known as "the Great Emancipator" for bringing freedom from sickness and hunger. They came to trust him even more than their own leaders, who had led them into such misery. Said MacArthur about the Japanese people: "As they increasingly sensed my insistence upon just treatment for them, even at times against the great nations I represented, they came to regard me as not as a conqueror but as a protector."

No way, however, was MacArthur running a charity operation. One thing that pleased him no end was how hard the Japanese people were working. "Never have I seen debris from bombing so quickly and cleanly cleared away," observed a *New York Times* reporter. When MacArthur returned to Manila for a day in mid-1946 to celebrate Philippine independence, he was depressed to note that the Filipinos seemed primarily interested in what they could extract from the Americans. With the Japanese it was different.

A major theme of the JCS policy memorandum was to help the Japanese help themselves. For Japan to become self-sufficient in food, land reform was imperative. Only 16 percent of Japanese land was fit for cultivation; the rest was mountains and urban areas. Japanese farmers were dirt-poor, making the bulk of Japanese farmland look like a Far Eastern Appalachia. The rural countryside had been a breeding ground for militarism as hundreds of thousands of young men sought to escape grinding poverty by joining the armed forces (almost all the kamikaze pilots came from impoverished rural areas).

To strike at the heart of militarism, MacArthur had to address the farmers' dire straits. For centuries they had toiled like feudal serfs, turning over the bulk of their meager crops to their landlords as rent. The rich got richer, the poor got poorer. It wasn't just land, it happened in trade and banking, too. In 1945 some fifty families controlled 90 percent of Japan's gross domestic product (GDP) through the economic monopolies known as *zaibatsu*. Going after the *zaibatsu* would have to wait for another day, however; the first priority was land reform.

Three months after taking over Japan, MacArthur issued a directive ordering the Japanese government to "take measures to insure that those who till the soil of Japan shall have a more equal opportunity to enjoy the fruits of their labor . . . and destroy the economic bondage which has enslaved the Japanese farmer through centuries of feudal oppression." The landlords, of course, didn't like this one bit. But what astounded MacArthur as he undertook this social engineering was how he got lambasted by the liberal Left in America. A blistering article in *The Nation* predicted that the bulk of Japanese farmers wouldn't be able to afford buying a plot as large as the new maximum of 12.5 acres, and so would slip from tenancy to the even lower status of farmhands. Furthermore, rich landlords could evade this limitation by buying excess land in the name of their relatives. What did SCAP's reformers from the U.S. Agriculture Department know? the magazine thundered. Their knowledge of land reform could be "balanced on the tip of a chopstick."

Frequently being able to see the obvious is more important than having a lot of knowledge. As Gen. William Marquat brusquely put it when he signed off on a proposed land reform program by SCAP agricultural economist Wolf Ladejinsky: "I may be dumb but I am not stupid." Few people understood how all the numbers would work in trying to resurrect the economy, but one thing MacArthur and Marquat did know: They had to do something, and achieving social reform was more important than balancing the budget. Nothing redistributes wealth like inflation. With Japan in the throes of hyperinflation, farmers could buy the land and pay it back at a fraction of what it would cost in times of price stability. In addition, a lot of farmers had cash because they were getting black-market prices for their food from desperate urban dwellers. This was a unique opportunity to knock out the power of the rural landlords once and for all and encourage broader landownership. Furthermore, farmers, once they had a vested interest in the land, would work harder and adopt improved methods of increasing yield, such as using insecticides and fertilizer and rebuilding irrigation dikes. The result turned out to be a win-win situation: The percentage of land owned by farmers soared from 10 to 89 percent, farmers were able to make their payments (most of them paying the whole amount up front), and they increased their yields to such an extent that by 1950 Japan was self-sufficient in food and people were consuming 1,800 calories a day. It was a five-year miracle: Hunger and famine had been eradicated for good. Admiring MacArthur's achievement in land reform, Chiang Kai-shek told him in 1950 that if he "could have done in China what [you] did in Japan, I would still be there today."

MacArthur, with his acute ear for historical drama, likened Japanese land reform to the efforts of the Roman Gracchi brothers in the second century B.C. "Dad would have liked this," he said proudly, thinking of his father's similar work as military governor of the Philippines in 1900.

MacArthur was not a man interested in the fine arts or the theater, but as an avid reader and book collector who had known the pain of cultural loss when the Japanese burned Manila and destroyed his personal library, he instituted measures to protect the Japanese patrimony. Given the grinding poverty right after the surrender and the widespread selling of antiques by city dwellers to the farmers, the loss of cultural treasures was a potential danger. To stop any vandalism or theft, SCAP ordered the Japanese to compile a list of the more than 150,000 temples and shrines throughout the country, identify the most important ones, and assign policemen to guard them. This was promptly done. In five years not a single important temple or museum was looted.

Not only the temples and shrines, also the artworks and cultural artifacts of Japan needed protection. Enter the Monuments Men, a group of some 350 soldiers and civilians assigned to protect artwork and cultural monuments in war-ravaged Europe. A handful of these specialists were sent to Japan to serve in the Civil Information and Education Section of GHQ. Led by the enigmatic Langdon Warner, allegedly the model for Indiana Jones, and curator of the Harvard Fogg Museum and advisor to the Boston Museum of Fine Arts, the group—together with the Japanese Ministry of Culture—conducted an inventory of all

Japanese arts and monuments, including temples, buildings, gardens, and national parks; evaluated war damage; and prepared plans for necessary restoration.

After the Monuments Men completed their work in 1947–48 and returned to America to resume their careers as museum curators, GHQ expanded this effort in an entirely new and imaginative way. Whereas in Europe and America artworks are generally perceived to be paintings and sculptures, in Japan the definition of artwork is much broader, and includes the performing arts (bunraku, kabuki) and crafts (pottery, lacquer boxes, paper making, bamboo weaving, metalwork, fabric dyeing, and embroidery). Exhibiting the Japanese penchant for exactness and detail, these crafts require practitioners of utmost patience and skill (a ceremonial samurai sword, for example, consists of metal worked over and folded several thousand times). Because of the dire economy, there was the very real danger that these crafts would die out and Japanese tradition would be lost forever.

Concern for the future stirred MacArthur to take action.

"Curiously," observed *National Geographic* magazine, "the idea of recognizing people as national treasures originated not with the Japanese but with an American—General of the Army Douglas MacArthur. Appalled by the wartime destruction of priceless works of art, he persuaded the Japanese to safeguard those who carried on the creative tradition." In MacArthur's view, art preservation involved more than just protecting ancient art, it required supporting future art by providing official recognition and financial assistance to living artists. Spurred by the supreme commander, the Diet passed a Law for the Protection of Cultural Properties. Included in the law was a designation of "Living National Treasures" for artists considered "Keepers of Important Intangible Cultural Properties." Such individuals received grants to enable them to continue their craft, and—most important of all—to hire apprentices and train them to be their successors. Such designation quickly became highly esteemed: artists nominated had to be approved by committees of experts and then by the minister of education, and finally by no less than the full cabinet of the Japanese government. No country in the world developed such a rigorous program for government support of the arts, certainly not America, be it at home or in subsequent military occupations such as Iraq.

Today, long after the occupation ended, Japanese traditional crafts have continued to flourish—a remarkable feat. "Few countries have inherited more art worth saving," says one art historian, "and fewer have matched what the Japanese have accomplished since World War Two in preserving their relics and artifacts."

All of which was engineered by one man who, when he returned to America, flooded his ten-room apartment with gifts of arts from the Japanese. A Japanese visitor to MacArthur's New York City premises would have rejoiced at being back home in Japan.

IN HIS ROLE as protector and builder, MacArthur had to contend with hard-liners in Washington outraged by Japan's wartime barbarism. The commissioner for reparations in Germany, oil executive Edwin Pauley, was given the job in Japan as well. He came to Japan for an inspection and issued a report to President Truman stating that the Allied Powers "should take no action to assist Japan in maintaining a standard of living higher than that of neighboring Asiatic countries injured by Japanese aggression." Pauley demanded the immediate seizure of half of Japan's twenty-seven plants making machine tools, a reduction in the country's annual steel-making capacity from 11 million to 2.5 million tons, and an even more severe cut in the airplane, shipbuilding, and ball bearing industries—with more restrictions to come later. MacArthur was aghast. Certainly there was merit in eliminating any war equipment manufacturing, but he had no intention of putting Japan back in the Stone Age. Japan was already in desperate straits: All people could think about was where their next meal was coming from. Not that it mattered to America's Pacific allies on the Far Eastern Commission: they demanded compensation for the havoc Japan had inflicted on them. MacArthur disagreed: He believed that the purpose of reparations was not punishment but security. As far as equity was concerned, to claim that Korea and Formosa should have a standard of living as high as Japan was so ridiculous as not to merit discussion. The Japanese, by dint of their culture, education, and hard work had built up one of the post powerful countries in the world in the forty years since the turn of the century (albeit with help by raiding Japan's neighbors for raw materials). MacArthur's job was to put Japan back on track and steer it in the right direction. No way could Korea or Formosa ever match Japan.

Pauley threw out a load of statistics to document his case. MacArthur, like any general thoroughly versed in logistics, looked at the statistics and found them wanting. The issue was a lot more complex than the numbers suggested, he said. What may work in transporting oil may not work when you're dealing with an entire country. To break up a huge industrial plant, move it to another country, and reassemble it was fine from an engineering point of view, but how about the support infrastructure? Did Korea or China have the trained labor force to operate such machinery? Who would be the suppliers? Where was the transport/supply network? What about fabrication of spare parts when the machines broke down? Generals managing a massive invasion deal with these issues; most business executives don't. So MacArthur resorted to a standard bureaucratic stunt: Do nothing and stall for time, even if it meant annoying his adversaries and making new enemies. Over the next four years much of the reform passion died out, and only a few of Pauley's industrial plants would get moved; the remaining ones stayed where they were, producing materials and equipment for peacetime purposes.

Besides the impoverished farmers, there was another group the supreme commander had JCS 1380/15 instructions to free: industrial workers. Like tenant farmers, they had been treated like vassals and their wages had fallen far behind the raging inflation. They posed a potential hotbed of trouble. On October 4, 1945, SCAP issued a "Bill of Rights" directive ordering the Japanese government to remove "restrictions on political, civil and religious liberties" and to release all political prisoners, including Communists. Another directive in November provided an expanded basis for collective activity, and a vast union movement was born. In a year's time the number of workers belonging to a union would skyrocket to more than four million, and workers would begin to hope for better days to come.

To ensure that they would, MacArthur gave the Japanese a gift, the best one America could possibly bestow: a new constitution. It would consolidate everything SCAP had attempted in land reform, labor rights, and political liberties to free Japan from hunger, fear, and feudalism. A year-end 1945 SCAP report called *Summation of Non-Military Activities in Japan* spelled out the challenge that lay ahead:

> Political activity is hampered by the concentration of the people on the paramount problems of food, clothing and shelter. Even if the essentials of life were adequate in Japan, it would be unrealistic to expect spontaneous and widespread participation of the people in politics. They would willingly punish the policy-makers and bureaucrats for *losing* the war, and that is about all.
>
> As for democracy, they have no experience with it in any way. Dignity of the individual is completely foreign to their background of feudalism and totalitarianism. The millions of peasants and the women in general are politically ignorant. Add to this the fact that real leaders are afraid to speak out, not knowing how long United States troops will be here to protect them against the dreaded secret police, and it will be readily understood why as yet there have been no significant political developments in Japan.

11

The Emperor Is Not a Kami

O N THE PLANE ride to Atsugi, MacArthur made no mention of Shinto, the state religion that extolled Japan's feudal past and proclaimed the emperor to be the sum of all verities. Yet if MacArthur was to break the hold of militarist sentiments and steer Japan into becoming a democracy, he must do something about Shinto, the national religious cult known as the Way of the Gods. He had his instructions from Washington: "Ultra-nationalistic and militaristic organizations and movements will not be permitted to hide behind the cloak of religion."

He made an initial foray with his October 4 civil liberties directive. Titled "Removal of Restrictions on Political, Civil, and Religious Liberties," it attacked the use of religion as wartime propaganda and ordered the Japanese government to abrogate those laws that restricted freedom of thought, of religion, of assembly, and of speech, "including the unrestricted discussion of the Emperor, the Imperial Institution, and the Imperial Japanese Government." Then came a public broadcast by John Carter Vincent, chief of the State Department's Division of Far Eastern Affairs. "Shintoism, insofar as it is a religion of individual Japanese, is not to be interfered with," said Vincent. "Shintoism, however, insofar as it is directed by the Japanese Government . . . is to be done away with."

Proceeding with care—any regulation of religion was a potential minefield, and this was the national religion—it took SCAP two months to finalize its policies. In mid-December it issued the Shinto directive, pronouncing the establishment of religious freedom:

All propagation and dissemination of militaristic and ultra-nationalistic ideology in Shinto doctrines, practices, rites, ceremonies, and observances of any other religion, faith, sect, creed, or philosophy, are prohibited and will cease immediately. . . . The purpose of this directive is to separate religion from the state, to prevent misuse of religion for political ends, and to put all religions, faiths, and creeds upon exactly the same legal basis, entitled to precisely the same opportunities and protection. It forbids affiliation with the government, and the propagation and dissemination of militaristic and ultra-nationalist ideology not only to Shinto but to followers of all religions, faiths, sects, creeds, or philosophies.

Particular reference was made to the emperor. The SCAP directive defined militaristic or ultranationalistic ideology as "the doctrine that the Emperor of Japan is superior to other heads of state because of ancestry, descent or special origin." Clearly, in trying to separate church from state, a major change had to be made to the role of the emperor. In the Shinto religion there is a fundamental word impossible to translate into English: *kami* (singular and/or plural), referring to spiritual entities and forces believed to be prevalent in man and in nature. *Kami*, evoking the deities, spirits, and gods, is and are everywhere, especially in the emperor.

For the military men in SCAP, dealing with a concept like this was a challenge none of them had ever run into before. When a battlefield commander has an enemy he can't see or comprehend, he moves gingerly. In their edicts on religion MacArthur and his team were very careful not to impugn the emperor's position and dignity. Yet it was the emperor's very position as an august being that had caused many Japanese militarists to accept the belief that war and any service to the state were fully justified. For the Japanese soldier, what higher calling than to fight for the emperor and to die in his service, even to the point of becoming a kamikaze?

A 1937 government proclamation defined the emperor's status as follows:

The Emperor is a deity incarnate who rules our country in unison with the august will of the Imperial Ancestors. We do not mean, when respectfully referring to him as deity incarnate—marvelous deity—or humanly manifested deity, the so-called absolute God, or omniscient and omnipotent God, but signify that the Imperial Ancestors have manifested themselves in the person of the Emperor, who is their divine offspring, that the Emperor in turn is one in essence with the Imperial Ancestors, that he is forever the fountainhead for the growth and development of his subjects and the country, and that he is endlessly a superb august person.

Clearly, something had to be done, but what? Mused MacArthur to Bonner Fellers shortly after his first meeting with the emperor: Wouldn't it be nice if he relinquished the throne? That wouldn't happen, of course, but no harm speculating. Hirohito was both the Son of God and the titular head of state, with vague decision-making powers that defied Western logic. For example, in listening to his cabinet's deliberations on declaring war, was his silence a form of assent, or was it just an opportunity for him to be informed? Such subtleties would be difficult for most outsiders to grasp, certainly for most Americans. If the supreme commander understood the Oriental mind as he boasted, surely he could find a way to clarify the emperor's role. The emperor's spiritual role as well as his executive role must be reduced. For the Japanese people to continue to venerate him like a deity, to consider him sacrosanct and indispensable, was unacceptable in a constitutional democracy.

MacArthur's meeting with the emperor had gone well. Now he must do more, and bring this man down to earth.

Every military organization has spies, which is why MacArthur had Charles Willoughby as one of his top aides. The supreme commander placed great emphasis on "intelligence." He must use it here. Having only limited options to reach out to the emperor discreetly, he needed help. He needed someone who knew what the emperor was thinking, and he needed a man who could contact the emperor without making it seem that the communication came from MacArthur himself.

The history of heroes and great deeds often turns on the minutest instances of coincidence, where the gods of good fortune (such as they are) exercise their sublime craft. Out of the clear blue, when MacArthur least expected it—he didn't even know the man—an Englishman appeared who had indirect access to the emperor. Actually, it wasn't just one man, it was several men—English, American, and Japanese—acting on a chain of events with Dr. Reginald Blyth as the common link. What followed would become known as "the 'secret history.'"

The Japanese have an expression where a man claps his hands loudly and exclaims: "Which hand made the sound?" In what would turn out to be the emperor's most significant public gesture during the occupation, many hands made the sound. It began in mid-November 1945, when Dr. Blyth, a teacher of English literature, was having discussions with the Civil Information and Education Section of SCAP about potential employment. He and Lt. Col. Harold Henderson, a Monuments Man and Columbia professor, discovered they had a common interest in Japanese literature, and Col. Ken Dyke, the head of the CI&E Section, offered Blyth a position. Several days later Blyth reappeared to thank Dyke and Henderson and to tell them that unfortunately he had decided to accept a position elsewhere at a prestigious private school in Tokyo, the Peers School. He also let them know that he had been requested to help Mrs. Vining tutor the crown prince in English and to act as informal liaison between the imperial household and CI&E. He had no idea what this all meant, if anything, but felt that at least he should tell them this. The two SCAP officers were intrigued, and agreed that such a liaison role could be mutually beneficial, and that Blyth would accept the teaching job and feel free to drop in at CI&E should he have anything interesting to report.

Within days Blyth started arriving at SCAP's offices twice a week, escorted in a limousine provided by the Japanese government, a form of transportation that undoubtedly raised eyebrows at SCAP. One day Blyth came for his usual meeting with Henderson, only this time he had some hot news. From the minister of the imperial household he had learned that the emperor had decided to renounce his divinity because it had been taken advantage of by the extremists, and such maneuverings had no place in the new world of peaceful coexistence symbolized by

MacArthur. More important, said Blyth, neither the emperor nor his advisers knew how to draft such an announcement—almost as if they were indirectly asking him for some suggestions.

Henderson was "flabbergasted." This was exciting. Because his boss, Ken Dyke, was out of the office on a trip, he proposed they wait a couple of days. That wouldn't do, Blyth told him, he needed it right away. Operating in a vacuum, Henderson duly wrote out some comments on a sheet of yellow memo paper—taking care not to sign it lest it seem official—and gave it to Blyth. Blyth in turn passed the handwritten note to the principal of the Peers School and a close friend of the emperor, Adm. Kakunoshin Yamanashi. Yamanashi would say little about his role in the unfolding drama, except that "the opportunity being ripe, a heaven-sent door was opened, and contact between the Imperial Household developed very naturally" before everyone was "fully aware of what was happening." "One or two persons," he said, making it clear he was talking about Blyth, "acting in great secrecy made an informal voluntary effort."

The next day held an even bigger surprise for Henderson: Blyth returned with the piece of yellow paper and told Henderson that the palace officials wanted the paper burned in Blyth's presence, and him to report back that this had been done. Henderson carried out this strange request, wondering what would come next. He didn't have to wait long. Within twenty-four hours, on December 7, Blyth was back in Henderson's office, this time with a draft he had cleared with the emperor's friend Admiral Yamanashi. The draft contained a paragraph almost exactly as Henderson had written it, word for word.

He called in Ken Dyke, who immediately took it to the supreme commander. MacArthur read it, said he was delighted, and handed it back to Dyke to return to the enigmatic Blyth. There the matter rested for several weeks. Other than Christmas greetings, there was no official communication between MacArthur and the emperor or between their staffs about what had just transpired. Everything remained hush-hush.

Meanwhile, activities were taking place in the Royal Palace. For some time the emperor had been reflecting on his imperial role and how it had been abused by aggressive militarists claiming implied approval by the ancestral deities. He even went so far as to exclaim to his aides: "I am not a *kami*, I am a human being with organs like other human beings!"

The emperor summoned his prime minister, Baron Kijuro Shidehara, for a meeting on December 10. Shidehara, who had a copy of Blyth's memorandum, which he knew had been seen by the supreme commander, had a good idea what was coming. Hirohito began by telling the story of a previous emperor who had abdicated in 1629 in order to get medical treatment because his own doctors weren't allowed to touch his holy body. "Wasn't that absurd?" he commented. The emperor went on to tell the prime minister that extremists had misused his divinity to promote their own ends, and unless the traditional ideas about his so-called divine nature were corrected, he could "never be the emperor of a democratized Japan." He instructed Shidehara to draft a rescript which he would deliver to the Japanese people on New Year's Day.

The choice of Shidehara to write the speech was an obvious one. The emperor knew his speech would be read carefully by MacArthur and by the U.S. government in Washington, and nobody in Japan had better command of English than Shidehara. His English was so good, in fact, that when he wrote a speech for a foreign audience, he wrote it in English—and then did the translation into Japanese. Such a man could be counted on to express Japanese thoughts in the simple language the emperor wanted for this epochal announcement.

On the morning of December 30 the cabinet approved the proposed proclamation, which was then relayed to GHQ for the supreme commander's approval. It was for his ears only—everything verbal, nothing put down on paper and permanently kept. MacArthur listened to the Japanese official reading out loud the English translation, and silently nodded his head. Two days later, on New Year's Day 1946, the emperor issued his rescript, which stunned the Japanese people. A new era had arrived: The emperor had renounced his divinity. The crucial paragraph, two times approved by MacArthur, read:

> The ties between Us and Our People have always stood upon
> mutual trust and affection. They do not depend upon mere

legends and myths. They are not predicated upon the false conception that the Emperor is divine, and that the Japanese people are superior to other races and fated to rule the world.

MacArthur's role behind the scenes was not what the public heard, nor was a word ever said about the other players involved: Blyth, Henderson, Dyke, Yamanashi, and Shidehara. The *New York Times* ran a story claiming that the general first learned of the rescript on December 30, and of course it got the story wrong in just the way MacArthur wanted: "That afternoon a representative of the government called the Commander-in-Chief's office, outlined the terms of the rescript and asked General MacArthur if there were any objections by the Allies. The General then was asked if I would read and approve the terms of the rescript and he promptly refused."*

The secret mating dance of MacArthur and the emperor had scored again.

It was more than just two men indirectly working in concert. Words matter. Precision of language can be all-important. Hirohito, borrowing from Henderson, was saying that the ties that bound the throne and the nation had always been based on mutual trust and affection and not on mere myth and legend. He was offering to modernize his office and to support whatever political and social changes Japan might be forced by the Americans to undergo; he was flexible and would adapt in the spirit of mutual trust.

A flurry of directives, already under way and with many more to come, would reach into every nook and cranny of Japanese life. The abolition of the military police, the purge of the militarists, the elimination of restrictions on labor, the creation of a new constitution, the enfranchisement of women and the reform of the education system, and the breakup of monopolistic family trusts would usher in a more modern and democratic state. Of all these changes, none was more revolutionary

---

*In his 1964 memoir MacArthur would continue this fiction of noninvolvement. He wrote that the emperor had issued the rescript renouncing his divinity "without any suggestion or discussion with me."

than the separation of church and state. From there on, there would be no more of Japan's religion of conquest.

FOLLOWING THESE TWO directives on civil liberties and Shinto, SCAP issued one on religious corporations, forbidding government control over the organization and activities of religious groups. This caused an unforeseen problem. Japan had some 46,000 temples and 109,000 shrines, most of which sat on state-owned property. Since the state could longer own religious property, it must sell these land parcels back to the temples and shrines. At what valuation? The temples and shrines, now cut off from any state financial support, lacked the money to pay fair-market value for the land. Either they would have to persuade the state to give away the land for free or, more likely, rely on contributions from individuals for the necessary money. However, people were telling SCAP officials that they didn't like being pressured by neighborhood associations to make a contribution, and they wanted MacArthur to "do something about it." It would take several years for SCAP to help resolve this complicated situation, whereby the state gradually relinquished its ownership of over 100,000 parcels of property.

Some of the Shinto shrines had to be treated with the utmost sensitivity. As pointed out by one of the U.S. naval officers in charge of education reform, the Yasukuni Shrine, alleged to represent the souls of the military dead, was revered "in the same way that Americans look on Arlington Cemetery." Even more formidable was a shrine honoring the war goddess Amaterasu, the mythical founder of Japan: the Ise Grand Shrine, "a Jerusalem, Mount Vernon and Vatican" all rolled into one.

Who owns Mount Fuji? This turned out to be the strangest dispute of all. The Fujinomiya Shrine claimed ownership of the summit— the last 2,000 feet up to the peak—where it had an inner sanctum for holy worship. Allowing the state to own such a place and let the public wander around, it argued, would be a profanity. The Japanese Ministry of Finance, representing the government, disagreed, claiming that the summit belonged to the Japanese people. The case would eventually be decided by the Japanese courts in 1967 in favor of the shrine; then it would go to the Supreme Court, where once again the government lost.

The Japanese people had an interesting reason to wonder about SCAP's religious policies in December 1945 and the turn of the New Year. It was hardly a festive time for a country still reeling from the war and people freezing in the cold, yet every occupation office building was adorned with bright Christmas lights. Two enormous Christmas trees flanked the entrance of the Dai Ichi Building. MacArthur adopted the position that such decorations were to communicate the festivity of the occasion, and not the religious significance of the Feast of the Nativity. The supreme commander was not a churchman, but he most definitely was religious: In his public utterances he consistently thanked God for divine guidance. In November 1945 he had welcomed four Protestant leaders with great enthusiasm: "Japan is a spiritual vacuum," he told them. "If you do not fill it with Christianity, it will be filled with Communism. Send me 1,000 missionaries!" He also asked for 10,000 Bibles. His staff members told him this was going too far: What would the Buddhists and Shintoists think? He should speak of "religious principles" rather than "Christian principles." Taking their advice, he eventually backed off, if only reluctantly. It wasn't until his New Year's Day message of 1948 that he managed to speak of religion only in the abstract. He never made public references to Christianity again.

Shinto as the state religion of Japan had ceased to exist. Shinto as practiced through the shrines could remain. All physical symbols of state Shinto were removed from public buildings, and public money could no longer be used to support the shrines. The Japanese people were freed from any state-sanctioned compulsion to believe in Shinto. Public education and all official propaganda were freed of Shinto teaching, and school textbooks were purged of Shinto-inspired nationalism.

In the spring of 1946 a mission of American educators, the Stoddard Commission, visited Japan. In its report to the supreme commander recommending reforms to Japan's education system, it sought to describe the American approach to reform: to work with the existing system in Japan as much as possible, not tear it all down and start anew. "We believe in the power of every race and every nation to create from its own cultural resources something good for itself and for the whole world. That is the liberal creed," the commission wrote. "It is the responsibility of all in authority to find out how much can be allowed rather than how much can be forbidden. That is the meaning of liberalism."

Shortly thereafter, in April of that year, the supreme commander spoke of the forthcoming elections where voters, for the first time, would include women and everyone could vote free of any influence from a state-sponsored religion. It was essential for the Japanese to understand the new ideology of democracy. Following the words of the Stoddard Commission, MacArthur sought to describe the opportunity and responsibility facing the Japanese people: "Pure democracy is immediately a spiritual quality which voluntarily must spring from the determined will of the people. It thus, if it is to become firmly rooted, may not be imposed upon a people by force, trickery, or coercion—nor is it a quality for barter or trade."

12

Drawing Up a Utopia

Two weeks after the Americans arrived at Atsugi, the Japanese government sent a senior official to meet the supreme commander. He was Prince Fumimaro Konoe, three-time prime minister and a man who had opposed going to war with the United States. Presumably this was meant as a "peace offering" to get relations off to a good start. Konoe's mission: to sound out MacArthur on his intentions for Japan. The two men met again on October 4, the day MacArthur issued his "Bill of Rights" directive ordering the Japanese government to remove restrictions on political, civil, and religious liberties and to release all political prisoners. Konoe asked if MacArthur had any ideas regarding the organization of the Japanese government and the composition of the Diet. MacArthur gave general responses about his directive issued that day, but on one item he was very specific: "The Japanese Constitution must be revised. It is essential to introduce into government sufficient liberal elements through constitutional revision." Without such revision, he argued, any reforms would be vulnerable to the whims of future cabinets after the occupation ended.

So startling was MacArthur's pronouncement that George Atcheson, who was at the meeting, immediately sent a telegram to his superiors at the State Department asking if this was new U.S. policy. The State Department was just as surprised as Atcheson and wanted to know what was going on. Two days later MacArthur sent Atcheson to meet again with Konoe to discuss desired changes in the Japanese constitution.

In the meantime the Lord Privy Seal, Marquis Kido, had selected a new prime minister, a man pulled out of retirement and given his new role largely because of his pro-American views and opposition to the war. He was Baron Kijuro Shidehara, a former foreign minister and ambassador to the United States who had appeared on the cover of *Time* in 1931 as "Japan's Man of Peace and War." His reemergence on the national scene at the age of seventy-five, after being out of the public eye for ten years, caught people by surprise. Some even asked, "Isn't Shidehara dead?" He came to pay his respects to the supreme commander, expecting this to be a courtesy call. No sooner had the gentleman sat down than MacArthur gave him a list of reforms he wanted put into effect. They included women's rights and independence, encouragement of labor unions, a wider distribution of income, an end to monopolies, and public ownership of production and trade. Schools should be liberalized and start teaching "a system under which government becomes the servant rather than the master of the people." Furthermore, there should be an end to "secret inquisition and abuse" by officials. The elderly diplomat made his way home in a daze: Never in his years in Washington had he met an American so predisposed to executive action.

On October 11, following his meeting with the prime minister, MacArthur issued a "Statement" to the Japanese government: "In the achievement of the Potsdam Declaration, the traditional order . . . will be corrected. This will undoubtedly involve a liberalization of the Constitution." Shidehara responded by creating a subcommittee with an interesting name, the Committee for the Investigation of Constitutional Problems, subsequently usually referred to as the Matsumoto Committee after its chairman, State Minister Joji Matsumoto.

That was three months ago. During this time the subcommittee had been working behind closed doors and never once sought SCAP advice. SCAP had informed the cabinet, both orally and in writing, that major reforms needed to be undertaken in areas such as parliamentary supremacy, legislative control of the budget, executive branch answerable to the legislature, and civilian control of the military. When no arguments or questions arose, SCAP assumed its suggestions were being followed. So when Matsumoto finally delivered the cabinet's draft of a revised constitution, the package was opened with great anticipation.

MacArthur rarely lost his temper. But on that cold, dreary day in early February 1946, he got very angry. He felt betrayed. For months he had put on the facade that he had taken no part in the deliberations of the Matsumoto Committee, whereas in actual fact he had held several personal conferences with state ministers, as had George Atcheson. And now this! The Japanese were either toying with him or ignoring him. Either way he didn't like it, especially since this was his major priority of the entire occupation.

He slammed his hand on the buzzer bell on his desk, the side door opened, and in scurried his ever-available top aide, Courtney Whitney.

Scanning the document with a legal eye, Whitney was dumbfounded. Here was this important document, and the cabinet had done zilch . . . Not a word to be found about any of the suggested reforms. There was no change in the power of the emperor; he was now "supreme and inviolable" whereas before he had been "sacred and inviolable." There was no new bill of rights, in fact some of the few rights that already existed had been taken away. Did the Japanese not know that a "suggestion" coming from SCAP was more than a suggestion?

MacArthur's problem was not that the Japanese were stalling or playing games—he could force reforms down their throat if he wanted to—his problem was that he was running out of time. Two threats loomed on the horizon: the Far Eastern Commission, due to start its supervisory function at the end of the month, and a general election coming up in April. Either event could undermine MacArthur's power as the supreme commander and reduce his entire occupation effort to a sideshow. MacArthur, staring at the calendar, knew that if he didn't control events, events would soon control him.

He had no choice, he had to go on an all-out offensive. Anticipating he might have to do this, he had already covered himself legally. Even though he was the supreme commander, and President Truman had told him "Your authority is supreme," could he go so far as change another country's constitution? This had never been done before, and he was sure the State Department or any of the Allied nations would jump all over him. To protect himself he had requested Whitney, Kades, and three members of SCAP's legal staff to prepare an official memorandum on the subject. He now had it, a lengthy and cogently reasoned memorandum stating he had "unrestricted authority to take any action you deem proper in effectuating changes in the Japanese constitutional structure—the only possible restriction being upon action taken by you toward removal of the Emperor, in which case you are required to consult with the Joint Chiefs of Staff." And, of course, no leaks to Washington. The less said, the better.

First thing next morning, Courtney Whitney called all twenty-five members of the Government Section into the conference room for an emergency meeting. "Ladies and gentlemen, today you have been called here as a constituent assembly. General MacArthur has given us orders to do the historic work of drafting a new constitution for the Japanese people."

The atmosphere was electric; everyone was stunned. They all knew the Japanese had been working on the constitution, progress was slow, and the supreme commander was known not to be a patient man—but this? Whitney pulled out a memo and started reading. Later dubbed "the MacArthur Note," the memo contained three principles. One, "The Emperor is the head of state, in accordance with the Constitution and responsible to the basic will of the people." Two, "War as a sovereign right of the nation is abolished." Three, "The feudal system of Japan will cease," meaning there would be no more hereditary rights of title (other than the emperor).

Then came the shocker: "This draft must be finished by February 12." Nine days. The Founding Fathers in Philadelphia had taken how long? Three months? The twenty-five people were jubilant and exhilarated: Writing a constitution—What heady stuff! "There are few students of political science," wrote John Gunther about this effort, "who have not wanted, at one time or another, to draw up a Utopia." Alas, the exhilaration of Utopia quickly dissipated as Whitney warned them what might be coming after February 12:

> On that date the foreign minister and other Japanese officials are to have an off-the-record meeting about the new constitution. We expect that the version produced by the Japanese government will have a strong right-wing bias. However, if they hope to protect the Emperor and to maintain political power, they have no choice but

to accept a constitution with a progressive approach, namely, the fruits of our current efforts. I expect we'll manage to persuade them. But if it looks as though it might prove impossible, General MacArthur has already authorized both the threat of force and the actual use of force.

Just as they had a deadline, so did the Japanese government. The government should approve the new constitution by February 22, specifically chosen because it was George Washington's birthday. What's more, the government ministers must act and publicly talk as if the constitution was their handiwork. "The complete text will be presented to General MacArthur by the Japanese for his endorsement," averred Whitney. "General MacArthur will then announce to the world that he recognizes this constitution as the work of the Japanese government."

This got people buzzing. They all knew presidents and generals rarely wrote their own speeches, but here was a man ordering a constitution written to his exact specifications, only to have it presented to him by the Japanese for his approval as if he'd never seen it!

Whitney announced the leader of the group would be Charles Kades. Heads nodded. It was an obvious choice: Kades, a Wall Street lawyer working for the U.S. Treasury, age thirty-nine, possessed dazzling energy and brilliance. Everyone in the GHQ liked Kades for the same reason they liked Whitney: He was friendly and eminently approachable.

Oh, and one last thing, said Whitney in closing. He told them their work was to be top secret, with no one—especially the Japanese—to know what they were doing. The doors would be locked, they must do all their work in the conference room, and in times of need, they were to bang on the door and a guard would escort them to the restroom. Sandwiches and coffee would be served, and Whitney would be always available. He'd be checking in every couple of hours. Best of luck, he told them.

THE SIGHT OF an American girl driving an army jeep bouncing through the potholed streets of Tokyo must have astonished Japanese pedestrians. They would have been even more astonished had they known she was the most powerful female in Japan. Had they surmised from the determined look on her face that she was a woman on a mission, they would have been correct.

The jeep slammed to a halt in front of a library, she hopped out, vanished into the library, and soon emerged lugging a stack of books. A quick stop at several embassies for more books, and her jeep roared back to the Dai Ichi Building where two army guards scooped up all the books and followed her inside.

In the 1940s, long before it became reasonably common in America, this woman with the unusual name was a true multicultural. Born to Russian Jewish parents in Vienna and raised in Japan, Beate Sirota attended Mills College in California (Phi Beta Kappa) and had two years' work experience for *Time* magazine when she landed a job with MacArthur's Government Section because she spoke Japanese (and five other languages). Only twenty-two years old, she had no interest in public affairs, she had never even voted; she took the job only because she wanted to return to Japan and see her parents, who were still alive. In Tokyo, in the high-pressure atmosphere of MacArthur's administration, she quickly established herself as more than just a translator. It was an environment offering bright young people enormous opportunities. "Beate," said Kades' aide Lt. Col. Pieter Roest, "you're a woman, why don't you write the woman's rights section?"

What did Miss Sirota know about women's rights? Not much, other than knowing it was a subject dear to the supreme commander, as he had issued a proclamation decreeing the emancipation of women and their right to vote. She loved the story of how MacArthur, warned before issuing this decree that it would upset a lot of Japanese men, had responded with a big grin and the comment that it served them right. In her visits to her parents and her trips through the countryside, she had spoken with many women and learned firsthand what a hard life they had, having no automatic rights to money, marriage, divorce, employment, or inheritance.

As she studied the constitutions of the United States, the Weimar Republic, France, Sweden, Norway, and other countries, Beate Sirota was amazed to find women's rights codified in only one of them: the Soviet Union's. She started writing. When she reviewed the Japanese Civil Code and read article 4—"Women are to be regarded as incompetent"—she resumed writing with passion.

Beate Sirota had stumbled into Utopia.

CHARLES KADES REVIEWED what Beate Sirota wrote and marveled, "My God, you have given Japanese women more rights than in the American Constitution!" Sirota responded dryly, "That's not very difficult to do, because women are not in the American Constitution."

Touché!

Describing the writing of a constitution does not make for exciting reading. It may be exciting for the lawyers arguing back and forth about the choice of words and whether this phrase or that phrase is redundant; for the outsider, the whole process can be tiresome. Once in a while a little inadvertent humor will emerge where people do things for reasons having nothing to do with thought or logic. When Whitney and Kades thought about the most important assignment of the whole project—writing the clause dealing with the status of the emperor—they assigned it to Ens. Richard Poole because he and the emperor had the same birthday.

Actually the drafters of the Japanese constitution did a very smart thing: They did not base their draft on the American political system. Surprisingly enough—nobody could explain why—it turned out that they based their proposed constitution more on the British parliamentary form of government. Supreme political power would be assigned to the Diet. The cabinet would be responsible to the Diet. The prime minister would be elected not by the people but by the lower house. Anybody looking for similarities to the American Constitution would have to look long and hard.

General Whitney came into the conference room every couple of hours to mediate disputes, fancying himself—as one of the staffers put it—"as a Thomas Jefferson." For the entire week everyone worked nonstop. Cigarette smoke fouled the air; empty bottles and food leftovers littered the room; many people stayed up all night. Finally, in just one week—two days ahead of schedule—the American drafters of the Japanese constitution were finished. They had produced a stupendous piece of work. The question was: How would the Japanese respond?

After MacArthur reviewed the document and signed off (Whitney had been feeding him drafts every day for his edits), Whitney, Kades, and two others went to the home of Foreign Minister Shigeru Yoshida to present copies of their document. Waiting for them were Yoshida, Minister of State Matsumoto, and liaison officer Jiro Shirasu. Whitney laid into Matsumoto, telling him that his draft was "totally unacceptable" and that he expected the three men to pay close attention to the American version about to be put in front of them. Shirasu straightened up "as if he had sat on something." Matsumoto took deep breaths. Yoshida scanned several pages, his face changed into a "black cloud"; this was an entirely new document. "You think you can make Japan a democratic country?" said Yoshida, holding up the document in his hand. "I don't think so."

"We can try," responded Charles Kades.

Knowing the conservative Yoshida didn't like him and thought him too liberal and progressive, not to mention blunt, General Whitney decided he had better leave the room. Leaving the Japanese ministers to digest the document's twenty pages, he went out into the garden to smoke a cigarette. Half an hour later Shirasu opened the door to inquire if Whitney needed anything. "Not at all," said Whitney. "We have been enjoying your atomic sunshine," at which point a big B-29 came roaring overhead, almost as if on cue, as aboard the *Missouri*.

For the Japanese official, Whitney's curt remark came as a jolt. Back inside, Whitney continued to put on the pressure. MacArthur did not require the Japanese government to adopt the SCAP draft literally, but he did want the draft's underlying principles incorporated. Time was now running short. The emperor might be tried as a war criminal, he warned; a lot of people in the United States still wanted Hirohito's head. Already the Joint Chiefs of Staff had informed MacArthur that the emperor was not immune from indictment as a war criminal: "The Supreme Commander has been unyielding in his defense of your Emperor," Whitney reminded the three Japanese officials, and "has defended the Emperor because he considered that was the cause of right and justice, and will continue along that course to the extent of his ability."

"But, gentlemen, the Supreme Commander is not omnipotent."

Going beyond MacArthur's instructions, Whitney went on to say that the supreme commander was willing to put the document to the Japanese people himself if the government wouldn't. Only by accepting this document could the government expect to survive and not get thrown out in the next election.

The meeting was quickly adjourned on a less than amicable note. Had Whitney gone too far? Afterward he returned to the Dai Ichi Building very nervous and told MacArthur what had happened. MacArthur reassured him it was okay, he had not overstepped. "Court, don't you know that I have never repudiated any action taken by me or by a member of my staff. Right or wrong, whether I like it or not, I accept the situation as it stands and determine my next move from there."

Two days later Shirasu wrote Whitney that the American way to achieve an objective was too "straight and direct" for the Japanese, whose way must be "round-about, twisted and narrow." The letter contained a vivid illustration.

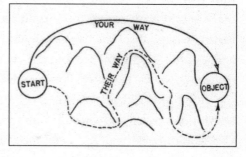

Whitney responded to Shirasu that the straight way was better than the crooked way, and that anybody who supported the supreme commander's principles could be assured that "the objectives can be reached promptly and directly." The next day Shirasu came to Whitney's office carrying a lengthy memorandum titled "Supplementary Explanation Concerning the Constitutional Revision." It was from Matsumoto, citing past failed efforts to transplant constitutions from one country to another, and warning that "too drastic a move . . . may . . . in the end retard the smooth and wholesome progress of democracy."

Included in the memo was a somewhat arch reminder that this was the Land of the Rising Sun, couched in lofty metaphors only a Japanese could muster: "Some of the roses of the West, when cultivated in Japan, lose their fragrance."

13

MacArthur Breaks the Impasse

T HE TWO SIDES were at an impasse. The gulf was huge. MacArthur knew he could go ahead and publish the American version, though he knew that doing so would smack of American tyranny. Even if he could break the impasse, he didn't want to make the first move any more than he had with the emperor. Such a gesture would upset the delicate dynamic between a powerful occupier and a proud supplicant seeking to become a full partner. Whitney had thrown down the gauntlet: The Japanese must deliver. If they feared the supreme commander, they would respond. MacArthur, with his insight into human psychology, would wait, confident that cooler heads in the Diet would prevail and they would come to him.

He held two aces. Whitney, he knew, had made it explicitly clear that as far as the Allies were concerned, the emperor was in jeopardy, whereas the Americans would protect him, albeit with reduced stature. The second ace was the Far Eastern Commission, soon to begin. Who did the Japanese prefer to deal with: a known entity like SCAP, or a remote and complex international agency likely to be dominated by the USSR and its veto power?

In the Diet a battle raged. Prime Minister Kijuro Shidehara and two other ministers read the beginning chapters of the translated SCAP draft and said they could never accept it. Welfare Minister Hitoshi Ashida disagreed and pointed out that if SCAP went ahead and published it, the people would be delighted, and they would all lose their jobs after the next election. Then a surprising voice piped up out of the blue: Joji Matsumoto, whose committee had written the draft rejected by MacArthur. As a scholar and a man with a modest understanding of English, he knew how easy it was to make mountains out of molehills in trying to use words precisely, especially in the difficult business of translating English into a language as different as Japanese. Sometimes it took a translator two days to get through a single page. "Turning Japanese into English, and vice-versa, with the precision of nuance required by lawyers is virtually impossible," observes one modern-day historian. "Japanese as a language bears no relation to English or any other European language, and the process of translation is more like describing a picture in words—creating an equivalent, not a replica. Not only is it difficult, it is also particularly time-consuming."

Maybe the two versions weren't so different, Matsumoto said. Heads must have turned at this startling pronouncement. Maybe with more time it might be possible for him to reconcile his document with the American one. However, by now Matsumoto had lost a lot of credibility, and had come under scathing criticism when it was revealed that SCAP had repeatedly warned him and he had failed to share these warnings with the cabinet. Matsumoto, courageous though he was in speaking up and admitting his failure, was now dead meat.

What to do? The cabinet couldn't go to Whitney, who had made his position unmistakably clear: No negotiation, "atomic sunshine." There could be only one solution: The prime minister, like the emperor, would have to go to the supreme commander.

THE MEETING LASTED three full hours. The two men had met twice before, both times productively: first in early October when MacArthur mentioned constitutional reform, and again in January after the emperor had denied his own divinity. In the second meeting Shidehara, whose wife—an heiress to the Mitsubishi fortune—was a Quaker, brought up the issue of renunciation of war, saying he had no problem including this in the constitution, since Japan had been a signatory to a similar provision in the 1919 League of Nations Covenant and the 1928 Kellogg-Briand Pact. Shidehara didn't know it, but by this gesture he had touched on MacArthur's soft spot. Back in 1930 he had refused to attend the Geneva disarmament conference, saying, "The way to end war is to outlaw war, not to disarm." MacArthur immediately agreed with the suggestion that there be a provision saying that "the right of belligerency of the state will not be recognized." Such a provision, he said, would relieve the concerns of the Soviet Union and Australia. On that positive note, the two men parted.

This time, in their third meeting, there would be no sweeping declarations of principle. The two men discussed everything face-to-face, openly and in confidence, made easier because Shidehara spoke perfect English. MacArthur reminded Shidehara that the FEC was beating down on him, he was personally concerned with "the good of Japan," and that Shidehara was undoubtedly doing "his best for the sake of his country." Did not the two men share the same goals? The danger to Japan, he told Shidehara, came not from the American government. It came from the Soviet Union and Australia, full of vengeance. "I don't know how long I can stay at my present position, and I feel great concern when I consider what might happen after I leave." Asked what Whitney had meant by saying that Japan must accept certain fundamental principles, MacArthur replied that the intent was to preserve the emperor, and that for the emperor position to work, it must be based on a clear statement of popular sovereignty.

Article 9 would become the most important and controversial part of the new constitution. Matsumoto liked it because he was a pacifist. The supreme commander, no pacifist himself, liked it for other reasons. War had become so deadly as to render the value of victory meaningless. "The enormous sacrifices that have been brought about by scientific methods of killing," he said, "have rendered war a fantastic and impossible method for the solution of international difficulties." Since there was no way to control war, the only other thing to do would be to abolish it.

As in MacArthur's meeting with the emperor, no transcript survives, a loss to future leaders in a similar situation. Such a transcript—a lesson in statesmanship—would merit careful study. MacArthur and

Shidehara had made a pact to "agree to agree." SCAP officials would sit down with their Japanese counterparts and make a deal, no matter what, and MacArthur would sign off on it.

Little did the two men know what a marathon it would turn out to be.

But MacArthur kept his word, and so did Shidehara. Out of a basic agreement in principle between two powerful adversaries, history was made, and Douglas MacArthur—the ultimate gambler—would achieve more than Washington ever dreamed of.

THE NEXT DAY, Shidehara made his report to the Japanese cabinet, inviting the other ministers to express their views. At first these were decidedly negative. This American document, protested one minister, was "like swallowing boiling water." Matsumoto complained that there wasn't enough time to reconcile divergent views, and he was fed up with the abrasive "Whitney group." Welfare Minister Ashida jumped in and disagreed: Why wasn't it possible for an esteemed man with Matsumoto's "scholarship and experience" to do what the Weimar Republic in Germany had done in 1919, write a constitution in three weeks?

With Matsumoto flummoxed and marginalized, the discussion assumed a cooler tone. The majority agreed that there was room to yield and maneuver. Shidehara would report to the emperor immediately, and to show his sincerity to the Americans he would send the two archconservatives Matsumoto and Yoshida to meet that afternoon with—of all people—the liberal Whitney. If that didn't send a signal of goodwill, what would? As for Charles Kades, who had never met MacArthur—he wouldn't until mid-1947—he had his plate full. The supreme commander had spoken from on high: Kades was to forget all his legalese, let what was past be past, compromise and make a deal. And of course, keep your mouth shut. "The revision has to be made by the Japanese themselves and it has to be done without coercion," MacArthur had decreed—fooling nobody while he snapped a whip over their heads.

When the Japanese met with Whitney and Kades, they quickly found they had a long way to go. In Whitney's office, behind his desk, was an enormous painting of a Filipino boy trying to defend his sister from being raped by a Japanese soldier. If the purpose of the painting was to intimidate a Japanese visitor, it certainly had that effect. Trying to avert his gaze from the terrified eyes of the young girl staring down at him, Matsumoto expressed optimism that a deal could be reached and the emperor would be pleased to present a new constitution. Whitney cut him short: A constitution, he said, "comes up from the people, not down to the people"—a fundamental and important distinction. Other, more specific differences dominated the remainder of the meeting. Whereas the Japanese wanted to keep the current constitution and amend it to include the two provisions about the emperor and war, plus whatever minor adjustments might be necessary, the Americans had a broader perspective. The SCAP document, explained Whitney, formed a whole and could not be reorganized or chopped up. Appropriate changes of small points would be permitted, but that was all. The more Matsumoto pressed with specific questions about details such as the preamble, amendment procedures, the Diet, elections, the imperial house law, and the rights and duties of the people, the more obvious it became that the two sides were coming from different directions. Whitney emphasized that the imperial family was not in control of the law, it was under the law, as in England. Matsumoto questioned why renunciation of war was an article of its own, couldn't it be inserted in the preamble as a principle? No, said Whitney, the supreme commander wanted it prominently displayed so as to attract the world's attention that Japan was now serious about its rehabilitation.

Translation remained a major problem. SCAP wanted the constitution to be written in colloquial Japanese to prevent obfuscation by classical rhetoric, whereas the Japanese argued that a literal translation of the American document would not achieve the formality and dignity of a Japanese legal document, especially a constitution. Making a translation into Japanese style would take weeks, and inevitably much of the American meaning might be lost. MacArthur was in a hurry; already months had been wasted; he needed the constitution completed before the FEC tried to take over constitutional reform and possibly deny the emperor's sovereignty.

On February 27 Matsumoto and his assistants started work on the judicial translation (actually more of a Japanese draft using the American one as a model). They had two documents to work with: the SCAP version in English, and a literal Japanese translation done by the Foreign Ministry. Their job was to make the Japanese translation legally correct according to Japanese law.

The Americans expected, when they got the Japanese version, to translate it back into English, match it up side by side with the American original, and find the two virtually the same. That didn't happen. For example, the American draft said in article 1: "The Emperor shall be the symbol of the State and of the Unity of the People, deriving his position from the sovereign will of the People, and from no other source." The Japanese version switched the two clauses around and made the emperor look godlike by using the word "supreme" in place of "sovereign": "The Emperor derives his position from the supreme will of the Japanese People, maintaining his position as a symbol of the State and as an emblem of the Unity of the People." In article 2, the American version said: "Succession to the Imperial Throne shall be dynastic and in accordance with such Imperial House Law as the Diet may enact." The Japanese version left out the Diet entirely: "The Imperial Throne shall be dynastic and succeeded to in accordance with the Imperial House Law."

Another problem for the Americans was that there were in reality two Japanese languages—the classical one and the conversational one. Like the Greeks, who use a modern rather than a classical form of their language, many Japanese could not understand the classical Japanese used by the emperor and the government. Indeed, when the emperor read his announcement of the surrender, the people in one particular village thought he was announcing a great victory and celebrated all night, only to wake up the next morning and realize they had been quite mistaken. When the emperor delivered his message to the first postwar Diet, fewer than half the members of that august body could understand him. When the list of Japanese war criminals was announced, only one out of ten Japanese could read the names. Americans were stunned to learn that the once-mighty country they had taken over was basically illiterate.*

Throughout the document the Americans found a host of omissions and differences, some of them critical. With time running out, the two sides got together to hash out an agreement. It was like writing a constitution all over again. Back and forth the two sides went, often so frustrated and exhausted that people were on the verge of exchanging physical blows. The Americans made many concessions, several of them by MacArthur personally. In what turned out to be the guiding principle of the constitution drafting, they would use "spoken Japanese instead of the traditional literary style of legal language," which they found to be "archaic, stilted and inelastic and could not be read, much less understood by the ordinary man." A constitution should be simple, MacArthur reminded his staffers; they were to remember what FDR said on the 150th anniversary of the U.S. Constitution in 1937: The American Constitution is "a layman's document, not a lawyer's."

In a thirty-two-hour nonstop, marathon session, the translation got done, bipartisanship at its best. On March 6 the government signed off on the "Japanese Government draft" and it became official on April 17, a week after the general election, which SCAP gladly interpreted as a popular ratification of the document.

Of course no SCAP deed occurred without an American-style dose of publicity and public relations, especially when Douglas MacArthur

---

*The complexity of the Japanese language was used as a tool by the Japanese government to control the people and keep them in ignorance and abeyance. There are 56,000 kanji ideographs in the classical Japanese language. To read a newspaper, one needs to know 2,400 of them. Yet most Japanese people (primary-school graduates) know only 600. SCAP conducted tests of primary-school children studying phonetic Japanese and found that in just two weeks they reached the same level of literacy as students studying kanji for six years. SCAP's efforts to promote the use of phonetic Japanese (romaji) were largely unavailing. Observed *Time* bureau chief Richard Lauterbach: "The Old Guard claimed that the large number of homonyms in the language would lead to ambiguity. And so millions of new textbooks were ordered in the old-style calligraphy. It was a victory for the traditionalists." Added the educator John Ashmead in a January 1947 issue of the *Atlantic Monthly*: "We may be able, by using the radio, to democratize Japan to a limited extent. But much of our present effort to re-educate the Japanese is just money down the drain."

was personally involved. To make sure the new constitution would be taken seriously and reverently, a Committee to Popularize the Constitution was organized in the Diet. Advised by Alfred Hussey and Ruth Ellerman of the Government Section, the committee put together an advisory board of prominent politicians and academicians and went into high gear. It divided the country into ten districts, sent experts to conduct training sessions for local public officials, and published twenty million booklets, one per household, titled "The New Constitution! A Bright Light!" The constitution, the booklet gushed, "is the compass of our daily lives . . . the splendid code which will be woven into our ideals and aspirations." Readers were pleased to learn that "The Japanese people mutually respect individual character. They will correctly practice democracy. With a spirit of love of peace, they will have warm and friendly relations with the countries of the world." The publicity committee made a special effort to reach out to the citizens of tomorrow. Grade-school and high-school children saw documentary films, put on plays using puppets, participated in essay-writing contests in the local newspaper, and sang musicals about peace and democracy marching onward like Christian soldiers.

No sooner had the March 6 draft appeared than MacArthur found himself in a fight over it. The State Department and the FEC, kept out of the loop by MacArthur, demanded to know what was going on and why they had not been consulted. The State Department was particularly frustrated: Because SCAP was a military operation, the only way to send an inquiry to MacArthur was through the Joint Chiefs of Staff and the army chief of staff, who didn't always move with the alacrity normally reserved for generals speaking to generals. This bureaucratic setup ensured delays, which was exactly what MacArthur wanted. The FEC, concerned that there was not enough time before the election for the Japanese people to "express their fully instructed, intelligent and authoritative views on their political future," sent a letter suggesting a postponement of the election. MacArthur responded with a lengthy essay pointing out that women had been given the right to vote, that the voting age had been lowered, that reactionary personnel had been purged from government, that Japan had several political parties in strong competition, and that there was no need for any special declaration, plus it probably wouldn't pass legal scrutiny. What else was there to discuss? The letter was so thorough and devastating, said one observer, that anyone reading it "began to suffer from spells of dizziness."

The truth of the matter, of course, was that MacArthur and conservative members of the Japanese government like Yoshida wanted the constitution put in place as quickly as possible before the liberals and especially the Communists got their hands on it. This was not an idle threat. Having freed the prisoners and the labor unions, MacArthur knew the dangers on the street and he was in a delicate position, but he could hardly admit this to Washington. Instead he resorted to legalisms, delays, and plain outright arrogance—of which he was a master. Like a general on the march, he would simply steamroll over anybody in his way. In war this wins plaudits; in peacetime politics it makes enemies.

On March 20 the Far Eastern Commission demanded that the April 10 election be postponed. MacArthur refused. Giving the FEC power to review and approve the constitution in advance of an election would "prejudice many Japanese people against the instrument itself" because they would "look upon it as a thing forced upon Japan at the point of Allied bayonets." MacArthur went on to demonstrate his propensity for mingling fiction with truth. The FEC had no executive power, he said. Speaking of himself as if he were another person, he reminded the FEC that such power was "reserved exclusively to the Supreme Commander." To cover himself with the U.S. secretary of state, who had gone on record that the responsibility of managing Japan rested with the FEC, MacArthur explained to Byrnes that the FEC's function in matters of constitutional reform was "limited to the formulation of guiding policy."

The supreme commander surely must have baffled Byrnes with his blubbery phrase. This was only typical of MacArthur. He could soar to Olympian heights with his majestic oratory; he could easily drown his listeners in vacuous and avuncular phraseology. Marveled one of his aides at the boss's ability to baffle the opposition and escape unscathed: "How do you fight someone you can't get your hands on?" MacArthur was in his element. He went on to tell the secretary of state that "in the absence of any such policy statement from the Far Eastern Commission, the Supreme Commander is clearly unrestricted in his authority to proceed."

"I have acted meticulously," he opined—lest the secretary of state think differently.

The FEC, getting tired of MacArthur's repeated evasions and ter-giversations, asked him on April 10—the day of the Japanese election, when the constitution was voted on and passed—to send a representative to Washington right away: "The Commission, in its concern that any constitution adopted by the Japanese should embody the 'freely expressed will of the Japanese people,' is particularly interested in the procedures by which it is contemplated a new constitution will be adopted." One can only imagine the supreme commander's reaction to such pretentious language when he was in a race against time and there was mounting political ferment in the streets. At the end of April a massive Communist-inspired labor demonstration electrified Tokyo. It attracted more than 400,000 people, giving General Eichelberger heart palpitations.

A month later, MacArthur deigned to respond to the FEC. In a twenty-page letter that was more like a thesis than a memo—the man liked to write!—he said he welcomed a closer working relationship but did not think dispatching an officer from his staff to confer with the commission would accomplish anything. In a repeat of his tactics with President Truman, where he said he was indispensable and could not leave Tokyo, he wrote: "As Supreme Commander, I have given my personal attention to the matter of constitutional reform, and there is no other officer in a position to express in detail my views on that subject."

How do you deal with a man like this? The State Department diplomatically held back on MacArthur's missive, and sent another directive. Again no response. The Department of the Army then jumped in and sent a telegram stating how essential it was for the Far Eastern Commission to be afforded an opportunity to examine the new constitution before it took effect. MacArthur responded with a soothing put-down: "This draft provides one of the most liberal constitutions in the world—far more liberal than is that of Russia or China, and certainly no less liberal than that of the United States or England."

By now the director of the State Department's Office of Far Eastern Affairs was in a state of despair. He informed the secretary of state: "No useful purpose would be served by any further discussion of this matter." The FEC came to a similar conclusion. With the new constitution now in force, on May 13 it sent MacArthur a memo basically raising the white flag in surrender: "Adequate time and opportunity should be allowed for the full discussion and consideration of the terms of the new Constitution."

Douglas MacArthur had outmaneuvered, worn down, and flummoxed the opposition. Now all he had to do was make sure the constitution was sufficiently "Japanese." Everyone knew the Americans had written most of it. There was even a joke going around town: "Have you read the new Constitution yet? . . . No, has it been translated into Japanese?" Yoshida, Shidehara, and Matsumoto worked behind the scenes to line up support and make sure no one questioned the constitution's legitimacy. The Japanese legislative bodies went through the motions of deliberation and ratification. The lower house, working closely with American lawyers from GHQ, made some minor modifications and passed the bill. The Privy Council conducted no fewer than eleven meetings, going into great detail so no one could say the document was being rubber-stamped. It gave its final approval at the end of October. In doing so it displayed one of the most remarkable examples of political courage and unselfishness ever seen in any country at any time: Because there was no place for it under the new constitution, by voting for the constitution it voted itself out of existence.

One must stop here and pause a moment. Yes, it actually happened—the Privy Council voted itself out of existence. How often do we see something like this today where a failed politician or leader of a country voluntarily relinquishes power? And puts aside personal gain for the long-term common good? If ever there was anyone in the occupation who deserved a peacetime Medal of Honor for courage and self-sacrifice, surely it would be the Japanese Privy Council.

As for Hirohito, who by now had become a "symbolic emperor," he had no problem with the new constitution. As a personal token of appreciation for their work, he sent Whitney and each of his colleagues who had helped draft the constitution a silver chalice bearing the imperial crest.

A constitution is only a written piece of paper: It cannot "give" people freedom any more than toppling a dictator does. In the April 1946 election the Japanese people signaled their participation in the new experiment of democracy. Women, enfranchised by the new constitution, ran for the first time (thirty-nine of eighty-two won). Of the 2,770 candidates competing for the 466 seats in the Diet, 95 percent were running for the first time. Due to the lowering of the voting age from twenty-five to twenty, the inclusion of women, and SCAP's promotion of the importance of the election, the number of people voting skyrocketed from 13.5 million to 37 million.

Going by this voter participation, MacArthur boldly predicted the constitution would last a hundred years. "Probably the single most important accomplishment of the occupation," he called it. To make sure he got the message across, on May 2, the day before the constitution went into effect, he sent a letter to Shigeru Yoshida, now prime minister, announcing an unexpected present:

> To mark this historic ascendancy of democratic freedom which events have made possible, I believe it particularly appropriate that henceforth the Japanese national flag be restored to the people of Japan for unrestricted display within and over the premises which house the National Diet, the Supreme Court, and the Prime Minister, as representative of the three main branches of constitutional government, and within and over the residence of the Emperor, who assumes his constitutional role as symbol of the State and of the unity of the people.
>
> Let this flag fly to signify the advent in Japanese life of a new and enduring era of peace based upon personal liberty, individual dignity, tolerance and justice.

14

His Most Radical Reform

WHEN MACARTHUR MET Prime Minister Shidehara for the first time on October 11 and demanded liberalization of the constitution, he also handed him a statement listing five necessary reforms. The fifth was the elimination of economic monopolies; the fourth, the abolition of the secret police; the third, more liberal education in schools; the second was the encouragement of labor unions; and at the top of the list was women's suffrage, "the emancipation of the women of Japan."

This idea did not originate in Washington but with the supreme commander himself. (Nothing like it was ever done by the American occupiers in Germany.) On the August 30 flight to Atsugi, MacArthur had announced as one of his commands: "Enfranchise the women"—the first time the subject of women ever came up in occupation policy. Just the day before he had received an advance copy of the September 6 *Initial Post-Surrender Policy Document for Japan.* All it said about human rights was that "laws, decrees and regulations which establish discrimination on grounds of race, nationality, creed or political opinion will be abrogated. . . . Policies shall be favored which permit a wide distribution of income and the ownership of the means of production and trade." Not a word was said about gender equality, much less anything about women having any property rights or claim on economic assets. Nor had anything been said about it in the Potsdam Declaration, nor in the detailed JCS 1380/15 memorandum of November 3. These three documents, taken together, presented a veritable laundry list of more than fifty demands and tasks for MacArthur, yet the subject of women was conspicuous in its absence.

Shidehara informed MacArthur that only two days earlier the Japanese cabinet had unanimously agreed with his demand to grant suffrage to women. Excellent, said MacArthur, adding that he hoped the other four reforms could be taken care of in the same manner.

At the next session of the Diet, in December, women's suffrage became the subject of heated discussion. Many members did not share the view of the Shidehara cabinet. Fumimaro Konoe, then the vice prime minister, argued that the enfranchisement of women "would retard the progress of Japanese politics." Prince Higashikuni, the emperor's uncle, was equally unreceptive. Clearly the Japanese government would not voluntarily grant suffrage; it would have to be imposed by the occupying authorities. Thanks to Beate Sirota and the backing of MacArthur, Whitney, and Kades, this had already been done by constitutional fiat. Still, the battle was not over: The constitution still had to pass the legislature. During the discussion in the Diet, one member of the House of Representatives looked into his crystal ball and found the future threatening: "These laws . . . will enable the son to marry a girl against the will of his parents, change his living place, spend money and other property ignoring the wishes of his parents, divorce a respectable wife without the consent of his parents. I fear the new constitution."

The British journalist Honor Tracy told the all-too-common story of a Japanese family. A woman whose husband had been killed in the war had a young son. Her family "wished her to marry again, and to send the small boy away to the dead man's people, to whom he legally belonged and by whom he was being repeatedly claimed. It was true that these people were only poor farmers, living in a province a long way off, but the child must go to them." The woman refused and said she would keep her child. She also said she would not marry the first man who happened to come along; she would be choosy and might never remarry. This made her family very upset: How could she be so unreasonable? Observed Tracy: "Her position seemed natural and straightforward enough; what was strange was only to find that [her older brother] did not think so."

The status of women in Japan was positively feudal. "Their supreme duty," observed one Japanese historian, "was to obey—obey their parents in childhood, their husbands in marriage and their sons in old age." Most women were married by the age of twenty, usually to a man chosen by her parents. It was difficult for a woman to file for divorce, and impossible for her to collect any alimony or make a claim on joint assets.

Under the new constitution pushed by MacArthur, parents were put in their proper place: in the far background. Everything would be different now. There would be no more marital bondage, parental tyranny, or male supremacy.

Once the constitution had been passed and women had the right to vote, SCAP launched a major campaign informing women of their new rights to make sure they took advantage of them. For the new experiment to work, a high turnout was essential, hopefully a lot higher than the anticipated 10 percent. Leading the effort was Lt. Ethel Weed, a public relations specialist sent to Japan by the Women's Army Corps (WAC). Her assignment: to develop "programs for the dissemination of information pertinent to the reorientation and democratization of Japanese women." Through round-the-clock use of press conferences, displays, radio shows, and motion pictures, Weed and her team of "Weed's Girls" helped generate a stunning 67 percent turnout among eligible female voters in the April 10, 1946, election.

In a gesture that aroused great envy among the male members of the Diet, MacArthur received a delegation of thirty-one of the thirty-nine females elected to this august body for the first time. The purpose of their visit: to express their appreciation to him personally for making women's suffrage possible. In remarks subsequently released to the *Nippon Times*, he said:

> Women of Japan are responding magnificently to the challenge of democracy; their record of participation in the general election on 10 April sets an example for the world . . . Japanese women are displaying an increasing interest in political, social and economic affairs which exceeds the most hopeful anticipation of political observers. It attests to the powerful appeal of the democratic idea and to the enthusiasm with which Japanese women are discarding the age-old bonds of convention.

In the informal discussion that followed, he urged the women to work as legislators and not as a women's bloc, that they "meet men on the [Diet] floor in complete equality, giving particular attention to the vital issues confronting the nation and accepting a full share of responsibility for their solution."

Responding for the female delegation was Kato Shidzue, a former baroness turned socialist, well known for her role in Japan's birth-control movement, who had lectured widely in the United States and had been jailed for her antimilitarist views during the war. The vote was only one step, she told MacArthur. "We are all hungry in Japan now . . . we Japanese women will never vote for the militarists, we shall never have war again." MacArthur nodded vigorously: In that statement Kato Shidzue had summed up why the supreme commander was such a proponent of women's rights. They were the people he would count on to make sure Japan would never go to war again.

Prodded by SCAP, the Japanese government passed additional regulations and acts. The Local Autonomy Act (October 1946) allowed women to be elected to local assemblies and local governments. In 1947 the Fundamental Law of Education required that nine years of compulsory schooling be available for females as well as males, and the Labor Standards Law mandated equal pay for equal work. In 1948 a special government agency was set up to protect women and children, the Women's and Minors' Bureau.

It was, says Susan Pharr, the former head of the Government Department of Harvard University, "one of the world's most radical experiments with women's rights." And a story rarely told even to this day: "Extraordinarily little has been written about the U.S. experiment with women's rights in Japan."

In undertaking radical change, constitutions and regulations are only a beginning; there must be grassroots involvement. The person normally expected to be involved, Beate Sirota, was no longer around. When her boyfriend, Joseph Gordon, a fellow SCAP officer, was transferred back to America in early 1947, she joined him and they got married. She published her memoir, *The Only Woman in the Room*, in 1997. Her contribution, while vital, was a one-shot achievement made possible only, as Gloria Steinem noted, because she had been fortunate enough to find herself a "presence in the corridors of power." More lasting power had to be earned through years of hard work.

However, other women were arriving in Japan from America, women older and considerably more experienced in community affairs than the twenty-two-year-old Sirota. They were the Women's Army Corps. The sight of several hundred women, all in army uniform, disembarking from a ship in Yokohama must have stunned the Japanese.

Unlike Sirota, these women didn't speak Japanese (other than six months' training for some), and had a difficult time adjusting to Japanese culture. But through perseverance and relentless energy, they showed Japanese women how to make the most of their new situation where, thanks to MacArthur and his strong position on gender equality, they enjoyed more rights than even women in America had or ever dreamed of. What emerged was one of the most remarkable stories in the history of women's liberation anywhere.

Not that it was easy. Weed, now a recipient of an Army Commendation Ribbon and promoted to be the Women's Information Officer of SCAP, had no real program budget to speak of. Making use of whatever SCAP resources she could round up, she led the women's outreach effort and stayed in Japan until 1952. She was not a radical feminist, but when she ran into the likes of Alfred Hussey, special assistant to the chief of the Government Section, who opposed a separate agency for women and feared it would create "a battle of the sexes," she let him have it. MacArthur, much to his discomfort, found himself drawn into the controversy, a fundamental one in politics: Do you work from within, or do you form an outside group and try to storm the ramparts? MacArthur believed in the former. He was not a man who liked unnecessary confrontation. But when he seemed to have no choice, he made one. To everyone's surprise he sided with Weed and against Hussey and permitted a separate government agency to serve solely women—an exception to his long-standing view that people with specific social grievances should not act as a bloc. The formation of this agency, the Women's and Minors' Bureau, proved instrumental in preserving the gains of women's rights long after the occupation ended.

Many people in the United States howled when it emerged that the newly appointed director was a Marxist. MacArthur let it go through: Even though he disagreed with the lady's politics, she was a proven leader who could be trusted to manage the bureau well.

In the meantime Weed had developed close relations with Margaret Sanger, the pioneer of American birth control and sex education efforts, and Mary Beard, the coauthor with her husband, Charles A. Beard, of the influential history of America, *The Rise of American Civilization*, and author of a book titled *The Force of Women in History* (and in 1953, another, *The Force of Women in Japanese History*). All three women supported Kato Shidzue's efforts to establish birth-control clinics, arguing that the best way to alleviate the poverty situation in Japan was for Japanese women to bear fewer children. Here, however, MacArthur refused to give his support, and instructed SCAP officers to do likewise, even to the point of denying Sanger a visa to enter the country. In his view abortion and birth control, while desirable, were personal issues best decided by the husbands and wives themselves. Shidzue could go ahead and introduce a bill in the Diet for the Japanese government to legalize abortion and provide contraceptives—unsuccessfully, it turned out—but no way should SCAP get involved in such a contentious issue.

Weed, in addition to helping SCAP's legal experts revise the Civil Code, led speaking groups to discuss women's freedom of choice in marriage, and how to attain equality under the new property, inheritance, and divorce laws. She acted as SCAP's watchdog to make sure the Japanese government kept the Women's and Minors' Bureau fully funded, and organized two major trips initiated by MacArthur for women leaders to visit the United States and meet high-ranking American politicians and women such as Eleanor Roosevelt and Maine's senator Margaret Chase Smith. MacArthur also supported her efforts by hiring a senior female State Department officer and personally inviting the head of the WAC to come to Japan for an official inspection visit. For a man who in 1935 as army chief of staff had eliminated the position of director of women's relations as having "no military value," this receptivity to women represented a major turnaround. In his memoirs MacArthur stated: "Of all the reforms accomplished by the occupation in Japan, none was more heartwarming to me than [the] change in the status of women." Mac-Arthur saw in Japanese women the counterweight he needed to help eliminate militarism. In addition to being much less militaristic than men, women were the major victims in the war, many now widows living in desperate economic circumstances. Winning their support and gratitude would be invaluable to the success of the occupation and acceptance of the American ideology of democracy. Recognizing their rights to a fair share and ownership of property would also combat the growing appeal of Communism. The Communists could tout Karl Marx and his definition of emancipation as equality of all citizens before the state, but no way could they match what the Americans had actually done with their article 24 of the new Japanese constitution in terms of "revolution":

> Marriage shall be based on the mutual consent of both sexes and it shall be maintained through mutual cooperation with the equal rights of husband and wife as a basis. With regard to choice of spouse, property rights, inheritance, choice of domicile, divorce and other matters pertaining to marriage and the family, laws shall be enacted from the standpoint of individual dignity and the essential equality of the sexes.

The Communists proceeded to hurt their own case, as when the secretary general of the Central Committee of the Communist Party, Kyiuchi Tokuda, made it clear which sex should have the upper hand. "Women's organizations," he said, "must not necessarily be run by women but should rather be guided by young men."

The constitution fostered by MacArthur took a totally different position. Article 14 banned "discrimination in political, economic, or social relations because of race, creed, sex, social status or family origin." Article 24 guaranteed equal rights within marriage in terms of property, inheritance, and divorce. At MacArthur's urging the Diet followed up in 1947 by passing a revised Civil Code giving wives full legal rights, and a Labor Standards Law stipulating equal pay for equal work and guaranteeing working women twelve weeks' maternity leave.

Today these rights may seem perfectly normal, but in the late 1940s they were radical. In America women did not acquire the right of non-discrimination until the Civil Rights Act of 1964 and subsequent legislation in the 1980s, and even today their rights to equal opportunity and equal economic privileges are ensnared in a tangle of federal and state legislation. Women do not have automatic rights to shared inheritance nor do they, depending on the particular state they live in, necessarily have equal division of property at divorce. In Japan they do. MacArthur was decades ahead of his time—and remains so to this day.

The most direct benefit SCAP provided women was reform of the education system, whereby females were provided nine years of compulsory schooling along with the males, and many universities were opened to coeducation. Members of the education team of the Civil Information and Education section—men as well as women—were given the task of visiting schools and advising female teachers how "equal education" would work. But here they ran into an obstacle: deeply ingrained Japanese cultural values centering on the importance of the home. A frequent question was: "If girl students take the same courses as boys, how will they ever learn the domestic arts of cooking, sewing, caring for children, and flower arrangement?" The logical answer to this question was that girls could learn these skills at home and in no more than an hour a day, and that it was easy enough for women to learn both the domestic arts and the normal curriculum simultaneously. Many Japanese teachers were skeptical that this could be done. One SCAP member told the delightful story of how he once visited a rural school to give his standard lecture on education, and at the end of the lecture he invited the women to discuss any questions and concerns. The women asked him if he knew how to make tea, and when he said no, they invited him to have tea with them, upon which they treated him to an elaborate ceremony where they instructed him on how to prepare, make, and serve tea in the proper manner. They were, he noted afterward, teaching him rather than him teaching them.

15

"He Has a Letter from God"

THE VISITOR TO MacArthur's office would find an office looking out at the enclosed grounds of the emperor's palace. For such a powerful man it was a surprisingly unprepossessing and small room, 581 square feet, formerly used for storage. It was now furnished with five items: a desk, a sofa, and three green leather chairs. Out in the hallway was a unique security feature found nowhere else in Japan: a shoot-the-chute tube for emergency exit to reach the ground floor in case of fire (or attempted assassination).

On the wall MacArthur had mounted a quotation by the historian Livy, attributed to the Roman general Lucius Aemilius Paulus (229?–160 B.C.). Paulus was talking about how a military commander should be counseled by people of known talent "whose knowledge is derived from experience . . . who are present at the scene of action, who see the country, who see the enemy, who see the advantages that occasions offer, and who, like people embarked on the same ship, are sharers of the danger." The quotation goes on:

> If, therefore, anyone thinks himself qualified to give advice respecting the war which I am to conduct . . . let him not refuse his assistance to the state, but let him come with me into Macedonia. He shall be furnished with a ship, a horse, a tent; even his travelling charges shall be defrayed. But if he thinks this too much trouble, and prefers the repose of a city life to the toils of war, let him not, on land, assume the office of pilot.

Such words about hands-on management are to be expected of a battlefield general, especially when the quotation ends with the stern warning: "We shall pay no attention to any councils but such as shall be framed within our camp."

Yet this was not how MacArthur ran his organization. Even as SCAP kept growing to the point where he had over five thousand people reporting to him, he spent a great deal of time with officials sent from Washington to observe and give advice. He was going out to the airport so frequently to meet visitors that one newspaperman remarked, "MacArthur should move his office to Haneda Air Force Base—he spends most of his time there."

Escorted to MacArthur's black Cadillac, the visitor might have noticed the license plate, "1." Or the two flags over the headlights: one was the Stars and Stripes; the other, a blue flag with five stars. Because there were so few cars on the road, the drive to downtown Tokyo took less than twenty minutes—plenty of time for MacArthur to exercise his legendary charm. He was a master of the one-on-one conversation, always asking questions and catching every nuance of his guest's words. He could charm birds off trees. The celebrated editor William Allen White had a two-hour lunch with him and was dazzled: "I never before met so vivid, so captivating, so magnetic a man." So captivating, apparently, that White was totally fooled. MacArthur, he wrote, "seemed to be entirely without vanity." Admiral Halsey, when he met MacArthur for the first time in Australia, had said: "Five minutes after I reported, I felt as if we were lifelong friends. I have seldom seen a man who makes a quicker, stronger, more favorable impression."

The general's charm worked equally well with women. The wealthy divorcée who became his first wife was smitten at first sight. "If he hadn't proposed the first time we met," she told reporters, "I would have done it myself."*

Joseph H. Choate Jr., a lawyer from California who visited Japan several times en route to Hong Kong to meet with a client, got to know

---

*The marriage lasted seven years. MacArthur's second marriage, in 1937 at the age of fifty-seven, lasted until his death in 1964.

MacArthur well. He tells the story of his first visit to Japan. He had arrived as a private citizen, and the military officers on duty at the airport were perplexed how a man with no "military status" could be in the country. They all gathered around and started peppering him with questions. Was he affiliated with a branch of the War Department? No. The State Department? No. How about the White House? No. Was he a member of a university faculty, here to teach? No. Was he an independent contractor of some sort? No. By now the questions were getting more hostile; this was becoming a very serious matter. Choate was definitely looking at getting deported on the next plane back home. "But I have a letter of introduction," he protested. That wouldn't do any good, he was told curtly: He had to be there on official business. Choate tried to explain, "Sir, I received letter from a fellow who invited me to come and see him." Impossible, said the military colonel, and anyway such a letter was meaningless. With great difficulty Choate extracted the letter from his briefcase and managed to get the colonel to read it. The colonel's face turned white as he skimmed down to the bottom of the page. Asked by one of his aides what was wrong, he pointed at the signature: "He has a letter from God."

It was reminiscent of what George Marshall had said to MacArthur in World War II. MacArthur was talking about his staff, and Marshall corrected him: "General, you don't have a staff, you have a court."

One of the advantages of being a god is that you can move walls. Which is what happened when MacArthur took an office on the top floor of the Dai Ichi Building in downtown Tokyo. The office was too small for MacArthur's carpet, just arrived from Manila. The Japanese building manager proposed to cut the rug to make it fit. No, he was told, you don't cut the carpet, you tear down a wall and move it. Several days later MacArthur had an office big enough for his carpet. The story got around, and added to the supreme commander's already considerable aura.

Another story that made its way around town was about the chair. When military translator Grant Goodman arrived in Tokyo in October, one of his first assignments was to procure a desk chair for General MacArthur. He found a suitable-looking one in the office of a Japanese company. The president of the company was sitting in the chair, working, when an American military officer marched in and ordered him to stand up. Before the poor gentleman could figure out what was going on, Goodman grabbed the chair and took off, leaving the businessman speechless. Told it was "by the orders of General MacArthur," he was even more astonished to learn that under the terms of the occupation, the Japanese were obliged to provide whatever the army wanted. And, of course, he would never see his chair again.

MacArthur's office was a spartan one, totally devoid of the autographed photos of famous celebrities so often found on the walls of ambassadors or politicians. One wall had two yacht paintings (though MacArthur had never owned a boat or lived near the sea). On another hung a painting of Washington and one of Lincoln—to be expected of a general who believed in the "great man" theory of history: "George Washington and Abraham Lincoln," he explained, "one founded the United States, the other saved it. If you go back in their lives, you can find all the answers."

The office helped him keep physically fit. Being on the sixth floor, whenever the elevator was busy or didn't work, he would run up the five flights of stairs and arrive "cool as a cucumber, followed by a very out-of-breath orderly officer." Because the office was scantily furnished, there was plenty of room to walk around. MacArthur was rarely at his desk, he was usually pacing back and forth from one end to the other. Multiplying the length by the number of paces, one aide calculated, MacArthur walked four to six miles a day. The Japanese prime minister Shigeru Yoshida had quite a different image: He compared the pacing to a lion prowling in its cage.

And it would be a young lion. Over MacArthur's desk was a framed message:

> Youth is not a time of life—it is a state of mind. Nobody grows old by merely living a number of years; people grow old only by deserting their ideals. . . . Whether seventy or sixteen, there is in every being's heart the love of wonder, the sweet amazement at the stars and the starlike things and thoughts, the undaunted challenge of the events, the unfailing childlike appetite for what's

next, and the joy and the game of life. . . . You are as young as your faith, as old as your doubt; as young as your self-confidence, as old as your fear; as young as your hope, as old as your despair.

The office had only two personal items: a picture of his wife, Jean, and a box containing some fifty pipes, mostly corncobs. What was surprising was his desk: It was a large table with no drawers, suggesting a man who abhorred clutter and liked to reduce everything to its barest essentials. Even more interesting, there was no telephone, just a buzzer. To receive a telephone call, MacArthur had to go into the next room. His office was a place of no interruptions, enabling him to give his visitor his complete attention. Not having a telephone also solved the security problem. During his days in the Philippines he very rarely used the telephone lest his calls be overhead by the enemy. In Japan this problem continued. For reasons no one in SCAP could figure out, it seemed that information communicated with Washington always seemed to end up in Moscow as well—sometimes getting there first. The problem was never solved, making face-to-face meetings all the more imperative.

The amount of work MacArthur had to do was staggering. In a foreign country with its own language and culture, he had to create a huge start-up operation of several thousand people, issue directives, manage hundreds of programs, coordinate with two different governments, and serve as the public spokesman for his administration. For a man who was sixty-five when the occupation started, he was in remarkably good shape. His only infirmity was trembling hands from advancing Parkinson's disease. He hadn't taken a vacation in thirty-five years; he wasn't about to take one now. He may have been foolish to turn down President Truman's two requests to come to Washington, but he really couldn't afford to take the time off. He worked seven days a week. Every day from ten to two thirty he was in his office, then off to the embassy for lunch and a nap, then back to the office from five until eight. He left his desk clean every night; when he could not, he took his work home with him to finish after dinner. He never drank coffee. His consumption of alcohol was limited: In the evenings before dinner, he would indulge in an Orange Blossom (a gin-and-orange-juice drink that had originated during Prohibition). Retiring to the master bedroom, he would read, usually history. He was a voracious—and fast—reader, capable of reading three books a day, which he proudly added to his small but growing collection. (Almost all of his original library of five thousand books had been destroyed when the Japanese sought out his home in Manila and set it on fire.)

He was totally dedicated to his job. His refusal to return to America annoyed many people, from President Truman on down. He got a letter from his friend Dr. James Conant, the president of Harvard University, informing him that Harvard had selected him for an honorary degree and he should plan on coming to the commencement exercises. MacArthur said he was too busy to leave Japan. Because Harvard only awards honorary degrees in person, he never got it.

He was the hardest-working man in the entire occupation. Considering that people who are very intelligent can work a lot faster than most people, one can only imagine the volume of work this exceptionally bright man was able to get done. His air chief, Gen. George Kenney, liked to remind people of the Luzon campaign, where, late one night, he noticed MacArthur was hardly eating, he was so tired. At dawn the next morning, Kenney had to leave. He called the orderly officer and told him to tell the general he was sorry he couldn't stay to bid him good-bye. "Oh," said the officer, "General MacArthur left for the front two hours ago."

General Whitney told a similar story: He and MacArthur were working in the office late one Sunday night, it was ten thirty, and MacArthur closed his notebook and told him, "Well, what do you say we take the rest of the weekend off?" With MacArthur you could never be sure whether he was being humorous or dead serious. This was the man who, when accused of working his staff too hard, had responded: "What better fate for a man than to die in performance of his duty!"

No job should pass without occasional moments of levity, however. One day MacArthur summoned the Japanese premier, the mayor of Tokyo, and the Tokyo fire chief to a meeting in his office. There were too many fires in Tokyo, he told them, and he wanted something done about it right away. The two senior government officials bowed in obeisance. The poor fire chief, losing face in front of his superiors, protested mightily and made furious hand gestures. "Sir," the translator explained to MacArthur, "the fire chief presents his respects and compliments and says that Japan has been famous for its fires for many centuries. Tokyo has always had the biggest and best conflagrations of any city, and he does not see why they should be prevented."

Suppressing his astonishment at such Oriental psychology, MacArthur ordered the fire department to start holding a Fire Prevention Week just like in the United States. The three men left. Within days the Tokyo Fire Department held its Fire Prevention Week. It built a huge pylon right next to MacArthur's office, painted with scenes of firemen and houses on fire. Every day when the general went home for lunch, the firemen set the pylon on fire and then climbed it and doused it with water, putting the fire out. MacArthur loved the joke and went over and personally thanked the firemen.

Other than a quick one-day trip to the Philippines in 1946 and another one to Seoul in 1948, he never left Japan during his five years before the Korean War started in June 1950. He never visited Hiroshima or Nagasaki. He never relaxed by going to a baseball game. He never toured Japan, not even Kyoto, the ancient capital and cultural center spared from the atom bomb by Secretary of War Henry Stimson. His wife and son's favorite holiday retreat was the Fujiya Hotel at Miyanoshita, a suburb of Tokyo. He rarely ever joined them. He was always in the city, glued to his desk. Very rarely did he go out or attend social functions. In a nation's capital where diplomatic receptions occur every week, he was nowhere to be seen. His idea of a good time was to stay home with his wife and young son and watch a movie, preferably a Western. He adored his son, Arthur, but he was so busy that the only meal he had with him was breakfast, which he made sure to do every day.

In keeping with his image as a man larger than life, he had a habit of describing himself in the majestic third person as if he were an institution: "MacArthur has decided to go into active command in the field," or "MacArthur thinks the time for action is at hand." His wife called him "General," not "Doug" or "Douglas." When she hosted a lunch at the embassy, she would chat with the guests by herself for a few minutes; when she saw the signal out of the corner of her eye, she would announce, "The general has arrived!" and MacArthur would stride into the room like a long-awaited potentate. Because of his demeanor and commanding presence, visitors perceived him to be taller than his actual five feet eleven inches.

He ordered his aides to schedule any appointments for the early evening; that way he would have dinner as his excuse for breaking away. Appointments were to be kept to the barest minimum, lest word get out that he was accessible, thus inviting a horde of visitors. "Don't want a fuss. Now that the war's over every Tom, Dick and his cat's coming over," he said. He met with the emperor twice a year, eleven times in total during his reign as supreme commander. According to a compilation of the appointments in MacArthur's office diary from September 3, 1945, to April 9, 1951, he met with William Sebald, his State Department adviser, 138 times, with Prime Minister Yoshida 75 times, with his aide Charles Willoughby 51 times, with State Department advisor George Atcheson 32 times, with war crimes prosecutor Joseph Keenan 31 times, fewer than 30 times each with Eichelberger and Sidney Huff, and fewer than 20 meetings with two members of the Associated Press and the United Press. Major General Whitney, though listed officially only 30 times, he saw unofficially almost every day (their offices were connected by a private door). All other frequent meetings were with various generals, primarily having to do with the outbreak of the Korean War in 1950.

What is remarkable about this compilation is how few meetings he had with key people. Many of his staffers resented his aloofness, but the Japanese respected him. "It indicated to them," said Elizabeth Vining, "a sacrificial devotion to duty that was comparable to their ideal of the samurai, the austere warrior." They flooded him with letters—almost one hundred thousand a year, two-thirds of them carefully written in English (the other one-third keeping SCAP's translators busy). MacArthur read them all. Just as Abraham Lincoln used to say that his once-a-week open-house sessions where the public could visit him at the White House were his "public opinion baths," so these letters were MacArthur's way of keeping in touch with his public, the Japanese people. To ensure he was getting unfiltered mail and not being censored by his own staff, he ordered all letters addressed to him to be delivered to him directly and not be opened (to save time and effort, he allowed his staff to slit open only half the edge of each envelope, and he would do the rest). He believed that as supreme commander he should not personally answer any letter; eventually he relented and answered a few that touched him most.

MacArthur was hardly a man to hide his own light. He enjoyed reading articles about himself, especially a *Fortune* 1946 poll of "Most Admired Military Leaders" showing him neck and neck with Eisenhower (Eisenhower at 39 percent and MacArthur at 37 percent, followed by Patton at 6 percent, Halsey at 4, Nimitz and Marshall at 3 each, and Bradley, King, and Spruance at less than 1 each). He was a man afflicted with what is known a "presidential disease," a state of mind that can cause many men to think foolish things. When Herbert Hoover visited him in 1946 to discuss Japan's food shortage, the most exciting part of their discussion was when Hoover exhorted him to run for president in 1948. The following month, MacArthur got a visit from his former aide Dwight Eisenhower, now army chief of staff. After dinner they talked till midnight, teasing each other about who would be the first to seek the 1948 Republican nomination. It was heady talk for "the Beau Brummell of the trenches," the "d'Artagnan of the battlefield," the "Napoleon of Luzon," the nonpolitician rated by Americans in a December 1945 Gallup poll as the "most qualified" to be U.S. president (ahead of Eisenhower) and the "most admired man in the world" according to a June 1946 Gallup poll (putting him ahead of Truman and Eisenhower). Both of these generals, both celebrated, both avid readers of history, knew they had history on their side. Out of the thirty-three presidents to date, eight had been generals.*

MacArthur had good reason to think he was looking at the end of the

---

*George Washington, Andrew Jackson, William Henry Harrison, Zachary Taylor, Ulysses Grant, Rutherford Hayes, James Garfield, and Benjamin Harrison. Another president who was prominent for his military exploits was Theodore Roosevelt in Cuba, though he was never a general.

rainbow. His accomplishments in Japan were attracting notice in America. In a June 1946 poll rating America's two occupations, 60 percent of Americans said the United States was doing "a good job" in Japan, compared with only 31 percent in Germany. MacArthur studied these polls like a general surveying the terrain. He was a vain man, puffed with his own brilliance, but he was not obtuse. The same Gallup poll that had him "most admired" also revealed that the number of people who had confidence in him as a civilian leader was extremely small. When asked their first choice of presidential nominee, the percentage of Republicans citing MacArthur was less than 10 percent.

The supreme commander had no serious intention of running for president. If he had, he would have returned to the United States, met with Republican leaders, and participated in rallies to get a bandwagon rolling. His apparent interest in doing so was a feint—to put the Truman administration on notice that he was not to be trifled with. He had seen enough of the office politics going on among the Joint Chiefs and especially the State Department to know he would need a lot of power to pull off his Tokyo job successfully. What better way to tell the bureaucrats in Washington "Hands off!" than to have in his pocket something none of them had—a lot of votes?

Talk of MacArthur running for president did not make him friends in the Truman administration, but it elevated his stature in Japan. Posters and banners appeared everywhere, promoting "MacArthur for President." The hoopla lasted until the 1948 Minnesota primary, where MacArthur's in-absentia campaign garnered only 1 percent of the vote and quickly fizzled.

FOR A MAN with such a huge ego, MacArthur was surprisingly human, a man with heart. When Admiral Halsey came to say good-bye after several days in Tokyo, MacArthur told him how much Halsey meant to him: "When you leave the Pacific, Bill, it becomes just another ocean." When Bob Eichelberger came out of the jungles of Buna the victor, MacArthur had a chocolate milkshake waiting for him. MacArthur did not flaunt his medals or act like a swashbuckler as did Pershing or Patton. He was a very private man, but he was not a statue. One day when he was walking to his car at lunchtime, a woman in a kimono broke free of the crowd and prostrated herself before MacArthur. Gently he picked her up, "Now, now," he said, "we don't do that sort of thing anymore," patted her on the shoulder, and sent her on her way. On another occasion he was walking into an elevator and saw a Japanese construction worker, embarrassed, stepping out so the supreme commander could have the elevator all to himself. MacArthur would have none of it, and insisted the man ride up in the elevator with him. Several days later MacArthur received a letter from this man: "I realize that no Japanese general would ever have done as you did."

Then there was the day of any leader's worst nightmare: A man with a knife tried to go after MacArthur. After the would-be assassin spent several days in jail, MacArthur invited him to his office for a cup of tea and to talk for an hour. MacArthur ordered the man released, and the man went away, MacArthur's greatest admirer. (For obvious reasons MacArthur refused to publicize the incident; it remained a secret for over forty years.) Like many great men, MacArthur was a man of contradictions. Said his air commander, General Kenney: MacArthur is "a hard-headed softie." (Another oxymoron for MacArthur: Calling this Medal of Honor general "Dugout Doug" was like calling a fat man "skinny.")

Best known in photographs for his corncob pipe, other than at Atsugi he never appeared with it in public when he ruled Japan. "They'd think I was a farmer," he joked. On the other hand, his practice of being driven back and forth to his office twice a day at the same time—"a target slower than a duck at an amusement park," he called it—scared his colonels but deterred him not at all: "I count on the Japanese people to protect me." As at Atsugi, his appearing unarmed in public was an essential part of his job description: to establish a bond with his followers. His obvious trust in the Japanese people made a powerful impression and brought out the best in them. When an American colonel, concerned about the large crowd being so close to the car, put up signs warning "Japanese stay away," MacArthur ordered the signs removed. To his Japanese subjects he was a distant man, yet a close one.

16

Russian Trouble

THERE WAS NO love lost between the Russians and the Japanese. Jumping into the war so suddenly at the last minute, just two days after Hiroshima, made the Russians look insidious and treacherous to the Japanese—just as the Japanese had appeared to the Americans after Pearl Harbor. MacArthur, who had welcomed the Russian entry into the Pacific War in 1943–44, when he needed all the help he could get, had a different reaction in August 1945, when the Soviets started claiming there should be two supreme commanders: the Russian marshal Aleksandr Vasilevsky as well as Douglas MacArthur. Averell Harriman, the American ambassador to the USSR, got so angry he walked out of a meeting with Stalin, resulting in a frantic message from Stalin's office saying there had been "a slight misunderstanding." Slight? Hardly: Harriman had called the Russians' bluff.

At the *Missouri* surrender signing, Rear Adm. Tomioka Sadatoshi, one of the official representatives of the Japanese navy, was watching the pompous body language of the Soviet representative, Lt. Gen. Kuzma Derevyanko. Sadatoshi whispered to his aide: "With the end of World War II, there is sure to be a confrontation between democracy and communism . . . between the U.S. and communism. In the rift between them Japan can find a chance to regain its feet."

In its one-week war with Japan after four years of neutrality since 1941, Russia had grabbed the Kuriles, Sakhalin, Manchuria, and North Korea and showed no signs of moving out. In February 1946 Harriman visited Japan and warned MacArthur of the Communist threat in Asia. The threat would bear careful watching, especially as it spread to

Japan. Already the Russians were demanding that their troops occupy the northern island of Japan, Hokkaido, thus dividing the country in two. General Derevyanko, in a heated meeting, threatened to send in his troops whether MacArthur liked it or not. You do that, replied MacArthur, you will regret it: "If the Soviets attempt to place any troops on those islands, I will throw seventeen divisions in that area, I'll decimate every Soviet soldier on the island and I will then throw you in jail." Derevyanko, knowing MacArthur's record as a general, stared at him and responded, "My God, I believe you would." MacArthur grinned: He liked this rogue. Derevyanko was a real ladies' man, reputed to be the best dancer in all of Tokyo. MacArthur was reminded of the time he was asked to leave the ballroom of the Waldorf-Astoria in New York for dancing with his boot spurs on.

Derevyanko had a huge staff of four hundred people, five times the size of any other embassy. What were these people doing? Enough to keep Willoughby's men busy (though they never did come up with much). The Soviets offered to send troops to help maintain the peace. There was peace already. MacArthur put them in their place by saying that any Allied troops would have to report to him; the Russians backed off. When the USSR sent a memo protesting SCAP's purge of the Japanese Communist leaders, MacArthur responded: "I have received your note, and have carefully considered its context in vain in search of some small semblance of merit and validity. Rarely indeed have I perused such a conglomeration of misstatement, misrepresentation, and prevarication of fact."

Such language did not make Stalin happy. He complained to Harriman that Derevyanko was being treated "like a piece of extra furniture." Harriman, who must have tried his hardest not to show his glee, was one of the few people in Washington who had always liked MacArthur. Now he liked MacArthur even more. He dashed off a cable to Secretary of State Byrnes reporting that Derevyanko was nothing but trouble:

He has endeavored to utilize Allied Council as inquisitorial and investigative body by presenting requests for unnecessary detailed information on wide range of subjects and making hypocritical statements. . . . His agents have encouraged mob violence by discontented elements and he himself has made public defense of demonstrations instigated or led by Japanese Communists and has persistently attacked Japanese government and its members as "reactionaries."

A story (best savored over several shots of vodka) that made the rounds of the Russian Embassy was about Derevyanko calling on the supreme commander before returning to Moscow to present a report. MacArthur took the opportunity to give the Soviet representative a full one-hour lecture on what was wrong with Russian foreign policy. Instructing him to be sure to tell Stalin exactly what he said, the supreme commander ordered the general to raise his right hand and repeat his comments. A year went by, no sign of Derevyanko. Finally he returned and paid MacArthur a courtesy visit. "Why, General Derevyanko! Delighted to see you!" teased MacArthur. "When you failed to return, I feared they had shot you!"

On another occasion Derevyanko went to the office of Gen. Elliott Thorpe and demanded that he censor the negative stories about Russian misconduct toward its Japanese prisoners in Manchuria; this was simply unacceptable. Thorpe asked if he denied the truth of these stories. Derevyanko said that was beside the point, the stories were negative and had to stop. Thorpe asked MacArthur what he should tell the Russians. "Tell them whatever you want to," said the supreme commander. "Why don't you just tell them to go to hell? . . . That's a good idea, just tell them to go to hell." The next day Thorpe met with Derevyanko: "General MacArthur says you can go to hell."

Without batting an eye Derevyanko responded: "Well, I had to ask, you know."

The Russians had their own ideas how to reform Japan. They wanted to treat the emperor as a war criminal, put in jail anyone suspected of war profiteering, redistribute the wealth, and deny the vote to anyone who was not a Communist. In the chaos and poverty of postwar Japan, stopping these fantasies at the gate required a vigilant sheriff. Commented Elizabeth Vining: "Japan is in heaven now, but sometimes a cold wind blows in from Russia."

What the Russians were hoping to do was what they had done in Germany: set up a separate zone of occupation. MacArthur refused to even consider it. As for the four hundred Russians already in Japan supposedly as part of the government mission, he devised an ingenious way to keep them in their place. Americans weren't allowed to travel more than twenty-five miles outside Moscow, so the same should apply here: No travel beyond twenty-five miles outside Tokyo. This put a crimp on the Russians and prevented them from interacting with the population in the countryside as the Americans could.

Even if they couldn't do much inside Japan, the Soviets could still hurt Japan abroad. They did this in two ways. In the dispute over reparations they claimed the Japanese property they had seized in Manchuria and Korea should be treated as war booty rather than reparations. This was not a minor dispute: MacArthur valued this property at $50 billion (Washington valued it much lower). He succeeded in getting this theft categorized as reparations, but he could do little about the second act, where the Russians stalled for four years before letting their Japanese prisoners in Manchuria come home. During this time they indoctrinated these prisoners to become Communist agents and stir up trouble when they eventually returned to Japan. This would cause MacArthur and Willoughby major problems in the later years of the occupation.

The Americans were in Japan to promote democracy. A basic tenet of democracy is freedom of speech, even if the privilege also applies to one's enemies. One of the supreme commander's very first acts was his October 3, 1945, directive, sometimes referred to as the "Japanese Bill of Rights," where he granted unprecedented freedom of thought and political action. The directive demanded that the government free all political prisoners—including Communists—and to "abrogate and immediately suspend the operation of all provisions of all laws, decrees, orders, ordinances, and regulations which establish or maintain restrictions on freedom of thought, of religion, of assembly, and of speech."

Many Japanese were puzzled at MacArthur letting the Communists out of jail. They would be even more mystified when the supreme commander, after releasing the Communist prisoners, started censoring their publications for potential treason. Why hadn't he kept them in jail in the first place? For the Japanese, how strange it must have seemed to see Communist speakers uttering their harangues in public parks and school auditoriums, flanked by red flags and protected by U.S. military police!

The only thanks MacArthur got from the Communists were blustering propaganda broadsides about subservience to the American occupation. He kept his cool and had George Atcheson launch attacks on Derevyanko and the lack of civil rights in the USSR. Democracy was a weapon, and he had no compunction about using it. He would permit democracy to the fullest.

If the Communists gained power and influence, so be it; if they gained too much power and threatened to take over Japan, well, that was a risk he would have to take. It would be up to him to communicate, with words and deeds, a more compelling political message. In early 1946 he instructed Atcheson to tell the ACJ that the United States "does not favor Communism at home or in Japan." He then followed up by making numerous pronouncements about the basic incompatibility of Communism and democracy, being careful to make the critical distinction between his views on Communism and the constitutional right of all Japanese to decide for themselves.

The first showdown came in the April 1946 national election. Because MacArthur and SCAP had moved so quickly in instituting land reform, they easily beat the Communists, who marched forth with the tired slogan "Land for the Toiling Farmer." What toiling farmer? The massive food shortage and black market prices had made farmers rich. A full 70 percent of them had paid for their land purchases with cash. "Japanese national farm debt melted away like snow under a spring sun," wrote one Japanese journalist, "and the hitherto downtrodden peasant emerged suddenly as a man of means." If the Communists were going to make headway in Japan, they would have to eschew their traditional target of land peasants and go after the office workers. There they struck pay dirt.

It so happened that another of MacArthur's early directives had encouraged the development and expansion of labor unions. Within a year more than a thousand labor unions emerged, boasting a membership of 6.6 million. Unlike the farmers, workers were getting hammered by inflation: 412 percent in 1946. Collective-bargaining efforts to achieve matching wages had gotten nowhere, leaving the door open for the Communists to march in.

MacArthur was no left-wing ideologue and certainly no socialist, but there were two reasons why he was allowing the labor union movement unrestrained growth. One, Washington had ordered him to support the development of labor unions; and two, he believed, like Henry Ford when he gave his auto workers the highest wages in the industry, that workers deserved a decent wage to live on. The prevailing average wage of twenty-five dollars a month simply didn't cut it.

In 1946 there was a looming showdown with government workers, who had not received a pay raise for months during a time of rampant inflation. The government was stalling, saying it had no money. Within the SCAP offices there was considerable debate about what to do. When it became apparent that the disagreements were becoming acrimonious, MacArthur called for a meeting of the two leading adversaries on his staff. One officer recommended a loose policy of doing nothing and letting the strikers and the Japanese government keep arguing; the other officer urged an overhaul of government compensation incorporating specific details about position classification, entrance examinations, training programs, performance evaluation, pay scales, tenure, transfer, retirement, and pensions. Each man, on his own initiative, announced he would resign if the decision went against him. Normally most executives would take offense at subordinates making such ultimatums. MacArthur, on the other hand, welcomed the opportunity to clarify the issue, even if one protagonist would have to go. The presentations were made, and MacArthur ruled in favor of the total, all-inclusive policy of compensation reform. He also announced that government employees would never be allowed "the use of so deadly a social weapon." He wrote a letter to the prime minister, quoting Franklin D. Roosevelt to the effect that "a strike of public employees is unthinkable and intolerable," and urged the Diet to revise the Civil Service Law and see to it that the new civil service commission ensured that government employees were properly compensated.

MacArthur described his job as managing "a controlled revolution." The drastic reforms he was imposing on the Japanese people amounted to nothing less. Revolutions are easy to start, which is why the history of mankind is replete with so many hundreds of them. Virtually all of them end badly: They spin out of control and devour their own children (the American Revolution of 1775–89 being the most notable exception). In controlling the revolution he had started, MacArthur must not impose more change than the Japanese could handle, lest revolutionary fervor get out of hand. He must always maintain control. In the case of labor unions, many officers in SCAP and back home in Washington fretted over the growing power of the Communists. Not MacArthur. He was willing to bet that the Communists would soon overreach. And when they did, he would be prepared to shoot them down, just like a general who has led the enemy into an ambush.

By now the Communist Party had grown to 60,000 members (even more than the Bolshevik Party in 1917 czarist Russia, with 49,000 members). Revolutionary slogans filled the air; every few days rallies took place in the plaza of the Imperial Palace, now renamed "the People's Palace" by the Communists. The Communists kept raising their wage demands beyond reason, thus revealing that their objective was not higher wages but an overthrow of the government. When SCAP civil affairs officer Carmen Johnson looked at a sample of labor union ballots, she was stunned to find that 80 percent were blank. When she demanded to know what was going on, the union leaders blithely told her "the Japanese cannot make up their minds how to vote." Clearly the union leaders were stuffing the ballot boxes.

The Communists, smelling victory, went for the jugular. Having attracted 3.4 million factory workers in addition to 2.6 million government employees, they announced they would proceed with a massive countrywide strike of 6 million people planned for February 1, 1947. Should this happen, MacArthur would have no choice but to use American troops to restore law and order—a most unwelcome prospect. He instructed General Marquat to warn the labor leaders that a strike of this magnitude—"a national calamity"—was against the country's interest and would not be tolerated. The next day Marquat received a petition signed with the blood of fifty strikers—a declaration of war. The supreme commander continued negotiating with Communist union leaders to get them to drop the strike; it became clear they had little incentive to do so.

A strike followed by American troops streaming in and beating up the strikers—a repeat of MacArthur's disastrous attack on the Washington Bonus Marchers in 1932—would be an enormous propaganda victory for the Communists. When the Japanese government reached a mediated settlement with the strikers on January 29, the Communist leaders shot the agreement down. Tensions rose as the hours approached for the nationwide strike. General Eichelberger, the commander of the occupying U.S. Eighth Army, alerted MacArthur that a strike by the railroads could "ruin the Occupation."

Waiting until the last minute—nine hours before the strike was due to start—MacArthur finally made his move, so dramatic that it arrived with "the impact of a bomb." But it was not what everyone expected: Instead of using force he would engage in a battle of wits with the union leaders over who had more power. "Under the authority vested in me as the Supreme Commander for the Allied Powers," he announced, "I have informed the labor leaders . . . that I will not permit the use of so deadly a social weapon in the present impoverished and emaciated condition of Japan and have accordingly directed them to desist from the furtherance of such action."

He didn't just inform them, he hit them over the head, accusing the Japanese Communists of being "undisciplined elements" operating "under organized leadership" to foment "physical violence." The gamble worked: so great was MacArthur's prestige, and so forceful was his message, that the workers capitulated. The union leaders, caught by surprise at their workers' response, were helpless. Efforts to rally their followers fell short. MacArthur had won the showdown, becoming more than ever a hero, not for busting the strike but for preserving order and doing it in a way that avoided any bloodshed. "We regret very much,"

wrote the *Mainichi* newspaper, "that we have had to trouble the Supreme Commander to avert the grave disaster that was sure to follow."
"In one stroke," said Blaine Hoover, SCAP's chief of civil service reform,
"General MacArthur had decapitated the creature which . . . had been
gaining strength and was, even then, twining itself around the throat of
the young Japanese democracy."

For the Communists, who had five seats in the House of Representatives and looked to get at least twenty in the forthcoming national
election in April, the result was an abject humiliation. In the election,
instead of a massive win they lost a seat. Never again would they be in a
position to take over Japan. George F. Kennan, the leading authority on
the worldwide Communist threat, could only marvel at what MacArthur had pulled off. Like the *Mainichi* newspaper, he admitted it, albeit
grudgingly. Note his use of the word "cursory": MacArthur's policies,
he wrote, "seemed, on cursory examination, to be such that if they had
been devised for the specific purpose of rending Japanese society vulnerable to communist political pressures and paving the way for a communist takeover, they could scarcely have been other than what they were."

MacArthur, recognizing that government unions were a fertile re-
cruiting ground for the Communists, followed up a year later by recommending to the prime minister that the National Public Service Law be
amended to prevent collective bargaining or strikes by government workers. Immediately he got a letter from the Army Department demanding
an explanation and implying that denial of collective-bargaining rights
to government workers was contrary to U.S. policy. MacArthur took
his time to develop a thorough response. This time he played hardball,
threatening indirectly to go to his Republican friends in Congress. He
explained that the issue in Japan had more to do with the danger of
self-appointed radical leaders using the vehicle of a strike for their own
personal ends than with the welfare of the workers—an issue recognized by the U.S. House of Representatives Appropriations Committee
in its concern about the behavior of the Communist-controlled labor
unions. "I know of nothing more calculated to impede recovery and
destroy occupation gains already made through painstaking effort and
heavy United States expense than to permit this trend toward disaster to

continue," he wrote. He went on to attribute the major source of trouble to a 1946 FEC decision encouraging trade unions to take part in political activities—a provision approved by the United States without his knowledge or, for that matter, the knowledge and approval of any senior official in the U.S. Army. . . .

MacArthur did not treat this issue of bargaining rights lightly. In his view it was an issue only because the officials in Washington were trying to appease friendly allies, notably the United Kingdom and Australia, where labor governments ruled. In the United States, government officials were not allowed to strike, so why in Japan of all places? To put this issue to rest, he had a staff meeting with his senior officials to go over every aspect. A meeting with MacArthur rarely lasted more than twenty minutes; this one went on for seven full hours. In the final of his many letters to Washington, he pointed out that he did not think it was possible for agencies as far away as Washington "to prescribe with wisdom details for the best course for government in Japan." Washington backed off, and when the Japanese Diet amended the Public Service Law as MacArthur requested, the issue finally went away.

While MacArthur was fighting Communism in Japan and labor officials in Washington, the Russians were busy stirring up trouble. Though they may have suffered a setback in the 1946 Japanese election, they still had another weapon: Japanese war prisoners. At the time of the surrender the USSR claimed to have 594,000 Japanese prisoners in China and Manchuria; Japan claimed there were three times as many. It wasn't until December 1946—fifteen months into the occupation—that Russia began to release its Japanese prisoners—only 71,000. Such prisoners, when they returned to Japan and were greeted by their families, were not the same men they had been. They had been thoroughly indoctrinated. (This loathsome practice, originating in Manchuria under the Soviets, is the origin of the phrase "Manchurian candidate.") The Japanese were outraged. This was brainwashing of prisoners on a massive scale and of course represented a complete violation of the Geneva Conventions' codes of conduct for treating prisoners of war.

The Japanese demanded answers. In a meeting of the FEC, they asked the Russian member, General Derevyanko: "What happened to

MacArthur, the supreme commander, arriving in Japan, is greeted by his number-two man, General Robert Eichelberger. "Bob," he says, "this is the payoff!"

MacArthur and his men, none wearing guns. "The most daring act of the entire war," said Winston Churchill.

MacArthur *(far right)* watches Shigemitsu sign the surrender document for Japan.

Everyone ready, waiting for the supreme commander to step forward and begin the surrender ceremony.

At the end of the ceremony, there was a deafening roar as planes flew overhead. The surrender was now complete. A new era for Japan had begun.

MacArthur and Emperor Hirohito at their first meeting, the only photograph ever taken of the two men together. The Japanese newspapers suppressed the picture because it made the emperor look inferior. MacArthur ordered them to print it.

The Japanese people gathered every day for a fleeting glimpse of MacArthur leaving his office for lunch.

Heartfelt gratitude for MacArthur's handling of emergency relief.

Children—the future citizens of Japan—were a high priority for the occupation.

If Douglas MacArthur was to achieve his major objective of eliminating Japanese militarism, then he needed to help women achieve positions of influence and power. Second to the constitution, this was his most successful reform of the entire occupation.

MacArthur was so popular in Japan that the Japanese posted billboards, hoping he might become the U.S. president.

Two brilliant men who changed Japan forever: Courtney Whitney and Charles Kades. They directed the drafting of a new constitution for Japan while overcoming Japanese resistance and keeping their activities secret from Washington. Their handiwork survives today.

MacArthur headquarters at the Dai Ichi Building. No checkpoints or fences were needed.

Under MacArthur, counter to the prevailing practices of the time, women were given a prominent role in the occupation.

Protecting Japan from nearby Russia proved to be MacArthur's greatest challenge.

MacArthur and John Foster Dulles.

MacArthur with an aide in his office.

"The Nuremberg of the East." The trial of Japanese war criminals lasted thirty-one months; all twenty-five defendants were found guilty.

John Foster Dulles and William Sebald talking with Prime Minister Shigeru Yoshida.

"Sayonara!" As MacArthur leaves Japan, 200,000 people line the streets to say farewell.

our sons?" Derevyanko refused to answer and walked out of the meeting. When asked why they were so slow to execute the 1945 repatriation agreement, the Russians resorted to numerous excuses, the lamest of which was that there was too much ice in the strait between Mongolia and Japan. MacArthur called this response nonsense, offering to send some icebreakers to Vladivostok. The Russians continued to stall, claiming the icebreakers were in bad condition and "would have endangered the lives of crew and passengers." When that didn't work they claimed that the Manchurian trains delivering prisoners to the ports were having engine trouble.

For the rest of the occupation U.S. relations with the Soviet Union continued to deteriorate, especially as the number of Japanese "spies" increased and the Russians launched radio broadcasts from Vladivostok, Khabarovsk, and Moscow, accusing American imperialists of exploiting Japan and threatening world peace. Then the Chinese joined in. They got upset when MacArthur ordered the entire politburo of the Japanese Communist Party to be purged. Undaunted, MacArthur went even further and ordered a purge of Communists from the newspapers. Mao Zedong, now in power in China, jumped in and denounced "the American imperialists and their Japanese jackals."

The jackals in the Japanese government thought differently. In 1949, they set up a Special Investigation Bureau within the attorney general's office to conduct surveillance of Communist activities. Its success in catching spies was limited. After the Korean War began, ten Communist leaders in Japan suddenly vanished into thin air; the bureau managed to find only one of them. Chortled a Russian military commander: "The Japanese and American bloodhounds have worn blisters on their feet searching for those loyal sons of Japanese people."

After MacArthur left Japan, the peace treaty between Japan and the Allied Powers was finally consummated in September 1951. Forty-nine countries signed. The Soviet Union was conspicuous in its absence: It refused to sign. For the rest of 1951 it made a major, largely unsuccessful effort to stimulate Japan-Soviet trade, and on January 1, 1952, Joseph Stalin sent a New Year's message to Japan sympathizing with the Japanese "who are in difficult straits due to foreign occupation." He could talk all he wanted; what mattered were the votes. From a high of 10 percent in the 1949 elections, the Communists dropped to 5.6 percent in 1950 and 2.5 percent in 1952. Never again would they threaten Japan. As he had in implementing a new Japanese constitution, Douglas MacArthur had won his war.

After he retired as Japanese prime minister, Shigeru Yoshida was asked what was possibly MacArthur's greatest contribution to Japan.

Preserving Japan's integrity and keeping the Russians out, he said.

TO UNDERSTAND WHY this was so, a little counterfactual speculation may be helpful:

Imagine that MacArthur had not been the supreme commander. Another man almost surely would have followed the State Department's original plan to let Prince Konoe prepare a revised constitution. "There being no provisions in the State Department's plan for establishing popular sovereignty and renouncing the right of belligerency, the corner stones of the subsequent MacArthur constitution," wrote SCAP legal officer Justin Williams, "it may be assumed that, had the State Department's revision plan been adopted, the old Japanese clique might very well have regained full control of post-occupation Japan."

The alternative supreme commander would have forwarded the Konoe draft to the State Department, which in turn, following Secretary of State Byrnes' December 1945 instructions that all constitutional matters be referred to the FEC, would have submitted the revisions to the USSR. Russia, sitting on the Far Eastern Commission, would have shared them with the Japanese Communist Party—and had a field day eviscerating them. The situation would have become very muddled indeed.

Washington had strongly advised MacArthur that if there was any domestic insurrection, the Eighth Army must not use its military force. The alternative supreme commander, lacking MacArthur's spine of steel, would have followed such instructions and permitted the strikers to take over the streets, create economic chaos, and overthrow the conservative Japanese government. The new government, in the hands of labor extremists and protected by the Soviet veto in the ACJ in Tokyo, immediately issued a new constitution eliminating the emperor and forcing the Diet to install a plural voting system. As the April 1946 national election approached, the State Department, strongly sympathetic to the "agrarian reformers" led by Mao in China, tolerated the growing insurrection of workers, shopkeepers, tenant farmers, and intellectuals. At the war crimes trial of 1948, the Russians put the emperor on trial, where he was found guilty and sentenced to death. The Russian Embassy, free of MacArthur's twenty-five-mile restriction, flooded the country with agents and provocateurs. The Japanese, ever respectful of power and seeking security at all costs, saw the handwriting on the wall: America's promise of support meant little. The use of Japan as a major supply port for America's massive invasion of Korea became impossible, hampering America's military effectiveness in trying to negotiate a cease-fire. By late 1950 (there had been no dramatic victory at Inchon) the cause was lost, and Korea became a united country under Kim Il Sung. When the occupation ended, America found itself in a very perilous situation in the power struggles in Asia. Congress, fed up with Japan's lack of loyalty, cut off any discussion of favorable trade terms with Japan. Japan had no choice but to look to Russia, not the United States, as its main trading partner. Other nations in Southeast Asia soon followed suit.

MacArthur made sure this did not happen.

17

"Where's Ishii?"

THE FIRST QUESTION MacArthur asked after landing at Atsugi was: "Where's Ishii?"

Nobody had any idea where Ishii was. He was nowhere to be found.

Ishii was Dr. Shiro Ishii, the founder and director of Japan's "secret of secrets"—Unit 731—a massive top-secret operation conducting research in biological weapons (BW). Only a handful of people in the American government knew about Japan's potential weapons of mass destruction, which they kept hidden from the American public lest it cause widespread panic. Already Japan, in one of the most daring military stunts ever attempted, had unleashed a fleet of a hundred anthrax-carrying balloons that floated with the winds across the Pacific and landed in California and Oregon. Fortunately most of the anthrax spores had died en route, but the War Department was beside itself worrying what might come next. Countries in the throes of defeat do desperate things, which is another of the reasons President Truman was anxious to end the war quickly with the atom bomb.

The first inkling the American public had that there was a BW war came the day after the *Missouri* signing. On the front page of the *New York Times*, beneath the huge story about the surrender, was an article headed "Enemy Tortured Dying Americans with Sadist Medical 'Experiments.'" The article revealed that American prisoners in a Tokyo hospital had been used as guinea pigs for "fantastic experiments recalling the sorcery and sadism of the Middle Ages." Medical research conducted by the hospital included injecting Americans with a mixture of acid and dried blood plasma from Red Cross supplies, exposing patients to malignant types of malaria, and observing how long it took for patients to die without proper drugs.

In Germany among the most diabolical of the Nazis was the infamous Dr. Josef Mengele, the "Angel of Death" who conducted experiments on live prisoners and quickly vanished before the surrender, now presumably hiding in Argentina. MacArthur would not countenance anything of the kind under his watch, he said. He wanted this monster Ishii, the Japanese Mengele, and he wanted him before the Russians got their hands on him.

Ishii was the most evil man in Japan—and potentially one of the most useful. MacArthur's job was to capture him alive and get him to talk. This did not mean bringing him to justice in a court of law, and it most definitely did not mean sending him to his maker. Ishii dead was useless, Ishii alive could be priceless.

America's cloak-and-dagger war with Japan had begun two years before Pearl Harbor, in New York City on a cold wintry day in November 1939. A team of Japanese researchers paid a visit to what was then the Rockefeller Institute for Medical Research, requesting stocks of yellow-fever virus. They were turned down, such a virus being on the prohibited list based on the Hague Convention of 1899 and the Geneva Protocol of 1925, banning biological weapons. The visit might have gone unnoticed had it not been for the fact that one of the Japanese researchers then foolishly tried more direct measures. In the institute's parking lot he offered one of the American scientists a very substantial bribe, and when that didn't work, he tripled the amount of money and threatened physical harm. The American, frightened out of his wits, ran back to the institute, which immediately reported the incident to the U.S. surgeon general and the War Department.

For years the United States had been following the progress in Japan of what is known as military medicine. In the Russo-Japanese War of 1904–5, an American army doctor, Louis Seaman, had been granted the privileges of a foreign military attaché and accompanied the Japanese troops in Manchuria. After the war he published a book in which he noted that the American fatalities in the Mexican War and the Civil War had been due 25 percent to bullets and 75 percent to disease, and that Japan had made remarkable strides in ensuring good health for its soldiers in the war with Russia, suffering only 18 percent of its fatalities from disease. Defensive hygiene and health had become an important, previously overlooked military tool.

Another American who noticed this development was Douglas MacArthur. In his visit to Japan with his father in 1905, when they witnessed an army general issue a command in the name of the emperor—the Voice of the Crane—that soldiers take their pills, the subject was military medicine.

So far so good, as long as military medicine was used for medical purposes. Except that in the late 1930s, as Japan became a militarist nation, a scientist named Shiro Ishii initiated an effort to build a network of laboratories to conduct disease research and dissect humans with the intent not to cure but to kill. Wealthy and politically well connected, he was extremely successful. His largest operation, known as Unit 731, was located in Pingfan, China, near Harbin, a major city 650 miles northeast of Beijing. The Pingfan facility was an enormous complex consisting of seventy buildings on 2.3 square miles. Inside the high walls were laboratories for breeding millions of fleas and other insects, vats capable of breeding eight tons of germs a month, large vegetable gardens, and enough land for livestock to graze. The complex was totally self-contained and closed to the outside world. To make sure no one learned about Pingfan, after it was built all the construction workers were lined up and shot.

Staffing this operation were three thousand doctors, technicians, and soldiers. It was like a small city; Unit 731 even had its own airport and a fleet of airplanes.

People in Harbin who wondered what was going on were told the facility was a lumber mill. The Japanese went so far as to call the five hundred prisoners *maruta*, or wooden logs. No prisoner ever escaped or left Pingfan alive. During their imprisonment patients were injected with deadly diseases and germs. To get the best test results on the germs' impact and how long it took for a patient to die, anesthesia was never used, and patients were operated on while alive and free of putrefaction bacteria. Once the five hundred prisoners were satisfactorily vivisected and dead, another five hundred were wheeled in and the cycle continued.

During the war Chinese spies and American missionaries had heard rumors about Pingfan and alerted the OSS. More than nine hundred incidents were reported. Chiang Kai-shek sent a letter to Winston Churchill, who passed it along to Franklin Roosevelt, who was already nervous about what biological weapons the Japanese might try to use. In a safety precaution kept secret from the public lest it cause panic, immediately after Pearl Harbor everyone in the White House had been issued a personal gas mask, even the president. (His gas mask was tied to his wheelchair, readily available at a moment's notice.) Throughout the Second World War, the threat of a gas attack on the White House hung in the air.

Another threat struck directly at the United States. In 1942 it was discovered that a group of Japanese saboteurs had tried to poison the Los Angeles city water supply with a mixture of typhoid and plague germs. President Roosevelt, on June 6, 1942, warned Japan against biological warfare and made it "unmistakably clear that if Japan persists in this inhuman form of warfare against China or any of the other United Nations, such actions will be regarded by this government as though taken against the United States, and retaliation in kind and in full measure will be meted out." For the same reason, countries don't try to assassinate other countries' leaders: fear of retaliation. Only with the Japanese, it didn't work. First they launched a small wave of balloons carrying anthrax; the result was nil because the anthrax spores froze at the high altitudes. Then, in December 1944, came a huge invasion: 9,300 balloons carrying incendiary devices. Some 200 landed in Alaska, Hawaii, Vancouver, the Aleutian Islands, and Michigan. One of the balloons, ninety-one feet in circumference, knocked out the power at the Hanford nuclear site in Washington State, causing a temporary delay in the construction of the atom bomb for Nagasaki. While the United States government played down the attack, the Japanese government told the Japanese public that the West Coast of the United States was a blazing inferno, with ten thousand dead.* Lest this message reach the already jumpy American public, on June 4, 1945, the War Department permitted *Newsweek* to run a small, barely noticeable four-inch article with the casual headline "Mustn't Touch!" (as if it was child's play). The article mentioned only scant details about the incendiary balloons. "These and other facts long have been known to many newspapers, magazines, and radio stations which, at the request of the Office of Censorship, have withheld publication or broadcasting of details," admitted *Newsweek*. Since news of the balloons' existence was out, might the public learn more? Hardly. Even then, "Papers and magazines were requested to withhold any specific information of the balloons; the time of arrival, locality, and effect of any incident connected with them." The balloons were to be kept secret (along with America's second-best-kept secret after the Manhattan Project: its own BW facility at Camp Detrick, Maryland, built in 1943).

In the final days of the war, the Japanese prepared their most daring plan yet, originally conceived by Adm. Isoroku Yamamoto of Pearl Harbor fame: to attack America with airplanes launched from submarines. By now the Japanese had developed the I-400 class, the biggest and most ingenious submarine ever seen. This massive, 400-foot-long sea monster had on its deck a watertight hangar 115 feet long, large enough to hold three seaplanes with wings folded. The deck also had a 200-foot runway ramp, and a derrick for hoisting a seaplane out of the water and into the hangar. The submarine carried enough fuel to cruise 35,000 miles, or one and a half times around the globe, meaning it could attack San Francisco and Los Angeles, then cross into the Atlantic Ocean via Cape Horn, attack Washington and New York, and return home. Two

---

*This propaganda bluff boomeranged after the Americans bombed Tokyo, Hiroshima, and Nagasaki. In 1946 a U.S. Army lieutenant conducted a survey asking Japanese people how they felt about the battering their cities took from American bombs. Were the attacks savage and unnecessary? Almost unanimously they said: "Oh no. Because first we bombed *your* cities that way."

of these monsters had been built and were ready to go. What kind of weaponry would they use? Yamamoto had planned to use conventional bombs. Given the way the war was going downhill for Japan, something much more drastic was needed.

Enter BW. Vice Adm. Jisaburo Ozawa hatched a plan with Shiro Ishii to use the I-400 and the I-401 to deliver germ bombs developed at Unit 731. Fortunately for the United States, Ozawa didn't have the authority to go ahead on his own; he had to run the scheme by a committee. Head of the war plans committee was the chief of the general staff, Gen. Yoshijiro Umezu. Umezu, who would later sign the *Missouri* surrender and subsequently be tried and convicted in the Tokyo War Crimes Trial and sentenced to life, didn't like the idea. In late March 1945 he blackballed it. This extreme kind of warfare was morally unacceptable, he said: "Germ warfare against the United States would escalate to war against all humanity. . . . Japan will earn the derision of the world."

The American general on the front line of Japan's potential BW attack, the one most worried about it, was Douglas MacArthur. As a veteran of World War I, he had seen the effects of poison gas both in its ability to kill and in its pernicious effects on military morale. He had nothing but contempt for the Nobel Prize Committee, which had awarded the 1918 chemistry prize to Fritz Haber, the inventor of poison gas, who in his acceptance speech had had the effrontery to call his chlorine weapons "a higher form of killing." This wasn't killing, this was barbarism.*

Aware that the major cause of death in war is disease—not enemy bullets—MacArthur was always very punctilious about the health of his soldiers. In early 1943 he had established the Combined Advisory Committee on Tropical Medicine, Hygiene and Sanitation to develop preemptive strategies for combating tropical diseases. In less than fifteen months he had reduced the malaria rate by 95 percent. As his troops made their victorious sweep up from Australia through the South Pacific, they conducted blood tests of their Japanese prisoners to see what medicines they were using, and were astonished to find they had been

---

* Haber's wife certainly thought so. Ashamed of her husband's work, she begged him to stop. He refused. The next day, she committed suicide.

inoculated against anthrax. There was no anthrax in the jungle: What was going on? Then it was discovered that a number of these Japanese had served in China at Pingfan and other facilities; now as prisoners they provided enough intelligence to generate eye-popping rumors. On the island of Morotai, American soldiers discovered a field manual on a dead Japanese soldier stating, "Great results can be obtained by contaminating their food and drink by bacterial strategy." On Luzon they captured a document outlining a plan to contaminate the island with cholera. Specific techniques included "spraying bacterial solutions by airplane," "firing shells and bullets containing pathogenic organisms," "dropping ampoules containing bacteria," "dropping infected insects and animals," "spraying powdered bacteria," and "spreading bacteria by agents."

Some of these sprays were actually used. Brig. Gen. Charles Loucks, the head of Pacific theater chemical warfare efforts such as smoke bombs and flamethrowers, had reported that the Japanese had used poison gas against American troops in a few isolated instances in New Guinea. MacArthur, when he got this report, resolved to do nothing retaliatory. The best solution was to stay on the move and keep capturing territory. But back in Washington, General Marshall had other ideas. The chief of staff told David E. Lilienthal, head of the Tennessee Valley Authority (and later head of the Atomic Energy Commission, 1946–51), that he favored the use of poison gas for the invasion of Okinawa. The only reason it wasn't used was opposition from Winston Churchill, who feared the Germans might feel free to do the same against Britain. Nonetheless, despite the views of MacArthur and Admiral Leahy, Marshall went ahead and ordered preparations to be made for BW warfare against Japanese rice crops should an invasion of Japan become necessary.

When MacArthur reached Manila and started making plans for the invasion of Japan, he demanded the services of Murray Sanders, Camp Detrick's top expert in biological warfare, then about to leave for Burma to investigate a plague caused by cholera ampoules dropped from Japanese airplanes. Unlike Marshall, the supreme commander had no intention of using BW, but he did need to know what to expect. Sanders flew to Manila and conducted a four-hour briefing with MacArthur, General

Willoughby, and Dr. Karl Compton, the former president of MIT, then President Truman's personal emissary in charge of reviewing Japanese BW. Compton reported his findings back to the president.

After the atom bombs were dropped and Japan surrendered, MacArthur sent Sanders to Japan a week ahead of him to start looking for Japan's BW criminals, which is why when he landed at Atsugi he asked about Ishii.

But the Japanese were one step ahead of the game. Waiting at the Yokohama dock to greet Sanders was none other than Ryoichi Naito, the man who had tried to bribe the Rockefeller Institute scientist in the parking lot.

This time Naito would be more successful.

ISHII KNEW HE was in deep trouble. No one, not even the emperor, could save him or even think of lifting a finger. He was on his own, the target of a massive manhunt. If he didn't want to spend the rest of his life in a cave somewhere, he would have to do what every "big fish" criminal does when the jig is up: cut a plea deal. He could embarrass a lot of important politicians with what he knew. As the war drew to an end, he got his team together and issued his final command: his comrades in arms were to go into hiding, never again to seek government employment, and never again to contact one another. After they departed the Unit 731 facility at Pingfan, he ordered all the buildings blown up and razed to the ground.

By the time the Russians, who had invaded Manchuria, got to Pingfan, everything was gone. But some evidence still remained: Even though the prisoners' bodies had been burned and then pulverized, skeletons from earlier days remained buried deep under the debris. The bullet holes, knife marks, and chemical residues indicated that this had been more than a lumber mill. Definitive proof came from the animals that the Japanese, in their haste to flee, had released into the countryside: thousands of plague-infested horses, monkeys, dogs, rats, even Mongolian camels.

What exactly had been going on at Pingfan? Allied investigators in Germany had it so much easier: the Germans have a well-known penchant for recording, documenting, and filming everything, so when it came time to prepare evidence for the Nuremberg trials, all the prosecutors had to do was collect and organize the available evidence. In Japan this was not the case. There were hardly any pictures or written records, and Ishii's doctors and lab technicians were lying low. Considering that Ishii's operation employed twenty thousand people in its various hospitals and factories of death in China, Japan, and the South Pacific, this was quite an accomplishment.

Ishii, who by now had escaped back to Japan, resorted to another stunt commonly used by most-wanted criminals. After burying many important documents in the garden of his Tokyo home, he arranged for the local mayor to issue a proclamation declaring that he was dead: He had been shot to death in Manchuria. His friends staged a massive funeral ceremony, complete with mourners, priests, burning incense, and prayers for his departed soul. By all eyewitness accounts it was an elaborate and moving event with many tears shed by mourners glancing at the sealed coffin.

Hearing that Ishii had beaten him to the grim reaper did not please MacArthur. Further news that he might have pulled a fast one made him even angrier. SCAP got an anonymous letter, written in Japanese, saying that the funeral had been a fake and that the writer, a former associate of Ishii, would reveal all if MacArthur's office would place a specially worded advertisement in a certain Japanese newspaper within three days. However, by the time SCAP translated this bombshell letter and got it to MacArthur, the deadline had passed. An utter and complete foul-up: SCAP never heard from the anonymous source again.

Frustrated that there would be no Ishii, MacArthur called Sanders into his office. Their best lead was Naito, and he was not being very cooperative. The investigation into BW was going nowhere; it was now time to use some imagination. MacArthur instructed Sanders to bluff: The next time Sanders met with Naito, he was to make his best effort to look worn out and dejected. He would tell Naito he had some very bad news: MacArthur was sending him home because he was being too weak and soft, and a Russian was replacing him.

The bluff worked, but for unexpected reasons. What the Americans didn't know was that Ryoichi Naito was hardly some bumbling scientist who had offered a bribe in New York City; he was a top man in Ishii's operation. No way could a man who knew so much let himself fall into the hands of the Russians and face a torture chamber. Within twenty-four hours he returned with a twelve-page handwritten memorandum, along with a pile of important documents. He was now being what MacArthur would call "a good boy": a cooperative witness.

But progress was still excruciatingly slow: Sanders was not an aggressive questioner able to unravel the nasty chiaroscuro of Japanese BW. He had none of a prosecutor's skills in asking leading questions. There are two basic ways to get information out of a reluctant defendant: Use torture, or provide immunity. MacArthur rejected the former: "We're not given to torture," he told Sanders. That left MacArthur with the very distasteful possibility that he would have to grant immunity to Ishii—assuming he was still alive—a man he must have despised as the lowest of the low, lacking any shred of honor. Be that as it may, as a general MacArthur had to recognize that Unit 731's research had serious potential military value; the Joint Chiefs wanted it, and his job was to get it—if possible.

Over at his hotel, Murray Sanders was getting ready to go to bed one evening when he heard a noise outside his room. Startled at seeing a Japanese face in the window, he quickly reached under his pillow and pulled out his gun. Keeping his revolver pointed at the intruder, he opened the window and ordered the man into the room. Apparently the man had climbed down a water pipe to reach Sanders's room in order to smuggle a blueprint for him. The drawing was of a bomb designed to carry biological germs, called the Uji bomb, and more than a hundred of them had been made. Over the next hour the visitor revealed further details about Japan's biological warfare, refused to give his name, climbed out the window, and vanished into the night, never to be seen again.

The next morning a shaken Sanders met with MacArthur. After hearing the story and lighting his pipe, MacArthur explained to Sanders: "We need more evidence. We simply can't act on that. Keep going. Ask more questions. And keep quiet about it."

Discretion was the key. In early 1946, knowing from Naito how little information the Americans had and how anxious they were to get it, a man surprised everyone by rising from the dead and walking in the front door, very much alive, Shiro Ishii himself. He proved to be sharp and shrewd: No matter how intense the questioning, he still managed to be vague. After numerous interrogations he put his conditions on the table: He wanted to be hired by the United States as a biological weapons expert! "I have given a great deal of thought to tactical problems in the defense of BW," he announced. "I have made studies on the best agents to be employed in various regions and in cold climates. I can write volumes about BW, including the little-thought-of strategic and tactical employment."

No doubt he could, but at a high price: He wanted a written promise of immunity. There was also a risk: What if he didn't deliver? He then played his trump card: "My experience would be a useful advantage to the United States in the event of a war with the Soviet Union."

DEALING WITH EVIL is never a pleasant experience. MacArthur must have choked at this sadist's consummate arrogance, but as supreme commander he had larger concerns than just putting Ishii in jail. The war with Japan was over, Russia was now the enemy, and Ishii had a lot of useful information about military medicine, both defensive and offensive, that was impossible to get in the United States (U.S. law prohibited medical experiments on live patients and any dispersal of harmful vaccines on U.S. soil). If the Russians got hold of this research, they could have a fearsome military weapon. The appeal of germ warfare, unlike the atom bomb, was that it was not only cheap, it was deniable and very difficult to trace. Finally there was the emperor to think about. Ishii, given the scale of his operation, clearly had powerful friends high up in the Japanese government, including possibly the emperor. If Hirohito knew, or if Ishii came out claiming he knew, about Japan's weapons of mass destruction and had sanctioned their use against the United States, there would be a huge hue and cry in America and certainly a congressional investigation—and a call for the emperor's head.

Complicating MacArthur's dilemma was the war crimes trial, the International Military Tribunal for the Far East (IMTFE), which had already opened on May 3, 1946. The Joint Chiefs and MacArthur didn't want any information about biological weapons to become public. On June 23 MacArthur cabled Washington that any pressure to put Ishii on trial for war crimes "will endanger present status of valuable intelligence" relating to biological warfare. A month later he had his instructions from Washington: "Under present circumstances intelligence relating to research and development in the field of science and war material should not be disclosed to nations other than the British Commonwealth." Another cable from Washington stated:

> Since it is believed that the USSR possesses only a small portion of this technical information, and since any "war crimes" trial would completely reveal such data to all nations, it is felt that publicity must be avoided in interests of defense and security of the United States. . . . The value to the U.S. of Japanese BW data is of such importance to national security as to far outweigh the value accruing from "war crimes" prosecution.

Unlike U.S. experiments performed on animals, this information was unique: "the only known source of data from scientifically controlled experiments showing the direct effect of BW agents on man."

In the meantime Sanders went back to America and was succeeded by another American investigator from Camp Detrick, Lt. Col. Arvo Thompson. Unlike Sanders, he refused to use Ryoichi Naito as his lead translator/interviewer. Naito was the last person he wanted in the room. Thompson, using American translators, spent many hours with Ishii and concluded that the man was being "guarded, concise, and often evasive." In other words, Ishii was lying. The investigation dragged on and on. The major sources of leads were letters addressed to SCAP, but unfortunately, in what apparently was a widespread Japanese cultural leaning toward secrecy, almost all of them were anonymous, thus hindering attempts to follow up and verify. Anonymous letters, hearsay affidavits, and rumors do not make for a sound investigation any more than did the mystery man who came shimmying down the water pipe to Murray Sanders' window.

The Joint Chiefs ordered MacArthur not to put Ishii on trial. They sent a memo to Tokyo instructing the BW investigation to be placed under the control of G-2, the intelligence arm of the U.S. Army: "The utmost secrecy is essential in order to protect the interests of the United States."

Ishii still continued to hem and haw, offering no hard information of value. No matter how tempting it must have been for MacArthur to have him subjected to torture, no efforts at coercion were made. Even though he was a supreme commander and could do virtually anything he wanted, even in secret, there were certain things he would not do. The only tool left at his disposal was a plea deal. On May 6, 1947, he cabled Washington: "Additional data, possibly some statements from Ishii probably can be obtained by informing Japanese involved that information will be retained in intelligence channels and will not be employed as 'War Crimes' evidence."

On June 23 a meeting took place in Washington to discuss the immunity request. Present in the room were senior members of the War, State, and Justice Departments. At the meeting it was informally agreed to accept the recommendation that all information be held in intelligence channels and not be used to prosecute war crimes trials. The decision was then kicked upstairs to the Joint Chiefs of Staff to implement. The Joint Chiefs, however, do not approve political policies, which meant that final authorization would have to come from President Truman.

For the rest of 1947 MacArthur's investigators went back and forth with Ishii. Where's the hard information on your BW?, they demanded. Where's the signed agreement?, responded Ishii.

Then an act of terrorism occurred, dominating Japanese newspapers for all of 1948. Fear gripped the population. Should such an attack happen again, widespread panic might ensue. For an occupation responsible for the health and safety of the Japanese people, this terrorist act was like a blow to the solar plexus, a threat to the very legitimacy of the occupation. The White House would have to make a decision.

18

"Cherry Blossoms at Night"

T HE STREETS OF Tokyo were cold and muddy on a late January day in 1948 when a well-dressed doctor walked into the Teikoku Bank at the three o'clock closing hour. He was from the Health Ministry, he said, and he had come to inoculate the bank employees against a local outbreak of dysentery. Stacks of money tempted the eye: 125,000 yen in the bank's open safe and 250,000 yen from the day's deposits piled high on the table in the middle of the room, waiting to be double-counted. This was a new drug, the doctor informed the employees, so they were to follow instructions carefully: Take the first drug by pouring two drops onto the middle of the tongue and swallow quickly before it got diluted by saliva, then after a minute drink a mouthful of the second drug from a teacup, and wash the cup immediately. The sixteen employees did as they were told, and as they collapsed and fell to the floor, the doctor grabbed the 125,000 yen from the safe, stuffed it in his medical suitcase, and beat a hasty retreat out the door. Why he didn't take the other 250,000 yen was never explained.

Ten minutes later one of the employees managed to crawl out into the street, clutching her throat and gasping for breath. Within hours twelve of the sixteen employees were dead, and newspapers had a field day. The mass murder became a sensation, and for months the Teikoku Bank poisoning dominated the news. The Japanese police assigned no less than twenty thousand out of one hundred thousand men solely to finding the killer. But because MacArthur has ordered the police force to be purged of militarists and undesirables, the majority of policemen were brand-new recruits who didn't even know how to lift a fingerprint, much less solve a difficult murder case. Because the teacups had been washed, and poison inside the body changes in chemical composition, identifying the specific agent was virtually impossible. It appeared to be a form of potassium cyanide, but nobody was sure. The Japanese police were stumped.

Across the street from General MacArthur's office was the Allied Occupation Public Safety Division (PSD), responsible for transforming Japan's police force into an effective crime-fighting unit. The PSD sprang into action. It was clear this was no normal bank robbery: Only a third of the cash was taken. Upon learning that there were two earlier instances of a health examiner walking into a bank branch and inoculating bank employees, though with no harmful results, the PSD concluded that this was a medical crime, not a financial one. Some madman was experimenting, trying to find the best way to kill people. The Americans did their own analysis of the minute portions of poison evidence and concluded it was not potassium cyanide but something quite different: acetone cyanohydrin, a very exotic poison that dissolves in less than sixty minutes, leaving virtually no trace.

Ishii, under house arrest by SCAP, was read the riot act: One of his men must be doing this, and it better be stopped, now. Ishii, who had been playing games with the Americans for almost two years, reminded them he wanted ironclad guarantees of freedom from war crimes prosecution. It was now time for the White House to make a decision. On March 13, 1948, the Joint Chiefs of Staff cabled MacArthur, granting immunity: "Information obtained from Ishii and associates may be retained in intelligence channels."

SCAP, of course, wanted this arrangement kept quiet.

So neither SCAP nor Ishii was happy when the Japanese police zeroed in on a doctor who had worked in Manchuria in Unit 731 and who matched the physical description given by the four survivors. The PSD stepped in and announced that the occupation authorities were holding all Ishii personnel under "special protection." At a meeting at PSD's offices the Americans surprised the head of the Japanese police by introducing him to the mastermind, Ishii. Ishii, a smooth talker, convinced the police chief that the police were going after the wrong man and should lay off. The Americans, who didn't want anyone to know any more than necessary about biological warfare, breathed a sigh of relief.

In August the police arrested a man long considered to be a serious suspect: Sadamichi Hirasawa, a struggling artist with an arrest record, who confessed after sixty-two interrogations during thirty-five days' confinement in a police station. No matter that he promptly recanted afterward, or that the signature at the bottom of the confession was not his, or that none of the four poison survivors could identify him in a police lineup, his arrest brought much-needed closure to a case causing the police a lot of headaches over their inability to solve a headline-grabbing crime. Hirasawa was due to be sentenced for execution any day. For unknown reasons he was not sentenced until 1954, and he was never executed. He spent practically all the rest of his life on death row—thirty-two years, a world record—until finally pardoned by the emperor in 1986. He died a year later, age ninety-five, proclaiming his innocence to the very end.

The mystery killer, whoever he was, never struck again.

THE RUSSIANS, PROBABLY because serious biological warfare had been conducted so close to their country's eastern border, wanted to put Ishii on trial themselves. The Americans refused. In a brief to MacArthur dated March 27, 1947, Charles Willoughby had written: "The United States has primary interest, has already interrogated this man, and his information is held by the U.S. Chemical Corps as TOP SECRET. The Russian [chief investigator] has made several attempts to get at this man. We have stalled. He now hopes to make his point by suddenly claiming the Japanese expert as a war criminal. Joint Chiefs of Staff direct that this not be done." MacArthur, because he headed a joint command, couldn't keep the Russians away from Ishii, but he could have his legal staff coach Ishii on what to say and what not to say to the Russians. Here Ishii—finally—kept his end of the bargain.

In 1949 the Russians went ahead with a full-blown trial of twelve Japanese military doctors associated with Unit 731. It was the only official inquiry conducted by any of the Allies, and thanks in part to presumed Russian methods of interrogation best not described, the information revealed was chilling. Ishii, it was proved beyond doubt, was a sociopath. He had proposed using biological weapons at Iwo Jima, only to be denied by the Tokyo surgeon general's office. He had proposed a germ attack on the West Coast of the United States; it was blocked by former prime minister Hideki Tojo. Then came his most blatant effort—what he called "Cherry Blossoms at Night"—an attempt to launch his latest germs on the United States in the waning days of the war. It would be a full-scale attack to bring America to its knees: Planes would attack San Diego with anthrax spores, sending the nation into panic. The attack was scheduled for September 22, 1945.

Before it could take place, America used the atom bomb on August 6 and August 9. President Truman had beaten the Japanese to the punch. Did he know specifically about "Cherry Blossoms"? No. But he certainly knew about all the gas masks in the White House. Truman also knew about Japan's desperate BW efforts from his friend Dr. Karl Compton, and that biological weapons would undoubtedly be used by the Japanese in defending the homeland. He certainly shared the pugnacity of Admiral Leahy, chief of staff to the president from 1942 to 1949 and America's highest-ranking military officer (even higher than Marshall, Eisenhower, or MacArthur), who had gone on record with FDR, during their trip to Honolulu for the MacArthur-Nimitz conference in July 1944, that any American plans to use germs and poison "would violate every Christian ethic I have ever heard of and all of the known laws of war." Yet in none of the volumes of Truman's memoirs is there any mention of this most sinister and terrifying weapon of the Second World War. "Why has Truman never mentioned the great war secret?" a British journalist asked years later. "Is it possible that the real planned reason he dropped the bomb on Hiroshima was the knowledge of the existence and planned use of frightful weapons developed over nine or ten years by the scientists of Japan?"

In 1950 the Russians released a partial 535-page trial transcript, *Materials on the Trial of Former Servicemen of the Japanese Army Charged with Manufacturing and Employing Bacteriological Weapons*. Among the evidence uncovered in court was the claim that the emperor had met Ishii twice and personally approved the construction of the facility at Pingfan (it was never disclosed precisely what kind of medical research Unit 731 was to be used for). Also mentioned was the fact that the emperor's brother Prince Mikasa had toured the Pingfan facility and witnessed experiments of prisoners choking on poison gas. Along with gruesome photographs, the trial revealed numerous crimes, including the fatal infection of more than one hundred thousand people with cholera in China.* It put to rest the American pretense that no BW offenses had been committed, and proved MacArthur's headquarters wrong when it reported that "the Japanese had done some experimentation with animals but that there was no evidence they ever had used human beings." To the contrary, said the Russians, Pingfan was "the Auschwitz before Auschwitz," a ruthless killing machine. According to one of the confessions:

> If a prisoner survived the inoculation of lethal bacteria, this did not save him from a repetition of the experiments, which were continued until death from infection supervened. The infected people were given medical treatment in order to test various methods of cure, they were fed normally, and after they had fully recovered, were used for the next experiment, but infected with another kind of germ. At any rate, no one ever left this death factory alive.

MacArthur and the Joint Chiefs downplayed the Russian trial by claiming it was a show of Communist propaganda. Such a blatant misstatement was clearly intentional. It was in no one's interest to make public how close the Japanese had come to terrorizing America. For almost two hundred years the United States had thought itself protected by two big oceans. No more: Any day hordes of balloons could come floating across the ocean, carrying firebombs and germs. The Russian trial revealed the magnitude of Japanese crimes against

---

*The number has continued to grow over the years as more research has been conducted. The commonly accepted figure, according to the International Symposium on the Crimes of Bacteriological Warfare held in China in 2002, is 580,000.

humanity, especially Ishii's vow to attack America with his "Cherry Blossoms": "In the summer of 1945, we shall have to employ our last means, among them the bacteriological weapon, in order to turn the tide in Japan's favor."

However, the Russians did in fact use their trial largely for propaganda purposes. Despite their heinous crimes against humanity, the dozen Japanese scientists tried and convicted were not put to death; they were imprisoned, and by 1956 most of them had been repatriated to Japan. To American intelligence, the short prison sentences suggested that the Russians had used the scientists for information just as the Americans had, and that MacArthur had probably been right in going along with the Joint Chiefs in granting leniency to Ishii. The horrors of BW were so unimaginable that they justified using extreme means to gain access to Unit 731's trove of secrets, especially after reading paragraphs from the Russian transcript like the following: "Experts have calculated . . . that it was capable of breeding, in the course of one production cycle, lasting only a few days, no less than 30,000,000 billion microbes. . . . That explains why . . . bacteria quantities [are given] in kilograms, thus referring to the weight of the thick, creamy bacteria mass skimmed directly from the surface of the culture medium."

With Ishii's cooperation, American investigators uncovered not only the treasure trove in his backyard but also another six hundred pages of reports and eight thousand slides of body parts, pathological diseases, and autopsy reports stashed away in temples and buried in the mountains of southern Japan. There was research data on anthrax, botulism, cholera, frostbite, gas gangrene, influenza, meningococcal diseases, mucins, mustard gas, scarlet fever, smallpox, tick encephalitis, tuberculosis, tularemia, typhoid fever, and typhus. The investigators' summary report, presented to MacArthur by General Willoughby, was read carefully and passed on to the experts at Camp Detrick in the hope that America forewarned would be America forearmed. Observed Dr. Edward Hill, Camp Detrick's technical director, who conducted the final investigation of Ishii:

Evidence gathered in this investigation has greatly supplemented and amplified previous aspects of this field. It represents data which have been obtained by Japanese scientists at the expenditure of many millions of dollars and years of work. Information has accrued with respect to human susceptibility to those diseases as indicated by specific infectious doses of bacteria. Such information could not be obtained in our own laboratories because of scruples attached to human experimentation.

The report went on to say: "It is hoped . . . that every effort will be made to prevent this information from falling into other hands."

Under MacArthur this was successfully done.

Distasteful though it must have been to make a plea deal, MacArthur's foremost priority was to do whatever it took to forestall the Russians, who were so anxious to get their hands on BW technology. This concern was well founded. Over the next forty years the Soviet Union would plunge ahead recklessly and build up the world's largest BW operation, with dubious safeguards, resulting in the 1979 outbreak of anthrax at Sverdlovsk, an accident that came to be known as the "biological Chernobyl."

As for the Americans who got hold of Ishii's research after so much effort had been expended, the result turned out to be a dud: There wasn't much there. The scientists at Camp Detrick spent a year poring over all the reports and photographs and came away singularly unimpressed. The Unit 731 experiments had been performed under sloppy conditions, the blood and tissue samples had been tested many hours after the experiments, thus making them worthless, and no new scientific revelations had emerged. The United States, the scientists concluded, was far ahead of Japan in understanding germs, disease, and military medicine. The four trunkloads of Ishii's files were promptly put into storage, never to be looked at again.

19

The Nuremberg of the East

Asia under the Japanese was a charnel house of atrocities. As soon as the war ended, evidence of war crimes began piling up, in mountains. POWs, civilian internees, and Asian natives starved, beaten, tortured, shot, beheaded. The water cure. Electric shock. Cannibalism. Men strung up over open flames or coiled in barbed wire and rolled along the ground, nails torn out, balls burned with cigarettes, dicks cut off and stuffed in mouths. Women dragged naked behind motorcycles, raped and ripped open, babies skewered on bayonets.

THE STORIES REACHING the supreme commander's desk were too sickening to read. No country in the world ever inflicted the human brutality Japan did on its neighbors: more than seventeen million people killed from 1931 to 1945, 95 percent of them civilians. And where was bushido, the honor code of the Japanese warrior? The conditions in Japanese POW camps made those of the Nazis pale by comparison. In German-run POW camps the death rate was 4 percent; in Japanese camps it was 27—almost seven times worse. And much of it was due to deliberate, outright sadism, like the prison guards having a contest to see who could lop off the most heads in a minute.

In January 1946 the supreme commander had issued a directive ordering the establishment of an international military court to try Japanese war criminals. The same day he approved a charter, based on Nuremberg, specifying the crimes to be charged and how the tribunal was to function and be organized. He appointed a panel of judges from eleven countries: Australia, Canada, China, France, British India, Netherlands, New Zealand, Philippines, Russia, and two from the United States, with Sir William Webb of Australia as president of the tribunal.

On May 3 of that year the prosecution made the opening statement of its case against twenty-eight war criminals. Already MacArthur had endured cries of "victor's justice" for his signing off on the guilty verdicts on the two Japanese generals Yamashita and Homma. With great reluctance he had agreed to a visit from Homma's wife, a very smart and articulate woman who spoke flawless English. She began by saying she hoped the trial hadn't been too much of a burden on him. That ticked him off, and he told her brusquely she needn't concern herself with how he did his job. The emperor had handled his situation so much better: Facing his judge, jury, and executioner in Douglas MacArthur, he had struck the right tone of humility and managed not to step in any minefields. Accepting full responsibility and acting like a leader, he had earned MacArthur's respect. The supreme commander would protect him and had succeeded in doing so—thus far. This trial could be a problem. Any one of the defendants could try to save his neck by pointing to the emperor and saying he was the one who gave the orders for war, in which case the courtroom would erupt and MacArthur would have a real mess on his hands. A lot of people among the Allies—especially the Chinese and the Russians—wanted the emperor's head.

Many people questioned the validity of the trial itself. Already this was happening at Nuremberg, now more than halfway over (November 20, 1945–October 1, 1946), where the victors put key figures of the losing nation on trial not only for conventional war crimes but also for "crimes against peace" and "crimes against humanity," two new and broadly defined crimes. Legal purists said this was ipso facto or "retroactive" justice, putting someone on trial for something that formerly had not been a crime. This, of course, was a specious argument, the kind of legal obfuscation that drove MacArthur up the wall. Rape, murder, wanton slaughter, genocide, killing hostages, violating Red Cross regulations, torture, and mutilation are war crimes, plain and simple. What the Nuremberg Trials contributed to legal theory was the application of precepts of criminal law to war crimes: If a person planned such crimes, or knew about such crimes and did nothing to stop them, or was in a position to know about them and deliberately avoided knowing (in law this is called "willful blindness"), then he became an accessory, a coconspirator, and therefore just as guilty as

the direct participant. Also established at Nuremberg was the principle that atrocities could be blamed on the specific individuals involved, not just on an amorphous entity like "the state."

The Japanese, like the Germans, had violated fundamental precepts
of humanity, certainly of every religion. This trial in Tokyo would be
the Nuremberg of the East.

MacArthur knew what was coming: The Japanese defendants never
had a chance for a fair trial; from day one the deck was stacked against
them. Let the lawyers fight that one out. One of the American lawyers
generously provided for the defense had already tried that stunt, saying
a fair trial was impossible because none of the judges were from neutral nations. Prosecutor Joseph Keenan had put him in his place, saying
no neutral nation could be found "until men landed on Mars." A more
serious threat to the trial's legitimacy would be the Japanese defense,
the only one even remotely possible: Japan had waged a war of defense
against the Allies, who had cut off its access to raw materials. Carried to
an extreme, this argument could claim it was the Americans who were
responsible for the attack on Pearl Harbor.

JAPAN NEEDED TO be taught the notion of personal responsibility. In a
military setting this is known as command responsibility, whereby an
officer is responsible for the conduct of his soldiers. It is an important
tradition in the U.S. Army: Gen. George B. McClellan, as commander
of the Union forces in 1861, warned all his officers they would "be held
responsible for punishing aggression by those under their command."
McClellan further directed that military commissions be established to
punish any soldiers who might engage in conduct "in contravention to
the established rules of war."

To set a precedent that would shape the outcome of most of the 2,200
war crimes trials soon to come throughout Asia and the Pacific, MacArthur personally took charge of the first two cases, both of them heard
by an American military tribunal rather than an international tribunal.
The trials would take place in Manila, where the atrocities had taken
place and anti-Japanese hatred was at a fever pitch. He instructed his
commander in the Philippines to appoint the prosecutor and five judges

from the ranks of the U.S. Army. None of the generals had any experience in the hand-to-hand combat or guerrilla warfare that defined the circumstances of the two defendants; they were "desk" generals. More important, none of them had any legal experience. Even though the rules stipulated that "if feasible, one or more members of a commission should have had legal training," MacArthur—for reasons he never disclosed—did not find it feasible.

But he did find it feasible to use legal gymnastics to protect himself. In a measure he carried out with what the State Department's George Kennan denounced as "flealike agility," MacArthur ordered war crimes trials by U.S. military courts to be placed under his jurisdiction as supreme commander rather than as a U.S. commander, thus further insulating himself from U.S. civil law and any possible overturn by the Supreme Court. Like any good general, MacArthur thought two steps ahead.

At the *Missouri* surrender signing, MacArthur had chosen Arthur Percival and Jonathan Wainwright to stand right behind him. Seeing the two generals they had earlier defeated on the other side of the table must have had a powerful impact on the humbled Japanese officials. The very next day, September 3, MacArthur had Percival and Wainwright flown down to Manila to witness a second surrender, this one of Percival's nemesis, Gen. Tomoyuki Yamashita. In 1942, with only 30,000 troops, Yamashita—"the Tiger of Malaya"—had captured Singapore in a stunning victory over the 85,000 British troops under Percival. It was the most shameful Allied debacle of the Pacific War after Pearl Harbor. In fact it was so embarrassing that when Prime Minister Winston Churchill informed the House of Commons, he asked the members to keep the details secret lest the news affect wartime morale. In 1944 Yamashita returned from a tour of duty in Manchuria to take over the defense of the Philippines against MacArthur's invading forces, and after heavy fighting retreated 150 miles into the mountains to conduct guerrilla warfare. In the meantime a naval group under Rear Adm. Sanji Iwabuchi, contravening Yamashita's explicit orders that hostilities be kept to a bare minimum, proceeded to slaughter 100,000 Filipinos in the infamous "Manila Massacre."

MacArthur, anxious to accommodate the Philippine people who

wanted revenge, could do nothing about Iwabuchi: He was dead. So he arrested Yamashita. For the supreme commander it was an opportunity to exorcise "Yamashita's Ghost," to bury the memory of his own two black marks: the Philippine "Pearl Harbor," where the Japanese caught all his planes on the ground and bombed them, and his flight to Australia, leaving 78,000 men behind.

The prosecutor filed a bill of sixty-four particulars (instances of alleged crimes). The defense had only two weeks to prepare for the trial. Yamashita's three American lawyers worked around the clock, only to get hit with another fifty-nine particulars three days before the trial, mostly involving new places, new persons, and new witnesses. The defense lawyers filed a motion for an extension, saying they needed more time to prepare; the judges said no, the trial would go ahead as scheduled, and they would reconsider the request at the end of the trial (it was denied). During the trial, standards of evidence were lax. Rumors, hearsay, uncorroborated statements, and anonymous witnesses became the norm: "He told me he was not sure, but he believed" . . . "I guess" . . . "I heard it from somebody."

Even with so many charges and low standards of "proof," the prosecutors had a hard time establishing Yamashita's guilt. He wasn't in Manila when the events happened, he had given written orders to treat prisoners decently, and communications in the mountains had completely broken down. The prosecutors argued he was guilty of criminal negligence for not controlling Iwabuchi, a man he had never met. In fact Iwabuchi didn't even report to Yamashita, the commanding Japanese general in charge of the Philippines; he reported to the Japanese navy. The trial became a circus: Day after day the prosecutors hauled into the courtroom a parade of Filipinos telling gut-wrenching stories of rape and beheadings. Observed a journalist in the London *Daily Express*: "Yamashita trial continued today—but it isn't a trial. I doubt it is even a hearing. Yesterday his name was mentioned once. Today it wasn't brought up at all." In the middle of the proceedings the head judge got a cablegram from MacArthur demanding to know why everything was taking so long, and why Yamashita hadn't been convicted yet.

When the judges brought the trial to an end, they announced they would have a decision in three days, on December 7, 1945 (the anniversary of Pearl Harbor). How did they know it would be exactly three days? They needed to consider and weigh 400,000 pages of testimony and 423 exhibits. In the interim the twelve international newspaper reporters covering the trial took a straw vote: All twelve predicted that Yamashita would be acquitted.

The verdict: guilty. The sentence: death by hanging. A petition for clemency signed by eighty thousand supporters of Yamashita was delivered to MacArthur; he rejected it. Yamashita's American lawyers then took the case to the U.S. Supreme Court. The Secretary of War suggested to MacArthur that he postpone the Yamashita execution until the Supreme Court had had the opportunity to decide what to do about the case. MacArthur refused. The War Department then overruled him and issued a direct order. This time MacArthur obeyed.

The U.S. Supreme Court voted 6–2 not to interfere in a court-martial proceeding, but not without the two dissenting justices issuing two of the most blistering opinions ever to come out of the Supreme Court (one of them, Frank Murphy, happened to be the former U.S. governor general of the Philippines: he called the trial "legalized lynching"). Focusing on the trial itself rather than the issue of jurisdiction, the two justices wrote a forty-five-page memorandum charging MacArthur with undue haste and deprival of basic rights. MacArthur, after receiving the verdict by cable and before he had a chance to read the dissenting memorandum, which arrived by plane a week later, announced that "the results are beyond challenge." Yamashita requested he be permitted the more honorable form of execution, being shot rather than hanged; MacArthur refused. In February 1946 Yamashita went to the gallows.

The *New York Times*, in explaining its opinion that "a fair verdict was reached," implied that the real issue was not justice but the need for a conviction, given all the allegations "too well documented in the broken bodies of their living victims and the mutilated corpses that lie in the hundreds of thousands of graves in Asia and the islands of the Pacific. . . . The trial of a general officer for the crimes committed by his troops sets an international precedent. It is high time."

MacArthur, prone to half-truths and evasions when convenient, announced that reviewing the sentencing of Yamashita was one of the most difficult decisions he ever had to make. One can only admire a man so capable of crocodile tears when the occasion demanded. But then, are not all great leaders great actors? Such a tribute in earlier days had been made by contemporaries of both George Washington and Franklin D. Roosevelt. Had not John Adams said the president was "one of the great actors of the age"? Had not Orson Welles, when he visited the White House for the first time, told the president: "There are two great actors in America, and it is a fine thing we have now met." MacArthur, too, could rise to that level of leadership prowess.

The hanging of Yamashita was the beginning of MacArthur's efforts to teach the Japanese a lesson. There was another general he was even more anxious to convict: Masaharu Homma, the man who had beaten him at Bataan and Wainwright at Corregidor, now accused of having ordered the infamous Bataan Death March. Homma's defense was that he had not known there were so many prisoners (he thought they numbered 15,000, not 78,000) and he had instructed that the prisoners receive decent treatment. The court refused to buy it: Homma, unlike Yamashita, had been in the immediate vicinity. All he had to do was keep his eyes open and see what was going on. He didn't. This made him guilty of failing to provide even the barest minimum of troop supervision. Once again the U.S. Supreme Court ruled 6–2 not to intervene, and MacArthur made no move to reduce the verdict. (He did make one concession to Homma's wife: He allowed the general to be shot rather than hanged.)

By these two trials MacArthur firmly established the principle of command accountability. On a battlefield this makes sense. But in a situation where the commanding general is far removed from the front and responsibilities are divided (as in the Yamashita case), the issue becomes murky. What about field generals who disobey written orders and conduct the actual atrocities? Is it fair to indict a senior commander if he did not order atrocities, did not know about them, or even lacked the means to stop them? By MacArthur's logic, violations of the Hague Convention, the Geneva Conventions, and other international codes of warfare could be traced up to a high-level commander if such commander had responsibility and did nothing to cure these violations. This far-reaching doctrine was subsequently applied in the 1990s to dozens of trials in the international tribunal for the former Yugoslavia, and also adopted by the International Criminal Court in The Hague in 2002.

However, what might therefore be called the MacArthur principle of command accountability remains unresolved to this day, as demonstrated by My Lai in Vietnam and Abu Ghraib in Iraq. If MacArthur had been running the U.S. Army in 2006, presumably a top general would have been put on trial for not knowing what was going on at the Abu Ghraib prison.

MACARTHUR WAS NOT present at the prosecutor's opening presentation. But his seven-year-old son, Arthur IV, was, eager to catch all the drama. The chief prosecutor, U.S. lawyer Joseph Keenan, strutted around the room, throwing thunderbolts. Referring to the Yamashita decision, he announced: "Individuals may be punished by a military tribunal for violations of international law, which, even though never codified by an international legislative body, have been sufficiently developed and crystallized to make them cognizable by courts of justice." He continued: "The personal liability of these high-ranking civil officials is one of the most important, and perhaps the only new question under international law, to be presented to this tribunal."

Not so, thought Japanese defense counsel Kenzo Takayanagi. A year later, when he finally got his chance to make the defense presentation, he said that any concept that crimes against peace incur personal responsibility is "perfectly revolutionary. . . . It is the general principle of the law of nations that duties and responsibilities are placed on states and nations and not on individuals."

One can only imagine MacArthur's reaction to such groupthink talk of personal immunity. The supreme commander took this trial very seriously. In his instructions to the American prosecutors, he insisted that no case be brought unless there was absolute confidence there would be a conviction. He wanted this trial to be over in three months as everyone expected. He also wanted no embarrassing acquittals that would make the prosecutors look like fools. The accounts of Japanese atrocities in Asia and the Pacific were so abundant and self-evident that anyone would conclude beyond a shadow of doubt that these incidents were a pattern, not an aberration, and that Japan had engaged in a deliberate and consistent program of destruction and brutality.

MacArthur did have one concern, however, and it was a major one: that the emperor not be dragged into this trial. Back in mid-September 1945, Prince Naruhiko Higashikuni, a distant uncle of the emperor and temporary prime minister for fifty-four days, had given a press conference. "The most interesting questions," said a *New York Times* editorial, "relate to the Emperor's role at the outset of the war." The newspaper was not about to let Higashikuni—much less his esteemed nephew—off the hook:

> The Premier [Higashikuni] asserts that the Emperor was "deceived." If so, it took the Emperor three and a half years and a complete Japanese defeat to discover the deception and to break with the deceivers. The Premier denies that the Emperor is a war criminal; even a negative association of the Japanese god with crime must set the Japanese thinking. But if he isn't, he is at the very least an accomplice after the fact. And the accomplice is usually regarded as no less guilty than the original perpetrator.

Complicity would become a major issue in the Tokyo War Crimes Trial, formally called the International Military Tribunal for the Far East (IMTFE). The first count of the indictment read as follows: "All the accused . . . participated . . . in the formulation or execution of a common plan or conspiracy, and are responsible for all acts performed by any person in execution of such plan."

"Responsible"—that was the key issue. The question then became: who is responsible? How far up or down the command line does responsibility go? Organizations vary greatly in their fluidity: some are tightly controlled, others are very loose. Complicating this question is the confusion caused by war, where organizational discipline can fall apart, sometimes completely. It is to the advantage of prosecutors to ignore context and simply cast a wide net as if everything was going according to "plan." "For all acts performed by any person" is standard prosecutorial language. The chief prosecutor, Joseph Keenan, said: "All the accused together with other persons." And who were these "other persons"? Keenan claimed they were "the large number of persons who might properly have been charged in this indictment." Still, who were they? Where had this "might properly" idea come from? Why had this "large number of persons" not been indicted, too? Keenan was essentially telling the Japanese he would be indicting a lot of other people, whenever he felt like it, whomever he felt like going after. The effect, carefully calculated, was chilling. Every Japanese military commander, ever senior government official knew he could be next.

The twenty-eight defendants included fifteen senior army officers, three admirals, five diplomats, four senior government officials, and one civilian. There were so many defendants, many of them playing a small role, that the attorneys constantly had to look at the official seating diagram to identify the defendants in question. Every group trial needs "a big fish," a man everyone loves to hate, like ancient Romans pointing their thumbs down at a fallen gladiator in the Coliseum. Nuremberg had Hermann Göring, Tokyo had Hideki Tojo. Tojo was charged with the Pearl Harbor attack and waging war in the absence of a declaration of war—a plain violation of the 1929 Hague Convention to which Japan had been a party. As the most visible leader of the war effort, Tojo had become the most hated man in the country, a convenient punching bag for Japanese to expiate their shame. Knowing what was coming, the day before he was due to enter prison and await trial, he swallowed a lethal dose of poison. Before it took full effect, American doctors got a hold of him and pumped out his stomach. Now under twenty-four-hour guard, he would be Joseph Keenan's prize prisoner. General Eichelberger was not so sure: better Tojo had succeeded, said Eichelberger, and saved the Americans a lot of trouble. Like the Supreme Commander, Eichelberger wanted the trial over with, the sooner the better.

It was not to be. The trial went on far beyond Nuremberg. Whereas the Nuremberg trial ended in ten months (December 1945–October 1946), this one lasted almost thirty-one months (April 1946–November 1948). State Department envoy William Sebald attended the opening day and had enough of it; he never returned.

Why did it take so long? Six months into the trial, MacArthur had a meeting with one of the most respected judges, Bernard V. A. Röling of the Netherlands. MacArthur expressed his impatience: "How long do you think the trial will last?" he asked.

"If the prosecution continues to proceed as it does now," Röling told him, "the prosecution phase will last a year and a 'fair trial' demands that the defense have about the same time at its disposal."

Röling was right. When the defense got the opportunity to present its case in April 1947, a year had passed and the international political dynamic had changed dramatically. China was turning Communist. The defense lawyers stalled every way they could, filing numerous motions in the expectation that the Allies would fall out among themselves and China, the United States, and Japan would align themselves against the Soviet Union, thereby enhancing their clients' prospects for leniency. Playing along were the defendants and defense witnesses, delivering meandering testimony. Observed Judge Röling, fed up: They responded to cross-examination "with prolix equivocations and evasions."

MacArthur was not happy, but there was little he could do. This was an international tribunal, consisting of a difficult judge from France and an even more difficult judge from British India who had serious issues about British colonialism and this new notion of crimes against peace. Chief Judge Sir William Webb called this "the trial of the century." Later he decided a century wasn't long enough: There had been "no more important criminal trial in history," he declared. For a trial so important, extra care had to be taken to ensure that all procedures were proper. MacArthur, after the flak he had gotten over the Yamashita trial, made sure everyone got the message: Leave me out of this. Frequently he was called on by the prosecutors to replace one of the judges or fire the head prosecutor (which he had the power to do). He refused every time. The trial would have to sink or swim on its own, he would do nothing to interfere or speed it along. In the meantime, as invariably happens when trials go on too long, fate intervened. Two of the defendants died and one was declared mentally unfit, reducing the number of defendants from twenty-eight to twenty-five.

The beauty of lengthy trials, however, is that one never knows what will turn up. Among the horrifying revelations to emerge in the testimony were orders to quickly execute all 30,000 American prisoners held in Japan should the Allies mount an invasion. That fact alone, thought many non-Japanese observers, was justification for using the atom bomb: a quick, massive strike.

Tokyo was not the most important trial in history—Nuremberg was—but it was certainly the biggest. The courtroom was huge: one hundred feet long by fifty feet wide, a third bigger than Nuremberg. There were eleven judges. Every day there were a thousand people in the courtroom. The lengthy indictment contained fifty-five counts against twenty-eight defendants, covering the seventeen-year period from 1928 to 1945. There were 419 witnesses and 4,336 documents. Keenan's prosecution team consisted of 340 lawyers, paralegals, and secretaries. For the defense there were 96 Japanese lawyers and 23 American lawyers. Whenever any important witness testified, nearly every defense lawyer, both American and Japanese, wanted to cross-examine him on behalf of his individual client. The days dragged on.

The trial, like all great trials, had its moments of high drama, which of course centered around the emperor. Hideki Tojo, the man with the Morse code teeth, was on the witness stand. He couldn't keep his mouth shut. In testimony under Keenan's withering cross-examination, he blew his cover and said there was no way the Japanese would have done anything against the emperor's wishes: "None of us would dare act against the Emperor's will."

Keenan had to move fast. Privately that evening, his lawyers beat up on Tojo to alter his testimony. Next day, in a carefull scripted cross-examination, Tojo sang a different tune: the emperor had always been a man of peace. The emperor's "love and desire for peace," he effused, "remained the same right up to the very moment when hostilities commenced, and even during the war his feelings remained the same."

For the emperor, it was a close call. As the trial moved along and stumbled its way to the end, there was the burden of language translation. In Nuremberg, everything was done via simultaneous translation; in Tokyo, this was very difficult because Japanese as a language bears no relation to English or any other European language. "The process of translating is more like describing a picture in words—creating an equivalent, not a replica," said one writer. "Not only is it difficult, it is also particularly time-consuming." Time and time again the trial ground to a halt while lawyers argued over what was being said. Translating a single page sometimes took two days, and what emerged rarely satisfied everyone. "I shall return," for example, came out as "I shall be back." *Senso sekinin sha* ("war responsible persons") does not mean "persons responsible for war" but rather "persons responsible in the course of war." To settle these interpretation disputes, the tribunal had to set up a Language Arbitration Board, incurring more delays. The Japanese often had the advantage in communication. The lead lawyer for the defendants, Kenzo Takayanagi, spoke and wrote flawless English—to be expected of a graduate of Harvard Law School. This wasn't the only time SCAP's lawyers were surprised. Another graduate of that school was Yamashita's best friend and personal translator, Masakatsu Hamamoto.

Another problem for the prosecution was the absence of many official documents and records—attributed to deliberate destruction by the government and the military after the surrender. Bonfires glowed day and night burning incriminating documents. Among the documents destroyed were the transcripts of all imperial conferences, all the records of the Privy Council, all the records of the Supreme War Council, all deliberations of the cabinet, and all files relating to prisoners of war. Unlike the Germans, who obsessively saved every scrap of paper, the Japanese made sure there were no "smoking guns" lying around. From the moment the emperor announced the surrender, the Japanese had been busy destroying evidence. They may have laid down their guns, but they picked up a match.

IT IS NOT KNOWN if Douglas MacArthur, while all the deliberations were going back and forth, ever encountered the seminal 1948 book on the Nuremberg Trial, F. J. P. Veale's *Advance to Barbarism: How the*

Reversion to Barbarism in Warfare and War-Trials Menaces Our Future. If he had, he would have been amused to find the author saying: "It must be freely admitted that the stage management at Nuremberg was excellent. . . . In fact, it seems unanimously agreed that, if a stranger, say from Patagonia, who understood no language but his own, had visited the Court during the proceedings, he might have well imagined that normal judicial processes were in operation—provided, of course, he did not tarry too long."

Tokyo was no different. There a reporter compared the trial to a Spanish bullfight—except that such comparison was unfair to the bull. At least the bullfight, in certain moments, was entertaining. The IMFTE was one long tedium, greeted at the end by a sigh of relief, even by the convicted.

So it was greeted by the supreme commander, relieved he had never pursued his boyhood dream of someday becoming a lawyer.

ON NOVEMBER 12, 1948, the tribunal delivered its verdicts. All twenty-five defendants were found guilty; seven were sentenced to execution, seventeen to life, and one to twenty years. The verdicts went to the supreme commander, who promptly rubber-stamped them. One of the defendants had bitter words for the supreme commander for not allowing those sentenced to death to be shot rather than hanged. MacArthur, he said, lacked "a scintilla of the so-called compassion of the warrior." He was wrong. MacArthur had the grace to preserve the dignity of those sentenced to death: In direct violation of an order from Washington that had been signed off by President Truman, he refused to allow photographers at the executions. In his five years managing Japan before the Korean War broke out, MacArthur received hundreds of orders from Washington. He disobeyed only two: this and an order concerning breaking up the *zaibatsu*.

Elsewhere in Japan and the Pacific, some 2,200 trials of 5,700 people were conducted. The conviction rate was 77 percent—not as high as MacArthur hoped, but certainly enough for him to get his message across, and to dispel any cries of kangaroo courts.

For many Americans, and especially the American military, there would be no great apology for what Japan had done, no great confessions of war guilt. MacArthur understood. An avid Civil War buff (every year for his birthday his wife, Jean, gave him a biography of a Confederate general), he fully agreed with his friend Admiral Spruance:

> There is nothing to indicate any feeling of war guilt on the part of either the Germans or the Japanese—only a feeling of regret at having lost. I think the most we can ever expect from them [the Japanese] is an admission that they made a bad mistake in start- ing the war. I never heard of a Southerner feeling that the South was in the wrong in starting the Civil War.

For what was supposed to be the most important trial in history, IMTFE's legacy proved to be disappointing. There were no unforget- table films of massacres or concentration camps, there were no great moments of stirring eloquence like the words of the U.S. chief prose- cutor at Nuremberg, Supreme Court Justice Robert H. Jackson. There was no trial of the emperor, the man to whom the Japanese army and navy were solely responsible. No one in Hollywood would make a movie. The Tokyo trial came too late, took too long, and failed to convey moral clarity.

There was no Shiro Ishii. But in the group of those convicted was the general who had blocked the infamous Ishii from attacking the United States with biological agents: Yoshijiro Umezu. His singular good deed, one of the very few instances of courage and humanity in the Japanese war machine, went unrecognized and unrewarded. The court's verdict on him, when it came to war crimes, simply said: "There is not suffi- cient evidence that Umezu was responsible for the commission of war crimes." Fair enough, but what about the fact that he had gone out of his way to *prevent* the commission of atrocities? It didn't matter: Because of his high position, he must go down with everyone else at the trial. Also with him were three peace advocates, accused for not having suc- ceeded. One was Prince Fumimaro Konoe, who had opposed the Pearl Harbor attack and had sought a meeting in September 1941 with Presi- dent Roosevelt to try to avert war (FDR refused to see him, even though both Ambassador Joseph Grew and British ambassador Robert Craigie strongly urged the men to meet). Konoe, before committing suicide the day he was arrested, delivered a blistering assault on Americans and Japanese alike: "The victors are too brutal, the losers too servile." Another peace advocate who was convicted was the Marquis Koichi Kido, Lord Keeper of the Privy Seal, the man who finally persuaded the emperor to order the war brought to an end. The third was the distinguished Mamoru Shigemitsu, the man who had represented Japan at the *Missouri* surrender signing. After four years Shigemitsu would be released from prison and once again become Japan's foreign minister. While in New York for a session of the United Nations in 1951, he called on MacArthur, who said to him: "I was always convinced that you were innocent and that your condemnation was a mistake."

Then why hadn't the supreme commander commuted the sentence when he had the power to do so?

PART THREE

WASHINGTON
TAKES OVER

20

George Kennan Pays a Visit

B Y MID-1947 AMERICA was comfortably ensconced in Japan. A diplomat from India, returning to Japan as his country's new ambassador, went to present his credentials to MacArthur. He found that Tokyo's street names had been changed. Bright new signs indicated B Avenue or 18th Street, and parks and movie theaters were now called Doolittle Field or the Ernie Pyle Theatre. Another sign pointed the way to Washington Heights, a housing settlement. "Americans," he told his daughter, "get homesick so easily."

Tokyo had so many movie theaters, nightclubs, and dance halls that life in Tokyo was like a perpetual Roman holiday. The country was safe from dangerous guns and arms, probably too much so. The Japanese government had successfully disarmed the military, to the point that all the samurai swords had been turned in. Even the wooden swords used in a kabuki play were confiscated, causing puzzlement among the Japanese as to why the Americans were so obsessed about security.

The legacy of the atom bomb had largely receded. The population—245,000 at the time of the bombing—was, after eighteen months, more than 250,000. Observed one journalist:

> As far as the people in the city itself were concerned, [the atom bomb] was a horrible disaster to be accepted and patiently borne, like a giant earthquake or flood. Only afterwards, when they began reading the foreign press, did they learn that a crime against humanity had been committed and that the martyrdom

of Hiroshima would ring down the ages. Then foreign notables, scientists and journalists all came pouring in, eager for horrors, American ladies wept in public and uttered beautiful thoughts, and the inhabitants of this modest capital of a modest province found the eyes of the whole world upon them.

Hiroshima was a growing tourist center, with an "Atomic Souvenir Shop" selling fused glassware, twisted metal, and other relics of the blast. An "Atomic Bookshop" sold Japanese literature on the bomb, and there was even a beauty salon called the "Atomic Beauty Shoppe." On New Year's Day 1946, a group of U.S. Marines, which included many college and pro football players (including the 1943 Heisman Trophy winner Angelo Bertelli of Notre Dame), had staged a football game in Nagasaki. They called it the "Atom Bowl." Nobody seemed to mind. Even the emperor was nonchalant. He visited Hiroshima and addressed the people like a kindly uncle: "There seems to have been considerable damage here."

Culture and freedom were beginning to flourish. Japan boasted no fewer than 168 periodicals in amusement and entertainment, 165 literary reviews, 132 science magazines, and 85 women's and children's magazines. By a margin of 58 percent, Japanese women said they preferred a love marriage (79 percent) to a family-arranged marriage (21 percent)—a major break with tradition.

The disarmament of the most heavily armed nation on earth had gone off without a hitch. In locating and eliminating all the arsenals and ordnance depots, American soldiers had stumbled on 100,000 tons of chemical warfare supplies that had been awaiting the invasion. Then they made an even bigger discovery, one straight out of Jules Verne: a mysterious, nonexistent island. It had been erased from all the Japanese maps, but still it existed—Okunoshima, off the mainland near Hiroshima—where the Japanese had constructed a huge poison gas factory. Gas manufactured at Okunoshima killed as many people in China (80,000) as did the atom bomb at Hiroshima. American soldiers found almost 5,000 tons of chemicals and quickly dumped them into the sea.

The Japanese armed forces had been totally disbanded. A purge of 180,000 military officers and 40,000 government officials, businessmen, and teachers had removed many militarists from positions of influence (and opened up job opportunities for younger people). Land reform had been accomplished. A new constitution had been installed and political rights codified. In record time—achieved in months what had taken America decades—the Japanese had in place the world's most liberal guarantees of civil rights: freedom of thought and conscience, academic freedom, the essential equality of the sexes, social security, and the right to work. Political parties were blossoming like dandelions after a spring rain. The voting in the country's national election had gone off without a hitch and brought fresh faces into the Diet.

SCAP had successfully cracked down on the hated *Kempeitai*, or military police. The Civil Administration and Education Section, nicknamed the "American Ministry of Japanese Education," was busy screening militarist doctrine from the education system and eliminating secondary-school courses on how to repair gliders, use bayonets, or throw hand grenades. Textbooks were being cleaned up, no longer allowing math questions like: "If one machine gun will kill ten Americans, how many will kill one hundred?" The books could discuss the atom bomb, so long as they also discussed the Rape of Manila or the Rape of Nanking. They also had to include an explanation of the war itself: America used the bomb only to terminate a war it did not start. Absolutely forbidden were statements like: "Japan might have won the war but for the atom bomb, a weapon only barbarians would use."

Movement in and out of the country was tightly controlled. No one, except with the personal permission and approval of General MacArthur, was allowed into the country, considered in military terms to be a highly restricted theater of operations. Visitors to Japan needed to carry their military permit number with them at all times; military police were everywhere and would ask for it. SCAP's chief of counterintelligence threatened censorship of any news or information that "disturbs the public tranquility." Forbidden topics included Emperor Hirohito as a ruler, SCAP's role in drafting the Japanese constitution, and the glory of the great emperor Meiji. No criticism or cartoon caricatures of MacArthur ever appeared in the newspapers. SCAP directives stated that "news must adhere strictly to the truth . . . there should be no destructive criticisms of the Allied Forces of Occupation."

One of the people invited to Japan was Roger Baldwin, the principal founder and executive director of the American Civil Liberties Union (ACLU). Baldwin came to Japan expecting to find all kinds of problems with SCAP's censorship restrictions. Instead, to his surprise, he fell under the MacArthur spell: "Why, that man knows more about civil liberties than I do!" Baldwin stayed in Japan for ten weeks and, with MacArthur's full support, created the Japan Civil Liberties Union.

The American military engineers conducted almost all the new construction and repairs to dams, dikes, roads, and bridges. SCAP's financial books were in perfect order. There were no procurement scandals, no corruption in the awarding of contracts, no embezzlement. MacArthur had reason to be pleased with himself. The peasant landholders, the factory workers, and the women—three large constituencies comprising 80 percent of the adult population—all appreciated what he had done. He had spared no one in his effort to democratize and demilitarize Japan. He had done more than just occupy the country, he had instituted widespread and massive reform.

IT IS WHEN everything is going well that the darkest clouds often appear on the horizon. From a distance they can sometimes be noticed, if only barely. Back in February 1946, presidential advisor John J. McCloy (later high commissioner of Germany and president of the World Bank) had visited Tokyo, gotten the full MacArthur charm treatment, and come away dazzled. "My God, how does he do it?" he sputtered to Faubion Bowers. "He's in better health than when I saw him before the war . . . more fascinating than when he was Chief of Staff [1930–35]. . . . What a man! What a man!"*

---

*The exact same words—by pure coincidence—were used by the highest-ranking member of the Soviet mission. According to Courtney Whitney, Col. Gen. S. A. Golunsky was arrested by the American military police for traveling outside the twenty-five-mile zone. The Russian general was outraged and demanded a written apology.

In his report, however, McCloy expressed concern that liberal reforms would drive Japan "further left" and the war criminals trial would be a total "fiasco." Given that wartime Japan had probably been the most right-wing nation on the face of the earth, it is hard to imagine how MacArthur could be accused of driving Japan too far to the left. (It reminds one of the quip that the Founding Fathers could never get the U.S. Constitution ratified today because it is too radical.)

For a man as brilliant as John McCloy to make such an off-target remark suggested that the problems were deeper than the liberal reforms or controversial war trials. His comment said more about Washington than about Japan. Trouble was brewing back home, and McCloy, the ultimate Washington insider, was a man in the know. What was occurring was a change of heart, a reordering of how to fit Japan into America's global priorities. MacArthur's expanding the purge of militarists, dissolving major industries, returning land to the peasants, and calling for an end of the occupation was not what Cold War warriors in Washington wanted to hear. Originally, when the occupation started, New Deal planners were in control in Washington. Now with Truman firmly ensconced as president, a new cast of characters was emerging who had little sympathy for MacArthur's moral crusade.

On March 17, 1946, the supreme commander gave his first press conference since the early days in Australia in 1942. "The time has now approached that we must talk peace with Japan," he announced. A prolonged occupation would only cause economic strangulation. This was also an opportunity for the newly created peace organization to show what it could do: "If the United Nations can't function now, it never will," he warned.

While almost everyone focused on the political implications of his speech, few paid attention to the thrust of what he was really saying: The occupation with all its restrictions was strangling Japan's economy.

For the supreme commander the issue was very simple: Could any foreigner travel around Russia without correct papers and not be arrested? Of course not. You tell the general, MacArthur instructed his aide, "There will be no apology, oral or written." When Golunsky got the message, he had only one thing to say: "What a man! . . . A real leader."

"Japan is not producing enough to satisfy her needs," he said. "The difference must be filled by the Allies. If we keep this economic blockade up, more and more we will have to support this country. It is an expensive luxury. But we will pay for it or let people die by the millions." The population of Japan, seventy-two million in 1945, was now eighty million after the return of soldiers and the postwar baby boom. The country, cut off from trade with adjoining countries, simply could not produce enough food to feed itself. Nor could its economy grow. "We do not allow Japan to trade," he complained. "She has got to be allowed to trade with the world. Japan is only permitted a barter system through the bottleneck of SCAP. We've got to take it out of the hands of the Government and put it in the hands of private traders." If Japan was to survive, it must be permitted to rebuild its manufacturing capacity, conduct international trade, and import food. Without major changes, Japan's economy would remain in the doldrums, leaving the United States no choice other than to provide massive amounts of foreign aid. "No weapon, not even the atom bomb, is as deadly in its final effect as economic warfare," he said. "The atom bomb kills by the thousands, starvation by the millions."

MacArthur's speech did little to calm Washington. To the contrary, it demonstrated once again his unique ability to stir up a hornets' nest back home. SCAP's program, said George Kennan, was causing "economic disaster, inflation . . . near anarchy which would be precisely what the Communists want." Secretary of the Army Kenneth Royall announced that it "really amounted to socialism, pure and simple, if not communism." The Army undersecretary, William Draper, a Wall Street bond trader, joined the fray: SCAP had turned Japan into an economic "morgue." James Lee Kauffman, a Wall Street lawyer and close friend of Royall and Draper, wrote a blistering article in *Newsweek* calling SCAP's economic program "far to the left of anything tolerated in America."

Be that as it may, these critics ignored the fact that MacArthur's original directive from Washington contained the specific instruction *not* to "assume any responsibility for the economic rehabilitation or the strengthening of the Japanese economy"—good advice at the time. Now, apparently, times had changed. MacArthur claimed that reviving Japan's economy required loosening its ties with the United States.

Washington policy makers argued the opposite, that economic revival required closer ties to resurrect the great Japanese enterprises of old, the family holding companies. What made the gulf between MacArthur and the policy makers so vast was that they were ten thousand miles apart. MacArthur thought primarily of what was best for Japan; the Washington policy makers thought of what was best for the United States. MacArthur thought of Asia; Marshall, now secretary of state, thought of the whole globe.

The supreme commander was becoming a major thorn in Washington's side, too independent for his own good. Marshall, Undersecretary of State Acheson, Defense Secretary Forrestal, Kennan—the head of the State Department's Policy Planning Staff—and President Truman (all "Europe first" proponents) concluded that the Soviet Union was a threat of the highest order. MacArthur, who had more firsthand experience dealing with the Russians than any of them, took a more sanguine view, feeling it was a threat that could be managed.

How could a conservative Republican be such a socialist? How could a military man be so unmilitaristic? MacArthur defied being pigeonholed. He was—and this is what most scared his superiors—unpredictable.

At a time when there was growing concern about the Communist trend in China and the need to make Japan a pinnacle in U.S. security, MacArthur was preaching independence for Japan. In early February 1947, he told a delegation of congressmen (headed by Secretary of the Interior Julius A. Krug) that a formal peace treaty would promote the democratization of Japan, and that the longer the occupation continued, the more dependent Japan's economy would become on the United States—which was not good. He wrote a letter to Congress saying

"We've Been Using More of a Roundish One"

that "military occupations serve their purpose at best for only a limited time, after which deterioration rapidly sets in." He followed up by sending his aide George Atcheson to Washington to make the case for independence; Atcheson's words fell on deaf ears. MacArthur was saying things Washington did not want to hear. It was now time for Washington to start exerting more control.

And rein in the "bunco man."

ENTER 1948, KNOWN in the Japanese calendar as the Year of the Mouse. Leading the charge was the army secretary, Kenneth Royall. On January 6, 1948, he gave a speech saying that "the men who were most active in building up and running Japan's war machine" were the ones most qualified to "contribute to the economic recovery of Japan." He went on to argue in favor of building up Japan to "serve as a deterrent against any other totalitarian war threat which might hereafter arise in the Far East."

A month later the barrage continued. This time it was from the State Department's George Kennan: "We should cease to talk about vague and—for the Far East—unreal objectives such as human rights, the raising of living standards, and democratization. The day is not far off when we are going to have to deal in straight power concepts. The less we are hampered by idealistic slogans, the better."

Needless to say, disparaging idealism was not a good way to win the supreme commander's good graces. He was delighted when one of his friends in the office of the Assistant Secretary of State for Occupied Areas responded that seeking to contain Soviet expansionism by abandoning democracy and economic reform was like arguing that "democracy must be abandoned in order to be defended."

In March, George Marshall, now secretary of state, sent Kennan to Japan. Before you leave, said Marshall to Kennan, let me give you some advice: You are going to meet a very difficult man with a colossal ego. So please do not get into an argument. The man is supersmart, probably even smarter than you are. Listen carefully, be sure to flatter him, and ignore his satraps—military officers, political advisors, and flunkies.

MacArthur, in the meantime, was not thrilled about Kennan's

forthcoming visit. He knew that Kennan, called "America's Global Planner" by the *New York Times* correspondent Brooks Atkinson, was the author of the famous "X" article published in a recent issue of *Foreign Affairs*, urging containment of Communism and the Soviet Union. MacArthur felt he was doing just fine in that area. If Kennan wanted a briefing, muttered MacArthur to his staff, "I'll have him briefed until it comes out of his ears!"

It would be a meeting of two of the sharpest minds in the American government, two men who couldn't have been more dissimilar, coming at a problem from different perspectives. No sooner had Kennan gotten off the plane than he was taken to lunch with MacArthur. Totally worn out after forty-eight hours without sleep on a freezing cold slowpoke propeller plane, Kennan viewed himself as "a civilian David" taking on "a military Goliath." For two hours the supreme commander conducted one of his nonstop monologues, this one comparing his occupation of Japan to Caesar's occupation of Gaul, "the only other historical example of a productive military occupation." He claimed the great events of the next thousand years were to take place in the Orient—not Europe— and that by planting the seeds of Christianity and democracy in Japan, America had a unique opportunity to "fundamentally alter the course of world history." The Japanese, MacArthur assured his visitor, were "thirsting for guidance and inspiration." The two hours, thought Kennan, reminded him of what Prime Minister Shigeru Yoshida had said after emerging from MacArthur's office for the first time: It was like hearing a lecture inside a lion's cage with a pacing lion. As Kennan stared at MacArthur, a quite different animal came to mind: a horse. A wild, strong horse that needed to be tethered.

And he, George Kennan, would have to be the one to do it. In his memoirs he would describe his mission to Japan as like being "an envoy charged with opening up communications and establishing diplomatic relations with a hostile and suspicious foreign government." He wasn't talking about Japan, he was talking about the MacArthur regime. The next day Kennan was treated to a lengthy briefing by two SCAP officers, which he regarded as bordering on an insult for a man in his senior position. He kept his cool, however, and following Marshall's advice to use flattery, sat down and wrote a letter. He reminded the supreme commander that he had come to Japan "to inquire—and to carry back to Gen. Marshall—your view of the broad framework of concepts which ought to underlie the decisions we shall soon have to take concerning our future course in Japan, and to give you any information that may be useful to you on the pattern of our over-all foreign policy problems, as we see them in Washington."

While MacArthur was digesting this sweet pabulum, one of Kennan's aides, who had served in the Tokyo Embassy before the war, met with one of his former colleagues now working at SCAP and arranged for Kennan to give a briefing on the Soviet Union for senior SCAP officers. Kennan delivered a stellar performance. General Willoughby immediately relayed his impressions to MacArthur, and the next day Kennan was summoned for a private dinner with the big man himself. In a congenial evening thoroughly enjoyed by both men, MacArthur informed Kennan that he had toned down some of the more radical democratization requests coming out of Foggy Bottom [the State Department]. He agreed with Kennan to ignore objections by the Allies and do his best to rehabilitate Japan's economy so the country could contribute constructively to the stability and prosperity of the Far Eastern region. The visiting diplomat noted that no proper provision had been made for Japan's defense, and that for America to sign a peace treaty and pull out, leaving Japan defenseless, would be premature. There was still a lot more work to do, especially in completing the land reform program (only one-seventh finished) and the strengthening of economic enterprises. MacArthur did not disagree.

There were still some occupation problems that had to be dealt with, such as the increase in gambling, prostitution, and narcotics traffic. Also troublesome was the booming black market, where the U.S. armed forces were getting favorable exchange rates for their dollars, enabling them to remit to America every month eight million dollars more than their total pay. Observed Kennan wryly: "The personal enrichment of members of the Occupation was not always absent."

They talked about Communism. MacArthur, of course, knew all about the "X" article and Kennan's position on the subject. He told

Kennan he valued civil liberties more than the possible threat of sub-versives, leftists, and even Communists. "We have probably got some of them. The War Department has some. So does the State Department. It doesn't mean very much."

Then Kennan pulled off a clever move. Knowing how the supreme commander detested the Far Eastern Commission and its Russian veto power—a feeling shared by Kennan—he pointed out that the FEC's scope was more limited than anyone had originally realized. The way Kennan interpreted the FEC's mandate, it applied only to supervising the surrender terms and not to determining Japan's postwar future—meaning that henceforth MacArthur need not worry about having to deal with the FEC. This was a revelation. MacArthur got so excited he slapped his thigh, as if to say, Well done, George! "From that moment," wrote Kennan, "things went very well."

Before leaving, Kennan praised MacArthur and his generals for using their great power responsibly and humanely. In a magnificent piece of rhapsody that surely must have thrilled the supreme commander, Kennan stated:

> They deserved the respect which must be paid in general to be-nevolent despotism wherever encountered. I am merely point-ing out that these commanders enjoyed something of the same sympathies which I suppose were once addressed to Belisarius by itinerant Byzantines visiting the Italy that rested under his com-mand, enjoying his hospitality, and listening to his complaints about the inept and ignorant interference he had to endure from the imperial court at Constantinople.

"We parted," concluded Kennan, "having reached a general meeting of the minds."

And MacArthur went to bed, no doubt imagining himself as a Belisar-ius coping with the imperial court at Washington.

Kennan was a man who had not only shaped American foreign policy with his "X" article, he had written the first draft of the Marshall Plan. Second to the Marshall Plan, he said, his handling of MacArthur was "the most significant constructive contribution I was ever able to make in government." Years later, however, after seeing how MacArthur responded and cooperated—"on no other occasion did my recommendations meet with such wide, indeed almost complete acceptance"—he downplayed his contribution. In his 1989 book *Sketches from a Life*, there was no mention at all of MacArthur or the trip to Japan.

Kennan's report to Marshall and the National Security Council became the basis for the formal policy statement NSC 13/2, on October 7, 1948, addressing the change of emphasis from political and social reform to economic revitalization. But the reforms did not die. The constitution stayed in place, women strengthened their newfound rights, the push to promote democracy and demilitarization continued as before. The emperor's status as symbolic ruler remained the same.

But here we run into one of the oddities of history, where a particular phrase takes on a life of its own, gets picked up by numerous historians, and contributes to a misleading and oversimplistic impression of what actually happened. That phrase—"reverse course"—is now so commonly used it has become a cliché. Yet it would have puzzled George Kennan, Kenneth Royall, and William Draper.

The term never appeared during the time of the occupation. Search all the government documents and memorandums of the MacArthur era; it doesn't exist. It was invented by Japanese scholars in the mid-1950s as a means of denigrating the occupation and asserting Japan's independence. Subsequently, in the late 1960s and early 1970s, the phrase got picked up by revisionist American historians critical of U.S. foreign policy in Asia.

Just because a phrase is pithy does not mean it's correct. In his choice of words in trying to change the focus of SCAP's efforts, Kennan was extremely precise: He called it a "shift." He did this numerous times verbally and twice in writing, first in his draft paper, "U.S. Policy Toward a Peace Settlement with Japan" talking about "a major shift in U.S. policy," and again in his report to the secretary of state: "The emphasis should shift from reform to economic recovery." The same for William Draper: when he sent MacArthur a directive announcing economic recovery as a primary objective of the United States, he called it an "immediate shift in emphasis." Likewise for the Department of the Army in its November 1947 "Statement of U.S. Policy," which spoke of an "appropriate shift of emphasis so as to facilitate the early revival of the Japanese economy." Even softer was Draper's substitution of "more emphasis" for "shift of emphasis" in the January 21, 1948, statement given by the U.S. representative to the FEC. Last and most explicit of all was the NSC 13/2 directive of October 1948, signed off by President Truman: "SCAP was to shift responsibilities to the Japanese."

That it was a shift rather than a reverse course was stated as such by Kennan: "The effect of the decisions in Japan was probably a gradual and to many an almost imperceptible one." There was no car screeching down the road, slamming on the brakes, and backing up, as a reverse course would imply: the change in policy was more like a car veering off to the right at a fork in the road.

Kennan had made seven specific recommendations: Revive the economy, stop reform legislation, reduce the number of purges, reduce occupation costs, halt the reparations, cease seeking a peace treaty, and strengthen Japan's police force. In agreeing with all but the last of these recommendations, the supreme commander surprised even his adversaries. In his subsequent New Year's message, he stressed the need for occupation "control of the Japanese economy." The disagreement with Washington, such as it was, was not about goals, it was about means.

21

A Shift in Emphasis

RRIVING IN JAPAN twenty days after Kennan, in March 1948,
was the second of a one-two punch, Kennan's strong ally, Undersecretary of the Army William Draper. A Wall Street investment banker who had served as economics advisor to Gen. Lucius Clay
in Germany, Draper was now the army's economics advisor for Japan.
The hope was that a way could be found to make Japan self-sufficient
without incurring the expense of an Asian "Marshall Plan." This was
Draper's second visit to Japan—a country he admitted he knew nothing
about. On his first visit the previous autumn, he had become alarmed
at the stagnation of the Japanese economy and the power of the labor
unions. Upon returning to Washington he instructed his staff to draw
up a position paper, "The Economic Recovery of Japan," calling for "the
necessary shift of emphasis to accomplish economic recovery." He also
ordered MacArthur to take it easy in his efforts to dissolve the *zaibatsu*.
MacArthur, in his second act of insubordination as supreme commander (after banning photographers from war crimes executions),
flatly refused. Instead of responding gracefully he caused a tempest by
sending Draper a ten-page radiogram accusing the *zaibatsu* of advocating "socialism in private hands."

. Thus the two sides engaged in a mud fight: Washington was accusing SCAP reformers of promoting political socialism, and MacArthur
accused Washington of promoting big-business socialism. Each side
accused the other of tampering with the development of so-called free
enterprise.

The *zaibatsu* were huge business combines that controlled hundreds of companies through holdings of stock, somewhat like the conglomerates of the 1970s in the United States. The major difference was that the *zaibatsu* owners were families. The ten top *zaibatsu* controlled nearly three-fourths of Japan's industrial, commercial, and financial resources. The two largest, Mitsui and Mitsubishi, had almost four million employees. SCAP's specialist on the *zaibatsu*, Eleanor M. Hadley, compared a *zaibatsu* enterprise to a hypothetical company in the United States that owned General Motors, United States Steel, Allis Chalmers, Western Electric, AT&T, RCA, U.S. Rubber, Douglas Aircraft, Dole Pineapple, the United States Lines, Grace Lines, the Woolworth stores, the Statler hotel chain, Westinghouse, National City Bank (now Citibank), Alcoa, DuPont, and Metropolitan Life.

Any company this size in America would violate every principle of American antitrust law and free trade. Particularly insidious was the close interaction between the *zaibatsu* and the Japanese government. In 1946 President Truman had sent Edwin W. Pauley to Japan to help MacArthur with the issue of reparations. Pauley, a former treasurer of the Democratic National Committee, knew the *zaibatsu* from first-hand experience, having sold oil to Japan while amassing a fortune in the 1930s as head of an oil company. He had strong words for the supreme commander: "Not only were the *zaibatsu* as responsible for Japan's militarism as the militarists themselves, but they profited immensely by it."

In response to the Kauffman article in *Newsweek* accusing him of causing the "virtual destruction of Japanese business," MacArthur came out firing his big guns: The Japanese system "permitted the family groups . . . to control, directly or indirectly, every phase of commerce and industry; all media of transportation, both internal and external; all domestic raw materials; and all coal and other power resources. . . . The record is thus one of economic oppression and exploitation at home, aggression and spoliation abroad."

MacArthur's views on the *zaibatsu* were based largely on the 1945 "U.S. Initial Post-Surrender Policy for Japan," which directed him to start dissolving them, and reinforced by the lengthy study prepared by Professor Corwin Edwards urging that several of them be broken up. But he couldn't execute Edwards's recommendations without Japanese cooperation: The *zaibatsu* were simply too big and complex. Here the Japanese used the time-honored technique of resistance: Admit the need to make changes, appoint a committee to study the problem and recommend cosmetic changes, and stall it to death, just as they had tried to do with the constitution.

By early 1948 the economy was still in the doldrums, and inflation was rampant. Something had to be done, even though MacArthur's original directive from the Joint Chiefs had stated very emphatically that the supreme commander would "not assume any responsibility for the economic rehabilitation of Japan or for the strengthening of the Japanese economy." MacArthur was not happy to see Draper, the Wall Street investment banker who had an accommodating view of huge corporate enterprises. But he knew he had no choice. He had managed to get along fine with Kennan; at least they both were intellectuals. Draper, on the other hand, was not given to big ideas; he was a nuts-and-bolts doer, and very opinionated and forceful. Being the point man for the army in making funding requests to Congress, he also had a lot of power.

Kennan stayed over in Japan to join Draper for his meeting with the supreme commander. MacArthur, one step ahead of Washington in his thinking, told them flat out that reparations had to go. A thousand industrial factories had been earmarked for removal to Asia, he said, and only twenty such transfers had begun, due to the difficulty of disassembly, the lack of ships, and lack of proper personnel, spare parts, and infrastructure at the receiving end. It would take twenty years to complete the process, and in the meantime metal parts were rusting and cement was hardening just sitting on the dock exposed to the elements. "Decision should be made now to abandon entirely the thought of future reparations," he urged. In keeping with what he had told the Chinese three months earlier, he justified this drastic move as a correction of an original policy gone awry: Reparations now had become "merely a camouflage method of subsidizing other nations from the U.S." Whatever was going out of Japan was being made up only by the largesse of the American taxpayer—clearly not the intent of the program.*

The Japanese economy was a more contentious issue. The dilemma facing both MacArthur and the Washington policy makers was that the industries most likely to lead the resurrection of Japan's economy were militarist related and controlled by the *zaibatsu*: steel, shipbuilding, construction, and heavy manufacturing. No matter, said Secretary of the Army Royall. The "conflict between the original concept of broad demilitarization and the new purpose of building a self-supporting nation" was "inevitable." Japan could not support itself as a nation of shopkeepers, craftsmen, and small artisans any more than it could as an agricultural nation. Added Gen. Frank McCoy, the U.S. representative to the FEC and a close friend of the supreme commander: New conditions required that "more emphasis be placed on such a program . . . to bring about the early revival of the Japanese economy." No matter what happened, something had to be done. Even George Marshall got involved: "Japan is costing us a great deal of money; that cannot go on indefinitely . . . what we have to be on our guard against is that we don't weaken ourselves economically so that the whole structure collapses."

On April 28, 1948, the day after he got Draper's formal report on reparations, MacArthur reacted quickly. Once again demonstrating his "flealike agility," he announced that the War Department—at his request (naturally)—had appointed a board of five Americans to oversee application of the report's recommendations. Since several congressmen were complaining about occupation costs and the drain on the U.S.

---

*In an October 1947 memo marked "secret" from SCAP's William Sebald to the State Department's deputy director for Far Eastern affairs (obviously seen by Kennan, the recipient's boss), Sebald wrote:

> Dr. Wang stated that the Chinese are most desirous of obtaining a larger share of reparations out of current production. In rebuttal of this statement, General MacArthur drew two parallel horizontal lines, the lower line representing Japan's present 45% production and the upper line a theoretical 100% production. He said the space between the two lines could be reached only at the expense of the United States and that the Chinese must consider us very stupid if they believe that we would fill in the gap only to have production turned over to the Chinese in the form of reparations.

Treasury, MacArthur had to cooperate, especially after the Wisconsin presidential primary earlier that month where his hopes of becoming a Republican candidate were dashed. His enemies rejoiced at his humiliation, and wondered if there might be an opportunity to drive a stake through his heart.

The Harvard Club of New York City is hardly a place where conspiracies are hatched, but June 28, 1948, was an exception. On that hot summer day several men met in the lobby and proceeded to make themselves comfortable in the magnificent Harvard Hall on the north side of the clubhouse. They lit their cigars and exchanged pleasantries while waiting for the rest of the group to arrive. Within a half hour all eighteen men were present, and the meeting was called to order. Assembled by Harry Kern, *Newsweek*'s foreign affairs editor, the group consisted of leading diplomats, journalists, investment bankers, and corporate CEOs unhappy with the perceived liberalism of Douglas MacArthur. Prominent members included Kenneth Royall, William Draper, James Lee Kauffman, and Joseph Grew, the ex-ambassador who had told President Truman in May 1945, "Democracy in Japan will never work." With democracy on the march under MacArthur, Grew missed the old Japan he used to know, and welcomed this new association of like-minded individuals. As their cigar smoke wafted up to the ceiling forty feet above, and basking in the stern gaze of trustbuster Theodore Roosevelt's portrait at the other end of the huge room, the men plotted how to minimize the power and influence of MacArthur and start making some serious money. Kauffman, who before the war had counted every major American corporation in Japan as a legal client, wanted back in on all the action. Draper, once again at Dillon Read (the former Wall Street firm of Royall and Secretary of Defense Forrestal), would soon return to Japan hunting for Japanese utilities in need of bond financing. Conspicuously absent was the world's leading authority on the *zaibatsu*, SCAP's Eleanor M. Hadley, whose lengthy article "Trust Busting in Japan" would appear in the July 1948 issue of the *Harvard Business Review*. Hadley had returned to Radcliffe to get her doctorate, aided by the support of Douglas MacArthur and Courtney Whitney, who had personally petitioned Harvard/Radcliffe to give her an extension so she could stay longer in Japan and continue working for them during 1947.*

All the men could speak freely: The room was so big no one could possibly overhear them. They would name their association the American Council on Japan, a lobbying group. There is no transcript of the meeting, but one can safely assume they readily agreed on their first mode of attack: a feature story in *Fortune*. "Two Billion Dollar Failure in Japan" would appear in April of the following year, at a time when two billion dollars wasted by the federal government was a lot of money.

Strikingly enough, just months earlier at the MacArthur-Kennan dinner in Tokyo, MacArthur had dropped an interesting phrase, little knowing how prescient it would be. In denouncing the *zaibatsu* executives he was purging, he called them "elderly incompetents," very much like "the most effete New York club men."

While the New York clubmen licked their chops contemplating his demise, the supreme commander regained his footing. Having lost much of his political aura and heft, he had no choice but to heed the new political winds. But he would do so gradually. Like FDR, who once said his policy was to have no policy, MacArthur operated on the premise that "major shifts in policy should be undertaken with the greatest caution." The original dissolution plan called for 325 companies to be liquidated. Edward Walsh, chief of the SCAP Anti-Trust and Cartels Division, recommended dropping 33 companies from the list developed by Eleanor Hadley. Gen. William Marquat, acting on MacArthur's orders, jacked up the exclusions to 300, leaving only 25 to be dissolved. By late 1948 the supreme commander had dissolved only 11, making sure to put a good face on the whole episode. He announced a victory: "It has always been my firm intention to implement the deconcentration program in such manner as will preclude any disruption of Japan's going economy and will insure rigorous limitation of the number of companies required to be subject to reorganization." In more ways than one the supreme

---

*It was just as well she was not invited to the meeting. Women in those days were not allowed in the Harvard Club (except in a "Women's Dining Room," with its own separate entry next to the main entrance).

commander was a man who rarely—if ever—knew defeat. He would simply announce a victory.

Meanwhile the American Council for Japan landed a big fish: Robert Eichelberger. On the "outs" with MacArthur, General Eichelberger had quickly found himself a new home as Draper's assistant, thus proving the adage that a leader need not fear his enemies but rather his closest friends. Eichelberger, using his military connections, would prove to be a most useful conduit of information and scuttlebutt about what was going on inside MacArthur's impenetrable GHQ.

In December 1948 the National Security Council issued NSC 13/2, announcing once and for all a shift in U.S. occupation policy from social reform to economic reconstruction. The supreme commander forwarded instructions from Washington to Prime Minister Yoshida: "Stop inflation, balance your budget, halt tax evasion, limit your credit facilities, stabilize wages and prices, and tighten your foreign exchange control." In early 1949 President Truman, rejecting a "Marshall Plan" for Japan, sent the banker Joseph Dodge to Japan, giving him ambassadorial rank so he could have direct access to MacArthur. Dodge, a self-made man from the Midwest who never went to college, was an enormously successful entrepreneur who had taken over a bank and grown it tenfold in twelve years. A former president of the American Banking Association and chairman of the U.S. War Contracts Board, he had acquired such a reputation that when the German monetary system collapsed after the war, General Eisenhower ordered: "Get Dodge to Germany fast!" Now President Truman was sending Dodge to Japan to pull off a second miracle.

Accompanying Dodge were Gen. Albert Wedemeyer and Army Secretary Kenneth Royall, the man who had such withering words about MacArthur and the Japanese economy. Here Royall got an object lesson on how not to conduct international diplomacy. In an unofficial press conference, he announced that America's major interest lay in Europe and the United States was fully prepared to withdraw its line of defense to the West Coast of the United States. This immediately sent shock waves throughout Japan, and made many Japanese, fearful they could not depend on the United States, wonder if it might not be wise to start exploring an amicable deal with the Russians. The Russians couldn't believe their good luck.

MacArthur, of course, was outraged but chose to keep his mouth shut. He was still the supreme commander; he would outfox his enemies by being sly and not giving the Russians a break. First, however, he had to deal with Joseph Dodge. Fortunately he and Dodge got along very well, both of them being conservative Republicans who believed in austerity and balanced budgets. Several days after they met and Dodge had taken a quick look around, Dodge brazenly announced that the Japanese economy was like a person "walking on stilts," about to collapse at any moment. MacArthur did not disagree. He liked the blunt-speaking banker even better when he had the temerity to admit, "I'm no colonel bucking to a brigadier—I can be objective, because the most I'll get out of this is a kick in the pants." A kick in the pants—so long as the speaker seemed to know what he was talking about—was the kind of language MacArthur could appreciate. Kennan, being so smart and savvy, MacArthur could respect and get along with. Draper, he could not. The dapper, smooth-talking Draper, in MacArthur's view, was a Wall Street hack.

Dodge's mission was to develop a plan to achieve economic self-sufficiency by promoting Japanese access to Asian markets. Even if it involved leaving the *zaibatsu* alone, placing strict curbs on labor unions, cutting the budget, and lowering the domestic standard of living, whatever it took to increase exports and tie Japan more closely with Asia, MacArthur would support. American aid now poured into industries previously restricted due to their military potential: steel, coal, iron, and ships. While this helped the big companies, the overall effect was to create a "stabilization depression," whereby many small and medium-size enterprises went bankrupt.

Fortune magazine, speaking for the newly formed American Council for Japan, came out with its "Two Billion Dollar Failure in Japan" article in April 1949. It claimed that the supreme commander was "an impressive gold-laced figurehead" living in an "Alice in Wonderland state," presiding over economic reforms that had been "massive failures." MacArthur responded two months later with a six-thousand-word reply. He began by stating he had been given strict directives to follow,* and admitted that under his strict control Japan's restricted economy had become "in effect a large concentration camp." His hands were tied, he said: "Until a peace treaty was consummated Japan would remain in more or less degree in the strait jacket of an economic blockade."

And how had Japan fared under an economic blockade? The issue, argued MacArthur, had to do with more than just the economy: It had to do with reforming the most militaristic country on earth and turning it into a democracy. On that "big picture" basis, he argued, the occupation was a success, perhaps not in everything but certainly in achieving its overriding priorities.

Then he went into specifics, refuting *Fortune*'s claims point by point. The two-billion-dollar figure was way off, he said, because much of it was for the pay and support of troops needed in a military occupation. That Japan depended "on the United States for better than three-fourths of its imports" was only to be expected since these imports were largely food and raw materials no longer available from Japan's neighbors, against whom it had waged war. Equally misleading was the claim that the Japanese bureaucracy numbered more than three million people. Not so, said MacArthur. Only 839,500 people worked in the government administration. Another 714,578 worked for the telephone companies, the railroads, the tobacco monopoly, and other government-owned enterprises that in America were privately held. The remaining jobs were make-work, in keeping with government policy to accommodate the oversupply of labor (due to millions of repatriates arriving from abroad) by dividing the work and keeping people off the dole. It was fine for *Fortune* to argue that "recovery comes first," but for such recovery to persist there must be political and social reform to eradicate the horrible exploitation workers had

---

*Given to him no fewer than three times: by the president's directive of September 6, 1945, by the Joint Chiefs' directive of November 3, 1945, and by the FEC's directive of June 19, 1947, all telling him to dissolve the *zaibatsu* (see brief excerpts in the endnotes).

endured in the past. With labor and capital now in proper balance due to SCAP reforms, it was incumbent on Japanese exporters to "find their markets on a more truly competitive basis." The days when Japan could flood the world with cheap Japanese goods, based on woefully underpaid labor, were over. Japan now must strive to move up the value-added scale in international trade.

The supreme commander had a personal reason for his hostility to the *zaibatsu*: They had flagrantly disobeyed the Potsdam Declaration. William Draper may have had no problem with this, but a military commander like MacArthur certainly did. Only recently had the truth come out, a violation so egregious it challenged a fundamental premise of MacArthur's entire occupation: that the Japanese, despite their infamous attack on Pearl Harbor, could be trusted.

It was a scandal he had tried his best to downplay in his efforts to protect the emperor. He made no mention of it in his public rebuttal to *Fortune*—he could not—but the facts were explosive. When the war ended, the military had stashed away in caves and hidden warehouses huge amounts of military supplies of precious metals, light and heavy oils, blankets, clothing, storage batteries, aluminum, zinc, mercury, wire rope, alcohol, sugar, and paper. Also included were enormous quantities of diamonds and family jewelry donated for the war effort. Apparently what had been going on was that the War and Navy Ministries, under cabinet authorization, had secretly parceled out the goods to their friends in the police, local governments, *zaibatsu*, and gangster groups for their personal use and resale in the black market. When the "hoarded goods" scandal came to light in late 1947, it was estimated by a Japanese House of Representatives special committee that the value of the stolen goods was three hundred billion yen—50 percent more than the entire government budget for that year. One witness testified that the moment the government order was given, "Trucks, wagons, railroad cars, carts, bicycles and porters swarmed into the arsenals; documents were forged, altered or destroyed. Thousands of tons of finished products, food, textiles, raw materials and machinery were hauled away." Observed *World Report* (later *U.S. News & World Report*): "Japan's war stockpiles have been looted of raw materials worth billions of dollars.* . . . There are indications that these stock-piles held enough iron, steel, and aluminum to supply Japan's peace-time economy for four years. Much of this has vanished. The *zaibatsu* companies, Japan's family monopolies, obtained the largest share of the spoils." The Japanese finance minister had the gall to admit: "Nobody knows where 100 billion yen worth of stuff has gone to."

Stuff!

That was not all. Also deceiving the Americans was the Japanese Central Bank. In the two weeks between the August 15, 1945, decision to surrender and the August 31 date when the occupation forces landed and took over the country, the government had flooded the country with yen, mostly to pay debts to the *zaibatsu*. Whereas on August 15 the volume of yen was 30 billion, on August 31 it was suddenly 42 billion—a 40 percent increase in two weeks. Such sleight-of-hand maneuvering by the government to help its friends was improper, undemocratic, and helped trigger the hyperinflation of the early years of the occupation.

MacArthur took particular exception to *Fortune's* claim that "the zaibatsu, alone, of all major groups in Japan . . . were . . . against war with the U.S. . . . The U.S. Army and the young bureaucrats, ignorant of this history, got rid of two thousand managers." Accusing MacArthur, a voracious reader of history, of not knowing his history was like waving a red cape before a bull. The supreme commander responded: "This statement is thoroughly refuted by the known facts, yet continues to crop up from one or another source, usually with a private ax to grind. There is a tendency to use the goal of economic recovery as a cover for special-interest pleading, sometimes insidiously persuasive to the uninformed." Had not the *zaibatsu* executives "uncorked their cham-pagne bottles and toasted the coming of a new 'industrialists' era'" the moment they learned the occupying power would be the United States, presumably offering leniency? Did not these men lack any guilt for all

---

*It is difficult to provide a dollar equivalent because there was severe inflation during the early years of the occupation, plus there was a substantial variation in the cost of dollars used for import as opposed to export, depending on the particular commodity being bought/sold. In August 1945 the estimated average value of the dollar was 13.6 yen; in June 1949, when Joseph Dodge created a fixed rate, he set the dollar at 360 yen.

the airplanes, gunpowder, cannons, and battleships they had manufactured in the cause of war? What about all the money and stolen goods they had gotten after the fighting stopped?

Yet the purpose of the purge was not to punish, it was to bring in new leadership. "The purgees were not excluded from all economic activity"—just the companies they had headed (with disastrous results). Just as well to get rid of them.

The magazine and the general came down to the wire at the end, their differences unresolved. "All the great social reform measures of SCAP become empty words unless the economic problem is solved," said *Fortune*. "Man still cannot live by reform alone; in Japan he must have rice too." MacArthur found this simplistic. He responded by paraphrasing *Fortune*: "Even in Japan," he said, "man cannot live by rice alone. He must have freedom."

From 1946 to 1948 inflation was 1200 percent. Compared with the old 1930–34 level, Japanese industrial production was 32 percent in 1946, 41 percent in 1947, and 64 percent in 1948. The economy was improving, but still had a long ways to go. The Communists, seeing an opportunity to regain some of their lost power, jumped in and called the Dodge Plan the "road to fascism," along with juicy language like "capitalist offensive . . . foreign monopolies . . . selling out of the country" and "semicolonial regime." MacArthur backed Dodge 100 percent. To make sure the Communists got the message, in 1949–50 he instituted the so-called Red Purge, costing 20,997 alleged Communists and sympathizers their jobs. (This was on top of the 210,288 citizens who had already been purged for their ties to militarism.)

There wasn't a whole lot the supreme commander could do about the *zaibatsu*, but one thing he could do was make sure they paid their taxes. Many of them paid nothing, indicative of the cozy relationships that existed between impoverished municipal tax collectors and wealthy corporations. In the last quarter of 1947, tax receipts were a third of what was due. The supreme commander decreed this to be totally unacceptable. To add muscle to the tax collection efforts, MacArthur ordered the U.S. Eighth Army troops throughout the country to go out on visits with the thirty thousand tax collectors. This show of force worked: Tax revenues escalated dramatically and helped slow down the currency inflation, thus providing much-needed monetary stability.

As he had with reparations, MacArthur demonstrated foresight in addressing foreign trade, the most pressing ingredient for a Japanese economic recovery. Just two years after the surrender, he had been talking in public about the need for a "co-prosperity sphere" for the Far East, with Japanese factories processing the raw materials of the less developed Asian nations. Unlike Washington, MacArthur never put great hopes on, or had much interest in, China. While the impending collapse of the Chiang Kai-shek regime in China had Washington on tenterhooks, and President Truman was urging Joseph Dodge to assess "the economic situation in Japan and its relation to what has been happening in China," MacArthur was relatively nonplussed, convinced that a Communist victory would have no bearing on Japanese Communism. "A nuisance factor," he called the China takeover, a view that certainly raised eyebrows. Eventually both Dean Acheson and George Kennan would agree that MacArthur was right. The only way to have a peaceful Japan friendly to the United States, said Acheson, would be for Japan to develop strong economic relations with the non-Communist Far East. While it was hoped that Japan and the United States could develop a strong trading relationship, the prospects looked bleak: What could Japan export? Japanese productivity was so low that only the cheapest items could find a market. Said John Foster Dulles in a scornful tone: "The Japanese couldn't make anything Americans would buy" . . . except maybe "paper napkins."

In the meantime Joseph Dodge continued his budget reforms. Unlike many economic advisors who advocate slashing expenditures or imposing high tax rates, Dodge stayed away from extremes and relied on basic fiscal discipline (pruning the budget, eliminating overambitious infrastructure projects, getting rid of surplus government workers, applying more effective collection of taxes, and paring down the national debt). The result was a near-miracle, where a government with lopsided financial outlays became fiscally responsible and transparent. For the fiscal year April 1949–April 1950, the budget finally generated a surplus. Borrowing MacArthur's flair for hyperbole, Dodge announced in his report to Congress, "In no other nation has so much been accomplished with so little." On MacArthur's recommendation the Department of the Army in 1950 awarded Dodge the Exceptional Civilian Service Medal.

Following MacArthur's orders to boost international trade, SCAP concluded some twenty trade agreements with South American, European, African, and Middle Eastern countries. Efforts to obtain most-favored-nation treaties for Japan were unsuccessful, however, largely because of the shortage of hard currency. It would not be until the Korean War that the Japanese economy would get the shot in the arm it desperately needed. Just as World War II pulled the United States out of the Depression, what eventually got Japan's motor going was the massive inflow of U.S. military dollars into Japan during the Korean War: $2.3 billion. "A gift from the gods," said Shigeru Yoshida.

With the loss of China, America's foreign policy came to rely on Japan as a strong ally. Regardless of what MacArthur's enemy Kenneth Royall said, MacArthur succeeded in extending the borders of America's defense perimeter to the other side of the Pacific. In January 1950 Secretary of State Dean Acheson, echoing MacArthur's 1946 words that Japan should be "the westernmost outpost of our defenses," announced that the defense of the United States included Japan, Okinawa, and the Philippines. The Pacific had become an American lake, and Japan would now be, in MacArthur's words, America's "unsinkable aircraft carrier in the Far East."

In projecting American military power and enhancing America's security, MacArthur's occupation was a financial bargain. Compared with the cost of $100 billion for fighting in the Pacific theater, U.S. expenses in Japan during 1945–50 were $2 billion—all more than covered by Japanese reparations of $5 billion. Even adding the $2.3 billion contributed by the United States during the Korean War, the cost to the United States was still zero.

22

"The Greatest Piece of Diplomacy, Ever"

I N 1949, SITTING in on a staff meeting of the Economic and Scientific Section, MacArthur vented his frustration over the poor economy and the continued low state of Japanese morale. "What can we do to get the morale of the Japanese people back?" he asked.

Cappy Harada, a first lieutenant, chirped: "I think baseball would be a wonderful thing."

MacArthur stared at Harada, a roly-poly fellow, clearly no athlete. MacArthur, a varsity baseball player at West Point, was curious. "Why do you think baseball's important?"

"Well, the Japanese people love baseball, and I think if we brought an American baseball team here, the Japanese people would love that, and it would really help bring the morale up."

"So what are you waiting for?"

End of discussion. The general—a former president of the American Olympic Committee in 1928—had spoken.

That very afternoon MacArthur sent a cable to San Francisco, and two days later Harada was on a plane to California. MacArthur had secured a meeting for him with the San Francisco Seals, a team managed by Lefty O'Doul. Like Babe Ruth, O'Doul had started out in baseball as a pitcher, then switched to become an outfielder. In seven major league seasons he hit .349 and won the 1929 batting title with a .398 average (leaving Ruth in the dust at .345). In 1931 O'Doul visited Japan as a member of an American baseball team and became enamored of the country. He participated in repeat visits over the next three years, and arranged for a Japanese baseball team to tour the United States in 1935 and 1936. The highlight of these exchanges was a 1934 visit to Japan by the U.S. Major League All-Star Team. In one particular game, a seventeen-year-old pitching phenomenon named Eiji Sawamura, killed in the war in 1944, made a lasting impression on the Americans when he struck out four Hall of Fame players in a row, including Babe Ruth and Lou Gehrig, in a losing 1–0 game. The American manager, Connie Mack, tried to sign him on the spot; Sawamura declined. The following year, a Japanese team toured the United States, and once again Sawamura turned down an offer of American riches.*

Even American colleges went on baseball tours of Japan. Before World War II intervened, teams from Yale, Harvard, Stanford, the University of Chicago, and the state universities of California, Washington, Wisconsin, Indiana, and Illinois participated in baseball exchanges.

The greatest ambassador of American baseball, of course, was the Sultan of Swat, "Babu Rusu," as the Japanese called him. When Ruth arrived in Japan in 1934, the emperor sent a private railway car to transport him from Yokohama to Tokyo. One man walked eighty miles to see him play in the first game. Ruth, marveled Ambassador Joseph Grew, was worth a hundred ambassadors. Some 75,000 Japanese fans came to the game in Osaka, and to commemorate that day and his towering home run, a bust of Babe Ruth was erected outside the stadium, where it still stood after World War II. That the Japanese never removed it or defaced it during the war spoke well for them as a people—all the more remarkable given how Imperial Army soldiers in the jungles of the South Pacific screamed the battle cry "To hell with Babe Ruth!" (probably the only English they ever knew). The War Department, recognizing Ruth's celebrity, had made plans in 1945 to fly him to Guam and have him make radio speeches urging the Japanese to surrender before MacArthur launched his invasion. He would be their "Tokyo Rose," the Japanese-American woman who had broadcast messages to American troops to

*The Japanese award for the best pitcher of the year, equivalent to the American Cy Young Award, is called the Sawamura Award.

surrender. It never happened, only because the atom bomb ended the war quickly. So great was Ruth's popularity in Japan that on Babe Ruth Day at Yankee Stadium (April 27, 1947), his words were broadcast live to every ballpark in America—and to every ballpark in Japan.

With Ruth now dead and knowing there was little chance of getting a major league team to come to Japan, MacArthur thought of O'Doul as a potential goodwill ambassador of American baseball. Would he be interested? You bet, said O'Doul. Asked many years later why he was so enthusiastic, he explained: "So many of my friends in Japan got killed in the war. So many. Awful. Right after the war I went back. I wanted to, because I knew if we brought a baseball team over there it would help cement friendship between them and us."

Twenty players, along with team officials and an umpire, flew to Japan for a monthlong visit. They arrived to a rousing reception: 100,000 people lined the streets of Tokyo, waving American flags. The next day they were invited to the American Embassy for lunch with the supreme commander. At the reception MacArthur spoke with each person individually. Recalled one player: "He made it a point to know something about all of us. I remember when he came to Al Lien he said, 'Al Lien, my god, I see where you finally won twenty games.' I said, 'Good night, here's a general taking care of the whole Pacific and he made it a point to know that Al Lien won twenty games."

"Gentlemen, there's no substitute for victory," MacArthur told them in his closing remarks at the end of lunch. "You are here representing America!"

MacArthur would not be at the Seals-Giants game. For a man who loved the limelight, this may seem strange. It is possible, however, to surmise an explanation from an incident that took place two years earlier. A Japanese newspaper had been about to publish an effusively flattering editorial about MacArthur when Willoughby had the article censored: "It was not in good taste." At this important game and with all the cameras clicking, for a man as supreme as MacArthur to throw out the first ball and yell "Let the game begin!" would detract from the event itself. There are times when celebrity is not called for.

Next day would be the opening ceremonies at Tokyo's Korakuen

Stadium. Representing MacArthur and SCAP would be Gen. William Marquat, the self-appointed commissioner of Japanese baseball. Cappy Harada was nervous; he knew the huge stadium would be packed to the roof. Tickets normally costing three hundred yen were going for as much as fifteen hundred to two thousand; scalpers were having a field day. Even the vendors were joining in, getting ready to sell Coca-Cola and American-style hot dogs. Harada went to MacArthur and asked if it would be appropriate to raise both the U.S. and Japanese flags before the commencement of the big game. Absolutely, said MacArthur, "Go ahead."

The U.S. national anthem was played first. As the Japanese anthem was played, Harada remained at attention and continued to salute. One of the colonels was so furious at Harada he went to the supreme commander after the game and demanded he be fired. "It's OK," MacArthur responded, "I told him to do it." That was vintage MacArthur, a man who always stuck by his subordinates. "If it is right at the top, it will be right at the bottom," he liked to say. By this he meant that because he had good people at the top the people at the bottom were good, too, because they would work hard to meet the high standards of their bosses.

The U.S. Goodwill Baseball Tour of Japan was a rousing success, drawing a full crowd for each game. Recalled Lefty O'Doul:

When I arrived it was terrible. The people were so depressed. When I had been in Japan before the war their cry had been "Banzai, Banzai." But when I got there this time they were so depressed that when I hollered "Banzai" they didn't respond at all. No reaction at all. Nothing. But when I left there, a few months later, all Japan was cheering and shouting "Banzai" again!

The emperor was so pleased he invited O'Doul and the team officials to the Imperial Palace to personally thank them for everything they had done. MacArthur, not a man to get giddy, got excited over this one. "The greatest piece of diplomacy, ever," he exulted. Move it up a notch, he told Harada. So back to San Francisco went Harada, to elicit the services of the great Joe DiMaggio, who had begun his career playing for Lefty

O'Doul and the San Francisco Seals and was now a star of the New York Yankees. DiMaggio was delighted, and accepted. The following year, MacArthur brought him to Japan. The reception was tumultuous.

A new bond, totally unexpected by the bureaucrats in Washington who could only wonder what the excitement was all about, had been established by a supreme commander who had an ear for the adoration of a crowd. Nothing touches the gut like a national sport, and baseball could be the one sport that evokes the concept of *wa* (group harmony) and the four principles of life practiced by the ancient samurai: *doryoku, konjo, nintai, chowa* (effort, fighting spirit, perseverance, and harmony). What better sport than baseball, MacArthur's own at West Point?

In 1951 Joe DiMaggio would return to Japan, this time with the Major League All-Star Team, and in 1954, when he married Marilyn Monroe (with O'Doul as best man), the place he chose for their honeymoon would be Japan.

Anybody who thinks baseball isn't the heart and soul of Japan should heed a Japanese newspaper poll of 1954. The newspaper asked its readers to list the most important people of the twentieth century. Babe Ruth came in higher than Douglas MacArthur.

For MacArthur and Marquat, their encouragement of baseball had been fruitful. Beginning with the GIs who coached young kids from the start of the occupation, baseball had grown into a new form of diplomacy. One of the unique features of sports is the concept of equality: When two teams line up and face each other at the start of a game, they do so as equals. In Japan one bows. The Americans did. This respect for the other team in pursuit of excellence—something few other Allied countries were prepared to do at the time—won the Americans many friends.

23

Occupier as Protector

FOR THE JAPANESE, MacArthur was not only their liberator from militarism, he was their protector. In his public message to the Japanese people on May 3, 1948, the anniversary of the Japanese constitution, he promised he would continue the transition of the occupation "from the stern rigidity of a military organization to the friendly guidance of a protective force."

One beneficiary of this new protective force was the emperor. Freed of weighty matters of state, he indulged in his pastime as an amateur marine biologist. He gave the supreme commander a signed copy of Dr. Kikutaro Baba's recent book that undoubtedly filled a gap in MacArthur's vast fount of knowledge. Titled *Opisthobranchia of the Sagami Bay Region: Collected by His Majesty the Emperor of Japan*, it contained a brief discussion and many paintings and drawings of specimens collected by the emperor of this large and morphologically diverse group of non-shell snails having the gills posterior to the heart.

The Russians still were not cooperating with the 1945 repatriation agreement. MacArthur wouldn't let them off the hook. By now it had become painfully obvious that the Russians were using these prisoners as slaves to perform hard labor and transferring the best of them to Moscow for indoctrination and "training." In 1949 they sent 95,000 of these prisoners back home to operate as a fifth column. "A vast centrifugal machine," MacArthur thundered, "designed to reconstruct the lives and political future of every prisoner within its scope." In April 1950 the Russians announced the "completion" of Japanese repatriation from the Soviet Union, saying there were no more Japanese POWs remaining in their custody. Still unaccounted for, and presumably dead, were 310,000 Japanese prisoners in Soviet territories, plus another 60,000 in Manchuria. The only Russian concession to the international community was to put Japanese scientists from Pingfan on trial. MacArthur was less interested in the Russian trial at Khabarovsk than in knowing where the missing 370,000 Japanese were. No answer was forthcoming. On the subject of Pingfan, MacArthur had wanted Murray Sanders to go inspect the place, but had to cancel the trip when there was no plane available other than a B-29. The Russians controlled Pingfan, and America's relationship with the Russians was so tenuous MacArthur couldn't afford the risk of a B-29 falling into their hands and giving the Russians access to the B-29's technology.

While everyone focused on Russia and China, nobody was paying attention to the small neighbors. Yet it is small, chaotic areas—like the Balkans in World War I—that have the capacity to cause the greatest mischief. Another analogy might be the 1962 Cuban Missile Crisis, when the biggest threat to America's mightily armed nuclear defenses came from a poverty-stricken offshore island taken over by Fidel Castro.

THE YEAR 1950 began on a positive note. Indeed, it might have been cause for celebration. "Contemplating his handiwork, MacArthur found the miracle of the Occupation a source of constant wonder," wrote the historians Richard Rovere and Arthur Schlesinger Jr. The supreme commander, they imagined, was "often in a philosophical mood, pulling on his corncob pipe, letting his mind roam freely along the spacious reaches of history."

One cannot know what was going through MacArthur's mind, but one thing we do know: He expected this would be his last year as supreme commander. The United States and Japan would sign a peace treaty, and he could finally go home. He was tired. For five years he had worked flat out, and now he looked forward to retiring and doing whatever he wanted, though like most workaholics he had no plan in mind. He hadn't taken a vacation in nearly twenty years. Certainly he could look back with satisfaction on what had been accomplished. How Japan had changed! What had once been a desolate city of Tokyo was now a thriving metropolis bustling with well-dressed, well-fed people. The country was still poor, but it was free of the shackles of feudalism and moving forward. The sooner the Americans got out and let Japan make it on its own, the better. He understood how Prime Minister Shigeru Yoshida, like many Japanese, increasingly felt about the occupation. For Yoshida, the initials GHQ didn't stand for General Headquarters, it stood for "Go Home Quickly!"

MacArthur was annoyed that the president, the secretary of state, and the Joint Chiefs all wanted to rearm Japan and increase—not decrease—America's footprint. He thought this was a great mistake. Together with Yoshida, he opposed any dramatic remilitarization of the country. As military commander of the entire Pacific in addition to his post as head of Japan, the supreme commander thought of the whole region—not just Japan. For Japan to have a large army, he said, would cause "convulsions" in Australia, New Zealand, Indonesia, and the Philippines. Japan should be "the Switzerland of the Pacific," with an army only for self-defense. Back in the States, Gen. Robert Eichelberger, who had retired in 1948, was telling members of the Allied Council that a Japanese force of 150,000 men would be sufficient to confront Russia in case of war. This was the same Eichelberger who considered Japanese soldiers to be cannon fodder: "Dollar for dollar there is no cheaper fighting man in the world than the Japanese. He is already a veteran. His food is simple." MacArthur had little tolerance for such condescension. Still, the ACJ and the National Security Council kept pushing for the supreme commander to create a massive "national police force." Together with Yoshida, MacArthur stalled. To them, Article 9 of the Japanese constitution was sacrosanct. Back in America, John Foster Dulles argued for a Japanese force of 300,000 men; MacArthur refused. The Japanese people didn't want an armed force; the Americans shouldn't force them to do it. "Japanese rearmament is contrary to many of the fundamental principles which have guided SCAP ever since the Japanese surrender," said MacArthur. "Abandonment of these principles now would dangerously weaken our prestige in Japan and place us in a ridiculous light before the Japanese people."

Japan was militarily secure. The supreme commander had kept the

Russians at bay and had even managed to have cordial relations with General Derevyanko and his troublemakers. He had succeeded in holding off the Chinese seeking to bleed Japan with reparations demands, legitimate though their claims might be. He gave scant thought to this talk coming out of Washington about the "domino theory," whereby the collapse of one country might lead to the collapse of neighbor countries. An issue of the *Saturday Evening Post* arrived on his desk in March 1950 featuring an article by the respected journalist Stewart Alsop, "We Are Losing the Far East":

> The pin head was China. It is down already. The two pins in the second row are Burma and Indo-China. If they go, the three pins in the third row, Siam, Malaya and Indonesia, are pretty sure to topple in their turn. And if all the rest of Asia goes, the resulting psychological, political and economic magnetism will almost certainly drag down the four pins of the fourth row, India, Pakistan, Japan and the Philippines.

MacArthur thought Alsop was talking nonsense. Asia was not like Europe, with countries packed closely together. The Asian countries were spread out over vast distances, often thousands of miles apart, many of them with distinct cultures and religions. To lump them together was wrong. The only thing they had in common was a history of colonialism under the British, the French, and the Dutch. A commission from Washington under the leadership of President Truman's friend Robert Griffin, a newspaper publisher and much-decorated army officer, had toured the region recently and reported seeing a huge sign in Saigon: "Communism, No! Colonialism, Never!"

The biggest threat to the region's economic future was European colonialism, not Russian Communism. Communism was a danger, all right, but could be managed as MacArthur had done: by promoting workers' rights. He had taken a big gamble. Even the State Department recognized that MacArthur had won his war with the Communists (just as he had with the FEC over the constitution and with the labor agitators over a national strike). In a letter to William Sebald, John M. Allison, director of the State Department's Office of Northeast Asian Affairs, had written: "Everyone in the Department who has been connected with Japanese affairs has been impressed by the way General MacArthur has handled the Communist problem . . . [it] demonstrates that the Communist Party, given a certain amount of rope, can be its own hangman." The holy grail of the occupation was in sight, the crown jewel in MacArthur's diadem, the one thing the supreme commander sought more than anything else: a peace treaty. Since 1947 he had been pushing for it. The timing then had not been right, with many Americans still fearful of any resurgent Japanese militarism. With the rise of worldwide Communism in 1949, priorities had changed. Of all the countries in Asia, America's most likely—and certainly most powerful—ally would be Japan. Knowing of his desire for a peace treaty, the Joint Chiefs had sent several delegations to Tokyo to persuade him to back off on his advocacy, with no success. His old friend Eichelberger, now back in America, had given a speech saying a peace treaty with Japan "would be disastrous to the United States in the Far East at this time." Just as well that Eichelberger was retired and no longer working for him, otherwise the supreme commander would have personally strangled him.

In June 1950 the supreme commander got a visit from a man who, had the Republican presidential candidate Thomas E. Dewey won the 1948 election, would have become secretary of state: John Foster Dulles. Truman, in a remarkable show of bipartisanship, had appointed Dulles to be his special emissary in charge of negotiating a peace treaty with Japan. It didn't take long for MacArthur and his visitor to bond: Both were extremely moral, bright, highly egotistical, and in full agreement about the obsolescence of European colonialism. Most important of all, they shared a rabid abhorrence of war as a tool of statecraft. A peace treaty would drive that point home.

During this visit Dulles met with Prime Minister Yoshida and repeated his request for allowing 300,000 American troops. Yoshida responded with stony silence. Dulles admitted the meeting had been a total failure. The next time he came to Japan, he would need all the help he could get. No way—tempting though it was—would he bully Japan. Dulles knew from his experience on the Reparations Commission at the 1919 Versailles Peace Conference that strong demands would not work. Like MacArthur, no matter how frustrated he might be at times, he would treat the other side as an equal.

WARS HAVE A way of beginning on a Sunday morning.

On June 25, 1950, North Korea sent 90,000 soldiers across the border and routed the poorly trained 38,000 South Korean troops. The invasion was so abrupt that the first news Washington heard came not from military personnel or American foreign service officers in Korea, but from the United Press.

Six months earlier, in January, Secretary of State Dean Acheson had publicly announced an "American defense perimeter" that excluded South Korea and Formosa. Considering how North Korea pounced on its neighbor after hearing this statement, it is easy to see how one historian would conclude that "delivering this speech was not the brightest idea Acheson ever had." During his tenure as secretary of state, Acheson visited Europe eleven times, Asia not once. "The Korean attack had stirred us all up like a stone thrown into a beehive," said George Kennan. "People went buzzing and milling around, each with his own idea of what we were trying to do. . . . Never before has there been such utter confusion in the public mind with respect to U.S. foreign policy. The President doesn't understand it; Congress doesn't understand it; nor does the public; nor does the press."

Nor, for that matter, did MacArthur. He, too, had paid little attention to Korea, though it fell within his sphere of responsibility. Possibly this was because he had too many jobs: SCAP, CINCFE (Commander in Chief, Far East), and CGFEC (Commanding General, Far East Command). He was responsible for the occupation of Japan, the deployment of U.S. troops in Okinawa and Taiwan, the use of Allied troops in Japan and Korea, and the U.S. naval and air forces stationed in the Far East. For most men, running Japan would have been job enough. On July 7, the UN passed a resolution establishing a unified military command under the United States (some eighteen countries would join the coalition). The following day President Truman appointed Douglas MacArthur to the position of CINUNC, Commander in Chief, United Nations

Command. MacArthur, the only five star-general to receive the Medal of Honor, now had another "first" on his glittering résumé: commander of a United Nations force. "Mars' last gift to an old warrior," he called it.

Consistently in his term as supreme commander for Japan, MacArthur had demonstrated a remarkable ability to be ahead of Washington in his strategic thinking. Concerning Korea, however—a country he had never visited—he was woefully ignorant. The United States had a Korea expert, Dr. Arthur Bunce, a State Department economic advisor to the military government in Seoul, who had spent six years in Korea before World War II and after. In 1947 Bunce contacted his superior in Tokyo, George Atcheson, and told him that the right wing, headed by the corrupt Syngman Rhee, was losing the support of the people. To save the situation it was essential for the supreme commander to come to Korea right away and "use his prestige and influence" to help the middle-of-the-road politicians. MacArthur never bothered to come.

His sole concern was Japan. Korea was just another spot on the map. He wanted nothing to do with it: "I wouldn't put my foot in Korea. It belongs to the State Department. They wanted it and got it. . . . The damn diplomats make the war and we win them. Why should I save their skin?" Like Dean Acheson, he thought America's defense perimeter ran through Japan and should not touch the Asian mainland. In 1950 there was a compelling reason for such a policy: no money. America's defense budget, under attack by members of Congress, was stretched super-thin, with not a dollar to spare for outposts of marginal utility. Truman was president, not Eisenhower or Kennedy, with their visions of American military power and global responsibilities. Said George Marshall, despairing that there were not enough troops to contain the Soviet Union: America was "playing with fire when we have nothing with which to put it out."

The United States had no choice but to go to war in Korea—to protect Japan. Russia held Sakhalin Island and the Kurile Islands on the north of Japan, and Korea was close to Honshu, the southernmost island of Japan. Any Russian move to conquer South Korea would place Japan "between the upper and lower jaws of the Russian bear."

America may have had no spare cash, but for important items there is always money. Japan needed to be protected against possible attack by the Soviets, who were already on the Kuriles. Yet Japan didn't want American air bases. The United States had to find another island. The United States had already taken over Okinawa, four hundred miles away; now it was time to make it into a military fortress. With MacArthur's strong support, Congress in October 1949 had come up with $58 million for military construction on Okinawa. Okinawa, along with the Seventh Fleet patrolling the Straits of Taiwan, would provide Japan's security against Communist aggression.

The supreme commander was not concerned about the outbreak of war in Korea. On the day the war started, he held a meeting with John Foster Dulles, John Allison, and William Sebald. "This is probably only a reconnaissance in force," he cheerily told them. "If Washington only will not hobble me, I can handle it with one hand tied behind my back."

Really? Then why had the United States been so unprepared? Why was the South Korean army getting clobbered? When Dulles (escorted by MacArthur) went to Haneda Airport to leave, four days after the invasion, an incident gave Dulles cause for concern about MacArthur's insouciance. A message had come through from the Joint Chiefs for the supreme commander to participate in a conference call at one o'clock that afternoon. MacArthur didn't want to take the call, which would presumably involve unpleasant questions. Dismayed at the supreme commander's cavalier treatment of Washington, Dulles and Sebald concocted a ruse to get MacArthur back to his office in time for the call. They arranged for the loudspeaker to broadcast a fictitious announcement that the plane was leaving. After everyone said good-bye and Dulles and Allison boarded the plane, MacArthur got into his limousine and returned to the Dai Ichi Building. The minute they got word he was on his way, Dulles and his party returned to the waiting room, gleefully slapping hands that they had pulled off their bluff and forced MacArthur to face the music.

Korea was second priority, Japan came first. On the day he was appointed head of the UN command, MacArthur sent a letter to Shigeru Yoshida. It was a long letter, written in a style aimed to obfuscate rather than clarify. He didn't say a single word about Korea, Russia, China, or national defense; the letter was all about domestic security.

To ensure that this favorable condition will continue unchallenged by lawless minorities, here as elsewhere committed to the subversion of the due process of law and assaults of opportunity against the peace and public welfare, I believe that the police system has reached that degree of efficiency in organization and training which will permit its augmentation to a strength which will bring it within the limits experience has shown to be essential to the safeguard of the public welfare in a democratic society.

MacArthur, a forceful writer, was clearly hiding something with all this verbiage. "Events disclose," he continued, "that safeguard of the long Japanese coastal line requires employment of a larger force under this agency than is presently provided by law." At the end of the letter he finally got to the point: He authorized the Japanese government to establish a national police reserve of 75,000 men and to increase the maritime forces by 8,000 men.

And what about Article 9 of the constitution? So long as the new police force and maritime force dealt only with domestic threats, there was no violation. All that was happening was a transfer. That the 75,000 new Japanese policemen matched almost exactly the number of American servicemen being sent to Korea was just a coincidence, nothing to worry about. Still, questions persisted: What kind of training was being provided? Where was the equipment coming from? The answer, best kept quiet, was that the equipment was coming from an office in the U.S. military called the Military Assistance Advisory Group; MacArthur arranged to bury its existence by having it report to the Civil Affairs Section. He also issued strict orders that this section keep the police reserve's activities secret.

In planning his invasion of North Korea, MacArthur drew on the resources of the Japanese navy. A fleet of twenty-nine Japanese minesweepers under the command of the U.S. Seventh Fleet conducted raids on North Korea's east and west coasts, disabling mines. When the boats returned, they received a message of commendation from the commander in chief of the U.S. Navy in the Far East. Exulted the Japanese commander: "Our great undertaking . . . should be recorded permanently on the history of the newly-born Japan." Indeed—albeit under tight supervision—Japan was back in the business of war. To lead the new military forces, SCAP instructed the Japanese government to offer high salaries to attract the best candidates; when that didn't work, it "depurged" former military officers and let them back into the military.

To deal with the war raging on the Korean mainland, the supreme commander developed a plan so daring, he said, that the odds against it were 5,000–1: an amphibious landing at the South Korean port of Inchon, beset by dramatic tides in the middle of a monsoon season that required utmost precision in timing. Everything—men, equipment, and supplies—had to be put ashore in exactly one hour. What appealed to MacArthur was that Inchon was only 18 miles from the capital, Seoul. The only other possible landing port was 135 miles from Seoul, separated by a huge mountain range, with only one road to the city: much too risky. It would have to be Inchon.

The invasion succeeded, a brilliant maneuver. In an operation even more impressive than the 73,000 American troops landing at Normandy on D-Day, 70,000 men were disembarked from 262 ships in just fifty-seven minutes. The enemy was totally taken by surprise. Afterward the principal generals gathered in the supreme commander's office to congratulate him, all vying for the appropriate superlatives. Said Gen. Paul Muller: "This is one of the greatest military achievements of all time. The only thing that I can think of comparable was Wolfe's victory over Montcalm at Quebec." Not to be outdone, General Willoughby said, "No, no. It was even greater. It was like the achievement of Hannibal in crossing the Alps." MacArthur, listening and enjoying it all and smoking his pipe, chimed in: "No. It was none of those. . . . It was Napoleonic."

If it was Napoleonic, the supreme commander might have paid more attention to what happened to Napoleon after he ventured into the heart of Russia and encountered winter. MacArthur's friend Herbert Hoover advised him to "stop and dig in on the short line across Korea—and then use his Air Force on any armies north of that area." And he should beware the "oncoming winter, the impossibility of an adequate campaign in those mountains and temperature."

Yet MacArthur was flying high, impervious to counsel urging caution. Thomas Dewey caught the mood well: "The Russians," he announced with glee, "promised not to use the atom bomb against us if we promise not to use MacArthur against them." Even the president and the Joint Chiefs got swept up in the euphoria. The North Korean army was in disarray; already 60,000 prisoners had been taken. Intoxicated by the prospect of victory, George Marshall and the Joint Chiefs—with Truman's approval and UN backing—ordered MacArthur to cross the 38th parallel and proceed up to the Chinese border. Acheson and Eisenhower agreed with this controversial decision. So, too, did 64 percent of the American people in a Gallup poll. The JCS instructions were very explicit: "Your military objective is the destruction of the North Korean armed forces." Two days later George Marshall—now secretary of defense—sent him a "for your eyes only" cable: "We want you to feel unhampered tactically and strategically to proceed north of the 38th parallel."

Ostensibly to make sure they were on the same wavelength, President Truman flew three-quarters of the way to Korea for an October 15 meeting with MacArthur at Wake Island. In reality the president wanted to bask in the aura of a military hero, especially with midterm elections coming up. The supreme commander played along. The two men listened to each other, smiled a lot, posed for a photo-op of the president pinning another medal on MacArthur's chest, and went their own ways, both satisfied. MacArthur promised that the boys would be home by Christmas. He also told the president that the Chinese wouldn't dare attack, and if they did, their corpses would be so numerous they would be piled six deep. Truman, a man who believed that presidents should not get involved in military details—a mistake later made by John F. Kennedy in the Bay of Pigs fiasco—took MacArthur at his word. No serious discussion was attempted: What were U.S. objectives? What if things didn't work out as expected? What if China entered the war? What about Russia? The meeting might as well never have taken place, a waste of time by two great men who failed to do their duty.

MacArthur would later claim that no direct instructions had been given him, and no official record made. This is incorrect. The formal discussion lasted an hour and thirty-six minutes. MacArthur did most of the talking, usually in response to questions. Seven different people took notes. General Bradley, at the president's request, compiled a transcript that was sent to MacArthur's office for confirmation. The transcript was returned signed, indicating agreement (despite MacArthur's later assertions of denial).

The president called the meeting a success, though he must have been miffed when MacArthur insisted on leaving and not staying for lunch. MacArthur thought most of the people from Washington were political lightweights. "Who was that young whippersnapper who was asking questions?" he badgered his aide. (It was the senior State Department official for Far Eastern affairs, Dean Rusk.)

By the end of the month the U.S./UN forces were well into North Korea. North Korea's army had been rendered virtually nonexistent, and two million refugees were fleeing south, clogging all the roads. The Communist government of Kim Il Sung was on the run, clearly on its last legs.

Weakness invites war, MacArthur had always said. It would seem he forgot the corollary: Excessive displays of strength, too, invite war. Korea may have been a poor country nobody wanted, but as a buffer state it was very useful. For Japan it was a buffer against China; for China it was a buffer against Japan and America. Korea and China were "as close as the lips to the teeth," said Mao Zedong. Had MacArthur stopped a hundred miles south of the border, leaving plenty of space between China and the allied forces, he might have avoided the teeth. But like Icarus flying too close to the sun, he ignored the Chinese warnings and proceeded to within thirty miles of the Chinese border. Because of the north-south configuration of the Korean mountain range, he had to divide his army in two, making coordination and resupply difficult, especially with winter fast approaching. He didn't know it, but he was leading his troops into the valley of death.

His march to the Yalu wasn't a strategy, it was a reckless gamble.

Hidden in the mountainous terrain were 300,000 Chinese troops. By being lightly armed and never lighting fires to cook food, either in the daytime or at night, they had managed to avoid detection by U.S.

reconnaissance planes. On the night of November 25–26, 180,000 troops launched a savage attack and sent the allied troops reeling. Within weeks the allies were driven down to well below the 38th parallel. In seeking total victory the supreme commander had managed to accomplish what few great generals ever do: snatch defeat from the jaws of victory. It was Napoleon's retreat from Moscow all over again, including temperatures of twenty below zero. One wonders how a man like MacArthur could let such a debacle happen. Had he not learned from his disastrous experience on December 8, 1941? The warnings from the Chinese had been numerous and explicit. And where was the intelligence? Observed Missouri congressman Dewey Short, a member of the House Armed Services Committee (and a MacArthur supporter): "It is difficult to understand how 200,000 to 300,000 troops could move in, and MacArthur not know anything about it."

The ebullient MacArthur, normally so self-assured, was now Gen. Gloom-and-Doom, predicting a bloodbath. His memos to the Joint Chiefs about the poor morale of his troops raised eyebrows in the Defense Department, leading George Marshall to observe sarcastically that when a general complains of the morale of his troops, the time has come to look into his own. Even more worrisome was MacArthur's admission that his command was "incapable of holding a position in Korea and at the same time protecting Japan against external attack." U.S. objectives in Korea may have been vacillating and murky, but no way was America going to do anything to jeopardize the security of Japan.

Truman, a man who had the rare ability of a leader to see the obvious clearly, agreed totally: Japan must be protected. Two things needed to be done: straighten out this military mess, and secure a peace treaty with Japan permitting occupation by a substantial number of U.S. troops. Shortly before Christmas 1950 the Joint Chiefs, acting on MacArthur's recommendation, appointed Gen. Matthew Ridgway to be the new commander of the Eighth Army. Ridgway proved to be a brilliant commander, and immediately launched a counterattack. Within three months the American/UN forces were back at the 38th parallel, and both sides dug in for the long haul, neither side able to make much headway.

In the meantime, in January 1951, John Foster Dulles returned, with several prominent Americans in tow. The job of the so-called Dulles Peace Mission was to pursue possibilities for a peace treaty. The first thing Dulles did was huddle with the supreme commander for two hours and go over all the issues, especially the people he should meet. Dulles was very clear on what he wanted to do: see as many people as possible from government, commerce, and academia, and observe and listen. From here on MacArthur—though this was his baby—would stay out of it. Dulles' guide would be MacArthur's State Department advisor, William Sebald. Given the importance of "soft power" in such a delicate situation, special consideration would be given to the philanthropist John D. Rockefeller III, who had been to Japan twice before and had come, at Dulles' request, to advise on promoting U.S.-Japan cultural exchange. Japanese newspapers that hoped for a rapid political resolution would be disappointed: The issues to be explored and resolved were farther-reaching than just military or political. This mission must be broad, open-ended, and fair. Any decisions to be made would be made only by the American president.

The toughest obstacle to overcome would be Shigeru Yoshida. No doubt Japan needed America's military protection after North Korea's invasion, but Article 9 was sacrosanct. The diminutive (five-foot-tall) cigar-smoking Yoshida—"the Winston Churchill of Japan," SCAP teased him (knowing he was sensitive about his height)—was tough and inscrutable. How to deal with this man who had been put in jail during World War II for his antimilitarism? How to win his support for an American military presence? MacArthur told Dulles he had figured out the answer: There were two parts to this peace treaty issue, Japanese sovereignty and American military protection, and they needed to be separated: Get a peace treaty first, and make American military protection a totally separate issue.

All recommendations from the Japanese government as to whom Dulles should see—and they were many—were rejected out of hand by SCAP. The choice should be solely up to Dulles, his assistant Allison, and Sebald. Among those considered, however, were the eight hundred Japanese people who had written letters hoping for an audience, a few of whom Dulles and Sebald met.

The supreme commander then held a meeting for the entire delegation and laid out the issues as he saw them. According to John D. Rockefeller III, everyone was "very much impressed by the general—with his knowledge, his forthright and hard-hitting approach, his clarity and forcefulness of expression, and his devotion to his assignment." Clarity certainly was needed: The issues were complicated. Was Japan ready for admission to the UN? What about the Philippines and other Asian countries that demanded massive reparations Japan could not afford to pay? How to guarantee the security of Japan without rearming the country and scaring its Asian neighbors? Was there any way to strengthen Japan's defense capability without violating Article 9? With the Communist nations offering Japan territorial concessions and access to raw materials, what economic incentives could the United States offer to keep Japan on the side of the free nations?

By the time the two-week marathon was over, Dulles' open-handed approach had won many friends in the Japanese newspapers, believing that he would be compassionate and fair. Like the supreme commander, he came across as a man who had their best interests at heart. Before leaving for the Philippines to try to get the Filipinos to tone down their demands for massive reparations, he thanked the Japanese for their courtesy. "I came here with a question. I go back with answers. . . . I'm grateful to the Japanese for [their] cooperation and particularly to General MacArthur for his wise counsel." In a letter he personally handed to the supreme commander, he wrote:

> As our peace mission leaves Japan, I wish to express my profound appreciation for the assistance you have rendered us. If we have made progress on the road to peace—as I think we have—it has been due to the foundation you have laid and the wise counsel you have given. Your policies as Supreme Commander have so combined justice and mercy as to bring our late enemies to perceive and desire to share the ideals which animate our free world that makes it possible for us reasonably to plan on a future era of peace, trust and opportunity to be shared by Japan. Without that foundation our present task would have been hopeless.

Comrades in this vital effort, little did the two men know they would never see each other again.

A GENERAL CAN be forgiven for making a military blunder like MacArthur's in walking into a Chinese ambush. But he cannot be forgiven for making unapproved public statements. MacArthur never disobeyed the Joint Chiefs' military directives. He did, however, on several occasions speak too freely in public about his opinions concerning Formosa and Korea. On April 11, acting on the unanimous recommendation of his closest advisors and the Joint Chiefs, President Truman made his decision to get rid of MacArthur. The supreme commander had become too much of a loose cannon. He had also outlived his usefulness: He had done his job in Japan so well there was nothing more for him to do. As a general in Korea, he had chosen a superb military successor in Ridgway, so he was no longer needed there either.

A cable was sent to Tokyo, to be delivered personally to MacArthur in a brown envelope stamped in red letters ACTION FOR MACARTHUR. Only it didn't work out that way. Because the cable had to go through several relay stations, there was a problem getting the message through. In the meantime one of the newspapers got wind of what was happening and made an inquiry to the White House press office, which quickly issued a denial. Fearful the reporter would leak the story (as it turned out, he didn't), the White House had to move quickly.

Not many press conferences get called for one o'clock in the morning. Had a head of state died? Had Russia declared war? The announcement of news at such an hour dragged reporters out of bed. To further compound the comedy of errors, the official brown envelope got delayed in the delivery. It didn't arrive until ten minutes after MacArthur learned the news from his wife, who had gotten it from a staffer listening to the president's announcement on the radio.

The Japanese people were stunned and dismayed to lose their father figure. Could the same fate befall them? Could the United States suddenly wake up one morning and say to Japan: We're leaving; handle Russia and China by yourself. Quickly, there was talk of monuments and statues to the only peacetime leader most of them had ever known.

First to act was the port of Yokohama: It put up a bronze bust near the waterfront: "General Douglas MacArthur—liberator of Japan." Similar accolades appeared in many newspaper editorials, lamenting Japan's loss of so great a leader. The *Asahi Shimbun* said he had been a great commander who had taught the Japanese people the value of peace and democracy. The Diet passed a resolution citing the general "who helped our country out of the confusion and poverty prevailing at the time the war ended." Prime Minister Yoshida wrote to express his "shock and sorrow beyond words," and came to the embassy to personally express his gratitude for everything MacArthur had done. Then a humongous Grosser Mercedes 770 pulled up to the American Embassy, and out stepped a surprise visitor: the emperor. It was their eleventh meeting in the two thousand days of MacArthur's reign. It was an emotional meeting for both men, and the supreme commander returned the gesture by personally escorting Hirohito back to his limousine.

In the United States, Republicans reached an agreement with the Democrats to issue an invitation for MacArthur to address a joint meeting of Congress, and for a gold medal to be struck in his honor: "Protector of Australia; Liberator of the Philippines; Conqueror of Japan; Defender of Korea." (One wishes the congressmen had been more accurate. No way would MacArthur have conceived of himself as the "conqueror" of Japan. "Protector" might be acceptable; "restorer" would be more accurate and all-inclusive.) Out at Haneda Airport, painters scrubbed out the letters "*SCAP*" on the Constellation airplane used by the Supreme Commander, and substituted the word "*Bataan*."

On April 16 MacArthur left Tokyo for good. Two hundred thousand Japanese lined the streets to see him off and wish him farewell. At the airport waiting for him was an imperial deputy, the prime minister, the cabinet, Diet members, and representatives of several countries. The wife of one of the American generals observed:

> From the gates of the Embassy to the doors of the plane, all six miles, there was a solid line of guards. Japanese police, soldiers, sailors and marines. And behind them thousands lined the streets the entire way. Everywhere he moved, people applauded,

everywhere he turned, eyes followed him, some weeping, some silent, and some I am sure, among the followers of Acheson, relieved. When he turned from the seventeen-gun salute, his eyes were wet, as when he spoke to me. At other times his eyes were quiet. But I did not see him smile ... the passengers boarded the plane and the MacArthurs stood waving from the top. A roar of "Bonsai!" went up from the Japanese in enthusiasm and love for the man who had saved them and their emperor and their country.

America's successful exercise in the occupation of a country was over, the greatest feat by America's greatest general. For Japan, back on its feet, it was time to move on.

And the same for Southeast Asia, then beginning to develop. Following Japan's lead, South Korea, Hong Kong, Thailand, Malaysia, and Singapore would turn into some of the most dynamic economies in the world, stopping Communism in its tracks and saving a billion-plus people from the poverty and brutality of a North Korean regime. Douglas MacArthur, in two thousand days, had done his work well. To the extent that he saved Japan, he also saved an entire region.

PART FOUR

EPILOGUE

24

Had He Died at Inchon

MACARTHUR NOT ONLY made a fatal misjudgment in wanting to cross the Yalu, he blew his hard-earned goodwill with the Japanese. On May 5, 1951, MacArthur, during three days of congressional testimony in Washington, used an unfortunate choice of words in describing the Japanese people. The discussion was about the differences between Germany and Japan. Here is what MacArthur said:

Well, the German problem is a completely and entirely different one from the Japanese problem. The German people were a mature race. If the Anglo-Saxon was say 45 years of age in his development in the sciences, the arts, divinity, culture, the Germans were quite as mature. The Japanese, however, in spite of their antiquity measured by time, were in a very tuitionary condition. Measured by the standards of modern civilization, they would be like a boy of twelve as compared to our development of forty-five years.

Like any tuitionary period, they were susceptible to following new models, new ideas. You can implant basic concepts there. They were still close enough to origin to be elastic and acceptable to new ideas.

MacArthur went on to say that "you are not going to change the German nature . . . but the Japanese were entirely different," meaning that in Japan the United States could undertake more extensive policies to eliminate militarism than they could in Germany. All of this seemed perfectly obvious to the senators, who didn't pursue the subject and moved on to other topics.

In Japan, however, MacArthur's "like a boy of twelve"—5 words out of 174,000 over three days—caused a firestorm. He had insulted the Japanese. Overnight his luster in Japan evaporated. *"Hyaku-nichi no seppo he hitotsu,"* the Japanese would say ("One hour's cold will spoil seven years' warming"). Plans to build a big monument in Japan were abandoned. No designation of "honorary citizen" would materialize. Several large companies got together and published an ad: "We Are Not Twelve-Year-Olds!"

To be sure, not all Japanese reacted so viscerally or emotionally. The famed Japanese novelist Yukio Mishima stated on national radio: "I had thought that Japan was an old country that now needed a cane to walk, so I was happy that some famous American kindly pointed out that it's only twelve years old. Among the words Americans have bestowed upon Japan, this one has delighted me the most." Mishima continued with his argument, almost tongue-in-cheek: "I'm told that by criminal law no one under the age of fourteen has the ability to take on criminal responsibilities," meaning that "the so-called war criminals" weren't responsible for their deeds.

MacArthur's reference to "a boy of twelve" was not misplaced; in fact it was part of Western perceptions of Japanese culture. Victor Hugo, who had never visited Japan, once described Japan as "the child of the world's old age." Many nineteenth-century travelers made similar comments based on the country's modest size, lack of development, and the short stature of its people. On a more practical note, an age of twelve made perfect sense compared to the timelines of most other nations, which are expressed in terms of centuries. From the time of Commodore Perry's visit to open Japan to the outside world in 1858 and the time Japan became a world sea power ready to challenge Britain and the United States, some eighty years had passed—a remarkably short time. In likening Japan to a twelve-year-old, MacArthur also was saying that Japan would rise again. Japan may have been underdeveloped in terms of liberalism and democratic government, but it would grow quickly. Unfortunately most Japanese, still smarting from the ignominy of defeat, did not see it that way. An outsider like Victor Hugo could make a comment like this, but not the man the Japanese people had considered a father. Coming from MacArthur, the words were a slap in the face.

Finally, in early September 1951, came the moment the supreme commander had been striving for: the signing of the peace treaty, along with a separate agreement, a U.S.-Japan Security Pact. The Americans had occupied Japan for six years—a year longer than the war. Conspicuous by his absence at the San Francisco meeting was the bold leader who had made it happen. "Perhaps someone just forgot to remember," MacArthur wistfully said. What he neglected to mention was that he had insisted that the invitation come from the UN—not from the United States. Angry at his arrogance, Secretary of State Acheson refused. This wasn't the only time MacArthur forgot who he was working for. Two months before his termination, Deputy Undersecretary of State Dean Rusk had slipped a warning to William Sebald: MacArthur needed to be reminded he was an American general working for the Joint Chiefs and the president. MacArthur's response to Sebald: SCAP was an international position, and he reported not to the president but to the eleven countries of the Far Eastern Commission (though he had been only too delighted to agree with George Kennan that the FEC could be ignored whenever he felt like it). Perhaps MacArthur just forgot to look at his paycheck and see who was paying his salary.

Today in Japan, MacArthur is largely forgotten. There is only one statue of MacArthur in the entire country (at Atsugi Air Force Base).

MacArthur once said, "It's the orders you disobey that make you famous." This was back in World War I when he arrived in France as head of the Rainbow Division and refused to wear a steel helmet, insisting on sporting a cap set at a rakish angle. Today, of course, he is famous for disobeying President Truman. The best thing for MacArthur's legacy would have been if he had died at Inchon—which he almost did when he foolhardily insisted on getting close to the firefight on the beach.

As Harry Truman said, a man's fame is often determined by when he dies. MacArthur was a great man who lived too long. He once told journalist Theodore White: "Wars are over, White, wars are over. There will never be another war. Men like me are obsolete." And what were

White's thoughts about this remark? "He could be magnificently right and magnificently wrong at the same time." F. Scott Fitzgerald once wrote: "Show me a hero and I'll write you a tragedy." The drama of MacArthur's demise makes most people focus on the tragedy, which is unfortunate because it obscures the more important aspect of the man's life: the hero. In his comment to White, he was correct in saying that wars are waged differently now, and generals who pursue their goals relentlessly and don't know when to stop are unwelcome. But he over-dramatized the situation. Generals fighting a total war may be obsolete in today's era of limited wars, but good supreme commanders of occupied countries are vital—and always will be. Just as the mission of every statesman is to prevent a small foreign affairs crisis from becoming a big one, so the mission of every general is to win a war in a way that wins the peace. "Total" victory is an elastic concept, with Japan being about as "total" a victory as anyone will ever see, yet a country with a strong spirit and a willingness to work hard—two traits essential for economic growth. MacArthur's genius in administering Japan was in convincing the Japanese people that he was working for them, not for the United States. A superb administrator with considerable sensitivity to local needs—"a hard-headed softie," as George Kenney liked to say—he was the right man for the job. Because he was a general with such an awesome reputation as to be politically untouchable, operating in an arena where he had enormous freedom, he could be bold. He could introduce changes and take risks that no politician in America could ever take. Edwin O. Reischauer, the eminent historian and U.S. ambassador to Japan from 1961 to 1966, had this description of MacArthur: "The most radical, one might say even socialistic, leader the United States ever produced, and also one of the most successful."

As might be expected of a man who, like Winston Churchill, had a re-markable gift for the written word, the supreme commander's best eulogy was written by himself. Certainly it describes what he achieved in Japan, the goal of any fighting general anywhere, anytime: "Could I have but a line a century hence crediting a contribution to the advance of peace, I would gladly yield every honor which has been accorded by war."

For Korea he was not the right man. He underestimated the dangers of war in a hostile mainland occupied by millions of soldiers, especially at a time when America's military resources were stretched thin. He ignored warnings, he refused to listen. Korea did not need a man puffed with his own glory who thought himself invincible, it needed a battlefield tactician to capture a hundred miles of territory. In choosing Gen. Matthew Ridgway to take over the fighting in Korea, MacArthur made a superb choice and fulfilled one of the most basic responsibilities of a leader: choosing a successor. In so doing, for the second time (his victory at Inchon being the first) he saved Korea from being a total disaster. It was his last military gift, and a most valuable one.

He not only chose the right successor, he gave him control of both American armies in Korea, the Eighth Army and the Tenth Corps, thus ending the split that had hindered the campaign until then. Under Ridgway's leadership, in a relatively short time the Communists— despite their enormous advantages in manpower and unlimited support logistics right next door—were beaten back to the 38th parallel. By inflicting as many as ten times the casualties as the enemy could inflict on him, Ridgway proved that America could fight a war anywhere on the globe and not be beaten. That in itself was a victory (though MacArthur would never admit it).

Besides his Inchon victory and his choice of successor, there was a third gift MacArthur made to America's "victory" in Korea: the moral one. When Ridgway arrived in Korea to take over the fighting and saw how desperate the situation was, he asked the supreme commander for permission to use poison gas. MacArthur turned him down cold: "U.S. inhibitions on its use are complete and drastic."

THE IMAGE OF Truman firing MacArthur and banishing him to purgatory on the spot is incorrect. Truman asked John Foster Dulles, who of course had nothing to do with the sacking of MacArthur, to keep lines of communication open and assume responsibility for completing the last major task of the occupation: Consummate the peace treaty. Said Dulles: "With the President's knowledge and approval, I continued regularly to consult with General MacArthur and I was constantly strengthened by the pledge of his support." The two men communicated several times by phone, and came up with an approach that took everybody off the hook: Instead of the United States asking Japan for permission to install troops, it would be the reverse. The treaty would have a provision whereby Japan would request American military aid, and the United States would accept. To counter the Communists' offer of raw materials, the United States would offer a better deal—unlimited access to the U.S. home market. To protect Japanese sovereignty, America would not ask for fixed military bases on Japanese soil; rather, it would ask for the right to use its troops anywhere in Japan as necessary.

In many ways the real loser in the MacArthur-Truman controversy was Truman. By sacking the popular general and doing it in such a crude way, he outraged the Republicans and blew his chances of running for reelection in 1952. The winner of the controversy would be a third party: the likable Eisenhower, who had no baggage or major question marks.

MacArthur would not go out quietly. The American people wouldn't let him. He received 150,000 letters and 20,000 telegrams. He found himself treated to thunderous motorcades in New York, Boston, Washington, Baltimore, Miami, Houston, Dallas, Cleveland, Detroit, Chicago, Milwaukee, Seattle, and San Francisco. In New York alone, the motorcade lasted seven hours. It was the greatest outpouring of hero worship ever seen in America. Subsequently he gave a powerful speech to Congress watched by thirty million Americans, then returned to testify during a ten-day congressional investigation about the situation in the Far East and the facts concerning his relief. One of the questions, asked at the very beginning, was what day he was born. "I was born when my parents were away," he joked, bringing down the house. Thanks to President Truman, he had become a martyr. So much Sturm und Drang would focus on MacArthur and how he deserved to be fired that one has to look hard to find out what caused the firing in the first place. Yes, he disobeyed the president in his public statements. Yes, he was guilty of horrible misjudgment. Yes, he failed to keep his mouth shut.

But he did not, despite what many people believe, lead his troops north to the Yalu River against the president's orders. He was doing as he was told.

In the Senate investigation he responded to heavy questioning, earning plaudits from almost all the senators for his answers. After he finished, the next person interrogated was George Marshall. Several senators, angry at MacArthur's termination, grilled Marshall. Had the supreme commander disobeyed the president's or the Joint Chiefs' orders? No, he had not, said Marshall: "What has brought about the necessity for General MacArthur's removal, is the wholly unprecedented situation of a local theater commander publicly expressing his displeasure at and his disagreement with the foreign and military policy of the United States." The senators were not satisfied. The committee chairman asked "whether or not General MacArthur directly or indirectly violated any orders or directives." Replied Marshall: "No, he has not. . . . In relation to public statements, he has." The next day, just to make sure everyone was on the same wavelength and there was no misunderstanding, the senators brought the subject up again. Senator Alexander Wiley, a Wisconsin Republican, asked if MacArthur had ever violated the administration's policy of not bombing north of the Yalu.

MARSHALL: He did not violate the policy by military action, but he took issue with the policy before the world.
SENATOR WILEY: And that was his major sin?
MARSHALL: And created a situation where apparently we had two voices speaking for this country.

The senators then asked questions of the chairman of the Joint Chiefs, Gen. Omar Bradley, an enemy of MacArthur. Korea, Bradley famously announced, was "the wrong war, in the wrong place, at the wrong time." Were it so simple: Wars rarely occur in convenient times or places. Japan had to be protected, even if it meant involving Korea in the dead of winter. Among those who completely objected to Bradley's flip remark was the esteemed military affairs editor of the *New York Times*, Hanson Baldwin. While he disagreed with MacArthur's notion of extending war into China, he said that "to stop the spread of Asiatic communism," Korea was the right war, in the right place, and at the right time. Had we established ourselves in control of North Korea, he said in 1956, our later difficulties in Asia, as the French were losing in Indochina and we were starting to send in advisors, might have been avoided.

A Man Deeply Flawed: How Did He Do It?

*"It would mean a great deal to me if you have a moment in which
to favor me with a letter from the man who, I think, is the greatest
general in the history of the United States Army."*

—AUTOGRAPH SEEKER,
February 1946

"Thanks—I only wish I merited so high an opinion."

—DOUGLAS MACARTHUR

DOUGLAS MACARTHUR'S BATTLEFIELD career rates him a seat of honor in any military Valhalla. But generals nowadays not only have to win wars, they have to win the peace. For his performance in Japan, Douglas MacArthur rates a seat of honor in the peace Valhalla as well. Richard Nixon, in his list of seven twentieth-century leaders who changed the world, cited Douglas MacArthur (along with Shigeru Yoshida).

Leaders can be classified as two types, normal and extreme. Normal leaders fit well in an organization and seek minimal risks and incremental returns. Extreme leaders are self-centered and narcissistic, and attribute success to their own unique capabilities. More than normal leaders, they will take risks that may have a low probability of success but offer exceptionally high rewards. When they are successful in concluding an enterprise nobody else would have undertaken, they are called geniuses—and fabulous reputations are made.

Military organizations rarely have an egotist like MacArthur at the top. They are, after all, highly homogenous institutions in which officers have gone to the same types of schools and undergone the same rigorous training and the same intense evaluations at every step of their careers—meaning that potential wild cards get weeded out. MacArthur in 1935 was essentially "finished," and so he took a job with Quezon in the Philippines. Only the onset of World War II brought him back into the U.S. Army full-time, and the only reason Truman chose him to run Japan was that he had just come back from Potsdam and knew he needed a general who would be tough with the Russians. In a sense, therefore, MacArthur owed his appointment as much to Joseph Stalin as to President Truman.

Truman knew he was taking a risk with MacArthur, but Japan was ten thousand miles away, a place safe to assign a man who might succeed brilliantly—or fail catastrophically. Said George Marshall to Henry Stimson in 1944: MacArthur was "so prone to exaggerate and so influenced by his own desires that it is difficult to trust his judgment." Be that as it may, no one could question the man's idealism, intellect, or capacity for hard work. The job was a big one, and called for a man who was aggressive and daring, not a yes-man. Japan in 1945 was in desperate straits. It needed a man capable of making a huge impact.

One might describe this situation as the "plight of the conqueror." In a book about her service during the occupation, Honor Tracy identified what MacArthur was up against:

> The people of an occupied country can have no sincere feeling towards the conqueror, except to wish him gone. No matter how laudable are his intentions, or even how useful he may sometimes be, his presence is odious; he is a blot on the landscape and a constant reminder of disgrace and defeat, and of the fact that one is nothing but a second-class citizen in one's own country.

The conqueror undertaking this task was a man with serious flaws. He compared himself to Alexander, Caesar, and Napoleon and excelled all of them, or so he thought. He was unsociable and not particularly likable, though he could also be a charmer and could pour it on thick in a one-on-one meeting. He was isolated and lived in his own dream world, reinforced by a wife who called him "General" and ate up every word he said. He was self-centered, egocentric, and vain. He told a group of historians: "I don't care how you write history, gentlemen, so long as it agrees with my communiqués." When he heard the band playing the "Star-Spangled Banner," he told his wife, "Listen, Jeannie, they are playing our song." He thought grandiose. He dreamed of being president of the United States. He wanted to be George Washington. The only reason he was not a tormented, unhappy man was that he loved to work and got immense satisfaction from doing it well.

Ironically for such a peacock, he tended to be underestimated. He invited derision and occasional scorn for his antics, such as the time he had a pontoon bridge flown all the way from the United States to Korea so he could cross a river, thus giving his enemies and skeptics another opportunity to exult: "Whatever else MacArthur could do he could not walk on water." So when he pulled off a brilliant stunt like Inchon and proved he sometimes could perform miracles, his mockers were doubly amazed. He insisted on total control of his image. Unlike the navy where the head commander, Nimitz, shared the glory with Halsey and King and Spruance, with MacArthur there could be only one ray of light—and woe to any man who might share part of it. The great jungle fight in the South Pacific was Buna—100 percent won by Eichelberger. MacArthur later told him, "Bob, those were great days when you and I were fighting at Buna, weren't they?"—and he laughed. It was a veiled warning: Woe to anyone who dared disclose that MacArthur had had nothing to do with Buna. When Eichelberger appeared on the cover of *Time*, MacArthur called him into his office and read him the riot act: "Do you realize I could reduce you to the grade of colonel tomorrow and send you home?" In 1948, Eichelberger got ready to leave Japan and came to MacArthur's office to say good-bye. MacArthur was too busy to see him.

As the most famous American general of the 1930s and 1940s, MacArthur had powerful enemies—not just Truman. Secretary of State Dean Acheson, State Department advisor George Kennan, and Army Secretary William Draper were out to get him—and George Marshall was no friend. World War II secretary of war Henry Stimson observed:

MacArthur stands out as the manifest personality who has won the right to command the final land attack on Japan by virtue of his skillful work in the Southwest Pacific and the Philippines, but his personality is so unpleasant and has affronted all the men of the Army and Navy with whom he has to work that it is difficult to get combined assent on the proposition.

Secretary of State and former general George Marshall accused MacArthur of surrounding himself with sycophants and creating a court befitting a satrap—biting words from someone as reserved and taciturn as Marshall. Another name given to MacArthur's men: "the Knights of MacArthur's Round Table." Eisenhower, who had worked for MacArthur in the Philippines for seven years, said he was a "man of no character" who had "spent a life of hate and envy." The list grows. Robert Eichelberger called his boss a "strange character who wonders why he has so few friends and eternally blames the other fellow." The Australian head representative to SCAP, Macmahon Ball, said the real fault of the occupation was not that it accomplished so little but that it claimed so much. Omar Bradley once teased Eichelberger that if he teamed up with Marshall and Eisenhower to write an exposé of the occupation, he would become the hottest item in Washington (an offer Eichelberger had the good grace to refuse).

The British historian Lord Acton is famous for the epigram "Absolute power corrupts absolutely"—a saying that most definitely did not apply to Douglas MacArthur, who until Korea was careful not to step on any Washington toes while enjoying the prerogatives of an emperor, a shogun, and a president all rolled into one. But Acton was closer to the mark in his next comment: "Great men are almost always bad men." With MacArthur the order needs to be reversed: a man of major weaknesses who managed to accomplish extraordinary things.

How did he do it?

FIRST A FLASH-FORWARD to a more recent occupation. After the victory in the Gulf War of 1991, the secretary of defense argued against taking over the country:

Once you've got Baghdad, it's not clear what you do with it. It's not clear what kind of government you would put in place of the one that's currently there now. Is it going to be a Shia regime, a Sunni regime or a Kurdish regime? Or one that tilts toward the Baathists, or one that tilts toward the Islamic fundamentalists? How much credibility is that government going to have if it's set up by the United States military when it's there? How long does the United States military have to stay?

So spoke Dick Cheney, who ten years later would have to answer these questions in the Iraq War. There is no evidence he ever examined the record of MacArthur, who called his occupation of Japan "the greatest reformation of a people ever attempted." Nor, it would appear, had Cheney considered how MacArthur would have handled an enemy on the run. A MacArthur fighting the 1991 Gulf War would not have stopped at the first victory and let Saddam Hussein escape and stay in power. Had MacArthur been fighting the 2003 Iraq War he would have fought just as Gen. Tommy Franks did: a "light footprint" blitzkrieg. But once in control, he would have had a plan and enough troops for the difficult part: the occupation. MacArthur's concept of "total victory" meant not only the fighting part, it also meant the follow-up. If you attack a country and you win, you have to repair and fix it, even if it involves top-to-bottom changes in the system of governance, the constitution, the civil code, the penal code, the status of women, the school system, censorship of the newspapers, property rights, separation of church and state, food distribution, and repairing the infrastructure. If he were around in 2013, he would be horrified about the 1,000 people killed by chemical warfare in Syria, but he would be even more appalled by the Obama administration's loose talk of using airstrikes and drones "to send a message." War is not a legitimate tool of statecraft. Nor is there any such thing as "war on the cheap."

When MacArthur started his assignment as supreme commander, the prospects of success were dismal. Military occupations are notorious for their lack of permanent impact. Japan looked like an especially difficult case, given how ferociously it had fought the war. Even after the occupation was up and running and MacArthur was saying it was time to go home, naysayers like Ball, the Australian delegate to the Allied Council, were claiming the exact opposite: "In my own view some form of Allied control of Japan will be necessary for many years." Talk of twenty, even fifty years was commonplace. The Japanese could stymie MacArthur, knowing time was on their side, as Shigeru Yoshida did when he told local authorities there was "no need of adopting SCAP's costly new education system, because the Americans soon will be gone anyway."

MacArthur understood this. Military occupations don't last long. He must move quickly and decisively. "The minute I left Japan," he said, "so would the changes. These things had to come from the Japanese themselves, and they had to come because the Japanese people sincerely wanted them."

Japan in late 1945 was a country where the red light had suddenly turned green. Due to the shock of the atom bomb and the final, belabored realization of total defeat, supported by the emperor's ability to influence people to accept the surrender, the spirit of militarism had miraculously evaporated overnight. Into this void stepped MacArthur, literally dropping out of the sky in his plane. Observed Rovere and Schlesinger: "The overpowering need was for faith, for a mystique, for a moral revival in the midst of moral collapse. The powerful and dedicated figure of MacArthur filled that need" in administering "neither a soft peace nor a hard peace."

All leadership is largely situational, the right man in the right place at the right time (Winston Churchill is a perfect example). What makes MacArthur an unusual leader is how significant his success was throughout his entire life. He was not a one-shot wonder. Beginning with West Point, where he was first in his class, he had always risen to the top. He was America's most decorated soldier in World War I. After delivering an even more brilliant performance in World War II, he faced a totally different challenge: winning the peace. Fortunately for him the factors for continued success were in place: a country that had surrendered without being invaded, an industrious people who admired success (as opposed to resenting it), a fully functioning local government, a cooperative emperor, and substantial Washington support in terms of staff, resources, and money. And, of course, unlimited power to feed his colossal ego and keep him happy. He was in his element.

In the late 1950s William Ganoe, a former aide to MacArthur at West Point, identified MacArthur's treatment of subordinates as key to his leadership. He shared his ideas with Gen. Jacob Devers, head of the 6th Army in Europe during World War II and one of America's top generals. Interestingly, Devers had never worked with or even met MacArthur, he only heard about him through his friend Ganoe and through Robert Eichelberger, his West Point classmate. But MacArthur's reputation was so well known throughout the army that Devers agreed to collaborate with Ganoe on a book about MacArthur's leadership. Together they developed what they called the "MacArthur Tenets." No explanation of the tenets was provided, just a list of questions. There were seventeen of them, mostly dealing with obvious fundamentals such as delegation and responsibility: Do I act in such a way as to make my subordinates want to follow me? Do I delegate tasks that should be mine? Do I arrogate everything to myself and delegate nothing? Do I understand my subordinates by placing on each one as much responsibility as he can stand? Is my door open to subordinates? Other tenets address matters of personal comportment. Am I a constant example to my subordinates in character, dress, deportment, and courtesy? Do I correct a subordinate in the presence of others? Am I interested in the personal welfare of each of my subordinates, as if he were a member of my family?

Several other tenets were quite specific, inviting response concerning MacArthur's performance:

Do I heckle my subordinates or strengthen and encourage them?

MacArthur looked after his men and let them know how much he valued them—at least when he needed them. He told Eichelberger: "Bob, if you get a bloody nose, I'll give you every man I have." When Cappy Harada came up with the idea of inviting American baseball players to Japan for a series of exhibition games, he put Harada on the plane to America and told him, "Get it done." In 1950 America's greatest baseball star came to Japan. The crowds went wild as the great Joe

DiMaggio came onto the field, and the man escorting him and basking in the limelight was not MacArthur, it was Harada.

He never threw his subordinates to the wolves to boost his own position. Informed by the president of the Scripps-Howard newspaper chain that so long as he kept "radicals" like labor advisor Theodore Cohen he could not hope to get the newspaper chain's support for the presidency, MacArthur stood his ground and gave his beleaguered employee a big promotion. Such supportive treatment of subordinates applied also to senior Japanese officials. When he had to overturn their draft of a new constitution and have his men redo it, he resisted attempts to call it "a MacArthur constitution" and insisted that the Japanese be given full credit.

Do I use moral courage in getting rid of subordinates who have proven themselves beyond doubt to be unfit?

MacArthur had a problem with his long-standing Bataan chief of staff, Richard Sutherland, because Sutherland was too narrow-minded and inflexible to handle diplomatic duties. When Sutherland committed the double sin of having an affair with a WAC officer and trying to go around his boss and build his own coterie of loyalists, MacArthur fired him on the spot.

Whenever someone was unfit, MacArthur always dealt with him face-to-face. "To take up a painful matter by letter or other communication," he said, "is not only the rankest cowardice but the ruination of morale."

Have I done all in my power by encouragement, incentive, and spur to salvage the weak and caring?

From day one, MacArthur made it clear that he was on a humanitarian mission. One of his very first commands was that American troops not consume any of Japan's precious food supplies. He ordered food and medical supplies to be brought into the country, and set up local distribution centers throughout Japan to provide relief and to stamp out the local black markets. It was done quickly, and compares in size only to Herbert Hoover's massive food relief in Belgium and France after World War I.

MacArthur knew that helping the weak and vulnerable required more than just providing handouts and freebies. In supporting the formation of labor unions and women's equal rights, he gave people who could not protect themselves the means to become self-reliant and independent.

Do I know by NAME and CHARACTER a maximum number of subordinates for whom I am responsible? Do I know them intimately?

MacArthur had a phenomenal memory that dazzled his staff. Just as he could read a memo and recite it back an hour later almost word for word, he carried in his head a huge bank of names and other valuable information from many years in the past.

Did MacArthur know people intimately? No. In Japan he adopted a totally different style of management from his days as a general, when he was everywhere, mingling with his troops and running to the scene of gunfire. No longer was he the general who had once said "a commanding officer is best when he has observed the situation himself." Instead he withdrew into the four walls of his office and ventured outside only for lunch. Observed General Willoughby: MacArthur "knew his authority would be greater if it came from a Jovian distance." Such distance would create a "deliberate mystique."

Am I thoroughly familiar with the technique, necessities, objectives, and administration of my job?

That there were no major foul-ups or charges of corruption during his reign is a tribute to his superb ability as an administrator. He may have been remote as a person, but as an administrator he was thoroughly involved and hands-on. None of his SCAPINS were half-baked or had to be recalled because they were poorly conceived.

Like a president of the United States, he knew the most important person in his administration was the chief of staff. In Courtney Whitney, he had a superb one. He divided his organization into sections, appointed top-class officers, and let them run the show. SCAP was a remarkably lean organization. Personal initiative and responsibility took precedence over procedure. "Rules," said MacArthur, "are mostly made to be broken and are too often for the lazy to hide behind."

More important than his performance as a manager was his performance as a leader. The two roles are different. The Harvard Business School professor John Kotter defines the difference in succinct fashion: One copes with complexity, and the other—leadership—copes with change. "Most organizations are overmanaged and underled," he says.

Nobody would say this about MacArthur's SCAP. It was an organization determined to shake up the status quo, rid Japan of feudalism and militarism, and protect the country from its major external threat, the Russians. These were extremely ambitious goals, the kind of goals that call for leadership rather than management.

Do I lose my temper at individuals?

MacArthur was a master of self-control. The same fearlessness he displayed in battle he carried over into his office. When he got word he had been fired by President Truman, he evinced no anger or outrage. No matter how upset he must have been at the callous way it was handled, he did not lash out. Minutes after he had left Tokyo for good, John Foster Dulles' plane passed by, coming from the opposite direction. By telephone in midair, they had a lengthy talk about what needed to be done in Japan. Dulles noted: "I never had greater admiration for a man. Under such provocation, he still uttered not a word of personal bitterness; he considered only the cause of his country. . . . As long as America can produce men of that stature and caliber it will be safe."

Have I the calmness of voice and manner to inspire confidence, or am I inclined to irascibility and excitability?

In keeping with the above tenet about self-control, MacArthur was a master of serenity—a quality rarely mentioned in books on leadership. MacArthur possessed what Voltaire praised in Marlborough: "that calm courage in the midst of tumult, that serenity of soul in danger, which is the greatest gift of nature for command."

He never lost his temper. He radiated calm and self-assurance throughout his tenure. According to John J. McCloy: "He was most impressive as he talked about the future and the forces that were playing around the Orient with which he was quite familiar. He was a man of tremendous discernment. . . . He was a thoughtful man, he was not a poseur."

Am I inclined to be nice to my superiors and mean to my subordinates?

Here the evidence is mixed. MacArthur was not a butt-kisser who toadied to the powers that be in Washington. He followed his own drummer, and got away it by being extremely charming with visitors from Washington. He was a master at seeming to agree with people when in fact he didn't. People could get frustrated with MacArthur, but it was hard to get angry at him.

Asked by his military secretary Faubion Bowers how he managed to make such a powerful impression on people who came to see him, he said: "I just give 'em a shot of truth. They're so unused to it, it knocks 'em for a loop."

There's a wonderful story about MacArthur in World War I that showed his compassion toward subordinates. Brig. Gen. Douglas MacArthur was in the trenches just before dawn; he took the Distinguished Service Cross ribbon from his own tunic and pinned it to the chest of a young major about to lead his battalion into battle, explaining that he knew the major would do heroic deeds that day.

Such displays of personal concern can spur followers to excel. MacArthur treated his subordinates decently; he never bullied or browbeat them. He had his personality differences with Eisenhower, his long-standing aide in the Philippines, but never let that interfere with his professional judgment. In a fitness report on Eisenhower, he wrote: "This is the best officer in the Army. When the next war comes, he should go right to the top."

With men his equal, however, MacArthur could be tough, even mean. He went after generals who beat him and demanded revenge. Instead of treating Yamashita and Homma like honorable warriors, he made sure the U.S. Military Tribunal sent them to the gallows. One of his closest colleagues was Robert Eichelberger, who had won the pivotal battle at Buna and who he insisted be the first to greet him at Atsugi. The two men had known each other since 1911. When Eichelberger emerged from the jungle after winning Buna, MacArthur was there to greet him—with a chocolate milk shake. Their relationship cooled in 1946, when Eichelberger expressed his wish to leave and go work in Washington for Eisenhower and hopefully succeed him as army chief of staff. MacArthur blocked the move, and when Eichelberger left Japan two years later, MacArthur gave him only a perfunctory send-off.

Do I think more of POSITION than JOB?

Twice he turned down invitations from Truman to appear in Washington as a hero, with all the publicity and visibility it would have generated. He was absolutely right: The situation in Tokyo was critical; this was not a time to run off and play crowd-pleaser. He couldn't even be bothered to pick up a Harvard honorary degree.

Other than president, there was no job big enough for a man of his ambition and talents. He knew his post in Japan was a last stop in his career, with no opportunity for promotion. Yet he took the job seriously, and put in hours that would have exhausted younger men.

MACARTHUR MADE EIGHT bold moves when he went against or vastly exceeded Washington's wishes, any one of which could have seriously jeopardized his tenure. They were:

- recommending an immediate, major reduction of troops
- initiating a massive food relief program
- rejecting repatriation demands
- pushing for Article 9
- blackballing the Japanese version of the new constitution
- giving free license to Communist agitators in labor unions
- vetoing Dulles's proposal for a 3,000-man police force
- launching the surprise amphibious attack at Inchon

In every single one of them MacArthur was right, and Washington was wrong.

He had "the gift of command," said William Randolph Hearst. The components of this gift were mastery of sound policy, sensitivity to the local culture, and personal traits of flexibility, persuasiveness, and idealism.

Sound Policy

AS EVERY CEO will agree, more important than "strategy" (goals and means) is "policy" (purpose and rationale). MacArthur's job was to develop permanent peace and democracy in Japan. Everything he did was directed toward this mission. When superiors in Washington wanted him to pursue specific Cold War objectives (preserve the *zaibatsu*, build up the Japanese military), he did so only with the greatest reluctance. Such objectives were not consistent with his mission.

He undertook bold new measures—labor unions and women's rights— that were disruptive but consistent with his mission. In promoting pro-democracy measures even more liberal than current practices in the United States, he was a man ahead of his time. He was a master of "soft power" in communicating America's culture, political ideals, and aspirations.

Walter Lippmann once said that effective leadership consists not of giving people what they want, but of giving them what they will learn to want. MacArthur was very much an agent of change, attempting to push Japan toward a new future. He ran a highly disciplined, well-behaved organization. His troops, on the whole, behaved superbly and became popular ambassadors for America and its values.

He was not reckless or impulsive. He took a tremendous risk at Atsugi, but it was a gamble based on a careful reading of the Japanese mood and situation. It was a risk worth taking because the rewards would be so extraordinarily high. Almost everything he did was according to plan. He announced eleven specific objectives to his fellow generals on the Okinawa-to-Atsugi flight—and he accomplished them all.

Sensitivity to the Local Culture

FROM THE MOMENT he landed at Atsugi not wearing a firearm, he let the Japanese people know he trusted them. They were a beaten people; he would not humiliate them by showing up with a lot of guns. He never strutted around in public wearing all his medals, reminding them he was a victorious general. He always dressed informally, like he did in his first meeting with Hirohito.

He jumped immediately to meet their desperate need for food. He preserved the emperor, even if he had to perform considerable gymnastics to do so. He let almost all Japanese government employees keep their jobs, and motivated them by giving them important tasks to do, under American guidance and supervision. He reduced American troop levels (making Japan happy, Washington unhappy). He read every single letter sent to him by the Japanese people, and went so far as to meet with a man who tried to assassinate him, so as to glean deeper insight into Japanese sensibilities, even perverted ones. He quashed public exposure of the atrocities of Unit 731, not only to keep the biological research away from the Russians but also to avoid damaging Japan's international image.

Seeing how the Japanese were having trouble developing a new constitution, he ordered his staff to jump in and do it in one week—no messing around. He never insulted the Japanese or put them down. He did not blow up and insist it was his way or no way. He entertained modifications, and when the final version finally came out he gave the Japanese full credit. According to Shigeru Yoshida:

> General MacArthur's headquarters did insist, with considerable vigor, on the speedy completion of the task and made certain demands in regard to the contents of the draft. But during our subsequent negotiations with GHQ there was nothing that could properly be termed coercive or overbearing in the attitude of the Occupation authorities towards us. They listened carefully . . . in many cases accepted our proposals.

Flexibility

WARNED THAT GEORGE Atcheson might be a State Department "pink," MacArthur kept an open mind and gave the man a chance. On another occasion when he issued three directives and Mamoru Shigemitsu came to him and said it wouldn't work, MacArthur revoked them immediately and set about revising them. When George Kennan came to see him with new demands from Washington, MacArthur cooperated. On the other hand, when the Communists stepped over the line and went too far in taking advantage of his labor union reforms, he went after them vigorously. He did not bluff.

The son of a general, and a military man all his life, he was unlike most generals who "think of the last war." He was always thinking ahead. Of all the World War II generals, he was the most aggressive in advocating new technologies in motorized transport, fast boats, and aircraft. He recognized the obsolescence of Clausewitz's "war is policy by other means" in a world of atom bombs, and became a fierce opponent of attempts to build up "offensive" military operations intended solely to intimidate.

Considerable credit for his success belongs to the Joint Chiefs in Washington, who gave him good plans to work with. But planning can only do so much. The idea of exhibition baseball games didn't come from Washington, or even from MacArthur, it came from a lowly lieutenant. Knowing a good idea when he saw one, MacArthur pounced on it—on the spot.

Persuasion

HE WAS AN extremely hard worker. Officials who conferred with him were astounded how well prepared he was and how much he knew about their particular areas of expertise. He outdueled Nimitz in persuading the president how to wage the Pacific war. One on one with important visitors like Hirohito, Shigemitsu, Yoshida, McCloy, Kennan, Dodge, and Dulles, even lesser visitors like Choate and Griffin, he dazzled them all. At the Wake Island meeting, where neither protagonist was at his best, he still managed to astound his audience with his mastery

of distances, temperatures, artillery, aircraft, and number and configuration of troops. Army Secretary Frank Pace, who had never met him
before, concluded MacArthur "was indeed a military genius . . . the
most impressive fellow I ever heard." Added Truman's special counsel
Charles Murphy: "I believed every word of it."

His speeches to the Japanese public, beginning with the surrender
signing, were inspirational and uplifting. He expressed big ideas—
nothing pedantic or parochial. He was a serious man: He never started
a speech with a silly joke or how honored he was to be there. He was a
superb communicator, with a rich vocabulary and a mastery of cadence.
He could be mesmerizing. Who else could write like he could? "He died
unquestioning and uncomplaining, with faith in his heart and victory
his end."

As manager of a large enterprise, he communicated his wishes to his
thousands of employees fully. Everybody knew what the boss wanted
done, and they did it. He assembled a staff that covered all the political bases. He had liberals and New Dealers under Whitney, counterbal-
anced by conservatives under Willoughby. Somehow they all managed
to work under one roof. There was remarkably little backstabbing. Why?
Because everyone feared him, they knew they must act professionally.

A number of visitors, observing how loyal MacArthur's staff members were to him, accused him of surrounding himself with yes-men.
This was a simplistic observation. MacArthur was so smart he usually
was right. People who rebutted him were welcome so long as they knew
their facts. Eisenhower stated that he argued with his commander for
the nine years they were together and they had no problem.

Idealism

"WARRIOR RAGE" WAS never part of his temperament. He was no William Tecumseh Sherman whose scorched-earth policies created Southern hatred that lasted for decades (as a Southerner, MacArthur was very
much aware of this). He had none of the attitude of Admiral Halsey,
who had posted signs in a Pacific seaport on the way to Japan: "Kill
Japs. Kill Japs. Kill All the Lousy Bastards." Like Ulysses Grant, he

fought relentlessly like a warrior, but had no admiration for generals who incurred massive casualties and needless deaths in pursuit of victory. He set a standard for moral conduct toward an enemy who in war had shown hardly any honor at all. He was betting—correctly, it turned out—that in peace the enemy would respond positively to his overtures and cooperate.

But it wasn't easy. The Japanese military and *zaibatsu*—with the government looking the other way—were having a field day stealing wartime supplies for their personal aggrandizement and benefit, while the masses were starving. Corruption was rampant. Ishii was playing games. The Communists were making trouble at every opportunity. The economy was a shambles. No country in Southeast Asia wanted to trade, they all wanted revenge.

Yet throughout it all, MacArthur never wavered. He was imbued with a strong sense of idealism and purpose. It may be fashionable in certain political circles today to knock idealism as causing America to get into foreign policy excesses, but properly applied in places like Japan after World War II, idealism brought out the best in American influence. For the final word on MacArthur as a transformational leader, a comment by the historian Kazuo Kawai:

> One reason for his influence on the Japanese was his dedicated sense of mission. The egoism fringed with mysticism, with which he regarded himself as the chosen instrument for the reformation and redemption of the Japanese people, might sometimes be ludicrous and sometimes irritating. But there was no mistaking the sincerity and intensity of his idealism. . . . He lifted the tone of the Occupation from a military operation, to a moral crusade.

26

Aftermath

Douglas MacArthur

FOR THE NEXT twelve years he lived a quiet life in a ten-room suite on the thirty-first floor of the Waldorf-Astoria Hotel in New York, paying a subsidized rent of $450 a month (thanks to the hotel owner Conrad Hilton). His neighbor, living one floor above him, was his old boss Herbert Hoover. Down the hall was his friend Courtney Whitney. On either side of the private entrance to the Waldorf Towers on East Fiftieth Street, one will find a plaque, one for MacArthur, one for Hoover.

He took a position as chairman of Remington Rand (later Sperry Rand), based in Stamford, Connecticut, and commuted by limousine two or three times a week. In 1964 he published his memoir, *Reminiscences*, which became a huge bestseller.

He never went back to Japan.

He did not wish to be buried in Arlington National Cemetery, as he put it, "surrounded by his enemies." He made arrangements for a huge memorial and library to be built in Norfolk, Virginia, a navy town. In this memorial he and his wife are now buried. He died on April 5, 1964. Only one head of state came to his funeral: former Japanese prime minister Shigeru Yoshida. Truman and Eisenhower declined to attend.

Every year his name comes up when the National Football Foundation, which he was instrumental in establishing in 1947 (with Army coach Red Blaik and journalist Grantland Rice), announces the top college football team in the nation. The winning team receives the MacArthur Bowl, a twenty-five-pound silver trophy shaped like a football stadium. On the trophy are inscribed the words "There is no substitute for victory." His legacy as a football fan lives on.

Jean MacArthur and Arthur MacArthur IV

JEAN WAS SIXTY-FOUR when her husband died. She stayed in the Waldorf Towers and lived until 2000. She died at the age of 101. She received the Medal of Freedom in 1988 from President Reagan, the Legion of Merit from the Philippines in 1993, and a visit by Emperor Akihito and Empress Michiko during their 1994 visit to the United States. Young Arthur MacArthur IV, who was seven at the start of the occupation and fourteen at the end, was one of the world's most publicized children (even appearing on the cover of *Life* magazine). He had no interest in following the illustrious career of his father and grandfather. He majored in music at Columbia and pursued a short career as a composer. He eventually drifted into the bohemian community of Greenwich Village, and faded from view. He is believed still to be living in New York, under an assumed name.

Japanese Constitution

MACARTHUR STARTLED MANY people when he predicted that the Japanese constitution would last a hundred years. May 3, the day the constitution became effective, was not a big day in 1947, but it is now. It's Japan's national holiday, when people celebrate a document that has survived intact for nearly seven decades, exactly the way MacArthur left it. No major amendment or revision has been made.

Japanese History of World War II

FOR TWENTY YEARS, in its published guidelines for the basic history textbooks for Japanese schools, Japan's Education Ministry devoted more than two hundred pages to World War II. In 1977 it abruptly reduced the guidelines to six pages, consisting mostly of photos of Hiroshima and Nagasaki, a table of Japanese war dead, and photographs of the firebombing of Tokyo.

This effort to rewrite history and present itself as a victim drew an immediate international reaction. Virtually every nation that had fought against Japan protested vehemently. What about all the wartime atrocities and seventeen million people killed by Japan? The United States said nothing. (A visitor to Hiroshima will be surprised to see a monument to the dead of Auschwitz. It is Japan's effort to align itself with the Jews as the war's victims.)

The occupation, like war guilt, is widely considered to be best forgotten. A publicity booklet put out by the Ministry of Foreign Relations, *The Japan of Today*, makes no mention of the occupation at all: "In August 1945 an exhausted and battle-weary nation accepted the surrender terms of the Allied powers and by Imperial edict the people laid down their arms. Seven years later, in September 1951, Japan signed the peace treaty."

State Shinto, banned by the occupation, continues to exist. The Yasukuni Shrine in Tokyo had in front two huge bronze lanterns bearing friezes engraved with figures of Japanese war heroes and scenes of celebrated battles. The Shinto priests were ordered by the Americans to cover the reliefs with cement. Several years after the Americans left, in 1957, the cement was removed.

Shiro Ishii

THE ISHII STORY, covered up during the occupation, remained in the shadows for many years. None of the major players of the occupation—MacArthur, Whitney, and Willoughby—mentioned it in their memoirs. Nor did Truman, Marshall, or Acheson. Even major books about MacArthur and Japan—William Manchester's *American Caesar* (1978), Clayton James' *The Years of MacArthur* (1985), John Dower's *Embracing Defeat* (2000), and Eiji Takemae's *Inside GHQ* (2002) contain only single lines, maybe a paragraph. The only information about Ishii is found in specialized books on bioterrorism.

Almost all of the latter, written many decades after the occupation, express horror at MacArthur's apparent lack of conscience and morality. It is easy to forget the circumstances at the time, plus no military commander would dare make such a decision on his own. MacArthur kicked the Ishii question upstairs to the Joint Chiefs and the White House, and they all went back and forth for two years before deciding what to do. The decision they made was unanimous; there was not a single voice of dissent. Leaders frequently have to do things they are not proud of.

A more interesting question, rarely asked by academics writing about MacArthur and the occupation, focuses on the amorality of the Japanese. After the 1951 peace treaty and the dissolution of SCAP, the Japanese government might have rescinded the immunity deal and gone after the Unit 731 scientists. It did not. In fact it did just the opposite: It leaned over backward: Many of these rogues attained high positions in academia and government, and some, like Ryoichi Naito, became CEOs of major pharmaceutical companies. One scientist, using his knowledge of frozen bodies, became chief advisor to a Japanese expedition to the South Pole, and another scientist became president of Japan's largest blood-processing facility. Ishii lived the rest of his life in quiet retirement, and died in 1967, at the age of sixty-seven, of natural causes. Rumors surfaced that the United States had brought Ishii to America to consult with scientists at Fort Detrick (originally called Camp Detrick). There is no evidence of this.

In 1982 China, protesting the rewriting of Japanese schoolbooks and elimination of any mention of atrocities, raised the case of germ warfare at Harbin. At Harbin it built a museum consisting of wax models of vivisections, which can be seen on the Internet under the heading "Pingfan."

For a nation not known for facing unpleasant truths, the Japanese people pulled a major surprise that year. A book came out in Japan by Seiichi Morimura and Masaki Shimozato exposing, for the first time, the Unit 731 atrocities, called *The Devil's Gluttony*. It became a Japanese bestseller. Apparently the Japanese people have a greater capacity to face the truth than the Japanese government.

Defendants Convicted at the IMTFE Trial

SIX OF THE eighteen sentenced to prison terms died in prison, one of them being General Umezu, the man who stopped Ishii and later signed the *Missouri* surrender. Shigemitsu was released in 1950. Most of the other prisoners were released in 1954. By 1958, all the remaining prisoners were free.

JFK and Vietnam

IN 1961 PRESIDENT John Kennedy met MacArthur for the first time, expecting to find "a stuffy and pompous egocentric." He was surprised: MacArthur was "one of the most fascinating conversationalists he had ever met, politically shrewd and intellectually sharp." He followed up by inviting MacArthur to lunch at the White House. It lasted almost three hours. According to presidential aide Kenneth O'Donnell, MacArthur implored JFK to stay out of Vietnam and any other part of the Asian mainland; the so-called domino theory was a ridiculous concept in a nuclear age; to maintain military security, America's domestic problems merited far more priority than Vietnam. Kennedy came out of the meeting "stunned" and "enormously impressed."

The Genie Comes Out of the Bottle

"NEVER PROPHESY, ESPECIALLY about the future," said the movie magnate Samuel Goldwyn. In 1950 Japan's future looked very uncertain. MacArthur was confident his efforts had been successful, but no one in his right mind could have predicted the economic juggernaut Japan would soon become. Certainly not John Foster Dulles, who advised the Japanese to export their cars to Asia because they would never be able to produce the type of vehicles that American consumers wanted.

By the mid-1960s, when Japanese cars and electronic goods appeared out of nowhere to capture global markets, it became obvious that the "boy of twelve" had grown up. During this time, the president of a Latin

American country visited Japan and asked a Japanese minister the reasons for Japan's success. "The best way to obtain freedom and prosperity," the minister replied, "was to wage war against the United States and lose it."

By 1990, Japan had the world's second-strongest economy after the United States, twice the size of Germany's and eighteen times the size of Great Britain's. Today Japan is the world's largest creditor nation and ranks among the top three countries on virtually every economic indicator: size of economy, private financial assets, R&D, patents, industrial output, manufacturing output, and services. On quality of life, it ranks number one in life expectancy and among the top three in book and music sales and international spending.

Lessons from Japan on How to Run an Occupation in Iraq

SADLY, THEY WERE LOST. Admirable though America's objectives were in going into Iraq and freeing the people from an oppressive regime, the effort fell short due to massive incompetence and fraud. Most regrettable was the total lack of planning, and the cavalier bet that American troops would be greeted with flowers. A bet is not a plan. Most unfortunate of all, the United States tried to undertake the mission without a heavyweight leader. As any executive recruiter knows, you don't undertake a difficult project if you don't have the right person to run it; otherwise it's best to stay away. As MacArthur would say, you don't undertake a war unless you absolutely have the resources to win it.

Iraq and Japan are obviously very different, but that's what good planning is supposed to do: analyze the situation and develop an appropriate strategy. Our occupation of Japan was one of the greatest feats of American leadership; our occupation of Iraq was the opposite. In 2003, as it prepared to invade Iraq in what hopefully would be no more than a few days, the United States had in its possession enough experience and know-how to write the definitive manual on how to run an occupation. Inexcusably and inexplicably, the United States ignored it. Nobody in the government bothered to open up a history book.

Yet one must not be so facile. MacArthur's greatest military triumph was Inchon. Virtually nobody thought it would work. The enemy was on a roll, the Allied forces were in bad shape. MacArthur knew he had to do something extraordinary and dramatic. To minimize the risks he developed a meticulous plan down to the last detail of a massive one-hour assault.

In 2006 in Iraq, the U.S. Army was in a similar situation: getting knocked about by the insurgents. Morale was low, Americans were losing hope. What to do? The Defense Department developed an equally detailed plan—an outrageous gamble—calling for an *increase* in troops, to be headed by the man in charge of counterinsurgency, Gen. David Petraeus. Washington was abuzz; more troops in Iraq was the last thing people wanted to hear. Yet President Bush authorized Petraeus to go ahead; he would take the heat if it failed. Naysayers in America—and they were legion, including presidential candidates Barack Obama and Hillary Clinton—said the surge would never work. . . .

How Douglas MacArthur would have jubilated at the result. When a plan is carefully thought out and the upside far outweighs the downside, a massive risk can be called "prudent."

So, too, was the American occupation of Japan. It was a gamble that few people thought would end well. Thanks to the supreme commander, it did.

Notes

PREFACE

xiii *"He is shrewd"*: Lewin, 178.

xiv *majestic title*: Dwight Eisenhower also went by the title of Supreme Commander, but it was solely in a military capacity, first as Supreme Allied Commander, Expeditionary Forces (for the Normandy invasion), and later as Supreme Commander when he was head of NATO for a brief period in 1951. MacArthur had the more exalted full title ("of the Allied Powers"). He also had substantially more responsibility, both civil and military.

xiv *"had such enormous"*: Sebald, 103. William Sebald, who carried the rank of ambassador, was the State Department representative in Japan during the occupation.

xiv *"The greatest gamble"*: Wildes, 12; Kelley and Ryan, 144.

xiv *"without a single shot"*: Yoshida, 50.

xv *"one of the worst-reported"*: Gunther, xiii.

xv *"MacArthur is our greatest"*: Schmidt, 192; Harvey, 207

xv *Jimmy Doolittle raids*: It should be noted today where there is controversy over the U.S. use of drones in Afghanistan and Pakistan that the Doolittle raids on Japan were extremely successful in avoiding off-limits targets such as schools, hospitals, and the Emperor's Palace—in sharp contrast to Japanese bombers that deliberately attacked Red Cross and Allied hospital ships.

xv *Japanese peace overtures and no need for atom bomb or invasion*: Walter Trohan, "Rare Peace Bid U.S. Rebuffed 7 Months Ago," *Chicago Tribune*, August 19, 1945; Evans and Romerstein, 202; Kubek, 116–20.

xvi *ten million Japanese might have starved*: Dower, 93; Frank, *Downfall*, 35; Irokawa, 37.

1: A PRESIDENT ROLLS THE DICE

6 *Truman wishing the Medal of Honor over the U.S. presidency*: Perret, 638. Just one month later, in presenting the Medal of Honor to Gen. Jonathan Wainwright, the president actually said this to several generals.

7 *"discussed . . . Supreme Commander"*: Truman Diaries, June 17, 1945, in *Off the Record*. Truman misquoted the expression by including the Lodge family. The original quote from John C. Bossidy's 1910 poem read: "And this is good old Boston, The home of the bean and the cod, Where the Lowells talk to the Cabots, And the Cabots talk only to God."

7 *"a play actor . . . how a country"*: Ibid.

7 *"MacArthur says"*: Manchester, 145.

7 *"a senior officer should not be"*: MacArthur, 85.

8 *Japanese attack on Clark, Iba, and Nichols airfields*: Bergamini, 856.

8 *"making a mistake"*: Truman Diaries, August 10, 1945, in *Off the Record*, 60.

2: FLYING NINE HUNDRED MILES FROM OKINAWA TO ATSUGI

10 *"My God, general"*: Manchester, 444; Breuer, 236.

10 *"You will exercise"*: U.S. Department of State, *Occupation of Japan*, Appendix 16, 89, in Perry, 63.

10 *"Manila is ours"*: Lee and Henschel, 178.

11 *C-54 marked* Bataan: There were actually two *Bataan*s. The famous one, used by MacArthur in the Philippines, was a B-17E Flying Fortress, at the time back in California undergoing a total overhaul. In need of a more modern aircraft, MacArthur accepted delivery of a new C-54, called *Bataan II*. This was the plane he used in Japan for two years until it was replaced by a Super G Constellation marked *SCAP*.

11 *"Harbor mined"*: Brines, 39–40.

11 *"a ghostly fox"*: Archer, 140.

12 *"Our experts"*: Mashbir, 22.

13 *"The winner of the next war"*: Hunt, 77.

13 *"Take Buna"*: Eichelberger, 21. This was vintage MacArthur language: "or not come back alive"—much more memorable than "don't come back alive."

13 *"the two best damn officers"*: Ibid., xviii.

13 *three Army positions appointed solely by FDR*: Ibid., xi.

14 *"pictures of cadets"*: Ibid., xviii.

14 *"We have stopped"*: Drape, 240.

14 *"deserved a team"*: Ibid., xix.

14 *"Had there been"*: Schoor, 27–28.

15 *"To take up"*: Ganoe, 48.

16 *"If at any time"*: Mashbir, 309.

17 *Imperial Order of Meiji (medals of Eichelberger)*: Cover story, "General Robert Eichelberger," *Time*, September 10, 1945, 32.

18 *"The Japanese High Command"*: Eichelberger, xii.

18 *"I am Commander Anatoliy Rodionov"*: Craig, 288.

18 *the Russians and General Yamashita*: Breuer, 185–86.

19 *"principal architect"*: Sidney Shalett, "Occupation of Japan Planned Like a Battle," *New York Times*, September 2, 1945, 1.

19 *"fool-proof"*: Ibid.

19 *"First destroy"*: Whitney, 213. In his memoirs, 282–83, MacArthur adds four more: "punish war criminals . . . modernize the constitution . . . hold free elections . . . separate church from state." Whitney's version is the correct one: There is no evidence that MacArthur thought about the Japanese constitution at the time.

20 *"From the moment"*: MacArthur, 282–83.

20 *Initial Post-Surrender Policy*: The Truman administration soon afterward released this document to the public. See "Text of White House Statement on Occupation Policy in Japan," *New York Times*, September 23, 1945, 3.

21 *"Resist with tooth and nail!"*: Okamoto, 14.

22 *"I met all"*: MacArthur, 30.

23 *"My soldiers will never"*: Choate, 66.

23 *"The Emperor requests"*: Ibid., 67.

23 *"We declared war"*: Toland, *The Rising Sun*, 838.

25 *"I could see . . . gambled blindly with death"*: Whitney, 214.

3: "THE MOST COURAGEOUS ACT OF THE ENTIRE WAR"

26 *"simply born"*: Choate, 67.

26 *"Homma may have"*: Miller, *Fighter for Freedom*, 12.

26 *"I'm glad to meet"*: Ibid., 278.

27 *"I have had"*: Grew, 534.

27 *"The naïveté of the Japanese"*: Ibid., 479.

28 *Churchill . . . "the most daring"*: Willoughby, 295; Whitney, 215.

29 *"Bob, this is payoff time"*: Craig, 292; Whitney, 215; the actual phrase, though slightly less colorful, is recalled by Eichelberger as "Bob, this is the payoff," Eichelberger, *Jungle Road*, 262.

29 *"It was a masterpiece"*: Kawai, 12.

29 *"Son, I think you're in the wrong army"*: Craig, 292–93.

31 *"The gauntlet must be run"*: Eichelberger, 262.

31 *"No one can live forever"*: Toland, 865.

31 *"their inability"*: Harries, 43.

31 *egg incident*: Sheldon, 29.

31 *2,185 SCAPINS*: General Headquarters, Supreme Commander for the Allied

Powers, *Catalog of Directives to the Japanese Government.* Considering that MacArthur was supreme commander for almost two thousand days, this volume works out to be a frequency of slightly more than one a day, every day of the week. These instructions covered countless government activities, ranging from the general to the specific. Examples include distribution of food, abolition of the Japanese general headquarters, proceedings of the Diet, apprehension of suspected war criminals, fishery inspection, supply of smallpox vaccine to repatriation ships, fire protection, hoisting of the national flag, shipment of Chinese cabbage seed to Korea, and application for permission to manufacture small-size passenger cars.

4: SWORD SHEATHED, BUT GLEAMING IN ITS SCABBARD

32 *Ieyasu Tokugawa "The right use"*: Wolfe, 89.

33 *Churchill, Montgomery, and Brooke*: James, 657; *Marshall*: Kelley and Ryan, 18.

35 *Toshikazu Kase*: The last name is pronounced *KAH-zay* (in Japanese, all syllables end with a vowel sound).

36 *"There were few men . . . Our journey"*: Kase, 5.

36 *"Were we not sorrowing men"*: Ibid., 4.

37 *"a majestic array . . . mighty pageant"*: Ibid., 5.

38 *"I suggest"*: Mashbir, 322. Mashbir in his book cites the translation as "nonchalant face," which surely was not his intention for such a momentous occasion. Obviously he was the victim of poor translators.

38 *"in this particularly"*: Ibid.

38 *"diplomats without flag"*: Kase, 6.

39 *"like penitent boys"*: Ibid., 7; Steinberg, 145.

39 *"The whole scene"*: Sakamoto, 58.

40 *Vandenberg and greatest speech since Gettysburg Address*: MacArthur, 289.

41 *"Here is the victor . . . an altar of peace"*: Kase, 5.

41 *"Sutherland, show him"*: Kenney, 188.

42 *the six pens*: Accounts vary as to the number of pens and who got them; some accounts say five, some say six, some say Truman got a pen, some say the battleship *Missouri* got a pen, and so on, all of which goes to show that even with hundreds of witnesses, eyewitness testimony varies and history—no matter how well recorded—is often less than 100 percent accurate, making the story of MacArthur's pens resemble a game of three-card monte.

43 *"Start 'em up, Bill,"* Lee and Henschel, 194.

46 *"Is it not rare"*: Kase, 12; Duffy, 16.

46 *"If ever a day"*: Halsey, 283.

46 *"We were not beaten"*: Kase, 14.

5: "DOWN BUT NOT OUT"

47 *"If we allow"*: Toland, 870.

47 *Hiroshima and Nagasaki deaths*: The original statistics come from the highly regarded U.S. Strategic Bombing Survey of 1946. Over the years the Japanese Ministry of Health has increased these figures substantially by including early deaths of the survivors. Because these estimates involve a high degree of subjectivity, no firm number can be agreed upon. According to historian and Pulitzer Prize winner John Dower, the best number to use is a general total for both cities: "over 200,000" (Dower, *Ways of Forgetting*, 145–56).

48 *mid-1944 war lost*: Irokawa, 29–31. Had Japan surrendered in mid-1944 following the fall of Saipan and defeat in Burma, 1.5 million Japanese lives would have been saved.

48 *"You are not the enemy"*: Schaffer, 142.

49 *"It's very simple . . . Women don't want war"*: Toland, 863.

50 *"Give me bread"*: MacArthur, 307.

50 *"The Japanese are"*: Sheldon, 40.

50 *"onion-skin economy"*: Harries, 25.

50 *Nagasaki . . . Osaka housing devastation statistics*: Kelley and Ryan, 150.

50 *"This city now"*: Gayn, 47.

51 *Even in Hiroshima*: MacIsaac, 17.

51 *"Dempsey damage"*: Perry, 117.

52 *"joyfully surprised"*: Shigemitsu, 376.

52 *"Should the government"*: James, 37.

53 *"General Eichelberger, have our"*: Eichelberger, 265; *PRJ*, 423.

53 *"Well, Bill . . ."*: Schoor, 32.

53 *"We are home now . . . moved me"*: Hunt, 407.

53 *"I'll never forget"*: Murray Sanders, in Williams and Wallace, 132.

54 *"Never underestimate"*: Beech, 56.

54 *"Oh, we washed her"*: Chase, 133.

54 *Halsey signing the check as "Hirohito"*: Thomas, 343.

55 *"But I was thinking of"*: Halsey, 287, 290.

55 *"Grew sat in this"*: Mashbir, 67.

55 *"We do not exclude"*: Grew, vol. 2, 1426. President Truman had two problems with Grew's advice about keeping the Japanese monarchy. During the war numerous blunt comments had been made about the emperor; suddenly to turn around and grant him immunity was seen as too much of a reversal. Even more important, the Battle of Okinawa had been raging for two months now, with no end in sight. (Truman got the memo on May 28; the Battle of Okinawa, which started on April 1, would not end until June 22.) The president, unsure if the Japanese were truly serious, feared that making a major concession at this time would be construed as an act of weakness. See Stimson and Bundy, 619–27.

56 *"would not want"*: Emmerson, 252.

56 "We shall have": Bishop, 518.

56 "to report at once": Mashbir, 280.

56 "Those authorized": Ibid., 281.

56 "The best we can": May 28, 1945, FRUS, vol. 6, 545.

6: HARRY TRUMAN THROWS A FIT

58 "Wait a minute": Arthur Krock, New York Times, September 23, 1945, E3.

59 "the occupation forces": Ibid; Acheson, 126.

59 "a political statement": James, 18.

59 "to do something": Ibid.

59 "I'm glad the general": Presidential news conference, September 18, 1945, in
    U.S. National Archives, Public Papers of the Presidents of the United States . . .
    Containing the Public Messages, Speeches, and Statements of the President (20
    vols.); Truman 1945, 326.

59 United States Initial Post-Defeat Policy for Japan: All seven versions are available
    at http://www.ndl.go.jp/constitution/e/shiryo/01/022shoshi.html.

60 "The authority of the Emperor": Seventh and final version, page 2, item 2, line 1.

61 "It seems funny": Eichelberger Diary, October 20, 1945, Eichelberger Papers; Mar-
    shall to MacArthur, October 12, 1945, Record Group (RG) 5, MacArthur Archives.

61 "to receive . . . the extraordinarily dangerous": Truman, Memoirs, vol. 1, 520–21.

62 "Your authority is supreme": "You will exercise your authority as you deem
    proper to carry out your mission. Our relations with Japan do not rest on
    a contractual basis but on unconditional surrender. Since your authority is
    supreme, you will not entertain questions on the part of the Japanese as to
    its scope." U.S. Joint Chiefs of Staff to MacArthur, September 6, 1945; State
    Department Publication 2671, Occupation of Japan: Policy and Progress, Ap-
    pendix 16; also in PRJ, 427.

62 "General MacArthur told Sutherland": Harvey, 313.

62 "greatest possible aid": James, 27.

63 "The most satisfactory": Ibid.

64 "consult and advise": Sheldon, 61.

64 "I welcome you": April 5, 1946, address to the Allied Council for Japan.

64 "Now there's a man!": Whitney, 306.

65 "quit and go home": Kelley and Ryan, 156.

65 "Baron Shidehara . . . Too clear": Hunt, 422; Leary, 253–54.

65 Bismarck and Polybius: The two quotes are from Willoughby, Maneuver in
    War, 2.

65 "the world's greatest laboratory . . . Military occupation was not new": MacAr-
    thur, 282.

7: THE PHOTOGRAPH THAT SAVED A THOUSAND SHIPS

68 *"As Emperor and acknowledged"*: Gallichio, 79; Kelley and Ryan, 145.

68 *"would be comparable"*: Gallichio, 79.

68 *"I am honored"*: Toland, 875.

69 *"frightened to death"*: Harvey, 15.

70 *"To avoid the frontal attack"*: Ibid., 244.

71 *"To do so"*: MacArthur, 287.

71 *"lover of peace"*: Bix, 542. Fellers had met one of the two Japanese Quakers when he was a college student in Indiana, and the other on a trip to Japan in 1920.

72 *"freely expressed will"*: Potsdam Declaration.

72 *Japanese Army chief of staff advice*: Haruo Iguchi, "The First Revisionists: Bonner Fellers, Herbert Hoover, and Japan's Decision to Surrender," in Gallichio, 72.

72 *Theodore Roosevelt "You must listen"*: Harvey, 107.

72 *"I come to you"*: MacArthur, 288.

73 *"A tremendous impression"*: Ibid.

73 *"To see someone"*: Faubion Bowers Papers (Columbia University Oral History Project), 20; Bowers, 166; Okamoto, 36.

73 *"The peace party"*: Bergamini, 148. The most complete report of Hirohito's conversation with MacArthur is given in the Far Eastern Commission, Australian Delegation, Interim Report, February 11, 1946.

74 *"without peer"*: Kelley and Ryan, 149.

8: WHAT TO DO WITH THE EMPEROR AND THE MILITARISTS?

75 *"erased the words"*: Schoor, 39–40.

76 *"There must be"*: Harvey, 314–15.

77 *"Did I think"*: Thorpe, 208.

77 *"I told Matsudaira . . . How could that be done?"*: Ibid.

78 *"Otherwise we would"*: Harvey, 400.

78 *"I could have humiliated him . . . I was born"*: Bowers, 166.

78 *"I don't trust"*: Ibid., 95.

78 *"The Emperor called"*: Harvey, 18.

79 *"Hirohito was so controlled"*: Kelley and Ryan, 153.

79 *Emperor needing permission to travel*: Terasaki, 222.

79 *"American woman of cultural background"*: Sheldon, 141.

79 *"the real reason"*: Schaller, 129.

80 *"the State Department report"*: *Time*, Sept. 17, 1945, 20–21.

82 *13 percent of Americans*: Cohen, 27; Perry, 28; Schaller, *Douglas MacArthur*, 108; *33 percent of Americans*: Schaller, ibid.

82 *"savage apes" . . . "bestial"*: Harries, 11.

82 *"If you in the United States will forget"*: Brines, 124–25; Sheldon, 309.

82 *"The surrender terms"*: Miller, *Soldier-Statesman*, 295.

82 *Tojo's dentures*: After three months word got out in the military about what the two dentists had done; to avoid an official reprimand, they retrieved the dentures and polished off the message.

9: ORGANIZING FOR SUCCESS

85 *"General MacNimitz"*: Hellegers, 405, 719.

85 *"Underground chaos"*: Jansen, 669.

86 *By 19590 the United States was ready*: The Allied occupation officially ended with the signing of the peace treaty of September 8, 1951, but the treaty did not come into force until April 28, 1952.

87 *"the happy soldiers"*: Rinjiro, 50.

87 *"Wherever Americans went"*: Vining, 116.

87 *"That was when we knew"*: Manchester, 474.

88 *"I fully agree"*: Kelley and Ryan, 150.

88 *"We Japanese were poorly led"*: Kato, 263.

88 *"The Japanese, accepting defeat"*: Nishi, x.

88 *"We are trying"*: Shacklock, 38.

89 *"From the moment"*: MacArthur, 282.

89 *Potsdam Declaration*: http://www.ndl.go.jp/constitution/e/etc/c06.html.

89 *SWNCC 1590/4*: http://www.ndl.go.jp/constitution/shiryo/01/022/022tx .html.

89 *JCS 13890/15*: http://www.ndl.go.jp/constitution/e/shiryo/01/036/036tx .html.

89 *"one of the great"*: Douglas MacArthur, "Comment on Far Eastern Commission Policy Decision," 13 July 1947, *PRJ*, 774.

89 *"Unless you deem it necessary"*: JCS 1380/15, 3 November 1945, PRJ, 428–39; http://www.ndl.go.jp/constitution/e/shiryo/01/036/036tx.html.

91 *SCAP chain of command*: Williams, 18.

93 *"It is difficult"*: "SCAP's Denial of Friction with FEC," 14 June 1946, *PRJ*, 751.

93 *FEC opposition to food relief for the Japanese*: Haley, 39.

94 *"a debating society"*: MacArthur, 293.

94 *"a policy-making body"*: MacArthur to McCoy, 13 April 1946, "Far Eastern Commission," MacArthur Archives, RG 9, 3.

94 *"We do not come"*: Nishi, 27.

94 *"extremely intelligent people"*: Stimson to President Truman, "Proposed Program of Japan," Truman Library, Naval Aide File, Box 4, 7.

94 *number of SCAP civilian and military employees*: Williams, 277.

95 *"a boatload of New Dealers"*: Harvey, 338.

96 *"After about the third . . . We won't do"*: Gunther, 123.

96 *278,594 pages to be translated*: Mashbir, 225.

96 *"It is by avoiding"*: Puryear, 263.

97 *"I've been looking"*: Woodard, 22.

97 *"With rare exceptions"*: Ibid., 25.

97 *"Such sophistry"*: Williams, 265.

98 *"a sharp businessman"*: Toland, *Occupation*, 60; Hellegers, 489.

98 *"A stuffed pig"*: Harvey, 307.

98 *"I want your reaction"*: Gordon, 21.

98 *"Everyone felt"*: Hellegers, 760.

99 *"made her weak at the knees"*: S. J. Morris, 431.

100 *"as easy"*: Vining, 115.

100 *"goggle-eyed"*: Eichelberger, *Dear Miss Em*, 300.

100 *"within a few days"*: Ibid., xxi.

101 *"I just wanted you"*: Hunt, 427.

10: OCCUPIER AS HUMANITARIAN

102 *"one of the two"*: Tugwell, 348, quoted in Buhite, 21, and Larrabee, 305: MacArthur was the second; the number one most dangerous man was the populist governor of Louisiana and later U.S. senator, Huey Long. For a full understanding of this often misunderstood comment, see Freidel, 128. This remark was made by FDR shortly after he became president and there was concern that Americans, losing all hope during the Depression, might turn to a "man on horseback." The president sent Gen. Hugh Johnson, a mutual friend, to check out MacArthur's loyalty. Satisfied that MacArthur had no intention of quitting the army and running for political office, he took the unprecedented step of extending MacArthur's term as army chief of staff. Later he rewarded MacArthur by sending him to the Philippines, a post MacArthur coveted. During World War II the two men developed a solid working relationship.

102 *"Bury the dead horses"*: Hellegers, 416.

103 *"Political parties, elections"*: John K. Emmerson, "Political Factors in the Present Japanese Situation," 8 February 1946, U.S. National Archives 740.0019 Control (Japan)/2-2546, 1.

103 *statistics on number of troops and citizens to be repatriated*: "Summary of Achievements During the First Year of Occupation," *PRJ*, 754.

103 *number of Japanese ships*: "Chapter VI: Overseas Repatriation Movements," 148, 150, http://www.history.army.mil/books/wwii/MacArthur%20Reports/MacArthur%20V1%20Sup/ch6.htm.

104 *"Japan's Fanatics"*: *New York Times*, August 25, 1945, E3.

105 *"eggs"*: Brines, 95.

106 *"You cannot teach democracy"*: Kawai, 181.

106 *"Thirty million people"*: Van Aduard, 59.

106 *"ill-treatment including starvation"*: Frank, 352.

106 *"comparable to"*: Ibid.

107 *"Life Expectancy under the Occupation" statistics*: Sams, 183. It should be

pointed out that such statistics can be very difficult to compile and will vary, especially during postwar years when wartime injuries and disease may cause premature death. Willoughby, on page 63 in his book, cites 42.8 years life expectancy for men and 60.2 in 1951 (a 41 percent increase), and 51.1 and 64.8 years for women (a 27 percent increase). The Japanese Ministry of Public Welfare gives 46.9 and 49.6 years for men and women in 1936, compared to 58 and 61.5 years in 1950—a 24 percent increase for both men and women (Sato, 22). Because Crawford Sams was extremely thorough and professional, and had no ax to grind, we use his statistics. Whatever statistics one uses, they all tell the same story: an amazing achievement in improving life longevity.

107 *Greater number of deaths from tuberculosis than from war*: Ibid., 109.

107 *Disease reduction statistics, 1946–1948*: Van Aduard, 287.

107 *Crawford Sams saving 3 million lives*: Takemae, 413.

108 *Food imports saving 11 million lives*: SCAP, *History of the Non-Military Activities of the Occupation of Japan, 1945–1951* (typescript on microfilm), Introduction, 23. The three leading academic scholars of the occupation—John Dower, Clayton James, and Eiji Takemae—concur with this figure.

108 *"As they increasingly"*: Harvey, 343.

108 *"Never have I seen"*: Perry, 118.

109 *"take measures"*: Daniel Berrigan and W. I. Ladejinsky, "Japan's Communists Lose a Battle," *Saturday Evening Post*, January 8, 1949, 101.

109 *"balanced on the tip"*: Harold Strauss, "MacArthur in the Paddy Fields," *The Nation*, November 9, 1946, 521.

109 *"I may be dumb"*: T. Cohen, 184.

110 *"could have done in China"*: Schaller, 130.

110 *"Dad would have liked"*: PRJ, 760; Yoshida, 201–3.

110 *Monuments Men*: www.monumentsmenfoundation.org. The Monuments Men sent to Japan were Lt. Col. Harold Henderson, Sherman Lee, Maj. Laurence Sickman, Lt. Cdr. George Stout, Lennox Tierney, and Langdon Warner. Henderson, as discussed in the next chapter, also played a key role in helping arrange for the emperor to renounce his divinity.

111 *"Curiously the idea"*: Graves, 370.

112 *"Few countries"*: Havens, 66.

112 *"should take no action"*: Edwin Pauley, United States Representative Mission to Japan, November 1945 to April 1946, *Report on Japanese Reparations to the President of the United States* (U.S. Government Printing Office, 1948), 6–7.

114 *"Political activity"*: Summation, *September–December 1945*, 26.

11: THE EMPEROR IS NOT A *KAMI*

115 *"Ultra-nationalistic"*: U.S. Initial Post-Surrender Policy for Japan, September 6, 1945, part 3, paragraph 3.

115 *"including the unrestricted"*: PRJ, vol. 2, Appendix B, 463.

115 *"Shintoism, insofar as"*: October 11, 1945, telegram from U.S. Secretary of State James Byrnes to George Atcheson, in Woodard, 55, 56–57, plate 2, http://news.google.com/newspapers?nid=888&dat=19451007&id=EL4wAAAAI BAJ&sd=pU4DAAAAIBAJ&pg=6846,2844223.

116 *"All propagation . . . the purpose . . . the doctrine"*: SCAPIN 448: SCAP Shinto Directive, 15 December 1945, PRJ, vol. 2, Appendix B, 3a, 467, paragraphs 1c, 2a, 2f(1).

117 *"The Emperor is a deity"*: Gauntlett and Hall, 71, in Creemers, 123.

118 *"the 'secret history'"*: This was the title given by Henderson to his private memorandum requested by General Dyke for the SCAP files in late 1946, "The 'Secret History' of the Japanese Emperor's Renunciation of 'Divinity' 1946"; full text in Creemers, 223–25.

118 *"Which hand"*: Harries, 81.

119 *"flabbergasted"*: Woodard, 261.

119 *"the opportunity being ripe . . . One or two persons"*: Kakunoshin Yamanashi, June 22, 1965, "Memorandum on the Imperial Rescript of January 1, 1946," Woodard, 255 (full text 320–21). Yamanashi was apparently unwilling to say anything more about "the secret history" than this, plus a tacit admission on his part that he knew about the paper and was relieved it had been burned per his instructions (Woodard, 261n).

120 *"I am not a kami"*: Ibid., 255.

120 *"Wasn't that absurd" . . . "never be"*: Ibid., 253–54.

120 *"The ties between Us"*: Fifth paragraph; the only change made by the emperor was in the second line, where the word "upon" replaced Henderson's "only on."

121 *"That afternoon"*: New York Times, January 3, 1946, 2.

122 *"in the same way"*: Hall, 75.

122 *"a Jerusalem, Mount Vernon and Vatican"*: Ibid.

123 *"Japan is a spiritual vacuum"*: Woodard, 243.

123 *"We believe in"*: Stoddard Commission, Report of the United States Education Mission to Japan, Submitted to the Supreme Commander for the Allied Powers, Tokyo, March 30, 1946, 4–5.

124 *"Pure democracy"*: U.S. Department of State Bulletin, June 27, 1946, 1067.

12: DRAWING UP A UTOPIA

125 *"The Japanese Constitution"*: Schoichi, 9.

126 *"Isn't Shidehara dead?"*: Finn, 39.

126 *"a system . . . secret inquisition"*: Brines, 48.

126 *"In the achievement"*: Statement to the Japanese Government, PRJ 741, Kades, 219.

128 *"unrestricted authority"*: Feb. 1, 1946, Whitney to MacArthur memo,

"Constitutional Reform," paragraph #6, http://www.ndl.go.jp/constitu
tion/e/shiryo/03/069/069tx.html.

128 *"Ladies and gentlemen"*: Gordon, 104.

128 *"There are few students"*: Gunther, 128.

128 *"On that date"*: Gordon, 105.

129 *Top-secret room for preparing constitution draft*: Sirota, 21, 107; Ward, 992.

130 *"Beate, you're a woman"*: Ibid., 106; see "Obituary: Beate Gordon," *The Economist*, January 12, 2013, 86.

131 *"My God, you have given"*: Stanley Weintraub, "American Proconsul: How
Douglas MacArthur Shaped Postwar Japan," *Military History*, January 2012,
vol. 28, no. 5, 44–51.

131 *"as a Thomas Jefferson"*: Wildes, 44.

132 *"totally unacceptable"*: Moore and Robinson, 106; Kades, 229.

132 *"as if he had"*: Whitney, 251.

132 *"black cloud"*: Ibid.

132 *"You think you can make . . . we can try"*: Vinacke, 65.

132 *"Not at all"*: Whitney, 248.

132 *"The Supreme Commander . . . But, gentlemen"*: Kades, 228.

133 *"Court, don't you know"*: Whitney, 251–52; a slightly different, more explicit
version of MacArthur's statement is from Hellegers, 778: "Have you ever
known me to repudiate anything that any of my officers has ever done? I
might ultimately decide if an officer did it too many times that I would replace him, but I wouldn't repudiate what he had done."

133 *"straight and direct"*: Kades, 231; Williams, 114; Hellegers, 530.

133 *"too drastic a move"*: Kades, 231.

133 *Some of the roses"*: Rodney Hussey, "The New Constitution of Japan," *PRJ*,
vol. 1, 106.

13: MACARTHUR BREAKS THE IMPASSE

135 *"Turning Japanese"*: Harries, 117.

136 *"The way to end war"*: Harvey, 185.

136 *"the good of Japan . . . his best . . . I don't know"*: Moore and Robinson, 112–13.

136 *"The enormous sacrifices"*: Pratt, 15–16.

137 *"like swallowing"*: Hellegers, 534.

137 *"Whitney group . . . scholarship and experience"*: Moore and Robinson, 114.

137 *"The revision"*: MacArthur, 299.

138 *"comes up from the people"*: Hellegers, 535.

140 *"spoken Japanese"*: Williams, 117.

140 *"archaic, stilted"*: Inoue, 31.

140 *"a layman's document"*: http://www.presidency.ucsb.edu/ws/index.php?pid
=15459.

140 *The complexity of*: Lauterbach, 82; R. Smith, 216–217.

141 *"is the compass"*: Schoichi, 218.

141 *"express their fully"*: U.S. Department of State, *Activities of the Far Eastern Commission, Reported by the Secretary General*, 1947, 58–59.

142 *"began to suffer"*: Schoichi, 147.

142 *"prejudice many Japanese . . . reserved exclusively"*: 13 April 1946 memo, MacArthur Archives, RG 9, 1–6.

142 *"limited to . . . in the absence of . . . I have acted meticulously"*: Nishi, 136.

143 *"The Commission"*: Memorandum for the State Department Members of the State-War-Navy Coordinating Committee (Hilldring) to the Committee, 12 April 1946, *FRUS* (1946), vol. 8, 195–96.

143 *"As Supreme Commander"*: MacArthur to the Joint Chiefs of Staff, 4 May 1946, *FRUS* (1946), vol. 8, 220.

143 *"This draft provides"*: Schoichi, 152.

144 *"No useful purpose"*: Memorandum by the Director of the Office of Far Eastern Affairs (Vincent) to Secretary of State, 19 April 1946, *FRUS* (1946), vol. 8, 211.

144 *"Adequate time"*: Schoichi, 152.

144 *"Have you read"*: Lauterbach, 67.

145 *"Probably the single most"*: MacArthur, 302.

145 *"To mark this historic"*: Letter from Douglas MacArthur to Prime Minister, May 2, 1947, http://www.ndl.go.jp/en/result.html?q=douglas%20macarthur.

14: HIS MOST RADICAL REFORM

146 *"the emancipation"*: "Statement to the Japanese Government Concerning Required Reforms," October 11, 1945, *PRJ*, 741.

146 *"laws, decrees and regulations"*: http://www.ndl.go.jp/constitution/shiryo/01/022/022tx.html, part 3, item 3, paragraph 4.

146 *"Policies shall be favored"*: http://www.ndl.go.jp/constitution/shiryo/01/022/022tx.html, part 4, item 2, paragraph 1.

147 *"would retard"*: Beauchamp, 425.

147 *"These laws"*: Ibid., 433.

147 *"wished her"*: Tracy, 45.

147 *"Their supreme duty"*: Sato, 80.

148 *"programs for the dissemination"*: Pharr, "Ethel Weed," 722.

148 *"Women of Japan"*: "Women of Japan Lauded by General MacArthur," quoted in Koikari, 51, and Beard, 177–78.

149 *"meet men"*: Hopper, 185.

149 *"We are all hungry"*: *PRJ*, 752.

149 *"one of the world's"*: Pharr, "The Politics of Women's Rights," 222.

150 *"presence in the corridors"*: Steinem, quoted in Gordon, back cover.

150 *"a battle of the sexes"*: SCAP, Government Section, "Memo 1," August 17, 1946, Papers of Alfred R. Hussey, Asia Library, University of Michigan.

151 *"no military value"*: Treadwell, 12.

151 *"Of all the reforms"*: MacArthur, 305.

152 *"Women's organizations"*: Swearingen and Langer, 175.

153 *"If girl students" and story of tea*: Van Staaveren, 78–79.

15: "HE HAS A LETTER FROM GOD"

154 *"whose knowledge is derived"*: Livy, "A Roman General's Opinion of Military Critics," *A History of Rome*, book 44, chap. 22.

155 *"MacArthur should move"*: Lee and Henschel, 195 (photo caption).

155 *"I never before met . . . seemed to be"*: Karnow, 262.

155 *"Five minutes"*: Halsey and Bryan, 154–55; Puryear, 116.

155 *"If he hadn't proposed"*: Karnow, 262.

155 *"He has a letter"*: Choate, 18.

156 *"General, you don't have"*: Acheson, 424.

156 *desk chair for General MacArthur*: Goodman, 42.

157 *"George Washington and Abraham Lincoln"*: Vincent Sheean, "MacArthur in Tokyo," *Holiday*, December 1949.

157 *"cool as a cucumber"*: Harries, 211.

157 *"Youth is not"*: Kelley and Ryan, 13. This quotation was based on a poem by one Samuel Ullman, of Birmingham, Alabama.

159 *"Oh, General MacArthur left"*: Willoughby, 267.

159 *"Well, what do you say"*: Whitney, 236.

159 *"What better fate"*: Gunther, 50.

160 *"Sir, the fire chief"*: Chase, 149.

160 *"MacArthur has decided"*: Karnow, 260.

161 *"Don't want a fuss"*: Bowers, 95.

161 *Compilation of MacArthur's appointments*: James, vol. 3, 693–94.

161 *"It indicated to them"*: Vining, 86.

162 *"most qualified"*: Gallup, 550, 582, 584.

163 *"When you leave the Pacific"*: Halsey and Bryan, 290.

163 *"Now, now, we don't"*: Sheldon, 46.

164 *"I realize that"*: Ibid., 83.

164 *"hard-headed softie"*: Kenney, 64.

164 *"They'd think"*: Sheldon, 210.

164 *"a target slower"*: Bowers, 91.

164 *"I count on the Japanese people"*: "Assassination Day," *Newsweek*, May 15, 1946.

16: RUSSIAN TROUBLE

165 *"With the end of World War II"*: Ritchie, 87.

166 *"If the Soviets attempt"*: Choate, 25–26.

166 *"My God, I believe you would"*: MacArthur, 285.

166   *"I have received your note"*: Gunther, 22.

166   *"like a piece"*: FRUS, vol. 1, 79; T. Cohen, 59.

166   *"He has endeavored"*: Atcheson to Byrnes, 10 September 1946, MacArthur Archives, RG 9, Box 146.

167   *"Why, General Derevyanko!"*: Whitney, 306.

167   *"tell them whatever . . . Well, I had to ask"*: Thorpe, 214.

168   *"Japan is in heaven now"*: Vining, 265.

168   *twenty-five-mile restriction*: T. Cohen, 114.

169   *"does not favor "*: New York Times, May 16, 1946, 1, 15.

169   *70 percent of farmers paying for land in cash*: Japanese Ministry of Agriculture and Forestry, October 1949, in Fearey, 88.

169   *"Japanese national farm debt melted"*: Costello, 190.

170   *412 percent inflation*: The 1946 price index went from 1,057 to 4,352, *Statistical Yearbook of Japan* (Tokyo, 1949), 639.

170   *"the use of"*: PRJ, 762.

170   *"a strike"*: Blaine Hoover, "Address to Civil Service Assembly of the United States and Canada," Ottawa, 6 October 1948, 5, quoted in Williams, 67.

171   *"a controlled revolution"*: Schaller, *Altered States*, 7.

171   *"the Japanese cannot"*: Johnson, 100.

172   *"a national calamity"*: T. Cohen, 286.

172   *"ruin the Occupation"*: Eichelberger letter to MacArthur, 25 January 1947, Eichelberger Papers, Duke University: Diaries, 22-D, Box 181.

172   *"the impact"*: T. Cohen, 295.

172   *"I have informed"*: T. Cohen, 294–95.

172   *"undisciplined elements"*: Nishi, 66.

172   *"We regret very much"*: T. Cohen, 297.

173   *"In one stroke"*: Blaine Hoover, "Address to Civil Service Assembly of the United States and Canada," Ottawa, Canada, 6 October 1948, 5–6.

173   *"seemed, on cursory examination"*: Redford, 62.

173   *"I know of nothing"*: National Public Service Law Revision Bill, August 18, 1948, MacArthur Archives, RG 9.

174   *"to prescribe with wisdom"*: Ibid.

174   *"What happened to our sons?"*: Eichelberger, 286.

175   *"would have endangered"*: Swearingen and Langer, 232.

175   *"the American imperialists"*: Deverall, 35.

175   *"The Japanese and American bloodhounds"*: Swearingen and Langer, 251.

175   *"who are in difficult"*: Ibid., 374.

176   *Yoshida on MacArthur's greatest contribution*: Finn, 70.

176   *"There being no"*: Williams, 272.

17: "WHERE'S ISHII?"

178 *"Where's Ishii?"*: Barenblatt, 209.

178 *"fantastic experiments"*: New York Times, September 3, 1945, 1.

180 *only 18 percent Japanese war fatalities from disease*: Seaman, 5.

181 *gas masks for White House personnel*: Wilson and Day, 150. This measure was kept secret from the American public lest it cause widespread alarm and panic.

181 *"unmistakably clear"*: New York Times, June 6, 1942, 1–2.

182 *"These and other facts"*: "Musn't Touch!," Newsweek, June 4, 1945, 34–35.

182 *Camp Detrick, Maryland*: Renamed Fort Detrick in 1956.

183 *"Germ warfare against"*: Warner and Warner, 283; Felton, 283.

183 *"a higher form"*: Harris and Paxman, 10–11.

183 *Disease—not bullets—major cause of death in war*: The seminal, pioneering work on this subject is *Rats, Lice and History* (1935) by Hans Zinsser, a member of the U.S. Army Medical Corps who served in France during World War I and was awarded, along with MacArthur, the Distinguished Cross and the French Légion d'Honneur.

184 *"Great results"*: Harris, 167; Barenblatt, 188.

184 *"spraying bacterial solutions"*: Barenblatt, ibid.

184 *Loucks and Japanese poison gas*: Hersh, 10.

184 *Marshall and bacteriological warfare*: Lilienthal, 199.

186 *Ishii funeral ceremony*: Report by Neal R. Smith, RG 331, Box 1434, 20, Case #330, National Archives.

187 *"We're not given"*: Williams and Wallace, 133.

187 *Nighttime visitor with blueprint and "We need more evidence"*: Ibid., 134.

188 *"I have given"*: Ibid., 196; Harris, 198.

188 *"My experience"*: Barenblatt, 210.

189 *"will endanger"*: Williams and Wallace, 207.

189 *"Under present circumstances"*: ibid., 185.

189 *"Since it is believed"*: August 1, 1947, memo from the SWNCC (State, War, Navy Coordinating Committee), McDermott, 136; Williams and Wallace, 207.

189 *"the only known"*: McDermott, 136.

189 *"guarded, concise"*: Arvo T. Thompson, "Report on Japanese Biological Warfare Activities, May 31, 1946, Army Service Forces," Camp Detrick, Frederick, MD, Fort Detrick Library Archives.

190 *"The utmost secrecy"*: SWNCC 351/1, March 5, 1947, Record Group 331, Box 1434.20, Case 330, National Archives.

190 *"Additional data"*: Gold, 109.

18: "CHERRY BLOSSOMS AT NIGHT"

192 *"Information obtained"*: Barenblatt, 223.

192 *"special protection"*: Triplett, 68.

193 *death of Hirasawa*: *New York Times* obituary, May 11, 1987.

193 *"The United States has primary interest"*: John W. Powell, "A Hidden Chapter in History," *Bulletin of the Atomic Scientists* 46 (October 1981), 46, exhibit.

194 *"Cherry Blossoms at Night"*: Nicholas Kristof, "Unmasking Horror—A Special Report," *New York Times*, March 17, 1995, http://www.nytimes .com/1995/03/17/world/unmasking-horror-a-special-report-japan-confronting-gruesome-war-atrocity.html?pagewanted=all&src=pm.

194 *"would violate every Christian ethic"*: Leahy, 440.

194 *"Why has Truman"*: Bilainkin, 233.

195 *"the Japanese had done"*: *New York Times*, December 27, 1949, 16.

195 *"If a prisoner"*: *Materials on the Trial of Former Servicemen of the Japanese Army Charged with Manufacturing and Employing Bacteriological Weapons* (Foreign Language Publishing House [Moscow], 1950), 115.

196 *"In the summer of 1945"*: Ibid., 290.

196 *"Experts have calculated"*: Powell, "A Hidden Chapter," 49–50.

197 *"Evidence gathered"*: McDermott, 137; Williams and Wallace, 215.

197 *"It is hoped"*: Barenblatt, 224; Harris, 215.

197 *U.S. scientists unimpressed by Ishii's information*: Regis, 225.

19: THE NUREMBERG OF THE EAST

198 *"Asia under the Japanese"*: Daws, 363.

198 *seventeen million people killed*: Newman, 138. The specific breakdown of 17.2 million deaths attributable to the Japanese Empire, 1931–45, is as follows: China, ten million; Java (Dutch Indies), three million; Bengal famine, 1.5 million; Vietnam, one million; Outer Islands, one million; India, 180,000; Philippines, 120,000; Malaya, 100,000; United States, 100,000; Burma-Siam Railway, 83,000; Korea, 70,000; Indonesia, 30,000; Australia, 30,000; New Zealand, 10,000.

198 *POW death rate*: In his book on Japanese prison camps, Gavin Daws concludes: "If the war had lasted another year, there would not have been a POW left alive" (Daws, 18).

199 *Homma's wife and MacArthur*: Taylor, 218.

200 *"men landed on Mars"*: Ginn, 46.

200 *"be held responsible . . . in contravention"*: Taylor, 53.

201 *"flealike agility"*: Kennan, 370.

201 *85,000 troops under Percival*: Yamashita thought Percival had 100,000 men. Yet this did not deter him from pulling off probably the greatest military bluff of all time. Back in England, Percival was ostracized, even though he had no air support, very

little ammunition, and only one day's supply of water left. By surrendering when he did, he avoided what would have been massive senseless slaughter of civilians. MacArthur, unlike Winston Churchill and British commander Sir Archibald Wavell, understood this and gave Percival a seat of honor at the surrender ceremonies, along with Wainwright. MacArthur could be very generous to men who may have failed through no fault of their own.

202 *"Yamashita's Ghost"*: Title of book by Allan Ryan.

202 *"Yamashita trial continued today"*: Reel, 93.

203 *"legalized lynching"*: Finn, 81; Manchester, 487.

203 *"the results are beyond challenge"*: Reel, 235; Lyon, 397; Weiner, 204.

203 *"a fair verdict . . . too well"*: *New York Times*, December 8, 1945, 8.

204 *"one of the great"*: McCullough, 146.

204 *"There are two"*: Barnet, 218.

205 *"Individuals may be punished . . . The personal"*: U.S. Department of State, *Trial of Japanese War Criminals*, publication 2613 (Washington, DC: U.S. Government Printing Office, 1946), 20, 21.

205 *"perfectly revolutionary . . . it is"*: Takayanagi, 59–60, 63; Minear, 45.

206 *"The most interesting questions . . . The Premier"*: *New York Times*, September 20, 1945, 22.

206 *"All the accused . . . all the accused together"*: *Trial of Japanese War Criminals*, 47.

208 *"with prolix equivocations"*: Röling and Rüter, 24.

208 *"the trial of the century"*: Brackman, 18.

208 *"no more important"*: *Official Transcript of the Proceedings*, 21, in Röling and Rüter, ix.

209 *30,000 American prisoners*: A document called *Outline for the Disposal of Prisoners of War*, introduced at the trial, stated that in the event of an Allied invasion of Japan the prisoners should "be set free." In Japanese this did not mean being set loose, it meant "set free from earthly concerns" (Brackman, 265).

209 *"None of us"*: Minear, 114.

209 *"love and desire"*: Buruma, 175; see also Minear, 114–15.

210 *"The process of translating"*: Harvey, 368.

210 *"I shall be back"*: Shigemitsu, 274.

210 Senso sekinin sha: Takayanagi, 77.

211 *"It must be freely"*: Veale, 184–85.

211 *"a scintilla"*: Röling and Rüter, 401.

211 *77 percent conviction rate*: Piccagallo, 264.

212 *"There is nothing"*: Buell, 370–71.

212 *No Hollywood movie*: Probably the most the Americans would get to see of Japanese wartime brutality was a 1957 movie about British prisoners of war forced to build a railway in Burma, *The Bridge on the River Kwai*.

212 *"There is not sufficient evidence"*: Röling and Rüter, 464.

212 *FDR refused to meet with Konoe*: Observation by Herbert Hoover, in Nash, 270–77, 879.

213 *"The victors are"*: Finn, 78.
213 *"I was always convinced"*: Röling, 82.

20: GEORGE KENNAN PAYS A VISIT

217 *"Americans get homesick"*: Rau, 3. The ambassador's daughter, Santha Rama Rau, subsequently married Major Faubion Bowers.
217 *"As far as"*: Tracy, 172.
218 *"Atomic Souvenir Shop"*: Brines, 32.
218 *"Atom Bowl"*: John D. Lukacs, "Nagasaki, 1946: Football Among the Ruins," *New York Times*, December 25, 2005, SP9.
218 *"There seems"*: Sheldon, 142.
218 *Number of periodicals and magazines*: Cohen, 33.
218 *Percentage of Japanese women in favor of love marriage*: Ibid., 335.
218 *Okunoshima*: Nicholas D. Kristof, "Okunoshima Journal: A Museum to Remind Japanese of Their Own Guilt," *New York Times*, August 12, 1995.
219 *purge*: These 220,000 people represented little more than a quarter of one percent of the Japanese population, compared to 2.5 percent in Germany. One of the men purged in 1946 was Akio Morita, a teacher at the Tokyo Institute of Technology. He found a job with a small start-up and eventually made it one of the largest consumer electronics companies in the world: Sony.
219 *"If one machine gun"*: Gunther, 147.
219 *"Japan might have won"*: Braw, 10.
219 *"disturbs the public tranquility"*: Hellegers, 427.
220 *"news must adhere"*: Harvey, 365.
220 *"Why, that man knows"*: Manchester, 481.
220 *"My God, how does"*: Bowers, 93.
220 *"What a man!"*: Whitney, 306.
221 *"further left . . . fiasco"*: Schaller, 45.
221 *"The time has now . . . If the United Nations . . . No weapon, not even"*: "MacArthur Favors Japan Treaty Now to End Occupation," *New York Times*, March 18, 1947, 1, 20; van Aduard, 63; Hall, 45.
222 *"economic disaster, inflation"*: Schaller, 145.
222 *"really amounted to"*: Ibid.
222 *"morgue"*: Schonberger, 185.
222 *"far to the left"*: James Lee Kauffman, "A Lawyer's Report on Japan Attacks Plan to Run Occupation," *Newsweek*, December 1, 1947, 36–40.
222 *"assume any responsibility"*: Whitney, 267.
224 *"military occupations serve"*: February 20, 1947, letter to U.S. Congress, "In Support of Appropriations for Occupation Purposes," *PRJ*, Sept. 1945–Sept. 1948, vol. 2, 764.
224 *"the men who . . . serve as a deterrent"*: Twenty-seventh paragraph and final paragraph.

224 *"We should cease"*: Takemae, 555.

224 *"democracy must be abandoned"*: Harvey, 386.

224 *Marshall to Kennan advice*: Memorandum of conversation between Marshall and Kennan, Feb. 19, 1948, PPS Records, Box 33.

225 *"America's Global Planner"*: *New York Times Magazine*, July 13, 1947, 9, 32–33.

225 *"I'll have him briefed"*: Kennan, 383.

225 *"a civilian David"*: Ibid., 382.

225 *"the only other"*: Ibid., 384.

225 *"fundamentally alter"*: Gaddis, 301.

225 *"thirsting"*: Kennan, 384; Kennan memorandum, "General MacArthur's Remarks at Lunch," March 1, 1948, *FRUS*(1948), vol. 6, 697.

225 *Yoshida on MacArthur as a pacing lion*: Finn, 23.

225 *Kennan on MacArthur as a horse*: Gaddis, 301.

225 *"an envoy charged"*: Kennan, 382.

226 *"to inquire"*: Kennan to MacArthur, March 2, 1948, MacArthur Archives, RG 5, Box 32.

226 *Kennan-MacArthur private dinner*: Kennan, 393; Gaddis 302.

226 *$8million/month black market*: Wildes, 36.

226 *"The personal enrichment"*: Kennan, 387.

227 *"We have probably got"*: Ibid., 390.

227 *"From that moment"*: Memo of conversation between Kennan and MacArthur, March 5, 1948, *FRUS* (1948), vol. 6, 699–706.

227 *"They deserved the respect"*: Kennan, 371; biographer John Lukacs calls this paragraph the kind of mellifluous prose "we are unlikely to see in a thousand years" (Lukacs, 67).

227 *"We parted"*: Kennan, 386; see memo of conversation between Kennan and MacArthur, March 5, 1948, *FRUS* (1948), vol. 6, 699–706.

228 *"the most significant constructive . . . on no other"*: Kennan, 393.

228 *"Reverse course" invented by Japanese scholars*: Bailey, 52; see also Perry, 122, and Tsutsui, 119. Many historians display a certain lack of rigor when they interpret the past and make judgments based on what we now know. In his book about Kennan and American foreign policy, Wilson Miscamble says: "One must avoid reading history backwards and imposing an artificial coherence" (Miscamble, xiii).

228 *"a major shift"*: Schaller, 104.

228 *"The emphasis should shift"*: Kennan, 391.

228 *"immediate shift"*: Schaller, 117.

229 *"appropriate shift"*: "Statement of U.S. Policy toward Economic Recovery of Japan," November 1947, Stimson Papers, Yale University.

229 *"more emphasis"*: FRUS (1948), vol. 6, 854–56.

229 *"SCAP was to shift"*: Ibid., 857–62.

229 *"The effect"*: Kennan, 393.

229 *Kennan's seven specific recommendations*: Ibid., 391.

229 *"control of"*: "General of the Army Douglas MacArthur's New Year Message, January 1, 1949," *Documents Concerning the Allied Occupation and Control of Japan*, vol. 2, 221.

21: A SHIFT IN EMPHASIS

230 *"the necessary shift"*: Schonberger, 167

230 *"socialism in private hands"*: MacArthur to Department of the Army, 24 October 1947, Stimson Papers, Yale University.

231 *Eleanor Hadley on the* zaibatsu: "Trust Busting in Japan," *Harvard Business Review* vol. 26, no. 4 (July 1948): 429. The reader may note that many of these corporations no longer exist due to divestiture or merger/acquisition. Only General Motors, U.S. Steel, Dole Pineapple, Alcoa, and DuPont still survive, along with two others that have been restructured (National City Bank, now Citibank, and Metropolitan Life, now MetLife). Such is the dynamic of American capitalism. In the late 1940s these eighteen companies were the industry leaders of America.

231 *"Not only"*: *Report on Japanese Reparations to the President of the United States*, 39.

231 *"virtual destruction"*: *Newsweek*, December 1, 1947, 37.

231 *"permitted the family groups"*: *PRJ*, 780–83.

232 *"Decision should be made"*: MacArthur March 21 meeting with Draper and Kennan, *FRUS* (1948), vol. 6, 711.

232 *"merely a camouflage"*: Ibid., 710.

233 *"conflict between"*: January 6, 1948, speech, quoted in Moore and Robinson, 117.

233 *"more emphasis"*: *FRUS* (1948), vol. 6, 654–56.

233 *"Japan is costing us"*: H. Alexander Smith Papers, 1949, Princeton University Library, 393–95; see also *U.S. News*, March 4, 1949, 24–25.

234 *Harvard Club meeting*: Schonberger, "The Japan Library in American Diplomacy, 1947–1952," *Pacific Historical Review* (August 1977): 339–44; Takemae, 459.

235 *"elderly incompetents . . . the most effete"*: Kennan, 702.

235 *"major shifts"*: Eichelberger, 288.

235 *"It has always"*: Sugita, 32.

236 *"Stop inflation"*: Van Aduard, 93.

236 *"Get Dodge"*: *New York Times*, December 3, 1964, obituary. When Eisenhower became president in 1953, he made Dodge the director of the Bureau of the Budget (now called the Office of Management and Budget [OMB]).

237 *"walking on stilts"*: Uchino, 49.

237 *"I'm no colonel"*: *American National Biography* 6, 1999, 690–92.

237 *"an impressive . . . Alice in Wonderland . . . massive failures"*: "Two Billion Dollar Failure in Japan," *Fortune*, April 1949, 206.

238 *"in effect . . . Until a peace"*: *Fortune*, June 1949, 188, 190. *the three directives*:

238 *the three directives*: the President Directive of September 6, 1945: "It shall be the policy of the Supreme Commander . . . to favor a program for the dissolution of the large industrial and banking combines"; the Joint Chiefs of Staff Directive of November 1, 1945: "You will require this agency to submit, for approval by you, plans for dissolving large Japanese and industrial banking combines, the FEC Directive of June 19, 1947: "It shall be the policy of the Supreme Commander . . . to require a program for the dissolution of the large industrial and banking combines" (Bisson, *Zaibatsu Dissolution*, Appendixes, 239–40).

238 *"on the United States"*: "General MacArthur Replies," Ibid., 194.

239 *"find their markets"*: Ibid., 74.

239 *three hundred billion yen stolen*: Dower, 117–18.

239 *"Trucks, wagons"*: Costello, 153; Aldous, 98.

239 *"Japan's war stockpiles"*: *World Report*, January 6, 1948.

240 *"Nobody knows"*: Bisson, *Prospects for Democracy*, 115.

240 *increase in yen from 30 billion to 42 billion*: Ibid., 13.

240 *"This statement"*: *Fortune*, June 1949, 198.

240 *"uncorked their champagne bottles"*: Montgomery, 106–7.

241 *"The purgees were not"*: *Fortune*, June 1949, 198.

241 *"All the great"*: *Fortune*, April 1949, 71.

241 *"Even in Japan"*: *Fortune*, June 1949, 202.

241 *"road to fascism"*: Swearingen and Langer, 162.

241 *Red Purge of 20,997*: Braw, 81.

241 *Purge of 210,288 for ties to militarism*: Harries, 43.

242 *"co-prosperity sphere"*: *Baltimore Sun*, August 1947.

242 *"the economic situation"*: Dodge to Cleveland Thurber, Dec. 13, 1948, Joseph M. Dodge Papers, 1949 Japan Box 1, Burton Historical Collection, Detroit Public Library.

242 *"A nuisance factor"*: Sebald to Robert Lovett, Jan. 3, 1949, *FRUS* (1949), vol. 7, 601–3.

242 *Dean Acheson in agreement with MacArthur*: Acheson, 556.

242 *George Kennan in agreement with MacArthur*: Kennan, 394.

242 *Acheson on Japan trade with the Far East*: Acheson, May 8, 1948, *FRUS* (1949), vol. 7, 736–37.

242 *"The Japanese couldn't"*: Prestowitz, 67.

242 *"paper napkins"*: Dower, 537.

243 *"In no other nation"*: Joseph M. Dodge statement to the National Advisory Council Staff Committee, January 12, 1950, *The Reports of General MacArthur*, 1994 ed., vol. 2, 295.

243 *$2.3 billion*: Harvey, 398.

243 *"A gift from the gods"*: Weintraub, 353.

243 *"the westernmost outpost"*: "MacArthur Pledges Defense of Japan," *New York Times*, March 22, 1949, 22. MacArthur in his 1949 statement elaborated on this thought: "Now the Pacific has become an Anglo-Saxon lake and our line

of defense runs through the chain of islands fringing the coast of Asia. It starts from the Philippines and continues through the Ryukyu archipelago which includes its broad main bastion, Okinawa. Then it bends back through Japan and the Aleutian Island chain to Alaska" (Ibid.).

243 *$2 billion aid, $5 billion reparations*: Perret, 523; Sebald, 72–74; Finn, 37. SCAP officer and historian Richard Finn performed a comprehensive study and concluded: "The best information seems to be that depending on the method of calculation Japan paid between $4.23 and $4.98 billion in occupation costs, while it received $1.95 billion in U.S. economic assistance" (Finn, 332). On a per capita basis, the $1.95 billion received by Japan was one-third the aid that Germany received.

22: "THE GREATEST PIECE OF DIPLOMACY, EVER"

244 *"What can we do . . . So what are you waiting for"*: Fitts, 3.

245 *Sawamura pitching feat*: American baseball enthusiasts may appreciate an even more impressive Japanese pitching feat: The 1942 marathon in Kora-kuen Stadium where Hall of Famer Michio Nishizawa pitched a twenty-eight-inning, 311-pitch complete game. (Like Babe Ruth, Nishizawa later switched to the outfield and became a feared hitter, setting a home run record in 1950 and winning the batting title and RBI title in 1952.)

245 *Ruth worth a hundred ambassadors*: Dawidoff, 91.

245 *"To hell with" and plan to use Babe Ruth for radio broadcasts*: Whiting, 46.

246 *Babe Ruth 1947 speech broadcast to Japan*: Ritter and Rucker, 263.

246 *"So many"*: Ritter, 250.

246 *"He made it a point"*: Kelley, 124.

246 *"Gentlemen, there's no"*: Ibid., 114.

246 *"It was not"*: Cohen, 482.

247 *"Go ahead"*: John B. Holway, "Lefty and the Geisha," http://baseballguru .com/jholway/analysisjholway32.html.

247 *"It's OK"*: Ibid.

247 *"If it is right"*: Bowers, 164.

247 *"When I arrived"*: Ritter, 250.

247 *"The greatest piece"*: http://www.californiapioneers.org/sanfran_seals.html and http://www.dickmeister.com/id135.html.

248 *DiMaggio-Monroe honeymoon in Japan*: For DiMaggio, this turned out to be a grave mistake. The Japanese went absolutely nuts over Marilyn Monroe, leaving her husband in the shadows. Depressed at his comparative obscurity, DiMaggio realized how difficult it would be being married to her.

248 *Japanese newspaper poll and Babe Ruth*: Van Staaveren, 266.

23: OCCUPIER AS PROTECTOR

249 *"from the stern rigidity"*: MacArthur public message, May 3, 1948.

249 *"A vast centrifugal machine"*: Willoughby, 319.

250 *Number of Japanese prisoners in Soviet territories and Manchuria*: SCAP press release, May 14, 1948, *FRUS* (1948), vol. 6, 757–759; Fearey, 194.

250 *"Contemplating his handiwork"*: Rovere and Schlesinger, 92.

251 *"Go Home Quickly!"*: Takemae, 143.

251 *"convulsions"*: *New York Times*, March 2, 1949, 22.

251 *"the Switzerland of the Pacific"*: Harries, 233.

251 *"Dollar for dollar"*: Ibid., 231.

251 *"Japanese rearmament"*: Ibid., 232–33.

252 *"The pin head"*: March 11, 1950; quoted in Schaller, *Altered States*, 21.

252 *"Communism, no!"*: *FRUS* (1950), vol. 6, 88; see also Hayes, 34.

253 *"Everyone in the Department"*: Allison to Sebald, May 24, 1950, *FRUS* (1950), vol. 6, 1203.

253 *1947 push for peace treaty*: As an indicator of how strongly he felt about the issue, MacArthur made it the subject of the one and only press conference of the entire occupation, on March 17, 1947.

253 *"would be disastrous"*: Sebald, 249.

253 *Highly egotistical*: Like MacArthur, Dulles had a habit of misstating the truth to make himself look good. In the course of his work negotiating the peace treaty, Dulles availed himself of three years' worth of government memos, drafts, and position papers on the subject—and studied them carefully as any lawyer would. But that is not what he told the press. In 1951, when a reporter asked if he had started with a blank slate or if he had the benefit of much of the work already done, Dulles responded: "There were, I suppose, a good many drafts of a Japanese peace treaty which had been the product of various stages of thinking over the preceding five years. I will have to admit I never read any of them" (Hoopes, 92).

254 *"American defense perimeter"*: Dean Acheson speech, San Francisco, Jan. 12, 1950, *FRUS, East Asia* (1950), 275; Acheson, 357.

254 *"delivering this speech"*: Perret, 537.

254 *"The Korean attack"*: Kennan, 500.

255 *"Mars' last gift"*: Lauterbach, 61.

255 *"use his prestige"*: Smith, 51.

255 *"I wouldn't put my foot"*: Bowers, 168.

255 *"playing with fire"*: Harries, 229.

255 *"between the upper and lower"*: U.S. Department of State *Bulletin* 23 (July 10, 1950), 50.

256 *"This is probably . . . If only"*: Allison, 129.

256 *MacArthur at the airport*: It was an important phone call that Dulles made MacArthur go back to his office and take. MacArthur was informed that

Truman had decided to authorize the use of American air and naval power in Korea, to put the Seventh Fleet off Formosa to deter any Chinese attack, and to increase military assistance to the French in Indochina. MacArthur was ordered to make a personal inspection of conditions in Korea and report his findings to the president right away.

257 *"To ensure . . . Events disclose"*: MacArthur letter to Yoshida, July 8, 1950, in Masuda, 253.

257 *"Our great undertaking"*: Ibid., 257.

258 *"This is one. . . . No, no. . . . No, it was none . . . It was Napoleonic"*: Hellegers, vol. 2, 758n.

258 *"stop and dig in"*: Hoover to Bonner Fellers, December 3, 1950, Hoover Papers, Stanford University; see also Best, 359.

259 *"The Russians"*: Lee and Henschel, 206.

259 *64 percent public approval:* Gallup, vol. 2, 943.

259 *"Your military objective"*: FRUS (1950), vol. 7, 781. Widening the Korean War into a war with China, says Bradley in his memoirs (558–59), would be "the wrong war, at the wrong place, at the wrong time, and with the wrong enemy." But Bradley didn't say this during the mid-July 1950 JCS meetings when the decision was being debated, he said it after the fact during the May 1951 "MacArthur Hearings" in Congress. During the decision time he played it both ways: MacArthur could proceed north seeking to destroy North Korean forces "provided there was no indication of Soviet or Chinese intervention." Fair enough, but what if there *was* an "indication"?

259 *"We want you"*: FRUS (1950), vol. 7, 826; Marshall to MacArthur, Sept. 20, 1950, Box 9, Folder 6, RG 6, MacArthur Archives. Here, too, the person giving MacArthur instructions is being coy. The wording is very strange for a military order: "We want you to feel . . . " What exactly does this mean? Of course the JCS wants the field commander to feel confident! This is not a military instruction but a cover-your-butt memo. Marshall is leaving MacArthur to hang out to dry: If he succeeds, great; if he doesn't, it's his fault for being reckless.

260 *transcript of Wake Island meeting*: Bradley, 575.

260 *"Who was that young whippersnapper"*: Hastings, 6.

260 *"as close as"*: Herring, 642.

261 *"It is difficult"*: Barrett, 94.

261 *Marshall's sarcastic comment about when a general complains*: Acheson, 515.

261 *"incapable of holding"*: Ibid.

262 *"the Winston Churchill of Japan"*: The similarities between the two men are remarkable: Both came from prominent families (though Yoshida was adopted), possessed a quick wit, and were always seen with a cigar. Like Churchill, Yoshida was a man of strong principles who had been thrown out of the government before the war for his unpopular political views. Like Churchill, his return to power was a remarkable feat, and he performed brilliantly. The

same debt the United States owes Winston Churchill for helping win World War II, it owes Shigeru Yoshida for helping win postwar Japan.

263 *"very much impressed by"*: John D. Rockefeller III, entry of January 27, 1951, Rockefeller Diaries, Rockefeller Center Archive, Sleepy Hollow, NY.

263 *"I came here"*: *Pacific Stars and Stripes*, February 11, 1951, 1, Dulles Collection.

263 *"As our peace mission"*: *Nippon Times*, February 12, 1951, 1, Dulles Collection.

265 *Yokohama bust of MacArthur*: Sheldon, 232.

265 *Diet resolution . . . "who helped"*: Weintraub, 353.

265 *"shock and sorrow"*: Ibid., 346.

265 *joint meeting*: The Democrats refused to grant MacArthur the more formal, more prestigious venue known as a joint session.

265 *Two hundred thousand Japanese*: MacArthur would claim it was two million, thus exaggerating by a factor of ten. Be that as it may, a turnout of two hundred thousand people—including every important political leader—was a remarkable tribute.

265 *"From the gates"*: Smith, 160; Weintraub, 353.

266 *Southeast Asia following Japan's lead*: See Thomas Friedman, *New York Times*, August 21, 2013, A19: "People in Southeast Asia looked up to Japan—the regional power—as a model: 'We're behind, what's wrong with us? We need to learn from those who are doing better.'"

24: HAD HE DIED AT INCHON

269 *"Well, the German problem . . . like a boy of twelve"*: "Military Situation in the Far East," May 5, 1951, part 1, 312.

270 *"I had thought"*: Hiroaki Sato, "Irony of Being in the Company of '12-Year-Olds,'" *Japan Times*, June 25, 2012.

270 *"the child"*: Richie, 20.

271 *"Perhaps someone just forgot"*: MacArthur, 383. Actually MacArthur's presence, in addition to being awkward, would have been inappropriate. The peace delegates were national representatives. MacArthur, even if he had continued to be supreme commander, would have had no proper role. Not even General Ridgway was invited.

271 *Rusk warning to Sebald*: Sebald, 221–22.

271 *"It is the orders you disobey"*: Karnow, 260; Pearlman, *Truman and MacArthur*, 3.

271 *"Wars are over, White"*: Theodore White, "Episode in Tokyo Bay," *Atlantic Monthly*, August 1970, 55.

272 *"He could be magnificently right"*: Ibid.

272 *"Show me a hero"*: Fitzgerald, 122.

272 *"The most radical"*: Reischauer, 229.

272 *"Could I have but"*: Pratt, 28.

273 *"U.S. inhibitions"*: Soffer, 118.

273 *"With the President's knowledge"*: Van Aduard, 184.

274 "*I was born when*": *Military Situation*, 91.

275 "*What has brought about*": Ibid., 325.

275 "*whether or not . . . No . . . In relation to*": Ibid., 341.

275 *He did not violate . . . And that . . . and created*": Ibid., 417.

275 "*the wrong war, in the wrong place*": Ibid., 732.

275 "*to stop the spread*": Hanson Baldwin, review of *MacArthur* by Courtney Whitney, *New York Times Book Review*, January 22, 1956, 24.

275 *legacy of the Korean War*: While the Korean War did not result in the decisive victory MacArthur sought, it can be argued that the Korean War was probably America's most successful war. In my previous book, *American History Revised*, I put it this way: "It may seem ironical to call the Korean War—'the forgotten war'—America's most successful military endeavor, but it achieved its objectives and had the most satisfying long-term results. The purpose of waging war is not just to win battles, but also to secure a political peace. . . . In terms of achieving a stable, long-lasting peace, the Korean War was remarkably fruitful. The country we saved, South Korea, eventually went on to become one of the world's strongest democracies. For more than a half-century, both the U.S. and the Soviets/Chinese have respected the thirty-eighth parallel that physically separates the two countries. Even more significant, both sides refrained from using nuclear weapons or launching massive invasions of a million men, which they easily could have done. By their conduct of the war, all parties—Americans, Koreans, Chinese, and Russians—signaled "limits" to each other. In so doing, they initiated the era of limited war that has characterized warfare to this day" (294).

25: A MAN DEEPLY FLAWED: HOW DID HE DO IT?

276 *MacArthur autograph letter*: Author's collection.

276 *Nixon*: Harries, xxviii.

276 *extreme leaders:* For this concept of extreme leaders and how they will take high risks offering exceptionally high rewards, see Mukunda, 14.

277 "*so prone to exaggerate*": Diary entry of December 27, 1944, Stimson Papers, Yale University.

277 "*The people*": Tracy, 33.

278 "*I don't care*": Sheldon, 26.

278 "*Listen, Jeannie*": Weintraub, 7.

278 "*Whatever else*": Beech, 58.

278 "*Bob, those were*": Eichelberger, *Dear Miss Em*, 65.

278 "*Do you realize*": Ibid.

279 "*MacArthur stands out*": Diary entry of March 30, 1945, Stimson Papers, Yale University.

279 "*the Knights of MacArthur's Round Table*": S. J. Morris, 430.

279 *Eisenhower and Eichelberger on MacArthur*: Diary entries of July 1 and 30, Aug. 2, Sept. 18, 19, and 20, 1948, and multiple entries, Feb.–March 1949, Eichelberger Papers, Duke University.

279 *Macmahon Ball*: Wildes, 28.

279 *Bradley teasing Eichelberger*: Schaller, 155.

280 *"Once you've got Baghdad"*: George Will, "Inoculated for Exuberance?," *Washington Post*, November 10, 2006, A31.

280 *"the greatest reformation"*: Gunther, xiii.

281 *"In my own view"*: Ball, 179.

281 *"no need of adopting"*: Brines, 241.

281 *"The minute I left Japan"*: MacArthur, *Reminiscences*, 147.

281 *red light turned to green*: Daws, 347.

281 *"The overpowering need"*: Rovere and Schlesinger, 95.

281 *"neither a soft peace"*: *Fortune*, January 1946.

282 *"MacArthur Tenets"*: Ganoe, 170–71.

282 *"Bob, if you get"*: Eichelberger, 223.

283 *"To take up"*: Ganoe, 48.

284 *"a commanding officer"*: Considine, 45.

284 *"knew his authority"*: Sheldon, 57.

285 *"Rules are mostly made"*: Rumsfeld, xiv.

285 *"Most organizations"*: John Kotter, "What Leaders Really Do," *Harvard Business Review*, vol. 68, no. 3 (May–June 1990),103.

285 *Dulles "I never had greater admiration"*: Rep. Walter H. Judd oral interview, 95, Harry S. Truman Library, http://www.trumanlibrary.org/oralhist/judd.htm.

285 *"that calm courage"*: Wavell, 18.

286 *"He was most impressive"*: Wolfe, 115, 127.

286 *"I just give 'em"*: Bowers, 93.

286 *awarding the Distinguished Service Cross to a young major*: Taylor and Rosenbach, 144–45.

286 *"This is the best officer"*: Frank, *MacArthur*, 21.

288 *"the gift of command"*: Choate, 35.

289 *"General MacArthur's headquarters"*: Yoshida, 143.

291 *"was indeed"*: Weintraub, 191.

291 *"I believed every word"*: Ibid.

291 *"He died unquestioning"*: Considine, 98.

291 *"Kill Japs"*: Nye, 83; Harries, 280.

292 *"One reason"*: Kawai, 446; Williams and Wallace, 118.

26: AFTERMATH

293 *"surrounded by his enemies"*: Perry, 69.

294 *Japan's Education Ministry*: Ginn, 244–45.

295 *"In August 1945"*: Harries, 267.

297 *"stunned . . . enormously impressed"*: O'Donnell and Powers, 15, in Schlesinger, 339.

297 *John Foster Dulles*: Ghani and Lockhart, 227.

298 *"The best way"*: Redford, 33.

298 *1990 country economy statistics*: Harvey, 455.

298 *world's largest creditor*: Economist Pocket World, 13, 24, 30, 76, 91.

Works Cited

The sources quoted in this book are voluminous. For readers who wish to pursue further, in boldface are those books and articles I found particularly insightful and stimulating.

Acheson, Dean. *Present at the Creation: My Years in the State Department.* W. W. Norton, 1969.

Aldous, Christopher. *The Police in Occupied Japan: Control, Corruption, and Resistance to Reform.* Routledge (UK), 1997.

Allison, John M. *Ambassador from the Prairie or Allison Wonderland.* Houghton Mifflin, 1973.

Appleman, Roy E. *Disaster in Korea: The Chinese Confront MacArthur.* Texas A&M University Press, 1989.

Archer, Jules. *Frontline General.* Julian Messner, 1963.

Bailey, Paul J. *Postwar Japan: 1945 to the Present.* Blackwell (UK), 1996.

Baldwin, Hanson W. *Great Mistakes of the War,* Harper & Bros., 1949.

Ball, W. Macmahon. *Japan: Enemy or Ally?* Cassell (Australia), 1949.

Barenblatt, Daniel. *A Plague Upon Humanity: The Secret Genocide of Axis Japan's Germ Warfare Operation.* HarperCollins, 2004.

Barnet, Richard J. *The Rockets' Red Glare: The Presidents and Their People.* Simon & Schuster, 1990.

Barrett, David M. *The CIA and Congress: The Untold Story from Truman to Kennedy.* University Press of Kansas, 2005.

Beard, Mary R. *The Force of Women in Japanese History.* Public Affairs Press, 1953.

Beauchamp, Edward R., ed. *Women and Women's Issues in Post–World War II Japan.* Garland Publishing, 1998.

Beech, Keyes. *Tokyo and Points East.* Doubleday, 1954.

Bergamini, David. *Japan's Imperial Conspiracy: How Emperor Hirohito Led Japan into War against the West.* William Morrow, 1971.

Best, Gary Dean. *The Life of Herbert Hoover: Keeper of the Torch, 1933–1964.* Palgrave Macmillan, 2013.

Bilainkin, George. *Destination Tokyo: A Famous Correspondent's Urgent Warning to the West about Tomorrow in Asia*. Odhams Books (UK), 1965.

Bishop, Jim. *FDR's Last Year*. William Morrow, 1974.

Bisson, Thomas A. *Prospects for Democracy in Japan*. Macmillan, 1949.

———. *Zaibatsu Dissolution in Japan*. University of California Press, 1954.

Bix, Herbert P. *Hirohito and the Making of Modern Japan*. HarperCollins, 2001.

Bowers, Faubion. "The Late Douglas MacArthur, Warts and All." *Esquire*, January 1967.

Brackman, Arnold C. *The Other Nuremberg: The Untold Story of the Tokyo War Crimes Trials*. William Morrow, 1987.

Bradley, Omar N., and Clay Blair. *A General's Life*. Simon & Schuster, 1983.

Braw, Monica. *The Atomic Bomb Suppressed: American Censorship in Occupied Japan 1945–1949*. Liber Intl. (Sweden), 1986.

Breuer, William B. *MacArthur's Undercover War: Spies, Saboteurs, Guerrillas, and Secret Missions*. John Wiley, 1995.

Brines, Russell. *MacArthur's Japan*. J. B. Lippincott, 1948.

Buell, Thomas B. *The Quiet Warrior: A Biography of Admiral Raymond A. Spruance*. Little, Brown, 1974.

Buhite, Russell D. *Douglas MacArthur: Statecraft and Stagecraft in East Asian Policy*. Rowman & Littlefield, 2008.

Buruma, Ian. *The Wages of Guilt: Memories of War in Germany and Japan*. Jonathan Cape (UK), 1994.

Chase, William C. *Front-Line General: An Autobiography*. Pacesetter Press. 1975.

Choate, Joseph. *Douglas MacArthur as I Knew Him*. Privately printed, 1986.

Christian Deputation to Japan. *The Return to Japan: Report of October–November 1945*. Friendship Press, 1945.

Cohen, Theodore. *Remaking Japan: The American Occupation as New Deal*. Free Press, 1987.

Considine, Bob. *MacArthur the Magnificent*. David McKay, 1942.

Columbia University Occupied Japan Oral History Project. Faubion Bowers, Charles Kades.

Costello, William. *Democracy vs. Feudalism in Postwar Japan*. Itagaki Shoten, 1948.

Cousins, Norman. *The Pathology of Power*. W. W. Norton, 1987.

Craig, William. *The Fall of Japan*. Dial Press, 1967.

Creemers, Wilhelmus H. M. *Shrine Shinto After World War II*. E. J. Brill (Leiden, Netherlands), 1968.

Dahlberg, William N. *A Tool for Diplomacy: Baseball in Occupied Japan 1945–1952* (a slide-show presentation to the 2010 Annual Convention of Baseball Statisticians, August 6, 2010, Atlanta, GA).

Dawidoff, Nicholas. *The Catcher Was a Spy: The Mysterious Life of Moe Berg*. Pantheon, 1994.

Daws, Gavan. *Prisoners of the Japanese: POWs of World War II in the Pacific*. William Morrow, 1994.

Deverall, Richard L.-G. *The Great Seduction: Red China's Drive to Bring Free Japan behind the Iron Curtain.* Intl. Literature Printing Co. (Japan), 1953.

Documents Concerning the Allied Occupation and Control of Japan. Section of Special Records, Foreign Office, Japanese Government. 6 vols. Tokyo, 1951.

Dower, John W. *Embracing Defeat: Japan in the Wake of World War II.* W. W. Norton, 2000.

———. *Ways of Forgetting, Ways of Remembering: Japan in the Modern World.* The New Press, 2012.

Drape, Joe. *Soldiers First: Duty, Honor, Country, and Football at West Point.* Times Books, 2012.

Drea, Edward, ed. *Researching Japanese War Crimes Records: Introductory Essays.* Nazi War Crimes and Japanese Imperial Government Records Interagency Working Group, Penny Hill Press (Congressional Research Service), 2006.

Duffy, Bernard K., and Ronald H. Carpenter. *Douglas MacArthur: Warrior as Wordsmith.* Greenwood Press, 1997.

Dulles, John Foster. *English Language Coverage of the Visit of the Dulles Mission to Japan* (bound collection of press articles, Tokyo, 1951); Dulles' personal copy, New York Public Library.

Economist Pocket World in Figures. The Economist and Profile Books, 2013.

Eichelberger, Robert L. Papers. Duke University.

———. *Dear Miss Em: General Eichelberger's War in the Pacific, 1942–1945.* Edited by Jay Luvaas. Greenwood Press, 1972.

———. *Our Jungle Road to Tokyo.* Viking, 1950.

Emmerson, John K. *The Japanese Thread: A Life in the U.S. Foreign Service.* Holt Rinehart & Winston, 1978.

Evans, Stanton, and Herbert Romerstein. *Stalin's Secret Agents: The Subversion of Roosevelt's Government.* Threshold, 2012.

Fearey, Robert A. *The Occupation of Japan, Second Phase: 1948–1950.* Macmillan, 1950.

Felton, Mark. *The Devil's Doctors: Japanese Human Experiments on Allied Prisoners of War.* Pen & Sword (UK), 2012.

Finn, Richard B. *Winners in Peace: MacArthur, Yoshida and Postwar Japan.* University of California Press, 1995.

Fitts, Robert. *Remembering Japanese Baseball: An Oral History of the Game.* Southern Illinois University Press, 2005.

Fitzgerald, F. Scott. *The Crack-Up, With Other Uncollected Pieces, Note-Books and Unpublished Letters.* Edited by Edmund Wilson. Charles Scribner's Sons, 1931. Reprint, New Directions, 1956.

Foreign Relations of the United States (FRUS), 1948, 1949. U.S. Department of State, U.S. Government Printing Office, 1976.

Frank, Richard B. *Downfall: The End of the Imperial Japanese Empire.* Random House, 1999.

Frank, Richard B. *MacArthur.* Palgrave Macmillan, 2007.

Freidel, Frank. *Franklin D. Roosevelt: Launching the New Deal*. Little, Brown, 1973.

Gaddis, John Lewis. *George F. Kennan: An American Life*. Penguin, 2011.

Gallicchio, Marc, ed. *The Unpredictability of the Past: Memories of the Asia-Pacific War in U.S.–East Asia Relations*. Duke University Press, 2007.

Gallup, George H. *The Gallup Poll: Public Opinion 1935–1948*. 2 vols. Random House, 1972.

Ganoe, William A. *MacArthur Close-Up: Much Then and Some Now*. Vantage Press, 1962.

Gauntlett, John Owen, and Robert King Hall. *Kokutai no Hongi, Cardinal Principles of the National Entity of Japan*. Harvard University Press, 1949.

Gayn, Mark. *Japan Diary*. William Sloane Assoc., 1948.

Ginn, John L. *Sugamo Prison: An Account of the Trial and Sentencing of Japanese War Criminals in 1948, by a U.S. Participant*. McFarland, 2011.

Gold, Hal. *Unit 731 Testimony: Japan's Wartime Human Experimentation Program*. Charles F. Tuttle, 1966.

Goodman, Grant K. *America's Japan: The First Year 1945–1946*. Fordham University Press, 2005.

Gordon, Beate Sirota. *The Only Woman in the Room*. Kodansha Intl., 1997.

Graves, William. "Human Treasures of Japan." *National Geographic* 142 (3) (September 1972), 370–79.

Grew, Joseph C. *Ten Years in Japan*. Simon & Schuster, 1944.

Gunther, John. *The Riddle of MacArthur: Japan, Korea and the Far East*. Harper & Bros., 1951.

Hadley, Eleanor M. "Trust Busting in Japan." *Harvard Business Review* 26, no. 4 (July 1948), 425–40.

———. *Memoir of a Trustbuster: A Lifelong Adventure with Japan*. University of Hawaii Press, 2002.

Haley, John Owen. *Antitrust in Germany and Japan: The First Fifty Years, 1947–1998*. University of Washington Press, 2001.

Hall, Robert King. *Education for a New Japan*. Yale University Press, 1949.

Halsey, William F., and J. Bryan. *Admiral Halsey's Story*. Whittlesey House, 1947.

Hanson, Victor Davis. "Matthew Ridgway." In *The Savior Generals: How Five Great Commanders Saved Wars That Were Lost—From Ancient Greece to Iraq*, edited by Victor Davis Hanson. Bloomsbury Press, 2013.

Harries, Meirion, and Susie Harries. *Sheathing the Sword: The Demilitarization of Japan*. Macmillan, 1987.

Harris, Robert, and Jeremy Paxman. *A Higher Form of Killing: The Secret Story of Gas and Germ Warfare*. Chatto & Windus (UK), 1982.

Harris, Sheldon. *Factories of Death: Japanese Biological Warfare 1932–1945 and the American Cover-up*. Routledge, 2002.

Harvey, Robert. *American Shogun: General MacArthur, Emperor Hirohito and the Drama of Modern Japan*. Overlook Press, 2006.

Hastings, Max. *The Korean War*. Simon & Schuster, 1980.

Havens, Thomas R. H. *Artist and Patron in Postwar Japan: Dance, Music, Theater, and the Visual Arts 1955–19890.* Princeton University Press, 1982.

Hayes, Samuel P. *The Beginning of American Aid to Southeast Asia: The Griffin Mission of 1950.* D. C. Heath, 1971.

Hellegers, Dale M. *We, the Japanese People: World War II and the Origins of the Japanese Constitution.* Stanford University Press, 2002.

Herring, George C. *From Colony to Superpower: U.S. Foreign Relations since 1776.* Oxford University Press, 2008.

Hersh, Seymour M. *Chemical and Biological Warfare: America's Hidden Arsenal.* Bobbs-Merrill, 1968.

Holton, Daniel C. *Modern Japan and Shinto Nationalism.* University of Chicago, 1947.

Hoopes, Townsend. *The Devil and John Foster Dulles.* Little, Brown, 1973.

Hopper, Helen. *A New Woman of Japan: A Political Biography of Kato Shidzue.* Westview (HarperCollins), 1996.

Hunt, Frazier. *The Untold Story of Douglas MacArthur.* Devon-Adair, 1954.

Imparato, Edward T. *MacArthur: Melbourne to Tokyo.* Burd Street Press, 1997.

Inoue, Kyoko. *MacArthur's Japanese Constitution: A Linguistic and Cultural Study of Its Making.* University of Chicago Press, 1991.

Irokawa, Daikichi. *The Age of Hirohito: In Search of Modern Japan.* Free Press, 1995.

James, Clayton. *The Years of MacArthur: Triumph and Disaster 1945–1964.* Houghton Mifflin, 1985.

Jansen, Marius B. *The Making of Modern Japan.* Harvard University Press, 2000.

Johnson, Carmen. *Rings in the Water: My Years with the Women of Postwar Japan.* Charles River Press, 1996.

Karnow, Stanley. *In Our Image: America's Empire in the Philippines.* Trafalgar Square, 1990.

Kase, Toshikazu. *Journey to the Missouri.* Yale University Press, 1950.

Kato, Masuo. *The Lost War, a Japanese Reporter's Inside Story.* Alfred A. Knopf, 1946.

Kawai, Kazuo. *Japan's American Interlude.* Chicago University Press, 1960.

Kelley, Brent. *The San Francisco Seals, 1946–1957: Interviews with 25 Former Baseballers.* McFarland, 2002.

Kelley, Frank R., and Cornelius Ryan. *MacArthur: Man of Action,* 1950.

Kennan, George F. *Memoirs 1925–1950.* Atlantic Monthly Press, 1967.

Kenney, George C. *The MacArthur I Know.* Duell, Sloan and Pearce, 1951.

Koikari, Mire. *Pedagogy of Democracy: Feminism and the Cold War in the U.S. Occupation of Japan.* Temple University Press, 2008.

Kubek, Anthony. *How the Far East Was Lost.* Regnery, 1963.

Larrabee, Eric. *Commander in Chief: Franklin Delano Roosevelt, His Lieutenants, and Their War.* Harper & Row, 1987.

Lauterbach, Richard E. *Danger from the East.* Harper & Bros., 1947.

Leahy, William D. *I Was There.* McGraw-Hill, Arno Press (New York Times Co.), 1950. Reprint, 1979.

Leary, William M., ed. *MacArthur and the American Century: A Reader.* University of Nebraska Press, 2001.

Lee, Clark, and Richard Henschel. *Douglas MacArthur.* Henry Holt, 1952.

Lewin, Ronald. *The American Magic: Codes, Ciphers and the Defeat of Japan.* Farrar Straus & Giroux, 1982.

Lilienthal, David E. *The Journals of David E. Lilienthal.* Vol. 2: *The Atomic Energy Years 1945–1950.* Harper & Row, 1964.

Lukacs, John. *George Kennan: A Study of Character.* Yale University Press, 2009.

Lyon, Charles. "Review of *The Case of General Yamashita* by A. Frank Reel." *Columbia Law Review,* March 1950.

MacArthur, Douglas. *Reminiscences.* McGraw-Hill, 1964.

MacArthur Memorial, Norfolk, VA. MacArthur Archives, Willoughby Papers, Faubion Bowers Oral History.

MacIsaac, David. *United States Strategic Bombing Survey.* Garland, 1976.

Maga, Timothy P. *Judgment at Tokyo: The Japanese War Crimes Trials.* University Press of Kentucky, 2001.

Manchester, William. *American Caesar: Douglas MacArthur, 1888–1964.* Little, Brown, 1978.

Mashbir, Sidney F. *I Was an American Spy.* Vantage, 1952.

Masuda, Hiroshu. *MacArthur in Asia: The General and His Staff in the Philippines, Japan, and Korea.* Cornell University Press, 2012.

McCullough, David. *Truman.* Simon & Schuster, 1992.

McDermott, Jeanne. *The Killing Winds: The Menace of Biological Warfare.* Arbor House, 1987.

Mears, Helen. *Mirror for Americans—Japan.* Houghton Mifflin, 1948.

Military Situation in the Far East: Hearings to Conduct an Inquiry into the Military Situation in the Far East and the Facts Surrounding the Relief of General of the Army Douglas MacArthur from His Assignments in That Area. Committee on Armed Services and the Committee on Foreign Relations, 82nd Congress. Part 1, May 3–5, 7–12, and 14, 1951.

Miller, Francis T. *General Douglas MacArthur, Fighter for Freedom.* John C. Winston, 1942.

———. *General Douglas MacArthur: Soldier-Statesman.* John C. Winston, 1951.

Minear, Richard H. *Victor's Justice: The Tokyo War Crimes Trial.* Princeton University Press, 1971. Reprint, University of Michigan Press, 2001.

Miscamble, Wilson D. *George F. Kennan and the Making of American Foreign Policy, 1947–1950.* Princeton University Press, 1992.

Montgomery, John D. *Forced to Be Free: The Artificial Revolution in Japan and Germany.* University of Chicago Press, 1957.

Moore, Ray A., and Donald L. Robinson. *Partners for Democracy: Crafting the New Japanese State under MacArthur.* Oxford University Press, 2002.

Morris, Seymour, Jr. *American History Revised.* Random House, 2010.

Morris, Sylvia Jukes. *Rage for Fame: The Ascent of Clare Boothe Luce.* Random House, 1997.

Mukunda, Gautam. *Indispensable: When Leaders Really Matter.* Harvard Business Review Press, 2012.

Nash, George H., ed. *Freedom Betrayed: Herbert Hoover's Secret History of the Second World War and Its Aftermath.* Hoover Institution Press, 2011.

National Archives. College Park, MD.

Newman, Robert P. *Truman and the Hiroshima Cult.* Michigan State University Press, 1995.

Nishi, Toshio. *Unconditional Democracy: Education and Politics in Occupied Japan 1945–1952.* Hoover Institution Press, 1982.

O'Donnell, Kenneth P., and David F. Powers. *Johnny, We Hardly Knew Ye.* Little, Brown, 1970.

Okamoto, Shiro. *The Man Who Saved Kabuki: Faubion Bowers and Theatre Censorship in Occupied Japan.* University of Hawaii Press, 2001.

Pearlman, Michael D. "Truman and MacArthur: The Winding Road to Dismissal." In *Korean War Anthology*, edited by Michael D. Pearlman. Combat Studies Institute, U.S. Army Command and General Staff College (Fort Leavenworth, KS), 2003.

———. *Truman and MacArthur: Policy, Politics and the Hunger for Honor and Renown.* Indiana University Press, 1976.

Perret, Geoffrey. *Old Soldiers Never Die: The Life of Douglas MacArthur.* Adams Media, 1996.

Perry, John Curtis. *Beneath the Eagle's Wings.* Dodd Mead, 1980.

Pharr, Susan J. "The Politics of Women's Rights." In *Democratizing Japan: The Allied Occupation*, edited by Robert E. Ward and Sakamoto Yoshikazu. University of Hawaii Press, 1987.

———. "A Radical U.S. Experiment: Women's Rights Laws and the Occupation of Japan." In *The Occupation of Japan: Impact of Legal Reform*, edited by L. H. Redford. MacArthur Memorial, 1978.

———. "Ethel Weed." In *Notable American Women, The Modern Period*, edited by Barbara Sicherman and Carol Hurd Green. Harvard University Press, 1980.

Piccigallo, Philip R. *The Japanese on Trial: Allied War Crimes Operations in the East 1945–1951.* University of Texas Press, 1979.

Political Reorientation of Japan: September 1945 to September 1948 (PRJ). 2 vols. Government Section, General Headquarters, Supreme Commander for the Allied Powers, U.S. Government Printing Office, 1949. Reprint, Greenwood Press, 1970.

Gordon W. Prange Collection. University of Maryland, College Park.

Pratt, John H., ed. *Revitalizing a Nation: A Statement of Beliefs, Opinions and Policies Embodied in the Public Pronouncements of General of the Army Douglas MacArthur.* Heritage Foundation, 1952.

Prestowitz, Clyde. *Rogue Nation: American Unilateralism and the Failure of Good Intentions.* Basic Books, 2003.

Puryear, Edgar. *American Generalship: Character Is Everything: The Art of Command.* Random House, 2001.

Rau, Santha Rama. *East of Home.* Harper & Bros., 1950.

Redford, L. K., ed. *The Proceedings of a Seminar on the Occupation and Its Legacy to the Post-War World, November 6–7, 1975.* MacArthur Memorial, 1976.

———. *The Occupation of Japan: Economic Policy and Reform.* MacArthur Memorial, 1980.

Reel, A. Frank. *The Case of General Yamashita.* University of Chicago Press, 1949.

Regis, Ed. *The Biology of Doom: The History of America's Secret Germ Warfare Project.* Henry Holt, 1999.

Reischauer, Edwin O. *Japan: The Story of a Nation.* Alfred A. Knopf, 1974.

Reports of General MacArthur. 2 vols. U.S. Government Printing Office, 1994.

Richie, Donald. *The Donald Richie Reader.* Stone Bridge Press, 2001.

Ricks, Thomas. *The Generals.* Penguin, 2012.

Ritter, Lawrence S. *The Glory of Their Times: The Story of the Early Days of Baseball Told by the Men Who Played It.* Macmillan, 1966.

Ritter, Lawrence S., and Mark Rucker. *The Babe: A Life in Pictures.* Ticknor & Fields, 1988.

Röling, Bernard V. A. *The Tokyo Trial and Beyond: Reflections of a Peacemonger.* Polity (UK), 1993.

Röling Bernard V. A., and C. F. Rüter, eds. *The Tokyo Judgment: The International Military Tribunal for the Far East (I.M.T.F.E.), 26 April 1946–12 November 1948.* 3 vols., APA-University Press Amsterdam BV (Netherlands), 1977.

Rotter, Andrew J. *The Path to Vietnam: Origins of the American Commitment to Southeast Asia.* Cornell University Press, 1987.

Rovere, Richard H., and Arthur M. Schlesinger Jr. *The General and the President, and the Future of Foreign Policy.* Farrar, Straus and Young, 1951.

Rumsfeld, Donald. *Rumsfeld's Rules: Leadership Lessons in Business, Politics, War, and Life.* Broadside, 2013.

Ryan, Allan A. *Yamashita's Ghost: War Crimes, MacArthur's Justice, and Command Accountability.* University Press of Kansas, 2012.

Sams, Crawford. *Medic: The Mission of an American Military Doctor in Occupied Japan and Wartorn Korea.* M. E. Sharpe, 1998.

Sato, Takeshi. *Businessman's Japan: A Survey of Japan's "Divine Wind" Economy in the 1960s.* Michael Joseph (UK), 1964.

Schaffer, Ronald. *Wings of Judgment: American Bombing in World War II.* Oxford University Press, 1985.

Schaller, Michael. *Altered States: The United States and Japan Since the Occupation.* Oxford University Press, 1997.

———. *Douglas MacArthur: The Far Eastern General.* Oxford University Press, 1989.

————. *The American Occupation of Japan: The Origins of the Cold War in Asia.* Oxford University Press, 1987.

Schmidt, Donald E. *The Folly of War: American Foreign Policy, 1898-2005.* Algora Publishing, 2005.

Schoichi, Koseki. *The Birth of Japan's Postwar Constitution.* Westview Press, 1997.

Schonberger, Howard B. "The Japan Library in American Diplomacy, 1947–1952." *Pacific Historical Review,* August 1977.

————. *Aftermath of War: Americans and the Remaking of Japan, 1945–1952.* Kent State University Press, 1989.

Schoor, Gene. *General Douglas MacArthur: A Pictorial Biography.* Rudolph Field, 1951.

Seaman, Louis L. *The Real Triumph of Japan: The Conquest of the Silent Foe.* Appleton, 1906.

Sebald, William J., with Russell Brines. *With MacArthur in Japan: A Personal History of the Occupation.* W. W. Norton, 1965.

Shacklock, Floyd. *Which Way Japan?* Friendship Press, 1949.

Sheldon, Walter J. *The Honorable Conquerors: The Occupation of Japan 1945–1952.* Macmillan, 1965.

Shigemitsu, Mamoru. *Japan and Her Destiny: My Struggle for Peace.* Hutchins (London), 1958.

Smith, Bradley F. *Sharing Secrets with Stalin: How the Allies Traded Intelligence, 1941–1945.* University Press of Kansas, 1996.

————. *The Shadow Warriors: The O.S.S. and the Origins of the C.I.A.* Basic Books, 1983.

Smith, H. Alexander. Papers. Princeton University.

Smith, Robert. *MacArthur in Korea: The Naked Emperor.* Simon & Schuster, 1982.

Smyth, Sir John. *Percival and the Tragedy of Singapore.* MacDonald & Co. (UK), 1971.

Sodei, Rinjiro. *Dear General MacArthur: Letters from the Japanese During the American Occupation.* Rowman & Littlefield, 2001.

Soffer, Jonathan M. *General Matthew B. Ridgway: From Progressivism to Reaganism, 1895–1993.* Praeger, 1998.

Spanier, John W. *The Truman-MacArthur Controversy and the Korean War.* W. W. Norton, 1965.

Staaveren, Jacob Van. *An American in Japan 1945-1948: A Civilian View of the Occupation.* University of Washington Press, 1994.

Steinberg, Alfred. *Douglas MacArthur.* G. P. Putnam's Sons, 1951.

Stimson, Henry L. Papers. Yale University.

Stimson, Henry L., and McGeorge Bundy. *On Active Service in Peace and War.* Harper and Bros., 1948.

Sugita, Yoneyuki. *Pitfall or Panacea: The Irony of U.S. Power in Occupied Japan 1945–1952.* Routledge (UK), 2003.

Summation—History of the Non-Military Activities in Japan, 1945–1948. Government Section, Supreme Commander for the Allied Powers. 8 vols. U.S. Government Printing Office, 1945.

Swearingen, Roger, and Paul Langer. *Red Flag in Japan: International Communism in Action, 1919–1951*. Harvard University Press, 1952.

Takayanagi, Kenzo. *The Tokio Trials and International Law: Answer to the Prosecution's Arguments on International Law Delivered at the International Military Tribunal for the Far East on 3 & 4 March, 1948*. Yuhikaku (Japan), 1948.

Takemae, Eiji. *Inside GHQ: The Allied Occupation of Japan and Its Legacy*. Continuum, 2002.

Taylor, Lawrence. *A Trial of Generals: Homma, Yamashita, MacArthur*. Icarus, 1981.

Taylor, Robert L., and William E. Rosenbach. *Military Leadership: In Search of Excellence*. 2nd ed. Westview Press, 1992.

Terasaki, Gwen. *Bridge to the Sun*. University of North Carolina Press, 1957.

Textor, Robert B. *Failure in Japan*. John Day, 1951.

Thomas, Evan. *Sea of Thunder: Four Commanders and the Last Great Naval Campaign, 1941–1945*. Simon & Schuster, 2006.

Thorpe, Elliott R. *East Wind, Rain: The Intimate Account of an Intelligence Officer in the Pacific 1939–49*. 1958. Reprint, Gambit, 1969.

Toland, John. *Occupation*. Doubleday, 1987.

———. *The Rising Sun: The Decline and Fall of the Japanese Empire 1936–1945*. Random House, 1970.

Tracy, Honor. *Kakemono: A Sketch Book of Postwar Japan*. Methuen (UK), 1950.

Treadwell, Mattie E. *The Women's Army Corps (The United States Army in World War II: Special Studies)*. Office of the Chief of Military History, Department of the Army, 1954.

Trial of Japanese War Criminals. United States Department of State Publication 2765. U.S. Government Printing Office, 1947.

Triplett, William. *Flowering of the Bamboo*. Woodbine Press, 1985.

Truman, Harry S. *Off the Record: The Private Papers of Harry S Truman*. Edited by Robert H. Ferrell. Harper & Row, 1980.

———. *Memoirs*. 2 vols. Doubleday, 1956.

Tsutsui, William M. *Banking Policy in Japan: American Efforts at Reform During the Occupation*. Routledge, 1988.

Tugwell, Rexford G. *The Democratic Roosevelt: A Biography of Franklin D. Roosevelt*. Doubleday, 1957.

Uchino, Tatsuro. *Japan's Postwar Economy: An Insider's View of Its History and Its Future*. Kodansha Intl. (Tokyo), 1983.

Van Aduard, E. J. Lewe. *Japan from Surrender to Peace*. Martinus Nijhoff (Netherlands), 1953.

Veale, F. J. P. *Advance to Barbarism: How the Reversion to Barbarism in Warfare and War-Trials Menaces Our Future*. C. C. Nelson, 1948. Reprint, 1953.

Vinacke, Harold M. *The United States and the Far East 1945–1951.* American Institute of Pacific Relations, 1952.

Vining, Elizabeth Gray. *Windows for the Crown Prince.* J. B. Lippincott, 1952.

Ward, Robert E. "The Origins of the Present Japanese Constitution." *American Political Science Review,* December 1956.

Warner, Denis, and Peggy Warner. *The Sacred Warriors: Japan's Suicide Legions.* Van Nostrand Reinhold, 1982.

Wavell, Archibald P. *Soldiers and Soldiering, or Epithets of War.* Jonathan Cape (UK), 1953.

Webb, James. *The Emperor's General: A Novel.* Broadway, 1999.

Weiner, Col. Frederick B. "MacArthur Unjustifiably Accused of Meting Out 'Victor's Justice' in War Crimes Cases." *Military Law Review* 113 (1986).

Weintraub, Stanley. *MacArthur's War: Korea and the Undoing of an American Hero.* Free Press, 2000.

Whelan, Richard. *Drawing the Line: The Korean War, 1950–1953.* Little, Brown, 1990.

White, Theodore H. *In Search of History: A Personal Adventure.* Harper & Row, 1978.

Whiting, Robert. *You Gotta Have War.* Macmillan, 1989.

Whitney, Courtney. *MacArthur: His Rendezvous with History.* Alfred A. Knopf, 1956.

Wildes, Harry Emerson. *Typhoon in Tokyo: The Occupation and Its Aftermath.* Macmillan, 1954.

Williams, Justin. *Japan's Political Revolution Under MacArthur: A Participant's Account.* University of Georgia Press, 1979.

Williams, Peter, and David Wallace. *Unit 731: The Japanese Army's Secret of Secrets.* Hodder and Stoughton (UK), 1988.

Willoughby, Charles A. *Maneuver in War.* Military Service Publishing Company, 1939.

Willoughby, Charles A., and John Chamberlain. *MacArthur, 1941–1951.* McGraw-Hill, 1954.

Wilson, Frank J., and Beth Day. *Special Agent: A Quarter Century with the Treasury Department and the Secret Service.* Holt Rinehart & Winston, 1965.

Wiltz, John Edward. "Truman and MacArthur: The Wake Island Meeting." *Military Affairs* 42 (December 1978).

Wolfe, Robert. *Americans as Proconsuls: United States Military Government in Germany and Japan, 1944–1952.* Southern Illinois University Press, 1984.

Woodard, William P. *The Allied Occupation of Japan 1945–1952 and Japanese Religions.* E. J. Brill (Leiden, Netherlands), 1972.

Yoshida, Shigeru. *The Yoshida Memoirs: The Story of Japan in Crisis.* Heinemann (UK), 1961.

Index